# Indigenous Rights in Modern Landscapes



'The Sámi Reindeer herders, whose flocks and cultural landscapes span Norway, Sweden, Finland and Russia, provide, in this book, an ideal comparative basis for understanding indigenous peoples' key role in breaking the monopoly of bureaucratic, wilderness-fixated nature management regimes, and the uniform, globalized nature conservation these regimes foster'.

Kenneth R. Olwig, Professor Emeritus, SLU-Alnarp,
Department of Landscape Architecture,
Planning and Management, Alnarp, Sweden

This book examines the diverse use of Indigenous customary rights in modern landscapes from a multidisciplinary perspective. Divided into two parts, the first deals explicitly with Sámi customary rights in relation to nature conservation in the Nordic countries and Russia from a legal and historical perspective. The authors investigate how longstanding Sámi customary territorial rights have been reassessed in the context of new kinds of legislation regarding Indigenous people. They also look at the ideas behind the historical models of nature conservation. The second part deals with the ideas and implementation of new kinds of postcolonial models of nature conservation. The case of the Sámi is compared with other Indigenous people internationally with cases from Australia, New Zealand, Canada and India. The work investigates how the governance of protected areas has been influenced by the principles of equality and positive discrimination, and how it has affected the possibilities of establishing adaptive co-management arrangements for specific areas. How the legal situation of Indigenous peoples has been recognised in an international context is also investigated. The volume provides a multidisciplinary analysis of how the customary livelihood of Indigenous people has adapted to modern industrialised landscapes and also how postcolonial approaches have contributed to global changes of Indigenous rights and nature conservation models.

**Lars Elenius** (PhD) is Professor of History and Education at Umeå University and Luleå University of Technology, Sweden. His specialist areas of interest are on national minorities and Indigenous people in northern Europe. His research interests generally are on history of education, Indigenous history, historical culture, minoritypolicy, ethnopolicy, nationalism, regionalism, history of Northern Europe. He has written widely on these and related topics.

**Christina Allard** (LLD) is Associate Professor in Law at Luleå University of Technology, Sweden, and at the Faculty of Law, UiT The Arctic University of Norway. Her research interests focus on natural resources use and environmental protection with special emphasis on Indigenous people's territorial rights as well as comparative legal aspects. She is the leader of the Nordic research network for Sámi and Indigenous people's law, NORSIL, and has a strong publication record on legal research related to Indigenous rights.

**Camilla Sandström** (PhD) is a Professor at the Department of Political Science, Umeå University, Sweden. She has a special interest in institutional aspects of natural resource governance and management, including how collaborative governance such as co-management and public private partnerships can be used to handle conflicts and trade-offs between different interests. She is the leader of an interdisciplinary team involved in research on sustainable rural development with a specific emphasis on natural resource management such as protected areas, forests, fish and wildlife.

# Indigenous Rights in Modern Landscapes

## Nordic Conservation Regimes in Global Context

**Edited by Lars Elenius, Christina Allard and Camilla Sandström**

Routledge
Taylor & Francis Group
LONDON AND NEW YORK

First published 2017
by Routledge

2 Park Square, Milton Park, Abingdon, Oxfordshire OX14 4RN
52 Vanderbilt Avenue, New York, NY 10017

*Routledge is an imprint of the Taylor & Francis Group, an informa business*

First issued in paperback 2020



*British Library Cataloguing in Publication Data*
A catalogue record for this book is available from the British Library

*Library of Congress Cataloging in Publication Data*
Names: Elenius, Lars, 1952– editor. | Sandström, Camilla, 1967– editor. | Allard, Christina, editor.
Title: Indigenous rights in modern landscapes : Nordic conservation regimes in global context / edited by Lars Elenius, Camilla Sandström, Christina Allard.
Description: New York, NY : Routledge, 2016. | Includes bibliographical references and index.
Identifiers: LCCN 2016019063 | ISBN 9781472464927 (hardback) | ISBN 9781315607559 (ebook) | ISBN 9781317059677 (epub) | ISBN 9781317059660 (mobipocket)
Subjects: LCSH: Sami (European people)—Legal status, laws, etc.—Scandinavia. | Sami (European people)—Legal status, laws, etc.—Russia (Federation). | Customary law—Scandinavia. | Indigenous peoples—Legal status, laws, etc.—Scandinavia. | Nature conservation—Law and legislation—Scandinavia. | Sami (European people)—Land tenure.
Classification: LCC KJC5144.M56 I53 2016 | DDC 323.1194/57—dc23
LC record available at https://lccn.loc.gov/2016019063

ISBN: 978-1-4724-6492-7 (hbk)
ISBN: 978-0-367-59569-2 (pbk)

Typeset in Galliard
by Apex CoVantage, LLC

# Contents

# Figures

# Short biographies of contributing authors

**Michael Adams** (b. 1955), PhD. Associate Professor in Human Geography at University of Wollongong, Australia. He is a member of the World Commission on Protected Areas and the Commission on Environmental, Economic and Social Policy of the IUCN. He is Associate Editor of *Conservation and Society.* Prior to joining the University of Wollongong he worked for Australian conservation agencies and environmental NGOs. His research interests include shared governance between government conservation agencies and indigenous communities in national parks and World Heritage areas; indigenous and local knowledge systems; the cultural dimensions of hunting; sacredness and nature; and the relationship between diving and environmentalism.

**Christina Allard** (b. 1971), LLD. Associate Professor at Luleå University of Technology, Sweden, and Associate Professor II at the Faculty of Law, UiT The Arctic University of Norway, Project Leader of the Nordic Research Network for Sámi and Indigenous Peoples' Law (NORSIL, www.uit.no/jurfak/norsil). Allard's research interests centre on Sámi and indigenous peoples' rights comparatively and within the context of the recognition of territorial rights, natural resource use and environmental protection. In her doctoral thesis Allard analysed and contrasted laws in Sweden, Aotearoa New Zealand and Canada. In 2015, Allard published the book *Renskötselrätt i nordisk belysning* [*The reindeer herding right from a Nordic perspective*] (Makadam förlag) and co-authored the anthology *Indigenous Rights in Scandinavia* (Ashgate). She also works in interdisciplinary research projects.

**Tore Andersson Hjulman** (b. 1984), Doctoral Student. Luleå University of Technology, Sweden. His doctoral thesis explores the way in which the disjunction of nature from culture has been used and renegotiated in connection with interbellum conflicts about Sámi rights in the Swedish national parks.

**Lars Elenius** (b. 1952), PhD. Professor in History and Education at Umeå University and Senior Lecturer at Luleå University of Technology, Sweden, specialising in research concerning national minorities and indigenous people in northern Europe. He is conducting the multidisciplinary research project 'Indigenous Rights and Nature Conservation in Northern Fennoscandinavia' (www.indigenous-nature.eu) and also the transnational project of Russian and Nordic historians (www.barentshistory.eu). In the latter he served as Chief Editor of the history book *The Barents Region. A Transnational History of Subarctic Northern Europe*, published in 2015, and the Assistant and Graphics Editor of *The Encyclopedia of the Barents Region*, to be published in 2016. His research interests are history of education, indigenous history, historical culture, minority policy, ethno policy, nationalism, regionalism, and the history of northern Europe.

**Carina Green** (b. 1969), PhD in Cultural Anthropology. Researcher at the Swedish Biodiversity Centre, the Swedish University of Agricultural Sciences and lecturer at the Department of Cultural Anthropology and Ethnology, Uppsala University. Her research focus is indigenous peoples and management of natural/cultural heritage, especially in connection to World Heritage areas. Geographically, her research mainly includes Northern Sweden (Sámi), Australia (Aboriginal) and Aotearoa/New Zealand (Maori). In her work she has touched upon themes such as identity politics, power structures, bureaucracy and political ecology. Her dissertation, finished in 2009, is called *Managing Laponia – A World Heritage as Arena for Sámi Ethno-Politics in Sweden*. She is currently studying the environmental discourse on indigenous peoples as holders of so-called traditional/indigenous knowledge as it is played out in various international knowledge integration processes.

**Leena Heinämäki** (b. 1974), LLD. Senior Researcher at the Northern Institute for Environmental and Minority Law in the Arctic Centre, University of Lapland, Finland. Heinämäki is also Vice Leader of the University of the Arctic Thematic Network on Arctic Law. Her research interests relate to indigenous peoples' human and environmental rights and the rights of Sámi people. Heinämäki is currently co-authoring and editing a book on the protection of sacred sites of indigenous peoples in the Arctic. She is also coordinating an international network on indigenous peoples' sacred sites and teaches indigenous peoples' rights and Sámi Law at the University of Lapland.

**Thora Herrmann** (b. 1977), DPhil. Associate Professor at the Département de géographie at the Université de Montréal (Canada) working with indigenous peoples in polar regions on the social-cultural dimensions of human–environment interactions, place–people relationships, the impacts of socio-environmental changes on societies, and the forms of values, knowledge and use practices of plants and animals by societies. She is co-editor (with Thibault Martin) of the book *Indigenous Peoples' Governance of Land and Protected Territories in the Arctic* (2016, Springer). She was the holder of the Canada Research Chair in Ethnoecology and Biodiversity Conservation (2006–2011). Previously, she worked at the United Nations Department of Economic and Social Affairs (UNDESA), and at the German Agency for International Development (GIZ) on biocultural diversity conservation policy.

**Panu Itkonen** (b. 1954), PhD. Post Doctoral Researcher in Anthropology. In his doctoral thesis at the University of Helsinki within Social and Cultural Anthropology he explored forms of cooperation and reciprocity in the Skolt Sámi reindeer herding community of Sevettijärvi Finland and actions of state administration in relation to the community. He has produced official social impact assessments on local reindeer herding in mining projects in northern Finland. He has worked in the research project 'Barents Area Glocal Governance and Human Rights' in Erik Castrén Institute for International Law University of Helsinki. He is currently studying social and environmental relations in his research project 'Skolt Sámi Survival' in the Arctic Centre University of Lapland. His research interests are directed to Arctic cultures, especially Sámi culture, including its economic dimension, its relation to nature and administration, to reindeer herding, collaboration, work communities, and indigenous land rights.

**Cindy Morin** (b. 1981), MA. Lecturer at the Department of Urban and Touristic Studies at Université du Québec à Montréal. She primarily specialises in the management of native sacred heritage sites in Canada, more specifically in the co-management of those sites by the natives and the government and the relation between the two groups. She is interested in the importance of local community involvement in regard to preservation. She also is a specialist in local architectural history and development and she works as a consultant for various administrations in the province of Québec in order to manage and present the local heritage.

**Antje Neumann** (b. 1968), LLM. Legal researcher specialising in Polar Law. She is affiliated to the University of Tilburg, the Netherlands, where she is currently conducting her PhD research on wilderness protection in polar regions. Her master's thesis, obtained from the University of Akureyri, Iceland, related to the recognition of Sámi rights in the context of area protection and management. Neumann's research interests principally include human–nature relationships. She is also involved in the book project on the protection of the sacred sites of indigenous peoples in the Arctic, led by Heinämäki and Herrmann.

**Jan Åge Riseth** (b. 1953), PhD. Senior researcher at the Northern Research Institute (NORUT), Tromsø, Norway. Riseth is also a judge on the Finnmark Land Tribunal, an appeal court for disputes concerning land rights in Finnmark County. Most of his research is interdisciplinary and includes Sámi reindeer herding, nature management and protection, sustainable resource use, modernisation, impact analyses, climate change, and traditional/indigenous knowledge. In 2015 Riseth published the book *Reindrift og ressursforvaltning* [*Reindeer herding and resource management*] (Vett & Viten). Riseth leads the research project 'Reindeer herding and impact analyses' that will be concluded in 2016. He is also responsible for the traditional knowledge part of the new NCoE project 'Climate change effects on the epidemiology of infectious diseases' (CLINF).

**Elsa Reimerson** (b. 1982), holds a PhD in Political Science from Umeå University, Sweden. Her research explores relationships of power, spaces for agency and indigenous rights in discourses of conservation and natural resource governance and management. In her doctoral thesis, Reimerson analysed how the discourses that govern nature conservation and protected areas shape the conditions for indigenous peoples' political influence and participation in relation to protected areas on their lands, with a special focus on the Swedish and Norwegian parts of Sápmi. Currently she is continuing her research in the overlapping fields of indigenous rights, natural resource governance and environmental politics at the Department of Political Science, Umeå University.

**Jacinta Ruru** (b. 1974) PhD. Professor of Law at the University of Otago, New Zealand, Co-Director of Nga Pae o te Maramatanga New Zealand's Maori Centre of Research Excellence, and Associate Researcher at the Indigenous Law Centre, University of New South Wales, Australia. She holds a PhD from the University of Victoria, Canada, is editor of *Resource Management Journal, Resource Management Theory & Practice*, and a consultative editor for the *Maori Law Review*. Ruru's research explores indigenous peoples' legal interests to own, manage and govern land and water. She is co-author of *Discovering Indigenous Lands* (Oxford University Press 2010). Ruru is of Maori descent; her tribes include Raukawa and Ngati Ranginui.

**Camilla Sandström** (b. 1967), PhD. Senior Lecturer and Associate Professor at the Department of Political Science, Umeå University, Sweden, is currently engaged in the research programme Future Forests (www.futureforests.se) focusing on forest policy and governance including indigenous rights. She has a special interest in institutional aspects of natural resource governance and management e.g. how collaborative governance such as co-management and public private partnerships can be used to handle conflicts and trade-offs between different interests. At present she is also leading an interdisciplinary team involved in research into sustainable rural development with a specific emphasis on natural resource management such as protected areas, forests, fish and wildlife.

**Jan Turtinen** (b. 1965), PhD. Senior Adviser at the Swedish National Heritage Board and Researcher at the Department of Cultural Anthropology and Ethnology at Uppsala University, Sweden. His research explores various aspects of the global implementation of UNESCO's World Heritage Convention. His most recent work focuses on the Convention's effects on indigenous peoples and how they are involved in the identification and management of protected World Heritage sites. He is also working with the implementation of the World Heritage Convention at the Swedish National Heritage Board.

**Vladislava Vladimirova** (b. 1975), PhD. Senior Lecturer at the Centre for Russian and Eurasian Studies and the Department of Cultural Anthropology and Ethnology at Uppsala University, Sweden. Her anthropological research in northern Russia since 2001 includes such topics as ethnicity and indigenism, citizenship and special rights for indigenous people, economic transformations in the post-Soviet North, natural resource use and climate change, and moral anthropology. She has investigated the organisational and institutional capacity of the indigenous Sámi community in northern Russia to effectively promote its political and economic interests and realise its legally protected economic and cultural rights. Her publications include the monograph *Just labor: labor ethic in a post-Soviet reindeer herding community* (2006), and a variety of book chapters and articles.

# Introduction

*Lars Elenius*

The Sámi people live in the northern parts of Scandinavia and Russia and, as is true for many other indigenous people, their traditional activities are often carried out within national parks and other areas of nature protection. Nature conservation and governance in relation to indigenous rights have, however, been designed in completely different ways in the countries where the Sámi live. This has created tensions between the countries involved as well as in relation to other ethnic groups and within the Sámi population. The Sámi landscape is therefore comparable to other indigenous landscapes throughout the world.

This edited volume is the outcome of the research project *Indigenous rights and nature conservation in Fenno-Scandinavia*, financed by the Swedish Research Council Formas 2010–2015, and the conference *Sámi Customary Rights in Modern Landscapes – Indigenous People and Nature Conservation* held at Luleå University of Technology in autumn 2013. The volume aims to explore the use of landscapes by indigenous peoples and their place in protected nature, in a historic, comparative and contemporary setting, but focusing on the Sámi in northern Scandinavia and Russia. The Yellowstone National Park was established in 1872 and served for a long period as an international model for nature conservation. However, the kinds of protected areas that were established on the lines of the Yellowstone model are now being reassessed in the context of the declining power of single nation states, strengthened indigenous rights and postcolonial identity policies, and also elaborated through the political and media organisations of indigenous peoples.

The overall objective of this book is to present a cross-disciplinary perspective on the complex interplay between the customary rights of indigenous people and nature conservation as implemented in a postcolonial discourse. The key feature is a collection of articles taking up nature conservation in modern industrialised landscapes where reindeer herding coexists with water and wind power constructions, communication infrastructures, forestry and tourism. Nature conservation is set in relation to historical customary rights and the history of the Sámi people in their different national settings. Although the main focus is on the Scandinavian context and the Sápmi region, the Scandinavian cases are contrasted with the situations discussed in articles covering Australia, Aotearoa/New Zealand, Canada and India. The case of the Sámi is compared with that of other indigenous peoples concerning how environmental protection can contribute to a sustainable livelihood.

Investigations into indigenous people and nature conservation cannot be carried out using blueprint, general, standard analyses. The policies towards the Sámi depend on how ethnic relations and nationalism within the nation state have developed historically. It is these that have determined the way the Sámi have been written into the historical memories and myths of each country. There are also political differences between the countries despite current cooperation. Sweden and Finland have joined the EU while Norway and Russia have not. Norway has ratified the ILO 169 Convention, but Sweden, Finland and Russia have not. The Nordic model of minority legislation and nature conservation differs from those of Russia and other parts of the world. On the other hand, internationally there are many similarities regarding the models of nature conservation that are now being reassessed in accordance with a postcolonial discourse.

The case of the Sámi is very interesting regarding the intertwined issues of indigenous history, politics and legal rights. The authors provide a multidisciplinary analysis of the ways in which the customary livelihoods of indigenous people have adapted to modern industrialised landscapes and also how postcolonial approaches have contributed to global change regarding indigenous rights and models for nature conservation.

The book covers the two aspects of nature conservation and the use of landscape.

## Part 1. Legislation and historically changed policies within Sápmi

The first issue, comprising Part 1 of the book, compares how Sámi customary rights have been adapted to new kinds of legislation and models for nature conservation arising from the historical and political changes in the Nordic countries and Russia. The traditional livelihood of reindeer herding is still an essential part of Sámi culture, although today only a minority among the Sámi are engaged in it.

How has policy regarding protected areas and customary rights influenced reindeer herding Sámi in a multi-ethnic setting? The ideas behind the historical models for nature conservation are also examined. Despite the shared roots of culture, customs and language, the regulatory framework affecting the Sámi is quite different among the countries. Sámi ethno-history within each nation is also different.

In the first article **Christina Allard** compares the current legislation governing protected areas among the Nordic countries, and asks how the differences affect reindeer herding and associated traditional activities. Her chapter offers new knowledge revealing differences in approach and legal rhetoric with respect to the indigenous Sámi. Even if conservation of land and species is an area of international concern, emphasised through various international conventions, it is obvious that protected area regimes and their underpinnings differ considerably.

**Lars Elenius** compares how the ethnic content of the nation states of Finland and Sweden changed during the long period of colonisation, and what consequences this had for the shaping of nature conservation in the Sámi reindeer herding areas in the two countries. In Sweden and Finland, with a common history and shared legislation before 1809, relations between the Sámi and the majority populations took different courses during the nineteenth and twentieth centuries. In Sweden a 'closed' system of Sámi reindeer herding emerged, but in Finland an 'open' system was developed where every citizen could be a reindeer herder. The article examines these differences in relation to the nationalism and national historiography of the two countries.

**Tore Andersson Hjulman** concentrates on how the Swedish Sámi, in conflict with national park representatives in the interwar period, responded to the threat of having their land use circumscribed and their legal situation interpreted by various authorities. Based on the binary concepts of 'primitive' and 'civilised' the category 'nature people' came to function as a mirror of the Other in the transformation of society into an integrative nationalism and modernity. The concept of 'naturisation' cleared the ground not only for domination and resource exploitation but also for the counter movements of nature romanticism and preservation.

The main question is how ideas of the Sámi as a 'nature people' were included in the National Park law and how it affected the possibilities reindeer herders had of maintaining land use and defending their rights.

**Thora Herrmann**, **Leena Heinämäki** and **Cindy Morin** look into the subject of indigenous landscapes as also being traditional spiritual landscapes. They use the S*G*ang Gwaay Haida Heritage Site in Canada as a case study. It is a UNESCO World Heritage site that is managed within the Gwaii Haanas National Park Reserve, and as such this site is reflecting the indigenous Haida identity and worldview. The authors examine the local indigenous community's participation in managing and conserving this site. They ask, for instance, whether governance, policy and management practices draw upon and integrate both indigenous conservation practices and state conservation practices when safeguarding cultural sites. The S*G*ang Gwaay is commonly identified as an example of best practices for indigenous co-management of World Heritage sites, and one explanation for this success is that the partnership was built not only on consultation, but also on engaging the Haida in a meaningful way right from the beginning.

**Panu Itkonen** reveals the problem of changed national borders that has affected so many of the Sámi population, demonstrated in the article by the case of the Skolt Sámi who live in the border areas of Norway, Russia and Finland. Current traditional property rights of the Skolt Sámi in the Sevettijärvi environment in Finland are investigated in relation to reindeer herding, fishing and gathering. Itkonen demonstrates that the share of environment based on reindeer herding has become more and more centralised into the hands of a few among the Skolt Sámi, while at the same time some parts of the culture have also been centralised, namely certain forms of cooperation that strengthen the coherence of the community. When people lose their share of the environment, they lose their corresponding share of culture. Itkonen argues that nature conservation should be part of all discussions about land rights of the Skolt Sámi people and other indigenous people, because it sets limits for the utilisation of natural resources in general.

**Vladislava Vladimirova**, in the last article in Part 1, analyses how Seidozero Lake, a sacred Sámi site on the Kola Peninsula, was converted into a nature reserve of local importance in 1982 and, after having suffered from uncontrolled 'wild' tourism and poaching during the 1990s, was re-confirmed in 2003. The new status was expected to provide economic opportunities for indigenous people, mostly through the development of private reindeer herding and tourism. Vladimirova demonstrates the complexities that arose when the Sámi tried to take advantage of the special rights to natural resources that Russian legislation promised. Broad legal formulations and the unwillingness of bureaucrats to cooperate with indigenous people created obstacles to the development of indigenous economic branches. Nevertheless, the case of Seidozero Lake marks a turning point in the relation between conserved territories and indigenous peoples' right to natural resources in Russia.

## Part 2. Governance of indigenous space in a global context

The second issue, comprising Part 2 of the book, moves the focus from northern Europe to the global environment of indigenous people, thus comparing the case of the Sámi with other indigenous peoples. It deals with the ideas and implementation of new kinds of postcolonial models for nature conservation. The global comparison aims to problematise the differentiation of governance models in Sápmi in order to clarify how national and global regulations work together.

Among the Sámi there is still a longstanding struggle to gain proper recognition within the national legal systems for the right to herd reindeer. Furthermore, in the last two to three decades the reindeer herders have been accused of destroying pristine nature and mountain areas through their use of modern vehicles and tools, as well as keeping herds that are too large. The environmental movement has put pressure on the sustainable use of reindeer pasture along with questioning the Sámi tradition, especially within protected areas.

**Jacinta Ruru** addresses the principal question of whether there is a new commitment to recognising indigenous peoples in law, and what this ought to mean in the context of owning and managing national parks. With a stance in current national park legislation in Aotearoa/New Zealand she offers five reasons why national parks are a useful modern landscape through which to explore indigenous peoples' customary rights and interests in law. After examining the State's general national park governance ideas she focuses on the national park Te Urewera, situated on the North Island of the country. This national park is valued for its historical and cultural heritage as well as spiritual reflection. Te Urewera is an excellent example of radical legislative reform made real, where a new, more respectful, approach to valuing and caring for landscapes is enshrined.

**Michael Adams** examines trajectories of shared governance in conservation between governments and indigenous peoples in Australia and India, as a contrast to Sweden. With a specific focus on the 'new conservation paradigm' which includes broad differences, ranging from increased indigenous involvement to increased private sector involvement, the aim of the article is to reveal geographic and cultural influences on conservation, and how these in combination with different kinds of knowledge might relate to forms of shared governance and Sámi customary rights in Sweden. According to Adams, the emerging trends in global conservation, including the 'new conservation paradigm' offer opportunities to consider the advantages of complementary approaches to knowledge. Each of the different traditions has strengths and limitations that could be used to expand the toolkit available for innovative responses to impending challenging environmental changes e.g. climate change.

**Jan Åge Riseth** aims to investigate why Sámi values have had hardly any impact on nature conservation in Norway, taking into account that nature conservation and traditional Sámi land use have, in the main, joint interests in protecting nature from encroachments and over-use. During the last half century, the Sámi of Norway have achieved considerable improvements in the recognition of their political and cultural rights including a constitutional amendment (1988), establishment of a Sámi Parliament (1989), ratification of the ILO Convention (1991), and the first land-claim settlement as well as a consultation agreement (2005). Despite all this, before 2009 there are hardly any signs that the Sámi view of nature conservation was taken into consideration. On the contrary, there are clear indications that modern reindeer herding is considered problematic by conservation authorities.

**Elsa Reimerson** concentrates on how discourses articulated in and through international arenas for protected areas and nature conservation affect indigenous peoples' space for political agency on national and local levels. Reimerson studies two cases of protected area governance and management in Swedish and Norwegian Sápmi – the Laponia World Heritage site in Sweden, and the recently implemented local National Park Boards in Norway – where international conventions have been central to the discursive production of Sámi subjects. She argues that international arenas for conservation can be used to strengthen indigenous peoples' claims to influence over the management of protected areas on their traditional lands, but that they may also set limits for the articulation of claims and the political strategies possible or acceptable on the national or local level.

**Carina Green** and **Jan Turtinen** examine how the framework of the World Heritage Convention shapes the conditions under which indigenous peoples can influence the nomination process for new World Heritage areas and participate in the management of already established sites. It aims to illuminate and analyse the link between World Heritage sites, identity processes, power relations and local management strategies. Within these sites many different interests and objectives intersect, giving rise to tension between cultural and natural conservation management, democratisation processes and ethno-political aspirations and changing power structures. Three case studies are included in the analysis, namely Laponia in Sweden, Cape York in Australia and Tongariro in Aotearoa/New Zealand. The authors argue that bureaucratic structures and practices are part of the reason for the slow rate at which indigenous peoples gain influence and control over World Heritage processes. However, the World Heritage Convention has the potential to have a profound effect on local situations and relations among stakeholders. Laponia is the clearest example of this.

In the last article **Antje Neumann** compares the adaption of the Convention on Biological Diversity (CBD) to indigenous participation in the context of area protection and management in Finland and Norway. The CBD recognises protected areas as cornerstones of biodiversity conservation, but does not see this as constituting indigenous peoples' rights and therefore clearly has numerous limitations in this respect. However, one of CBD's targets reflects the relation between indigenous peoples and area protection, specifically focusing on the involvement of indigenous and local communities in the management of protected areas. She concludes that despite the progress in both countries, deficiencies remain regarding the full and effective participation of Sámi people in area protection and management in both Finland and Norway.

Indigenous people are living in modern landscapes in an interconnected global society where economic forces are regarded as strong actors and politicians, especially on local and national level, have lost much of their former power. Northern Scandinavia is breaking fresh ground through the development of new kinds of conservation models in which the Sámi people are taking an active part. This is partly known by other countries, but not in detail and not in a comprehensive way through the lenses of different scientific topics and global comparison. We hope this book will contribute to a better understanding of these issues.

# Part 1

# Legislation and historically changed policies within Sápmi

# 1 Nordic legislation on protected areas

## How does it affect Sámi customary rights?

*Christina Allard*

### Introduction

This chapter addresses the different legal frameworks for protected area regimes in Sweden, Norway and Finland and analyses, with an emphasis on the longstanding Sámi tradition of reindeer herding, how these frameworks take into account Sámi culture and customary activities. Chiefly examined are environmental provisions for protected areas within Sápmi, the Sámi homeland region located predominantly in the north of Sweden, Norway, Finland and Russia.[1] Sweden has practised area protection since the early eighteenth century; Norway and Finland have had designated protected areas since the middle of the twentieth century. The Sámi exist as one Indigenous people residing within and across the state borders of Sweden, Norway, Finland and Russia, hence the importance of examining the diverse legal contexts under which the Sámi live.

The legal framework in any given jurisdiction illuminates the standing of affairs in a state, including matters concerning nature conservation. Sweden, Norway and Finland have their own histories regarding protected area legislation, and the extent to which Sámi rights and culture are recognised within their legal systems. The two main areas of law – conservation legislation and systems of recognition of Sámi customary rights – coexist in the Nordic states, with the ensuing results influenced to a greater or lesser degree by the roles and legal status the Sámi have in relation to state aims and policies for designating protected areas. Where Sámi inhabitants and land-use practices are not sufficiently addressed legally or territorial rights[2] properly recognised, there is a risk of limiting Sámi customary activities, as a result of externally imposed restrictions within designated protected areas, potentially weakening Sámi ways of life.

As other authors in this volume have pointed out,[3] over recent decades there has been, through various binding and non-binding legal instruments, a growing emphasis internationally (and at times nationally) on the importance of traditional knowledge, sustainable uses and the participation of Indigenous peoples in the context of nature conservation.[4]

1 For an examination of the situation of the Sámi people in the Russian Kola peninsula see Vladislava Vladimirova's chapter in this volume.

2 Rights to land and natural resources are commonly referred to as territorial rights. See e.g. Anaya, *Indigenous Peoples in International Law*, 143.

3 E.g. the chapters by Elsa Reimerson, Antje Neumann, Carina Green and Jan Turtinen.

4 The most prominent are the Convention on Biological Diversity 1992 (CBD), the World Heritage Convention 1972, ILO Convention No. 169 Concerning Indigenous and Tribal Peoples in Independent Countries 1989 (ILO 169), the UN Declaration on the Rights of Indigenous Peoples 2007 (UNDRIP) as well as linked protocols and guidelines to those instruments.

Despite such efforts, however, the gap between 'theory and practice' – that is, between international standards and the implementation and interpretation of such standards on domestic and local levels – is still wide, as is revealed throughout this book.[5] A former UN Special Rapporteur on the rights of Indigenous peoples, James Anaya, has, for example, expressed concern about World Heritage sites and the lack of Indigenous peoples' participation in the nomination, declaration and management of such sites, as well as the non-recognition of Indigenous peoples' territorial rights regarding them.[6] However, such deficiencies are also seen in other protected-area legal categories on domestic levels. The right to participation, rooted in other basic human rights principles (such as self-determination, equality, cultural integrity and right to property), is generally understood as key for the effective exercise of the basic human rights of Indigenous peoples.[7] In the context of protected area regimes, the right to participation signifies adequate protection of customary rights, consultation with affected Indigenous groups and their free, prior and informed consent.[8]

The aim of this comparative study is to analyse and contrast the extent to which relevant conservation legislation in the three states takes into account Sámi cultural and territorial rights in the designation of protected areas. My main focus is on the legal rhetoric itself used in the statutes and the preparatory works[9] for such statutes, not how the rules play out in society. Here I examine categories most often applied to the protected areas in the region of Sápmi, where national parks and nature reserves are a common category in all three states, and where Norway and Finland also have designated protected landscapes and wilderness areas, respectively. In Sweden and Finland there is an additional 'layer' of area protection in the Natura 2000 areas, established under European Union (EU) environmental law which, although relevant to some extent, will not be analysed at length here.[10] This study, thus, includes an analysis of state legal sources,[11] in this case environmental legislation on various levels, preparatory works to Acts and legal literature.[12]

My guiding question is: *Does conservation legislation generally take into account Sámi culture, interests and/or territorial rights in the context of protected areas and, if so, in what ways?* Given the focus on the designation of protected areas, I will not address the management or co-management arrangements of protected areas or the influence of Sámi actors in such decision-making, as other authors in this volume have covered this.[13] The specific arrangements for the Laponia World Heritage site in Sweden are also not included in my analyses, mainly because Laponia must be regarded as a particular and unique example within the

5 Cf. Stevens, ed., *Indigenous Peoples, National Parks*; Chatty and Colchester, eds., *Conservation and Mobile Indigenous Peoples*; Stevens, ed., *Conservation through Cultural Survival.*
6 UN Doc. A/67/301, 2012, paras. 33, 34–37.
7 UN Doc. A/65/264, 2010, para. 39.
8 The principle of free, prior and informed consent (FPIC) is incorporated into the UNDRIP in several articles, most noteworthy here in Articles 19 and 32, but its current meaning and scope are much debated. See further e.g. Heinämäki, 'The rapidly evolving international status', 196–198.
9 This is an important legal source among the Nordic countries, and referred to below as SOU, Prop. (Sweden), NOU, Ot.prp. (Norway) and RP (Finland).
10 Habitats Directive 92/43 and Birds Directive 2009/147 (previous 79/409).
11 Legislation and most preparatory works in Finland are commonly available in Swedish. Translations of statutory texts into English are based either on unofficial government translations or translations by the author. All other translations from Scandinavian languages are by the author.
12 There are only a few court cases related to Sámi customary rights and protected areas; given the limited space here and the purpose of this chapter, case law will not be considered as relevant.
13 See the chapters by Jan Åge Riseth, Antje Neumann and Elsa Reimerson.

Swedish protected area regime, and thus far it has not influenced any general amendments to existing conservation legislation with respect to the Sámi.

The chapter is structured as follows: after a short background, I address the legislative frameworks for protected areas in Sweden, Norway and Finland and their history, followed by respective conclusions.

## Short background – Conservation tensions and national traits

There are tensions between nature conservation norms and traditional Sámi activities, especially reindeer herding. Increasingly, over the last three decades Sámi reindeer herders have been accused of destroying pristine nature and mountain areas, notably through their use of modern vehicles and equipment and having herds too large for the grazing areas to sustain.[14] The environmental movement has pressed for sustainable use of reindeer grazing areas and the conservation of large predators, while questioning Sámi traditions, within protected areas. Adding to the complexity, the Sámi in all three states are still struggling to gain proper recognition and protection for reindeer herding rights whereas, in national legislation, reindeer herding often has to yield to other land-use interests and exploitation.[15]

As an age-old culture and traditional Sámi livelihood and industry, reindeer herding is carried out over vast tracts of land, covering as much as 35–55 per cent of the northernmost regions in each of the three states, and the right to engage in reindeer herding is treated as a strong usufruct right covering both publicly and privately owned lands.[16] This usufruct right includes a number of additional entitlements, such as hunting and fishing rights for reindeer herders. Also important in the Nordic context is that there have been no historical treaties between the states and Sámi groups and therefore no equivalents to reserve lands. Moreover, there are no areas recognised by the state as existing under collective Sámi ownership.[17]

Although the three states are all parties to major conservation conventions, there are differences between them concerning State–Sámi relations. Only Norway is party to ILO 169; Finland has come close to ratifying ILO 169, but the Finnish Parliament rejected the corresponding bill in 2015. Sweden has been considering ratifying ILO 169 since the late 1990s, but has not yet formulated a bill. At the same time, these three states and the corresponding three Sámi parliaments are currently negotiating a Nordic Sámi Convention, the draft text of which builds on ILO 169 and other relevant human rights law but the prospect of ratification is uncertain. Sweden and Finland are, however, full members of the EU and are thus bound by EU law.

Nordic states have traditionally weak constitutions, even if Norway is, to some extent, an exception.[18] Sámi culture is protected in the texts of the constitutions, even if, as is the

14 The modernisation of the industry from the 1960s onwards has increased the use of various forms of motor vehicles in outlying lands which, if used on bare ground, may cause damage to plants and soil. See e.g. NOU 2004:28, 463, 466; Prop. 1995/96:226, 15. This corresponds generally to the situation in all three countries.

15 For Sweden see Torp, 'Det rättsliga skyddet av samisk renskötsel'.

16 Allard, 'The Nordic countries' law', 163–164; Sandström, *A Toolbox for Co-production*, 15.

17 The notion of 'aboriginal title' does not exist in Real Property Law. The only recognition of communal (Sámi) ownership is based in the Norwegian Supreme Court case *Svartskogen* (Rt 2001 p 1229). The case concerned a dispute over a claim of ownership between the State and a local community with a Sámi majority population. After complex assessment the court held that the local community was the rightful owner.

18 Cf. Allard, *Renskötselrätt i nordisk belysning*, 321–322.

case in Sweden and Norway, the protection is to be realised by the state authorities.[19] In Finland, protection is built into the legal text as a classic 'rights-provision', but has yet to be properly applied.[20]

In Norway, consultations between the state and the Sámi are legally founded on a consultation agreement between the government and the Sámi Parliament from 2005, which in practice accords Norwegian Sámi substantial influence, for example in the drafting of legislation affecting Sámi.[21] In addition, there is a specific consultation agreement from 2007 between the Sámi Parliament in Norway and the Norwegian Ministry of the Environment, applicable to traditional Sámi regions and securing the active participation of the Sámi in planning and decisions related to protected areas. Consultation as a duty in Finland is based in an Act and includes such issues as protected areas and legislative drafts or public policy related to traditional Sámi livelihoods.[22] Sweden lacks legislation and other documents concerning State–Sámi consultations in matters that affect the Sámi.

There has been a distinct Nordic trait to trust the resolving of competing land uses and Sámi rights claims to state government commissions and bills, not court cases; however Sámi rights are increasingly being pursued through national courts and international legal venues. The Nordic states have a positive reputation internationally for their progress in environmental protection generally, as well as in securing basic human rights. However, environmental law historically has its roots in the nation state which defines legislation and protected area regimes, resulting also in particular ways of solving State–Sámi issues, as will be explained below.

## The Swedish system of area protection

### *Introduction*

Sweden has a long tradition of establishing nature areas for conservation, and the state created the first national parks in Europe as early as 1909, when nine national parks were designated, on land largely located in traditional Sámi mountain areas. Fourteen of Sweden's first national parks were designated under the Act of 1909.[23] Scenic beauty and outdoor recreational interests have been strong since the start in Sweden and are still evident in current legislation. Nature reserves (originally nature parks), a later conservation category initiated in the 1950s and 1960s, emphasised social recreational needs particularly in areas adjacent to populated places in central and southern Sweden; eventually the scope was broadened to include conservation interests.[24] Because of the initial intent, land use conflicts with reindeer herding were not addressed in the preparatory works.[25] Today, nature

19 Swedish Instrument of Government 1974, ch. 1 s. 2 Norwegian Constitution Act 1814, s. 108.

20 Constitution of Finland 1999, s. 17.

21 NOU 2007:13, 824. All legislative proposals after 2005 of direct Sámi interest have been subject to consultations, including the Nature Diversity Act from 2009 that encompasses provisions regarding protected areas. The Agreement is an instrument for implementing the state's duty under international law, especially ILO 169.

22 Sámi Parliament Act 1995, s. 9.

23 *Nationalparksplan för Sverige*, 87–88. The first Swedish nature conservation legislation encompassed two acts, one concerning natural monuments (*naturminnesmärken*) and one regarding national parks, both from 1909. These were revoked by Nature Conservation Acts from 1952 and 1964, preceding the current legislation. See Elenius' and Hjulman's chapters in this volume for a historical account.

24 See e.g. Torp, 'Rennäringens rättigheter', 182–185; Michanek, *Svensk miljörätt*, 77.

25 Torp, 'Rennäringens rättigheter', 188.

reserves are the most common protection category in Sweden, and a large number exist within Swedish Sápmi.

During the nineteenth and early twentieth centuries both the Sámi and traditional reindeer herding were more or less seen as part of nature, or at least as no threat to nature-based interests aimed at preservation and, apart from hunting rights, the entitlements inherent in the reindeer herding right were allowed for within national parks until 1991, when a specific provision was repealed. However, Sámi hunting was increasingly restricted from the early twentieth century onwards, and over time nature conservation interests came into conflict with the modernisation of reindeer herding practices.[26] No provision protecting the right to herd reindeer has ever existed within nature reserves, as mentioned above; reindeer herding could be infringed in the same ways as other usufruct rights.

The current statute, the Environmental Code of 1998, includes basic rules concerning area protection. It is a comprehensive and integrated environmental protection statute, comprising 15 older and repealed acts. According to its very first section, para. 1, the overall aim is to

> promote sustainable development which will assure a healthy and sound environment for present and future generations. Such development will be based on recognition of the fact that nature is worthy of protection and that our right to modify and exploit nature carries with it a responsibility for wise management of natural resources.

The second paragraph states that the Act shall be applied to ensure, among other things, that 'valuable natural and cultural environments are protected and preserved' as well as biological diversity. The rules regarding national parks and nature reserves have a continuity having been transferred from the former 1964 Act with few major amendments. The ten current area-protection categories, in Chapter 7 of the Environmental Code, include shore protection areas and Natura 2000 areas; national parks and nature reserves are most important for Sápmi. More detailed provisions are given in regulations issued by the Swedish government;[27] by-laws are issued by competent Swedish authorities with specific requirements concerning each protected area and various guidelines from the Swedish Environmental Protection Agency. Thus, there is a hierarchy of rules concerning what is allowed and what activities are prohibited in each area, including with respect to Sámi customary activities.

For national parks, this hierarchy has resulted in a peculiar set of requirements that noticeably limit Sámi customary rights and activities. According to by-laws for individual parks, Sámi hunting and commercial fishing are often restricted or prohibited; in a newer park reindeer grazing has been prohibited. Despite a general prohibition on the use of motor vehicles, the Sámi may, with some exceptions, use snowmobiles in direct relation to the management of reindeer. Although no commercial activities are allowed within parks, Sámi are usually allowed to sell Sámi bread and fish to tourists.[28]

Swedish legislation draws strongly on the ideas of nature conservation as ecological protection along with outdoor recreation as a social concern. In contrast to current Norwegian legal sources, the Swedish bill concerning the Environmental Code does not discuss cultural land uses in general, or Sámi customary uses in particular; as if the conflict does

26 Ibid., 164–166.
27 Notably the Regulation on Protected Areas for the Environmental Code, 1998, and the Regulation on National Parks 1987.
28 Cf. e.g. the by-laws for the national parks of Sarek, Padjelanta, Abisko and Fulufjället.

not exist or present problems. Sámi and reindeer herding is hardly mentioned in the text. A new category, culture reserves, was added in 1998 meant to 'preserve valuable cultural landscapes'.[29] Even if older legislation had encompassed cultural aspects of the natural environment, nature reserves were not used to preserving cultural heritage; the bill stressed the need to include 'historical landscapes' in the system of protected areas, seen as an addition to biological diversity and aesthetic landscape concerns.[30] Among some 40 cultural reserves in existence today only two relate to Sámi cultural remains and landscapes.[31]

### *National parks and nature reserves*

As said at the beginning, common forms of area protection in Swedish Sápmi are national parks, nature reserves and areas relating to the EU ecological network, the Natura 2000 areas.[32] These latter areas, appointed and established under the EU Habitats and Birds Directives, are mainly conserved via national categories of protected areas. As Natura 2000 areas have no implied independent protection, they need to be conserved by domestic forms of area protection, commonly nature reserves.[33] Neither the provisions in the EU directives nor the Swedish rules implementing the two directives mention Sámi culture or reindeer herding, nor do they take into account such considerations during area designation processes. For this reason I will not discuss Natura 2000 further.

The provisions for national parks have been transferred to the Environmental Code; regarding interpretation, the bill refers to the preparatory works for the two former Acts from 1952 and 1964.[34] The prerequisites for designating a national park are stated in one sentence in the Environmental Code, ch. 7 s. 2:

> A land or water area that belongs to the state may with the consent of Parliament be designated a national park by the Government for the purpose of preserving a large contiguous area of a certain landscape type in its natural state or essentially unchanged.

It is made clear that national parks must comprise larger areas owned by the state and be of a certain landscape type, more or less untouched by human cultural activities; nothing prevents two or more landscape types co-existing in large national parks. The parks are usually to be open and accessible for tourism, but should not cause their original natural character to be lost.[35] In the Regulation on National Parks, 1987, all national parks are listed with a short description of the purpose of protection; commonly there are references to each area's

29 Environmental Code, ch. 7 s. 9. Like nature reserves, the County Administrative Board and Municipalities have the authority to designate them.

30 Prop. 1997/98:45 Part 1, 323–324. The main objective of cultural reserves is to preserve 'historical landscapes' and their cultural heritage, and is a complement to both natural reserves and cultural heritage in the Cultural Environment Act 1988. See ibid., 325.

31 They are Atoklimpen and Fatmomakke Church town, established in 2005 and 2014 respectively. The former aims to preserve an old Sámi reindeer herding landscape, and the latter to preserve the old Church town built for Sámi and settlers. See information on the webpage of the Swedish National Heritage Board, http://www.raa.se/kulturarvet/landskap/kulturreservat/forteckning-3/. The vast majority of culture reserves relate to farmsteads, older agricultural landscapes and old industrial sites.

32 See further in Krämer, *EU Environmental Law*, 189–192.

33 Prop. 1997/98:45 Part 1, 308–309.

34 Prop. 1997/98:45 Part 2, 69.

35 Ibid.

'natural state' or that it is 'essentially unchanged'. The Environmental Protection Agency is authorised to make by-laws concerning restrictions on the rights to use land and water areas within national parks, as well as passage rights, etc. Such restrictions may be directed toward all usufruct rights, including the right to herd reindeer.

Nature reserves are currently the most common form of protection, designated on the basis of the Environmental Code, ch. 7 s. 4:

> A land or water area may be declared a nature reserve by a county administrative board or a municipality for the purpose of preserving biological diversity, protecting and preserving valuable natural environments or satisfying the need for areas for outdoor recreation.

Nature reserves can be designated also on privately owned lands and in general for three reasons – biological diversity, valuable natural areas or outdoor recreation, or any combination of these three. Generally, there must be a strong public interest in establishing a nature reserve;[36] however, it is a simpler procedure in that the decision is made by either by the municipality or a county administrative board, and there is no need for land purchase as there is in creating national parks. The area of a nature reserve may be large or small, depending on the need. In the decision to designate a nature reserve, a statement of reasons must be made in accordance with Environmental Code ch. 7 s. 5, and the decision must specify restrictions on rights to use land and water areas as necessary, in order to meet the original purpose of the protection.

In the decision-making process related to area protection under chapter 7 of the Code, there is to be a balancing of interests with s. 25 stating that 'private interests shall also be taken into account' and that restrictions 'must . . . not be more stringent than is necessary in order to achieve the purpose of the protection'. However, there is little guidance as to how this balancing should be carried out, or how Sámi rights and customs should be weighted. As said, Sámi customs and reindeer herding are barely mentioned in either the Code or the bill, leaving the authorising authority with a wide margin in balancing rights. An additional complicating factor is that environmental legislation commonly regards reindeer herding (industry) as a public interest and seldom as a private interest (civil right). All in all, there are no specific provisions concentrating on matters related to Sámi culture or customary activities in Sweden's protected area regime.

## The Norwegian system of area protection

### *Introduction*

Norway was relatively late in designating special protected areas, with the state's first national park, Rondane, being established in 1962.[37] The common forms of protected areas in Norway have historical roots, while categories and rules have developed through state praxis and are codified in the former Nature Protection Act of 1970. Previous legislation (1910 and 1954) included a more general authority to designate protected areas.[38]

36 Ibid., 71.
37 NOU 2004:28, 294.
38 Backer, *Naturmangfoldloven*, 265.

What is striking in area protection in Norway is the greater focus on continued use of protected areas and the relationship, and often correlation, between historic and current uses and protection.[39] As a general rule, traditional uses have been, and still are, allowed to continue after a nature protection area has been designated.[40] This approach also applies to traditional non-Sámi uses, as Norway's geography and topography, with extensive high mountain areas and fjords, have favoured traditional industries that are small-scale and scattered.[41] With respect to an accentuated focus on conservation of biological diversity along the lines of the Convention on Biological Diversity (CBD), Norwegian legislation emphasises the importance of dynamic and flexible rules, so as to enable a sliding scale between use and protection, a balance determined in advance through legal provisions.[42]

The basic statute for designating protected areas is the Nature Diversity Act, 2009. It is the key statute for environmental considerations in Norway with a comprehensive and integrated approach.[43] In the Commission Report, comprising background material and considerations relevant for revision of the law, Sámi issues are highlighted throughout wherever relevant, but particularly in Chapter 21, which is dedicated to challenges with respect to the Sámi and local communities.[44] International obligations related to Indigenous rights law are comprehensively examined in the preparatory works. There have been consultations with the Norwegian Sámi Parliament in the law-making process based on the consultation agreement from 2005.[45] The Commission also investigated whether there was a need for a new specific Sámi protection category related to reindeer herding or other customary activities, but rejected the idea as national parks and protected landscapes allow for Sámi customary uses to continue.[46]

In both the Commission Report and the bill a whole chapter is devoted to addressing international environmental treaties that Norway has ratified, in particular the CBD, which the Nature Diversity Act seeks to implement.[47] In looking to the International Union for Conservation of Nature (IUCN) guidelines on categories of protected areas, the Commission found that there was generally a good correlation between the domestic provisions and IUCN equivalents.[48] Despite the fact that Norway is not a full member of the EU and thus not bound by its conservation legislation, the preparatory works still take some EU rules into consideration, particularly regarding Natura 2000, as this is the EU's response to both the Bern Convention[49] and the CBD.[50]

39 Cf. Ot.prp. No. 52 (2008–2009), 41.
40 NOU 2004:28, 154, 473–74, 486.
41 Allard, *Renskötselrätt i nordisk belysning*, 66–68.
42 NOU 2004:28, 154, 156.
43 Ot.prp. No. 52 (2008–2009), 51, 53. The Act's preparatory works are of substantial length. See further Backer, *Naturmangfoldloven*, 2–4, 12–13.
44 It should be noted that the Nature Diversity Act does not regulate the collective and individual territorial rights of the Sámi. This was not part of the mandate for the Commission, see NOU 2004:28, 463. Sámi rights were examined by the Sámi Rights Commission II appointed in 2001 and summarised in their extensive Commission Report NOU 2007:13 Part A–B. There is no space here to go into the resulting recommendations regarding protective areas, which have not yet influenced changes in legislation.
45 A summary of the consultations is available in Ot.prp. No. 52 (2008–2009), 33–39.
46 NOU 2004:28, 485.
47 Ot.prp. nr. 52 (2008–2009), 44; NOU 2004:28, 158.
48 NOU 2004:28, 310–311, 367–368, 373, 376.
49 The Bern Convention on the Conservation of European Wildlife and Natural Habitats, 1979.
50 Ot.prp. nr. 52 (2008–2009), 49–50; Backer, *Naturmangfoldloven*, 9.

The Act's emphasis is on sustainable use;[51] its aim is enshrined in s. 1 where it is stated that the Act's purpose is to:

> protect biological, geological and landscape diversity and ecological processes through conservation and sustainable use, and in such a way that the environment provides a basis for human activity, culture, health and well-being, now and in the future, *including a basis for Sámi culture.* [my emphasis]

In the phrasing of s. 1, the Act itself combines both eco-centric and anthropocentric views on nature and, especially in the government bill, emphasis is placed on the relationship between nature and people as a means for developing Norwegian culture and identity and equally relevant on national and local levels, including Sámi cultural aspects.[52] Hence, the italicised phrase in s. 1 above should be understood as a clarification, founded in Indigenous rights. The Norwegian state must secure a sufficient natural resource base for the Sámi to carry on their own cultural activities and livelihoods.[53]

Section 14 of the Act stresses the need to take into account other important public interests in decision-making, meaning that economic, social and cultural needs should be weighed against conservation interests. According to para. 2 of s. 14, in the interpretation of individual provisions directly affecting Sámi interests, 'due importance shall be attached . . . to the natural resource base for Sámi culture'. The bill refers here to Article 27, regarding the protection of minority cultures, of the UN International Covenant on Civil and Political Rights (ICCPR), 1966, and related safeguards the state must provide.[54] In s. 14, the balance between conservation and the use of biological resources is evident. With respect to protected areas, Sámi resistance has generally gathered around the principal issues: i) that Sámi territorial rights remain unresolved; ii) that protection is seen as being in breach of Sámi self-determination; iii) the concepts of 'wilderness' and 'untouched'; iv) discontent with the designation process; and, v) fear of future limitations on customary uses.[55]

The legal framework for area protection is characterised by the perception that Norway has been shaped by humans for millennia, evidenced in Norwegian nature by the many visible cultural remains, cultural landscapes and biological diversity itself.[56] The agricultural landscapes are also more varied and long-lived than those of the rest of northern Europe. It is also acknowledged that reindeer is a natural species that impacts on vegetation and landscape forming a part of the ecosystem, acknowledging the Sámi position – that reindeer herding areas are cultural landscapes.[57]

### *National parks, protected landscapes and nature reserves*

Relevant forms of protected areas in Norwegian Sápmi are national parks, protected landscapes and nature reserves. These can be designated on both state-owned and private lands. Protected areas in Norway are designated through a regulation, a decision by the

51 Ot.prp. nr. 52 (2008–2009), 51, 371.
52 Ot.prp. No. 52 (2008–2009), 43, 371; Backer, *Naturmangfoldloven*, 19, 47.
53 NOU 2004:28, 468, 471.
54 Ot.prp. No. 52 (2008–2009), 384; NOU 2004:28, 471; Backer, *Naturmangfoldloven*, 118–119.
55 NOU 2004:28, 478.
56 Ot.prp. No. 52 (2008–2009), 41.
57 Ibid.

King-in-Council, following s. 34 of the Nature Diversity Act. Chapter V of the Nature Diversity Act is devoted to area protection, and s. 33 sets out eight objectives that should be reflected in the designation of protected areas. Importantly, cultural landscapes are mentioned here: 'natural environments that reflect human use through the ages', relevant to generations of Sámi uses. Cultural–historical values can, thus, be included as part of area protection.[58]

The category, protected landscapes, contains the measures that least limit the use of the land, whereas the category nature reserve can entail the complete cessation of any use and passage rights; a national park typically lies in between the two regarding use-allowance.[59] Traditional peripheral land uses (*utmarksbruk*), including recreational fishing, hunting, small-scale farming, reindeer herding and berry picking, etc., can often continue after the establishment of protected landscapes as well as in national parks.[60] Nature reserves normally prohibit the use of motor vehicles and area uses are restricted to hunting, trapping, fishing and berry picking.[61]

With respect to Sámi reindeer herding in protected areas, in principle only a few restrictions exist, notably those concerning the use of motor vehicles (particularly on land not covered by snow); normally grazing, hunting, trapping, fishing, and use of timber for fires and necessary structures can continue. Restrictions on other forms of Sámi customary uses are more difficult to foresee, since no distinctions are made within use regulations between Sámi and other customary uses; thus, the Sámi may be subject to limitations on hunting and fishing, especially in nature reserves.[62]

Because the very concept of national parks is historically embedded in ideas of protecting the 'wilderness' and 'untouched' nature areas from human devastation (cf. Yellowstone National Park), Indigenous peoples, including the Sámi, have long questioned the foundations for protected areas. The Norwegian Sámi Parliament criticised the description 'untouched' and 'beautiful' in earlier legislation, signalling the neglect of age-old uses and the Sámi presence. Following that criticism, wordings were slightly amended in the new Act with respect to the three categories of protection.[63] Instead of referring to 'untouched' nature, the qualifications for designating a national park (s. 35 para. 1) now refer to, '[l]arge areas of natural habitat that contain distinctive or representative ecosystems or landscapes and where there is *no major infrastructure development*'[64] (my emphasis). Following para. 2, the park shall be shielded from 'development, installations, pollution and other activity' that may hamper its protection. One important amendment in the new Act is that there is no longer a requirement for national parks to be established on state lands.[65]

The purpose of protected landscapes is stated in s. 36, para. 1 and relates to '[n]atural or cultural landscapes that are important in ecological or cultural terms, as a source of enjoyment *or as a basis for forming an identity*' (my emphasis). In para. 2 it is reaffirmed that current activities may be continued and developed within protected landscapes. The focus on human enjoyment of the natural–cultural environment is stronger for both national parks and protected landscapes than for nature reserves.[66] Nature reserves have stricter criteria

58 Ot.prp. No. 52 (2008–2009), 405–406.
59 Cf. Nature Diversity Act, 35–37. See also NOU 2004:28, 154, 369.
60 NOU 2004:28, 311, 363, 473.
61 NOU 2004:28, 375–376.
62 NOU 2004:28, 473–474.
63 NOU 2004:28, 295, 472, 478, 486.
64 See further Backer, *Naturmangfoldloven*, 315.
65 NOU 2004:28, 297; Backer, *Naturmangfoldloven*, 266, 315–316.
66 See also NOU 2004:28, 147.

that are more directly tied to the conservation of biological diversity, based on s. 37 para. 1 of the Act.[67] Paragraph 3 declares that 'no person must do anything that reduces the conservation value', and, as explained, absolute protection from all activity and access is possible.

Among the provisions analysed there are no general exemption clauses for Sámi reindeer herding rights or other Sámi customary uses in the restrictions imposed under ss. 33–37 of the Nature Diversity Act. At least for national parks and protected landscapes, the general practice regarding specific regulations is to allow continued customary use. All in all, the emphasis on protection and sustainable uses, as well as a natural resource base for Sámi culture, must, I argue, be seen as strengthening the Norwegian area protection system.

## The Finnish system of area protection

### *Introduction*

Finland designated its first four national parks and six nature reserves in 1938 after prolonged public debates and legislative shortcomings. After the Second World War and forced land transfers to the Soviet Union only two parks and reserves remained within Finnish territory.[68] Since then, new protected areas have been continuously added, especially within the last three decades. The original reason for conserving nature and nature areas is stated as being the preservation of scenic beauty and, even if new goals have been added such as protection of biological diversity, the bill for the current Act retained the reference to natural beauty.[69] On their websites national parks are described as Finland's most beautiful natural and recreational areas,[70] and these parks, as in most states, carry symbolic values. In Finnish legislation there are a few general exemptions from restrictions on usage, including reindeer herding.

The protected areas in Finland are made up of national parks and nature reserves, including Finnish Sápmi. In addition, there is also a specific category labelled wilderness areas. The Natura 2000 areas are important, but these do not constitute an autonomous protection category since the EU system requires protection of such designated areas through normal national protection categories. In Finland, as in Sweden, most Natura 2000 areas are legally protected as national parks and nature reserves, as well as through being parts of wilderness areas.[71] There are no general exemptions relating to minority or Indigenous cultures or livelihoods, and therefore I will not expand on this category.

The basic area protection statute in Finland is the Nature Conservation Act 1996, and when it came into force it replaced the former Act from 1923.[72] The new Act is intended to implement the two EU directives, the Habitats and Birds Directives, as is clearly stated in s. 3 of the Act, but also partially to implement the CBD and its focus on sustainable use.[73]

67 Ot.prp. No. 52 (2008–2009), 415.

68 See the online Finnish dictionary at http://www.uppslagsverket.fi , word '*nationalparker*', and the public website on Finland's protected areas and their history, http://www.utinaturen.fi/sv/varanationalparkershistoria. See Elenius' chapter in this volume for a historical account.

69 RP 79/1996, 26.

70 See e.g. the web page of the Ministry of the Environment at http://www.ym.fi/sv-FI/Natur/Naturens_mangfald/Naturskyddsomraden/Nationalparker_och_naturreservat.

71 See the website of the state owned enterprise Metsähallitus', which manages protected areas, http://www.metsa.fi/web/sv/natura2000omraden.

72 See Nature Conservation Act 1996, s. 76.

73 RP 79/1996, 1, 26.

The Act is not a comprehensive 'catch-all' environmental statute, as are the Norwegian and Swedish statutes but, rather, a specific legislation for the designation, protection and management of area and species conservation.[74]

The bill, which is the essential correlating preparatory work, is short and does not include specific sections related to Sámi culture or reindeer herding, as Sámi interests and reindeer herding are mentioned only briefly in a few instances.[75] Notably, the bill declares that, with the new Act, reindeer herding, in accordance with the Finnish Reindeer Husbandry Act 1990, shall be permitted in national parks and nature reserves.[76] One has to remember, however, that reindeer herding is practised in Finland by both Sámi and Finns.[77] Lack of acknowledgement of Sámi and Sámi livelihoods is not surprising, as the Act and its bill are from the mid-1990s, a time when considerations of Indigenous rights and culture were not so developed. The Act, however, was amended in 2011 to include a specific provision giving protection to the exercise of Sámi culture when protected areas are designated within the administratively demarcated 'Sámi homeland'.[78] On the other hand, as we shall see below, the Wilderness Act of 1991, establishing 12 demarcated wilderness areas, does refer to Sámi livelihoods.

The aim of the Nature Conservation Act is stated in s. 1 as five goals, and the most relevant here are that the aims are to 'maintain biological diversity; conserve the beauty and scenic values of nature; and, promote the sustainable use of natural resources and the natural environment'. The Act also introduced a new protection category, landscape conservation areas, in a separate chapter, and with somewhat more lenient restrictions than the traditional categories, as is examined below.[79] What is protected here is not nature in its original state, but the cultural landscape scenery, its beauty, and its specific land-use history. To this day, only a handful of areas have been established under this category,[80] mostly in southern Finland with no connection to traditional Sámi land uses. I will not mention them further.

### *National parks and nature reserves*

National parks and nature reserves can only be designated on state-owned lands, normally through an act, whereas the so-called 'other nature protection categories' can be established on both private and public lands.[81] A number of common prerequisites for the establishment of these three categories are stated in the Nature Conservation Act, s. 10 para. 2, and mostly comprise ecological criteria, such as that the area to be protected, among other

74 Cf. RP 79/1996, 27. Finland has supplementary environmental statutes tasked with regulating other aspects.

75 The bill (RP 79/1996) comprises 100 pages; however, Finnish preparatory works are normally shorter than their Norwegian and Swedish equivalents. It can be compared to the Norwegian NOU, taking up 800 pages, and the corresponding bill covering 480 pages, and the Swedish bill which is in three parts covering roughly 1,400 pages.

76 RP 79/1996, 31, 51.

77 Reindeer Husbandry Act, s. 4.

78 Nature Conservation Act, s. 16; RP 99/2009.

79 RP 79/1996, 1, 37.

80 See the Ministry of the Environment's web page at http://www.ym.fi/sv-FI/Natur/Naturens_mangfald/Naturskyddsomraden/Landskapsvardsomraden; mentioned uses include agriculture, gardening, buildings and roads, but not traditional Sámi livelihoods – even if such landscapes could be included. See also RP 79/1996, 37.

81 Nature Conservation Act, ss. 10–12, 17 and 24.

things, hosts an endangered or rare species, that protection is necessary in order to maintain the favourable conservation status of a natural habitat or species, or that the area is a site of outstanding natural beauty. At least one of the seven qualifications mentioned must be met in order to designate land as a protected area in Finland. It is clear that it is the natural and ecological aspects of the nature areas that are important, not the cultural aspects (or a combination). The designation process is normally preceded by a planning process led by the Ministry for the Environment, through nature conservation programmes subject to the provisions in Chapter 2 of the Act.[82]

Apart from the general requirements mentioned above, there are specific criteria for each category. A national park (s. 11) must hold 'general interest as a natural attraction', or be capable of 'raising general awareness of or interest in nature'. In turn, a nature reserve (s. 12) must 'hold significance as a means of safeguarding undisturbed natural development, or for scientific research or education'. All activities and industries that alter natural surroundings are prohibited in national parks or nature reserves, including the construction of buildings and roads, drainage, and removal or destruction of fungi, trees, bushes and other plants.[83] Exemptions are made in s. 14 for reindeer herding, fishing in alignment with the Fishing Act of 2015, and the picking of berries and mushrooms. Through an application process reindeer herders may also be permitted to construct buildings or other fixed installations for the purpose of reindeer herding.[84] Fishing is more likely to be restricted in nature reserves than in national parks, as many nature reserves are closed to the public. Permanent inhabitants of Lapland, and a few other municipalities in the Finnish north, are entitled to hunting rights on state-owned lands, in accordance with the Hunting Act 1993 (s. 8), and hunting is in such cases allowed in national parks. In Finland there are no autonomous Sámi hunting rights attached to reindeer herding rights.

Since an amendment in 2011, as mentioned above, traditional Sámi rights have been safeguarded within the administratively demarcated Sámi homeland region whenever national parks and nature reserves are designated. Pursuant to s. 16 of the Act, 'the maintenance and development of the Sámi culture shall be secured' within this homeland area, although 'the interests of visitors to the area shall be taken into account'. The Sámi homeland is referred to in s. 4 of the Act on the Sámi Parliament 1995, and is situated in the far north of Finland.[85] Even if this means protection for Sámi culture within the Sámi homeland, Sámi residing outside this area are not granted special protection for their culture and customary rights with respect to protected areas schemes.

### *Wilderness areas*

Wilderness areas were, when they were introduced in the Wilderness Act of 1991, a new and less strict form of area protection in Finland. Through the Act, 12 large wilderness areas, comprising some 15 per cent of the County of Lapland, were established on state-owned lands in the far north, each chosen for their pristine nature and with the aim of keeping

82 RP 79/1996, 29. Public hearings are part of the drafting of these programmes and the decision-making 'shall take into account financial, social and cultural considerations' as well as 'characteristic local and regional features'. Nature Conservation Act p. 2 para. 3. See further RP 79/1996, 27.

83 Nature Conservation Act, s. 13.

84 Nature Conservation Act, s. 15 para. 1 point 6.

85 The area consists, essentially, of the Municipalities of Enontekis, Enare and Utsjoki. For more on the demarcation process see Joona, 'The definition of a Sámi person', 165–166.

them as close to their natural state as possible.[86] The reasons behind the protection were concerns that such areas would soon vanish in the wake of civilisation. One defining characteristic was, thus, the absence of roads, as well as 'vast, ***uninhabited*** and remote areas' (my emphasis).[87] Such an understanding of these areas explains their being labelled 'wilderness' areas. As a consequence, building new roads is not permitted in these areas, pursuant to s. 5 of the Act.

The Act's purpose, set out in s. 1, is that, apart from preserving the 'wilderness' character of these areas, the designation 'shall secure the Sámi culture and traditional livelihoods', as well as develop and support a multitude of uses of nature in these areas. A few interests and intentions are addressed in the bill, including what is described as 'natural industries' (*naturnäringar*), meaning varied and more or less traditional forms of uses where the natural resources constitute the basis of the use, tourism and recreational uses, and in certain areas moderate forestry.[88] Reindeer herding is mentioned as one important natural industry, but it is not elaborated upon further with respect to the consequences the protection of an area has for Sámi culture, Sámi reindeer herding and other customary uses.

During the bill's hearing process, the organisation prior to the Finnish Sámi Parliament (*Delegationen för sameärenden*) put forward the view that, due to conflicting opinions concerning the ownership of these lands, it was too early to establish the wilderness areas.[89] This intervention reveals lingering questions of Sámi land rights in the north – a question that commonly arises during the designation process of protected areas.[90] The Sámi claim ownership of these vast areas, even if no cases as such have been brought to Finnish courts.

## Conclusions

Although the conservation of land and species is an area of international concern, emphasised through various international conventions, it is obvious that protected area regimes and their underpinnings differ considerably, as shown with respect to Sweden, Norway and Finland in this chapter. While earlier studies have focused on comparative case studies among these states, this chapter offers new knowledge revealing differences in approach and legal rhetoric with respect to the Indigenous Sámi. The Nordic states may in general seem rather similar on the surface, but their similarities are based on a community of values rather than a common history of law.[91]

National parks and nature reserves are common in Sweden, Norway and Finland, but, despite the sameness of the labels, their differences regarding aim and content of area protection are obvious. First, there is a difference with respect to whether national parks and nature reserves can be established on private or public lands, where only Norway may designate parks on privately owned lands. Secondly, nature reserves in Norway and Finland are both smaller, and more strictly protected areas, often closed to human activities. Nature

86 RP 42/1990, 1, 8. Wilderness areas comprise some five percent of Finland's total territory. See ibid.
87 RP 42/1990, 3.
88 RP 42/1990, 1, 3, 8.
89 RP 42/1990, 6.
90 See e.g. the GrUU 29/2004 rd, 4, where the Constitutional Committee, commenting on the bill to designate an Act concerning Pallas-Yllästunturi National Park in 2004, remarked on the disputed state ownership within the park area and correlating research on Sámi customary rights.
91 See generally Husa et al., *Nordic law* and, specifically related to Sámi reindeer herding, Allard, *Renskötselrätt i nordisk belysning*.

reserves in Sweden are common and may be designated for several (at times conflicting) purposes, with vast areas protected, especially in the Swedish north. Thirdly, protected landscapes and wilderness areas in Norwegian and Finnish legislation offer a compromise, as these areas allow for and protect traditional land uses, including Sámi customary activities. Such a category is absent in the Swedish protected area regime.

Consultation with affected Sámi also differs among the states. Swedish legislation lacks altogether provisions for consultation between the Sámi and the state or state authorities, and, as a result, decision-making follows general public administrative law. In Sweden, the Sámi are not singled out as an Indigenous people in area protection, but are rather treated as stakeholders among many others. In Norway, two consultation agreements from 2005 and 2007 guide matters between the state and the Sámi, and in Finland consultation with the Sámi is required by an Act and is related to protected areas, among other things. A common denominator among the three states is, however, lingering conflict regarding Sámi territorial rights, which commonly arises during the designation processes for protected areas.

To answer my guiding question as to whether conservation legislation generally takes into account Sámi culture, interests and/or territorial rights in the Nordic states, the conclusion is that Norway stands out positively. Both Norway and Finland have, in their protected area regimes, explicit provisions that safeguard Sámi culture and reindeer herding, even if the newly established Finnish provision is limited in scope to the demarcated Sámi homeland. In Norway's Nature Diversity Act there is a reminder in the Act's aim that nature is an important resource base for Sámi culture and livelihoods. The Act also contains a general requirement that, in decision-making, social and cultural needs are weighed against conservation interests, explicitly stating that due importance shall be attached to the natural resource base of Sámi culture, with reindeer herding marked as significant.

Of the three states, Norway has a more sophisticated system that acknowledges and protects Sámi customary area uses and territorial rights, as is evident in its Act's wording and even more so in its preparatory works. Thorough investigation of the law-making process proves that there is an understanding of Sámi matters in Norway, including conservation tensions related to Sámi uses, and consultations with the Norwegian Sámi Parliament improve both dialogue and outcome. Sweden, on the other hand, has no explicit provisions in conservation legislation protecting Sámi culture or reindeer herding.

Sweden has a strong and proud history of early protection, and within that has been – and still is – a strong focus on conserving pristine nature. Scenic beauty and recreational interests are still emphasised within Swedish area protection, much like in the Finnish regime. In contrast, Norway has, to a greater extent, acknowledged the correlation between nature and cultural uses through the generations that have shaped the state's nature and landscapes. The legal rhetoric is quite different; the relative emphasis placed on cultural manifestations in nature conservation legislation (the nature–culture dichotomy) is a point of divergence. This divergence influences the weight placed on Sámi customary activities within protected nature areas, affecting reindeer herding, hunting and fishing among other activities.

To conclude, this study has highlighted how the distinct national traits of these Nordic states, expressed in their respective conservation legislations, reveal differences with respect to protected areas and the recognition of Sámi culture and customary law in each of the three states and, within them, Sápmi. Strong state historical roots have not been removed with the implementation of international and European laws; instead, they linger. There is a strong path dependency also in conservation legislation.

## Bibliography


Allard, Christina. 'The Nordic Countries' Law on Sámi Territorial Rights'. *Arctic Review on Law and Politics* 2 (2011): 159–183.

Allard, Christina. *Renskötselrätt i nordisk belysning*. Göteborg: Makadam förlag, 2015.

Anaya, James. *Indigenous Peoples in International Law*. Oxford: Oxford University Press, 2004.

Backer, Inge Loranger. *Naturmangfoldloven: Kommentarutgave*. Oslo: Universitetsforlaget, 2010.

Chatty, Dawn and Marcus Colchester, eds. *Conservation and Mobile Indigenous Peoples: Displacement, Forced Settlement and Sustainable Development*. Oxford: Berghahn Books, 2002.

Consultation Agreement, 2005. *Prosedyrer for konsultasjoner mellom statlige myndigheter og Sametinget*, 2005.

Consultation Agreement, 2007. *Avtale mellom Sametinget og Miljøverndepartementet om retningslinjer for verneplanarbeid etter naturvernloven i samiske områder*.

Heinämäki, Leena. 'The Rapidly Evolving International Status of Indigenous Peoples: The Example of the Sámi People in Finland'. In *Indigenous Rights in Scandinavia: Autonomous Sámi Law*, eds. Christina Allard and Susann F. Skogvang, 189–204. Farnham: Ashgate, 2015.

Husa, Jaakko, Kimmo Nuotio and Heikki Pihlajamäki *Nordic Law – Between Tradition and Dynamism*. Antwerp: Intersentia, 2007.

Jentoft, Svein, Henry Minde and Ragnar Nilsen. *Indigenous Peoples: Resource Management and Global Rights*. Delft: Eburon, 2003.

Joona, Tanja. 'The Definition of a Sámi Person in Finland and Its Application'. In *Indigenous Rights in Scandinavia: Autonomous Sámi Law*, eds. Christina Allard and Susann F. Skogvang, 155–172. Farnham: Ashgate, 2015.

Krämer, Ludwig. *EU Environmental Law* (7th edn). London: Sweet & Maxwell, 2011.

Michanek, Gabriel. *Svensk miljörätt*. Uppsala: Iustus, 1997.

Minnerup, Günter and Pia Solberg, eds. *First World, First Nations. Internal Colonialism and Indigenous Self-determination in Northern Europe and Australia*. Brighton: Sussex Academic Press, 2011.

*Nationalparksplan för Sverige – Långsiktig Plan*. Stockholm: Naturvårdsverket, 2008.

Prop. 1997/98:45 Part 1. *Miljöbalk*.

Prop. 1997/98:45 Part 2. *Miljöbalk: Författningskommentar och bilaga 1*.

Ravna, Øyvind. *Finnmarksloven og retten til jorden i Finnmark*. Oslo: Gyldendal, 2013.

RP 79/1996. *Regeringens proposition med förslag till revidering av naturvårdslagstiftningen*.

RP 99/2009. *Regeringens proposition till Riksdagen med förslag till lag om ändring av naturvårdslagen*.

Sandström, Per. 'A Toolbox for Co-production of Knowledge and Improved Land Use Dialogues. The Perspective of Reindeer Husbandry'. PhD diss., Umeå: Swedish University of Agricultural Sciences, 2015.

Stevens, Stan, ed. *Conservation through Cultural Survival: Indigenous Peoples and Protected Areas*. Washington, DC: Island Press, 1997.

Stevens, Stan, ed. *Indigenous Peoples, National Parks, and Protected Areas: A New Paradigm Linking Conservation, Culture, and Rights*. Tucson: The University of Arizona Press, 2014.

Torp, Eivind. 'Rennäringens rättigheter i nationalparker och naturreservat'. *Förvaltningsrättslig tidskrift* 2 (2005): 155–192.

Torp, Eivind. 'Det rättsliga skyddet av samisk renskötsel'. *Svensk Juristtidning* (2014): 122–148.

United Nations. UN Doc. A/HRC/18/35/Add.2. *Report of the Special Rapporteur on the Rights of Indigenous Peoples, James Anaya. The Situation of the Sámi People in the Sápmi Region in Norway, Sweden and Finland*, 2011.

United Nations. UN Doc. A/67/301. Anaya, James. *Report of the Special Rapporteur on the Rights of Indigenous Peoples* (Report to the General Assembly), 2012.

# 2 Conceptions of ethnicity and nature conservation in reindeer herding areas in Sweden and Finland

*Lars Elenius*

## Introduction

Legislative protection of nature is a modern phenomenon linked to the legitimation of the nation state from the end of the nineteenth century. In this national and nationalistic discourse the launching of preserved nature associated the territory of the state with a politically defined nation state based on the power of a unified people. One way of preserving the long-term history of the nation was to establish national parks. It was the ultimate way of linking the territory of the nation state with the sacred feeling of the nation. The use of preserved nature had to be defined in relation to various ethnic groups and their history in the making of the nation state.

It is particularly rewarding to compare Sweden and Finland in this context because they have a common history, lasting more than 600 years up to 1809 when Finland first became a Russian Grand Duchy and then, in 1917, an independent state. Large and sparsely populated areas were set aside for national parks in the northernmost parts of both countries from the beginning of the twentieth century. The largest national parks were established in the reindeer herding areas where groups of Sámi, Finnish and Swedish ethnicity had for a long time lived closely with each other. The aim of this article is to investigate why ethnically determined rights in connection with preserved nature have been defined and framed so differently in Finland and Sweden during the twentieth century. It comprises the significance of ethnicity in the colonisation process of reindeer herding areas and the conception of national identity.[1]

This is done by examining how the area of settlement changed for different ethnic groups and how their livelihoods were altered in relation to each other during the colonisation period, and also how inter-ethnic contacts shifted. Subsequently, the motivation for the ethnic content of nature conservation legislation is investigated and how the ethnic mobilisation of Sámi people influenced that legislation. Finally the status attributed to the ethnic groups in the history of the nation is examined.

In this chapter, ethnicity is defined as the social boundaries between groups that are culturally distinguishable from each other. They are not fixed and vary over time.[2] In addition ethnicity is also part of the national identification, which in this chapter is regarded as a hybrid identification within a single territory, created by bringing together various ethnic groups, which manifest the many parallel ethnic identifications within one single national identification.[3] The link between territory, ethnicity and nation is crucial when analysing

1 The main focus in the article is on Finland with concomitant comparisons with Sweden.
2 Barth, 'Introduction', 9–38; Hylland Eriksen, *Ethnicity and Nationalism*, 18 35.
3 Spira, 'Ethnicity and nationality', 248–264.

the ethnic content of the criteria for founding national parks, and the way they are used. There are many constructed elements in the making of nations, as has been pointed out by several scholars[4] but the nation is not ethnically neutral. Apart from a common economic and political system within a confined territory there are also the histories, memories and myths of the most influential groups within the territory which make people feel a loyalty to the nation.[5]

## Colonisation and assimilation

It is open to debate whether Finland was colonised by Sweden in the early Middle Ages, in the sense that non-European countries were colonised by Crusades at the same time. The Swedish conquest took place simultaneously with the start of the evolution of a global colonial system. It was definitely a military enterprise, which aimed at consolidating control over the territory, and it was met with resistance from kin-ship organised Finnish people.[6] It was also legitimised by the *doctrine of discovery*, which was one of two main methods by which European nations legitimised European title to the new discoveries. The other one was the *doctrine of terra nullius.*[7] Both were used in Norway during the colonisation of the Sámi territory in northern Norway[8] and also when Denmark occupied Livonia.[9] None of these people, neither the Sámi, nor the Finnish or Estonian tribes, were unknown to the Scandinavian people. Swedish, Danish and Norwegian Vikings had already travelled eastward along the Finnish Gulf and Baltic Sea for many hundreds of years.

In the eleventh century, however, these enterprises were blocked by new powers and the Scandinavians had to find other routes for trade and for geographical expansion. The conquest of Finnish territory was one such new enterprise as well as the further colonisation of northern Sweden. At that time both Sámi and Finnish tribes were living in southernmost Finland; the Finns making their living from agriculture, hunting and fishing, and the Sámi from hunting, fishing, reindeer herding and probably small-scale shifting cultivation.[10] Both of these groups became part of the centralised Swedish kingdom that took shape at that time.

The conquest of the territory of Finland was a state expansion like many others within Europe, motivated to some extent by Christian arguments, but also by geo-political and economic goals. The city state of Novgorod, the Kingdom of Sweden and the Kingdom of Denmark were at this time fighting over hegemony of the Gulf of Finland and the

4 Gellner, *Nations and Nationalism*; Hobsbawm, *Nations and Nationalism*; Anderson, *Imagined Communities.*
5 Smith, *Ethnic Origins of Nations*; Smith, *National Identity.*
6 Edgren, *Finlands historia I*, 282–301; Lindkvist, *Sveriges medeltid*, 107–108.
7 The doctrine of discovery was invented by the European empires to legalise their conquest of non-Christian countries. From the beginning it was sanctioned by the Pope during the Crusades to recover the Holy lands in 1096–1271. It fostered the idea of justified holy wars by Christians against infidels, but it also led, in practice, to an international agreement by which European Christian nations gained sovereignty and property rights over the non-European, non-Christian lands when they discovered them, see Newcomb, *Pagans in the Promised Land.* The doctrine of terra nullius meant that lands that were not possessed by any person or nation of European descent, or were occupied by non-Europeans but were not being used in a fashion that European legal systems understood and/or approved, were considered to be empty and waste and available to be claimed, see Miller et al., *Discovering Indigenous*, 1–15.
8 Niemi, 'Sámi history', 62 ff.
9 Lönnroth, *Från svensk medeltid*, 13 ff.; Leinberg, *Finlands territoriala*, 1 ff.
10 Bergman and Hörnberg, 'Early cereal cultivation', 57–66.

surrounding areas. The establishment of Swedish power in Finland profoundly changed the traditional life of the tribes who had formed distinctive ethnic communities since at least the Iron Age.[11]

They were integrated into the Catholic fiscal system, and into the Swedish kingdom through a legal system and a political and administrative hegemony. From the fourteenth century the Finns were allowed to participate in the election of the king with the same political rights as the Swedes.[12] The Sámi people were loosely incorporated into the state. The tributes they had paid earlier to trading and looting bands of Scandinavian or Finno-Ugric descent they now paid as taxes to either the king's bailiffs or to private traders, so called *birkarlar*, who had received the monopoly from the king to trade with the Sámi. The *birkarlar* were coastal farmers of Swedish and Finnish decent and, at least from the thirteenth century, a patron–client trading relation was established between them and the Sámi. In the sixteenth century this patron–client system was dissolved by the king and the traders became government Lap bayliffs. At the same time the vast untaxed land of forests, lakes and rivers was declared the property of the king.[13] In that way the *doctrine of terra nullius* was applied to the vast territories of the kingdom. It did not affect only a single ethnic group; it affected all the common people, Swedes, Finns or Sámi. It is, therefore, not wholly comparable with the use of the doctrine for non-European colonies.

One distinction in the colonial system is that between *transplantive* or *replicative colonialism*, which reproduces the culture, society, polity and economy of the imperial power in the colony, and *intrusive* and *oppressive colonialism*, which dominates the colony but leads to the withdrawal of the imperial power.[14] Neither of the models is relevant to the Nordic countries or Europe in general. The expansion of the European states within Europe was, as Charles Tilly has described in detail, a combination of state coercion and the engagement of private capital in a constant military struggle with other states.[15] It is not helpful for the analysis of the incorporation of different minorities into the state to reduce Europe to a large area made up of colonies.

This is not to deny the need to analyse subordinated subjects within those territories and the related power relations using discursive and post-colonial methods.[16] The European colonial system became widespread throughout the world and transmitted specific ideas, values, ideologies and power relations within the European countries.

The hegemonic state system taking form in Sweden was based on both ethnic and social criteria. At the top of the pyramid were the Swedes, below were the Finns and Sámi who did not belong to the 'symbolic core' of the nation. Socially the nobles formed an upper stratum in society, followed by priests, merchants, peasants and at the bottom nomads and semi-nomads of various kinds. Keeping the discussion on a general level, the Finnish peasants thus occupied a middle position. Together with the Sámi they were ethnically inferior to the Swedes, but as peasants they had a higher status than the nomadic and hunting Sámi. As mentioned, there was still in the Middle Ages a Sámi population in southern Finland who

11 Edgren, *Finlands historia I*, 282 ff. These distinguishable tribes that survived to present time were the Sámi, Finn, Häme, Savolax and Karelian.

12 Lönnroth, *Från svensk medeltid*, 13 ff; Leinberg, *Finlands territoriala*, 1 ff.

13 Jutikkala, *Finlands historia 3*, 33; Bergman and Edlund, 'Birkarlar and Sámi'.

14 Oommen, 'Introduction: Conceptualizing', 27–51.

15 Tilly, *Coercion, Capital*.

16 Here exemplified with Said, *Orientalism*; Chatterjee, *Nationalist Thought*; Bhabha, *Nation and Narration*; Loomba, *Colonialism/postcolonialism*.

were engaged in hunting, fishing and probably small-scale reindeer herding. At the same time, at the same latitude on the Swedish side of the kingdom, there were also Sámi living in approximately the same way as in Finland.[17]

Today, 800 years later, reindeer herding is still carried out by Sámi on about the same latitude in Sweden, but in Finland both the Sámi settlements and reindeer herding have been dramatically limited to the most northern part of the country i.e. the County of Lapland and the northern part of the County of Oulu. The withdrawal of the Sámi from the southern to the northern area of Finland has been described in earlier research in terms of a continuously expanding Finnish frontier of new settlements northward, and a concomitant Sámi retreat in the same direction.[18] It is a kind of 'push and retreat' theory in which the Finns, through the spread of agriculture and permanent settlements, and by means of violence, pushed the semi-nomadic Sámi away out of their former areas.

We do not know very much about how Finns and Sámi coexisted in southern Finland during the early Middle Ages, but the ethnic mosaic in pre-history has, both in Finland and Sweden, been elaborated in current research and is now pictured as more dynamic and changeable than earlier. Ethnic groups are not seen as static entities, but as intermingling and changeable. In Finland the archaeologists are open to the ideas that there were both cultural assimilation processes and large language shifts among the early inhabitants of southern Finland.[19] In a similar way the coexistence of reindeer herding and experimental agriculture in northern Sweden in prehistoric and early historic time has been detected by archaeologists and paleo-botanists through pollen analyses and other methods.[20] These kinds of cultural encounters were not dictated by the state, but were a spontaneous process that could involve different kinds of local people, no matter how they were categorised ethnically by themselves or by others.

Burn-beating was used in many Nordic environments as an early form of agriculture, but in Finland it prevailed until modern times. It has been described both as a complex system of using the landscape in various ways, and as the creator of the East-Finnish expansion northwards during the Middle Ages. This culture is described as relying on hunting and fishing as well as on agriculture in a semi-nomadic way.[21] When the slash and burn farmers in the 16th century expanded northward they came into conflict with the semi-nomadic Sámi over the lakes and hunting places the latter used, for which they paid taxes to the Crown. They also came into conflict with farmers from the Häme region who, by customary rights, had used vast areas, called wilderness areas (Fin. *Erämaa*), for fishing, hunting and trading with the Sámi. Thirdly they also came into conflict with the *birkarlar* over both their fishing in the lakes and trading with the Sámi.[22]

The expanding slash and burn farming has been seen as the main explanation for the extinction of the Kemi Sámi culture from the sixteenth century onwards. The burning of

17 The historical southern boundary of Sámi settlement in Sweden is contested, see Kjellström, *Sameforskning i dag*; Zachrisson, *Möten i gränsland*; Lundström, *Historisk rätt?* Tunón, *Uppsala mitt i Sápmi*. In the context of this article the interesting point is to notice the enormous difference between Sweden and Finland regarding Sámi settlement in the Middle Ages compared with today, not to go into the debate over exact boundaries of Sámi settlements in pre-history. The main focus is on the changes in Finland since it illustrates how nationalism in the new state after 1809 influenced nature conservation.

18 Itkonen, *Mamme lappalaisen*; *Bebyggelsen i Finland*; Tegengren, *En utdöd lappkultur*, 232–273.

19 Tarkiainen, *Sveriges österland*, 42–43, 282 ff.

20 Josefsson, Ramqvist and Hörnberg, 'The history of early cereal cultivation', 821–840; Hörnberg et al., 'Indications of shifting cultivation', 989–1001.

21 Larsson, *Svedjebruk*.

22 Edgren, *Finlands historia I*, 312 ff.; Elenius, 'Det vilda som gränsmarkör', 32–69.

large forest areas and the concomitant agricultural settlement by Finns eroded the base for wild reindeer and other game that were the central element in the Kemi Sámi way of living. These Sámi were a hunting society with none of the large semi-domesticated reindeer herds that the mountain Sámi in Sweden and Norway developed from this time onwards.[23] This was the reason the Kemi Sámi culture was assimilated into Finnish culture. It could have happened that a Sámi in a state of destitution started to combine hunting and reindeer breeding with agriculture, and later became established as a full-time farmer. At the same time the Finnish population adopted elements of Sámi livelihood into their daily life as farmers, for example using reindeer for transportation.[24] It was the similarities in the cultures of Finns and Sámi in close relation to nature that explains the quick assimilation of Sámi into the Finnish population in southern Finland.[25] It also created a hybrid culture of reindeer keeping, agriculture, fishing and hunting in a mixture of Finnish and Sámi cultural elements.[26]

The expansion of Finnish farmers continued northward during the eighteenth, nineteenth and even into the twentieth centuries, so that northernmost Sweden and Finland and the shores of the Arctic Ocean in Norway were settled by Finnish-speaking farmers who also relied on hunting, fishing and keeping some reindeer.[27] In this respect there is a difference between Finns and Swedes. While Swedish farmers stopped their expansion south of the Polar Circle the Finns continued to the extreme ecological limit at which agriculture was possible.

Mixed marriages are regarded as a crucial factor in assimilation processes, and marriage patterns in the nineteenth century reveal that the ethnic boundary between Swedes and Sámi was much stricter than that between Finns and Sámi. It was easier for a Finnish-speaking woman in northernmost Karesuando to cross the ethnic boundary to Sámi than for a Swedish-speaking woman in Jokkmokk to do so. A closer examination of cross-marriage patterns among mountain and forest Sámi in the parish of Jokkmokk reveals that the endogamous pattern was stronger among the former than the latter. The same endogamous pattern can be found among mountain Sámi in Karesuando and in Finnish Utsjoki[28] suggesting that it was the culture of nomadic reindeer herding that was the big barrier to inter-ethnic marriages, not Sámi ethnicity in general.

The first-generation Finnish settlers in the lake district of Inari, which was more of a fishing Sámi district, very often married their daughters to settlers of Sámi descent, but in the latter part of the nineteenth century they more often married them to Finnish families. At this stage it was newly arrived Finns from the south who married Sámi. Local conflicts with Sámi and economic reason lay behind the change in pattern. Finns who settled in northernmost Inari mostly became assimilated into the mountain Sámi, not the other way around.[29]

23 Tegengren, *En utdöd lappkultur*; Lundmark, *Uppbörd, utarmning*.

24 Kortesalmi, *Pohjois-Vienan*, 63–79; Ruotsala, *Muuttuvat palkiset*, 92–100, 402–403.

25 Edgren, *Finlands historia I*, 304 ff.; Tarkiainen, *Sveriges Österland*; Lähteenmäki, *Peoples of Lapland*, 194–207.

26 Lähteenmäki, *Peoples of Lapland*, 197–205; Enbuske, *Vanhan Lapin*; Enbuske, 'Bosättningen och markanvändningen', 83–101; Hiltunen, 'En värld mellan världar', 102–121; Lehtola, *Saamelaiset Suomalaiset*.

27 About the Finnish settlers in northernmost Sweden, but also the assimilation of Sámi into a Finnish identity, see Högström, *Beskrifning öfwer Sweriges*, 40–42, 52–54; Laestadius, *Om uppodlingar*, 83, 89; Paulaharju, *Ödebygdsfolk*; For the connection between Sámi and Finns in northern Norway, see Bjørklund, *Fjordfolket*, 171–230; Thuen, 'Acculturation and Ethnic'.

28 Nordin, *Äktenskap i Sápmi*, 80–101. In Nordin's study the category 'Non-Sámi' has no ethnicity in Karesuando, but my interpretation is that almost all of them were Finnish speakers, cf. note 25.

29 Aikio, 'Marriage among the Saame', 54–56; Müller-Wille, *Lappen und Finnen* 26–31, 41–42, 54–71.

One general conclusion that can be drawn is that the ethnic barrier between Finns and Sámi was more easily crossed than that between Swedes and Sámi. Another observation is that when reindeer herding was more specialised and nomadic, as among the mountain Sámi, Sámi marriages were more endogamous, but this did not apply to the forest or fishing Sámi. This helps to explain why the assimilation process of Sámi in southern and middle Finland was so rapid.

## Nature conservation and ethnicity

To understand the ethnic aspect of natural parks in Sweden and Finland it is first necessary to compare the development of reindeer herding legislation in the two countries. From earlier times, when Sweden and Finland were a single state, the Sámi paid taxes for so-called Lap tax lands (Swe. *Lappskatteland*).[30] In Sweden these individual rights were transformed into the collective administrative right for reindeer herding communities, which were granted the right to use land and water for reindeer herding; a right that was first regulated in the Reindeer Herding Act of 1886. In the follow-up Act of 1898 it was explicitly stated that only Sámi people were allowed to engage in reindeer herding.[31]

In Finland there was no such legislation at that time, but in 1888 the Committee for the Colonisation of State-Owned Forests for Farming (Swe. *Kommittén för kolonisation av statens skogsmark till jordbruk*) remarked that the establishment of colonies in Finnish Lapland had in some respects impacted negatively on reindeer herding. The committee therefore suggested that reindeer herding should be some consideration when cultivable land was separated from state forests, and also when that land was parcelled out to colonies.[32] In 1898 the Finnish Senate decided that from then on reindeer herding had to be organised into reindeer herding districts, which resembled the legislation in Sweden.[33] The first Reindeer Herding Act in Finland was passed as late as in 1932, but did not contain any major changes to earlier practices. The main difference from Sweden was that no ethnic limitations were associated with reindeer herding. The law stated in §3 that every Finnish citizen had the right to own reindeer, and also to participate in a reindeer herding team.[34]

The national differences in reindeer legislation also influenced the ethnic content of the nature conservation legislation that was carried out parallel to that regulating reindeer herding. As early as in 1881 a proposal for the establishment of a national park in Finland was launched by the botanist and geographer Ragnar Hult, referring to a speech one year earlier by the famous Finnish–Swedish scientist and polar explorer Adolf Erik Nordenskiöld. The German biologist Hugo Conwentz was another influential person with his idea that nature was not only worth protecting for aesthetic and nationalistic reasons, but also because of its value for science.[35] This was a common starting point for the nature conservation movement in the two countries.

### *Development in Sweden*

In Sweden the first national parks were established in 1909. Most, such as Abisko, Sarek, Stora Sjöfallet and Pieljekaise, were established in the Sámi reindeer herding area in northern

30 Päiviö, *Från skattemannarätt.*
31 Lantto, 'Sámi rights', 26–51.
32 *Kommittén för kolonisation*, 23.
33 Kortesalmi, *Pohjois-Vienan*, 189; Lähteenmäki, *Peoples of Lapland*, 202.
34 Heikkila, *Reindeer Talk*, 113–114; Act 1932/239, Lag om renskötsel (Finland).
35 Lundgren, *Staten och naturen*, 40 ff.; Palmgren, *Naturskydd och kultur.*

Sweden. It was inscribed in the legislation that Sámi reindeer herders had the right to pasture for their reindeers, to use the forest for private ends and to take with them the dogs used in the herding. They were also allowed to hunt and fish, but not to hunt bear. These rights were referred to as private rights that could not be restricted. The possibility the government had to deny access to the national parks in general was not applicable to the Sámi.[36] The aim of national parks was to preserve large continuous types of landscapes in natural or mainly unchanged conditions. They were given the double role of being both natural sights and areas for tourism.[37] In addition they had to adhere to the reindeer herding legislation. Later national parks established in the Sámi reindeer herding area in Sweden were Vadvetjåkka in 1920, Muddus in 1942 and Padjelanta in 1962. The concept of 'park' was borrowed from England denoting something both private but at the same time a common aspect of the landscape. Parks were created as a counter measure when commoners were thrown off the common land by the nobility.[38] In Sweden the wilderness within the national parks was regarded as a natural landscape for research, the imagined organic space between people and landscape, and the scenic landscape for leisure and recreation.[39]

## *Development in Finland*

In Finland Ragnar Hult worked out a guideline for managing national parks in 1891. It was followed by a proposal from the organisation Societas pro Fauna et Flora Fennica to establish national parks. When a committee was appointed by the Senate in 1910 to set up a proposal concerning protected forests it suggested the establishment of three national parks; Pallas-Yllästunturi, Pyhätunturi-Luostotunturi and the Oulankajoki district. They were all situated in Finnish Lapland in the area where reindeer herding was carried out. At the same time the National Board of Forestry took the lead in 1916 by putting the mountain of Malla, in the northwestern corner, the so-called 'Finnish arm', under protection. In the preparatory work for the Nature Preservation Act of 1923, Pisavaara, the Oulankijoki district and Pallastunturi were mentioned as areas that were already protected by the National Board of Forestry, and should later be included in the category of national parks.

The notion *national park* was used in the preparatory work for legislation by the Committee on Law and Economy, but the board drafting the law rejected the idea. It argued that the areas in Lapland could not be regarded as parks because they were wilderness areas and therefore should be treated as untouched nature. They were now called 'restricted areas' and the National Board of Forestry was tasked with parcelling off for protection appropriate areas of state land.[40] When the first Nature Conservation Act was passed in 1923 the areas set aside were first and foremost depicted as worthy of protection for their beauty and 'for the protection of nature against interference by human hand'. Protected areas of nature were now called 'general restricted areas'. Cultivation and cattle grazing were forbidden on these areas, but exceptions were made for local people living in or adjacent to them and for nomadic Sámi. Thus, the Sámi in Finland did not receive exclusive rights to the protected areas as the Sámi did in Sweden. The protected areas were, somewhat contradictorily,

36 Act 1909/56 Lag angående nationalparker (Sweden).

37 Hedberg, *Naturskydd*, 14; *Naturen och samhället*, 37–40, 87–88; Act 1909/56 Lag angående nationalparker (Sweden); About different opinions on the legislation, see Lundgren, *Staten och naturen*, 280–306.

38 Olwig, 'The landscape of justice', 39–63.

39 Mels, *Wild Landscapes*, 88–89.

40 Act 1923/71 Lag om naturskydd (Finland); Committee report 1976:88, *Nationalparkskommitténs betänkande*, 9 ff.; *SOU 1962:36*, *Naturen och samhället*, 49–50.

regarded as distant and untouched wilderness areas, but at the same time as areas where local people and Sámi could carry out cattle and reindeer herding.[41]

When the first national parks were marked off and established in 1938 the affinity between Finns and Sámi was emphasised even more. In the Ordinance for the Law on the Setting up of Nature Preservation Areas a pragmatic approach guided the implementation and the general harsh restrictions were softened. It was now permitted to set up a plantation in the close environment of constructed houses for the park's rangers and in connection with scientific arrangements. Farmers' meadows could be maintained and wood used for fences, hay-drying racks, barns and Lap cots could also be erected. Permission was given for reindeer, horses and cows to graze, to the extent that they had been allowed to do so earlier and was still regarded as necessary, to use wood for fences needed in reindeer herding and to kill or trap wolf, wolverine, bear and lynx.

It is clear that the Finnish national parks in the north were regarded as an area inhabited by both reindeer herders and farmers who were supposed to engage in their livelihoods in the landscape as they had before. Actually no ethnic group was mentioned in the ordinance, only the means of livelihood that were allowed within the parks; i.e. reindeer herding, hunting, fishing and farming, which were supposed to be carried out irrespective of ethnicity. Other tolerated activities were the management of the park, scientific activities and works by land surveyors.[42] The notion of 'national park' was now used under the overarching category 'specific restricted areas' and the nature parks, created at the same time, were categorised as 'general restricted areas'. The latter were primarily reserved for the purposes of scientific research.[43]

The parallel between Finland and Sweden regarding the establishment of national parks is striking, both regarding ideological influences, the timing of the proposals and the suggested location of protected nature in the reindeer herding areas of the north. The ethnic content of the legislation, however, differed and also the way in which activities of daily life were integrated. The Finnish way of inscribing reindeer herding and farming into the nature legislation continued in the Nature Preservation Act of 1956. The new legislation was largely enacted because of the loss of territory after the Second World War, when four of the six nature parks and two of the four national parks were ceded to the Soviet Union. To compensate for the losses the two large national parks of Lemmenjoki and Oulanka, among others, were established. They were both located within the reindeer herding area of Sámi. Large nature parks like Kevo and Sompio were also established within reindeer herding areas.[44]

### *From preservation to conservation*

From the 1960s nature protection in Finland and Sweden changed. The earlier policy, principally concerned with preservation, changed in favour of a conservation policy, manifested in Sweden by the establishment of the new Nature Conservation Act in 1964, followed by the establishment of the National Environmental Protection agency in 1967.[45] In Sweden the policy towards Sámi reindeer herding in the national parks continued as before, but with the setting up of a Sámi Parliament in 1993 and the establishment of the World

41 Act 1923/71 Lag om naturskydd (Finland).

42 Act 1938/83 Lag om inrättande av vissa nya naturskyddsområden å staten tillhörig mark (Finland).

43 Act 1938/83 Lag om inrättande av vissa nya naturskyddsområden å staten tillhörig mark (Finland); SOU 1962:36, 49–50; Committee report 1976:88, *Nationalparkskommitténs betänkande*, 9.

44 Act 1956/634 Lag om inrättande av vissa nya naturskyddsområden på staten tillhörig mark (Finland).

45 Act 1964:882 Naturvårdslag (Sweden); Hermansson, *Miljövårdens institutionalisering*, 19.

Heritage site of Laponia in 1996 out of already existing national parks, the management of the parks came into focus, as described in the chapters by Green and Turtinen, Reimerson and Adams in this book.[46]

In Finland a major shift took place when the Ministry of the Environment was established in 1983.[47] In Finnish Lapland recurrent controversies regarding the exploitation of rivers came to public attention in the shift of the 1970s and 1980s, and the conservation of old forests became a hot issue in the 1990s. At that time 47 per cent of the Lapland population was still working in nature-related occupations. Reindeer breeding was an important part of the solidarity within village communities and about 1,000 households derived their main income, and 800 a vital part of their income, from reindeer breeding. It also contributed to the social life of the villages. The general tendency after the Second World War was the very rapid transformation from a traditional to a modern and late-modern society.[48] The institutionalisation of environmental issues came a decade later in Finland than in Sweden, but followed the same path, broadening the concept of nature into a more complex societal context.[49]

The shift from preservation to conservation can be symbolised by the establishment of two large protected areas; the Urho Kekkonen National Park, named after the former president of the republic, and the establishment of 12 wilderness areas, all situated in the northernmost Sámi part of the country. They illustrate the continuation of the Finnish conservation policy, but also the changes that took place. Power over national parks had politically and administratively resided in the field of forestry, but it was now transferred to the new political field of the environment.

In the Urho Kekkonen National Park the ideas of nature conservation were combined with measures to stimulate outdoor life. It was a very different approach compared with the earlier parks. Reindeer herding and its activities were allowed as before, together with fishing and hunting for the local people, but the construction of buildings and roads necessary for managing the park, for information, walking-tours, skiing, research and 'observing nature', were allowed, as was the construction of huts for accommodation. Also allowed were: the picking of berries and mushrooms, panning for gold, making fires, the catching and killing of animals for scientific purposes, collecting cones, necessary elimination of plants and culling of animals, measures for maintaining traditional types of environment and for fire control, rescue services, and supervision of the national border. In addition measures for telegraph, telephone and radio activities, geological research and ore-prospecting were allowed. There were no regulations preventing the preparation of an area on the mountain of Isakkipää for slalom skiing, the erection of houses, constructions and other necessary installations. From a Sámi point of view reindeer herding was still allowed, but now there were so many other activities that reindeer herding became a minor subject.[50]

The aim of the Wilderness Act, which led to the establishment of 12 wilderness areas in 1991, was to preserve the feature of wilderness in the areas, to secure Sámi culture and the livelihoods that were close to nature, and also to develop a many-sided utilisation of nature together with the necessary preconditions.[51] All the 12 areas are within the extreme

46 See also Nilsson Dahlström, *Negotiating Wilderness*; Green, *Managing Laponia*; Reimerson, *Nature, Culture, Rights.*

47 Hermansson, *Miljövårdens institutionalisering*, 19.

48 Suopajärvi, 'Lapin luonnon', 138–145.

49 Hermansson, *Miljövårdens institutionalisering*, 18–22, 291–315.

50 Act 1983/228 Lag om Urho Kekkonens nationalpark (Finland); Ordinance 1983/229, *Förordningen för Urho Kekkonens nationalpark.*

51 Act 1991:62 Ödemarkslag (Finland).

northernmost part of the country in the area where Sámi is still used as a vernacular language and reindeer herding is carried out. They are also located within the, so-called, Sámi Homeland established in 1995.[52] The naming of the areas as *Wilderness Areas* has direct connotations with the description of preserved nature in 1923 as areas unexplored and untouched by human hand. The contrast between the poetic name and the expressions of industrialisation, tourism and late modern technologies that took place in northern Lapland at this time is very strong.[53] It represents the contrast between the Finnish romantic national approach to nature and the rational approach to nature in a late modern industrial and communication society.

## *The political mobilisation of Sámi*

Both these new kinds of protected areas must be seen in the light of Sámi political mobilisation and changing strategies. The state policy towards the Sámi during the first part of the twentieth century was one of meeting a general welfare goal, as for other citizens, and the Sámi movement responded positive to this. In general there was no conscious assimilation or segregation policy like in Sweden and Norway, but an integration policy, however with no decisive support for specific Sámi issues. In the 1960s the Sámi movement was radicalised and their voices were raised. This was connected with the intensified industrialisation of northern Lapland's natural resources and the ongoing modernisation.[54] This caused conflicts throughout the area of reindeer herding, especially regarding old forests in areas where it took a long time for forests to grow. The Sámi reindeer herders wanted all forestry to stop in these areas, arguing that they were needed as reserves for their reindeer. The Forest and Park Service argued that a state-owned business had to be run at a profit even in local areas where reindeer herding was carried out.[55] At issue was an ethnic claim for specific Sámi needs set against legalistic claims that treated the Sámi like any other citizens.

The Kessi dispute in eastern Inari, starting in the 1970s and reaching its peak in the late 1980s, was an important conflict for the radicalisation of the Sámi movement in Finland. It took place in an area that was chosen in 1991 as one of the 12 wilderness areas, at the same time as being an area where forestry was carried out by the Forest and Park Service. The Wilderness Committee had taken its starting point in the Finnish concept of wilderness as a mutual space for ancient Sámi and Finnish activities, to which both forestry and reindeer herding belonged. On the other hand there was also an argument about the concept of wilderness as something natural and untouched worthy of being protected in its own right.[56] The Sámi idea of wilderness lay somewhere in between, as a cultural/natural area and a resource to be sustained for coming generations.

In the Sámi political struggle nature conservation was on one hand a threat regarding land usage and land rights, on the other hand a guarantee against further external encroachment. The arguments about conservation being an external encroachment were, however, rare before the 1980s. There was a fear among both Sámi and Finns in the region of Lapland that their use of natural resources would be too restricted by outsiders

52 The Sámi are guaranteed cultural autonomy in this area regarding the Sámi language and culture, administered by the Sámi council, cf. http://www.finlex.fi/sv/laki/ajantasa/2003/20031086.

53 Linjakumpu and Suopajärvi, *Sellainen Seutu*.

54 Nyssönen, 'Everybody recognized'; Lehtola, 'Organiserad samepolitik', 299–304; Lehtola, *Saamelaisten paralamentti*.

55 Raitio, 'Konflikten mellan rennäring', 227–247.

56 Nyyssönen, *Everybody Recognized*, 291–330.

'from the south'. Two main discourses concerning forestry appeared among the Sámi: one stating that restricted logging was not a major problem for reindeer herding and that employment in logging was necessary even for Sámi; the other asserting that logging had destroyed reindeer herding and the Sámi culture.

During the conflict a shift emerged from self-representation and external representation of a 'natural people', where Sámi leaders were in alliance with the early conservation movement, to a more powerful discourse of environmentalism in alliance with younger and more militant activists. Politically it was paralleled by a shift from a national welfare discourse of cooperation within the nation to a global, indigenous discourse of confrontation arising out of legal arguments for self-representation.[57]

In 1973 the Sámi Delegation was created in Finland, referred to as the Sámi Parliament. It was a first step towards self-representation even if it had no direct power in decision making. The mandate was to serve as an advisory board on issues of direct or indirect concern to the Sámi, such as environmental protection, development of industrial enterprises within the Sámi homeland area, reindeer herding and the organisation of education.[58] In 1995 the Sámi Parliament was granted a new kind of legislative framework to provide a statutory basis similar to the Sámi Parliaments in Sweden and Norway. The strategy among members of the Sámi Parliament seems to have been to build a base of support among politicians and administrators in both the county of Lapland and in the capital of Helsinki.[59] This emphasises the specific role the Sámi had in Finland as very much integrated with Finns on the local and regional levels, while at the same time coming together politically on the national and international level as a unified Sámi people. The established Wilderness Areas helped the arguments for specific needs for reindeer herding against efficient industrialised forestry, but on the other hand positioned the Sámi as a 'nature people' in the discourse of wilderness outside modernisation.

## Conclusions: Narrating the territory of the nation

The national parks were inscribed into the narration of the nation, but these narrations were not ethnically neutral accounts. They were woven into the myth of the chosen people i.e. the dominant ethnic group of the state. A nation is formed, in an ethno-symbolic interpretation, in a process in which a named population, within a historic territory, sharing historical memories and myths, a mass-public culture, a common economy and legal rights and duties for all members come together.[60] It must be added that the named population constituting the nation does not necessarily have to be the only named population within the territory. Most nations are actually multi-ethnic, but in order to maintain the national identity that binds different ethnic groups together in a sense of solidarity the dominant ethnic group must hold the necessary power to carry forward the binding myths, historical narrations and memories of national identity.

Anthony D. Smith has sorted Sweden and Finland into two types of nation formation, which he defines as the two main roads of nation building. Sweden is categorised into the *lateral* way of nation building, together with other old nations such as England, France, Holland and Spain. It is characterised as directed by an ethnically dominant group composed of aristocrats and higher clergy that had close links to other laterally dominant ethnic

57 Nyyssönen, *Everybody Recognized*, 291–330; Lehtola, 'Organiserad samepolitik', 299–304; Brantenberg, *Becoming Visible*.

58 Sillanpää, *Political and Administrative*, 113–116.

59 Sillanpää, 'Government responses', 95–97.

60 Smith, *National Identity*, 43.

groups in the geographical surroundings. Through administrative, economic and cultural progress the outlying regions, with elite groups and middle and lower classes, were incorporated into the dominant lateral culture. It was done through the agency of the bureaucratic state in which the public, mass education system played an important role.

Finland, on the other hand, is categorised into the *vertical* way of nation building. The Finns formed a subordinated, vertical ethnic community within the Swedish kingdom. For vertical ethnic groups there were two main ways for the ethnic intelligentsia to 'wake up' the people to their destiny as a nation: through a return to 'nature' and its 'poetic spaces', and through the use of a history of golden ages. The intelligentsia needed to implement a moral and political revolution out of the new vernacular historical culture that they had rediscovered.[61]

Smith's ethno-symbolic concept has been debated within historiography for decades now and questioned by the modernist approach to nation building, which sees the nation merely as a modern construct by elite groups dating from the middle of the nineteenth century. Regarding Finland his theory has also been tested empirically and criticised for not fitting the Finnish case. It was elite groups that compiled the scattered Fennic folklore from the different regions and from abroad into the concept of a Finnish nation.[62] But the question remains: why did they have to gather Finnish identifications? Why not Swedish or Sámi who also lived within the same state borders?

Empirical investigations into the antiquity of the nation-building process in Sweden conclude that the nation is both a set of cultural historical identifications and an elite project among those who put them into action in one direction or another.[63] There is a problem in talking about common, uniform communities over time, whether they are nations, ethnic groups, language fellowships or other types – it leads to static and essentialist thinking.[64] The nation must be regarded as more complex and relational, consisting of the multiplicity of ethnic groups involved in a negotiation about what the nation is and will become. The narration about the connection between nation, territory and ethnicity is one such a negotiation.

The historiography of Sweden had to adapt to a new kind of territorial national identity in 1809 after Finland became a Russian Grand Duchy and the Tsar raised the new entity to a 'nation among other nations'. Firstly the Scandinavian peninsula, with Denmark as the third party, became a new kind of Scandinavian and Nordic national identification, in contrast to the Finnish nation. Secondly the total dominance of the Swedes as the carriers of history, memory and myths of the nation was stressed.

For Swedes the wilderness of the north represented something distant and strange, situated in an inaccessible mountainous area. At the same time the Sámi in northern Sweden and the Finnish minority in Tornedalen represented alien cultures in relation to Scandinavians. In the late nineteenth century the Nordic landscape was painted by national, romantic artists with a distance to nature, placing people, dramatically alien, in the forefront of the landscape. These landscapes could have Old Norse mythological figures foregrounded, dressed in the fashion of antiquity, drawing a parallel between the Nordic and Hellenistic cultural heritage.[65] The dramatic mountain landscape was associated with Western culture. Sámi or Finnish people could be put into the landscape towards an illustrative fond, or the

61 Smith, *National identity*, 54–70.

62 Fewster, *Visions of Past*, 401–05.

63 Hall, *Social Construction of Nationalism*; Hall, *Den svenskaste historien*, 291–303.

64 Burke, *Languages and Communities*, 5–7; Elenius, 'Minoritetsspråken', 13–16.

65 Grandien, 'Fornnordiskt i konsten', 110–123.

landscape itself could represent a dramatic scenery.[66] It was therefore logical to relate to these areas as scenic *parks* when the first national parks were established.

Finland started its history writing from year zero in 1809. Over one night the ethnic groups of the territory received a state of their own with their own state finances, a separate tariff area and a senate as the body for political decision making, even if subordinated to the governor-general under Russia. The creation of Finland has been described as a gift from the Tsar, i.e. the state came first, and then the nation.[67] The epic of Kalevala brought an imagined antiquity for the nationalists and created a historic (ethnic) Finnish past for the nation. Väinömöinen, in the founding myth of Kalevala, represents the potential farmer whose destiny is to spread agriculture to the waste land.[68] In Finnish mythology the wilderness and emptiness of the landscape represent the symbolic lack of a history, and at the same time an empty space that has been filled with pioneering settlers of Finnish descent. The Karelians, Ingrians, Sámi and other Fenno-Ugric people, who provided the ingredients for the myth, were however regarded by the Finnish elite groups as more primitive in relation to the state-bearing proper Finns. By gathering up the lost folklore and contrasting these Fenno-Ugric people as marginal to the nation-building proper Finns, the latter could be regarded as modern, with a future to develop.[69]

It can explain why the national planners in the early twentieth century repudiated the notion of 'park' in favour of 'untouched restricted areas', and why the 12 specific areas created for the purposes of the Sámi and local people in 1991 were called *wilderness areas*. It also explains why this attitude towards nature as something untouched and pure was simultaneously combined with an advanced modern system of national park administration that was imported from the US.[70] The national narration of the lonely archaic settler in the wilderness is dichotomised with the Finns as a modern people in a state of constant progress, expressing the two essential sides of Finnish national identification. The advent of the Sámi foundation myth and narrative, showing the Sámi as an even older 'indigenous people' than the Finns, has contested the Finnish myth of the empty wilderness.[71] It has been met by arguments from ethnic Finns in Lapland that indigenous nomadic people are not the first-comers to the region because they did not settle there, or that the Sámi view regarding land rights is a turning back from progress to ancient hard times that no one wants to return to.[72] Both in Finland and Sweden the big narration of the nation has been contested by particular narrations of politically ethnified sub-groups. In the same time the idea of the nation as the only legitimate basis for nature conservation is contested.

## Bibliography

Act 1909/56. *Lag angående nationalparker* (Sweden).
Act 1923/71. *Lag om naturskydd* (Finland).
Act 1932/239. *Lag om renskötsel* (Finland).

66 Tham, *Lappland och Tornedalen*.
67 Engman, 'Den unge falkens flykt', 421–436.
68 Elenius, 'Det vilda', 32–69.
69 Anttonen, *Tradition through Modernity*, 155–177.
70 Perttula, *Suomen kansallispuistojärjestelmän*.
71 Elenius, 'Det vilda', 32–69.
72 Tuulentie, 'For and against', 275–295. Tuulentie calls the local interpretations of history 'local narratives of the nation'.

Act 1938/83. *Lag om inrättande av vissa nya naturskyddsområden å staten tillhörig mark* (Finland).

Act 1956/634. *Lag om inrättande av vissa nya naturskyddsområden på staten tillhörig mark* (Finland).

Act 1964:882. *Naturvårdslag* (Sweden).

Act 1983/228. *Lag om Urho Kekkonens nationalpark* (Finland).

Act 1991/62. *Ödemarkslag* (Finland).

Act 2003/1086. *Samisk språklag* (Finland). http://www.finlex.fi/sv/laki/ajantasa/2003/20031086

Aikio, Aslak. 'Marriage among the Saame of the Kemi Region of Lapland in 1750–1900'. In *Family Life on the Northwestern Margins of Imperial Russia*, eds. Tapio Hämynen, Jukka Partanen and Yury Shikalov. Joensuu: Joensuu University Press, 2004: 39–66.

Anderson, Benedict. *Imagined Communities: Reflections on the Origin and Spread of Nationalism*, Rev. and extended ed. London: Verso, 1991.

Anttonen, Pertti J. *Tradition through Modernity: Postmodernism and the Nation-state in Folklore Scholarship*. Helsinki: Finnish Literature Society, 2005.

Barth, Fredrik. 'Introduction'. In *Ethnic Groups and Boundaries: The Social Organization of Culture Difference*, ed. Fredrik Barth, 9–38. Oslo: Univ.-forl., 1969.

*Bebyggelsen i Finland på 1500-talet. Atlas* (Nordiska ödegårdsprojektets finländsk avdelning). Forssa, 1973.

Bergman, I. & L-E. Edlund. 'Birkarlar and Sámi – Inter-cultural Contacts beyond State Control: Reconsidering the Standing of External Tradesmen (Birkarlar) in Medieval Sámi Societies'. *Acta Borealia* (2016). DOI:10.1080/08003831.2016.1154676.

Bergman, I. & G. Hörnberg. 'Early Cereal Cultivation at Sámi Settlements: Challenging the Hunter-herder Paradigm?'. *Arctic Anthropology* 52 (2015): 57–66.

Bhabha, H. K., ed. *Nation and Narration*. London and New York: Routledge, 1990.

Bjørklund, Ivar. *Fjordfolket i Kvænangen: fra samisk samfunn til norsk utkant 1550–1980*. Tromsø: Universitetsforl, 1985.

Brantenberg, Terje, Hansen, Janne & Henry Minde, eds. *Becoming Visible: Indigenous Politics and Self-Government*. Tromsø: University of Tromsø, 1995.

Burke, Peter. *Languages and Communities in Early Modern Europe*. Cambridge: Cambridge University Press, 2004.

Chatterjee, P. *Nationalist Thought and the Colonial World: A Derivative Discourse?* London: Zed Books, 1986.

Committee Report 1976:88. *Nationalparkskommitténs betänkande*. Helsingfors: Statens tryckningscentral, 1976.

Edgren, Torsten & Lena Törnblom, eds. *Finlands Historia I*. Helsingfors: Schilds, 1998.

Elenius, Lars. 'Det vilda som gränsmarkör mellan nomader och bofasta i kolonisationsprocessen i Finland, Sverige och Norge'. In *Nordiska gränser i historien. Linjer och rum, konstruktion och dekonstruktion*, ed. Lars Elenius, 32–69. Joensuu: University Press of Eastern Finland, 2014.

Elenius, Lars, 'Minoritetsspråken i nationalistisk växelverkan: Samiska och finska som kyrkospråk och medborgarspråk'. In *Gränsöverskridande kyrkohistoria: De språkliga minoriteterna på Nordkalotten*, ed. Daniel Lindmark, 13–16. Umeå: Umeå universitet, 2016.

Enbuske, Matti. 'Bosättningen och markanvändningen i mellersta Lappland och Enontekis fram till början av 1900-talet'. In *Yhteenveto ja tiivistelmä Lapinmaan maaoikeudet- tutkimuksesta*, ed. Jouko Vahtola Helsinki: Oikeusministeriö, 2006: 83–101.

Enbuske, Matti. *Vanhan Lapin valtaanmailla. Asutus ja maakäyttö Kemin Lapin ja Enontekiön aluella 1500-luvulta 1900-luvun alkuun*. Helsinki: Suomalaisen Kirjalisuuden Seura, 2008.

Engman, Max. 'Den unge falkens flykt. Brott och kontinuitet kring Finland 1809'. In *Maktens mosaik: enhet, särart och självbild i det svenska riket*, eds. Max Engman & Nils Erik Villstrand. Helsingfors: Svenska litteratursällskapet i Finland, 2008: 421–436.

Eriksen, Thomas Hylland. *Ethnicity and Nationalism*. London: Pluto Press, 1993.

Fewster, Derek. 'Visions of Past Glory: Nationalism and the Construction of Early Finnish History'. Diss. Helsinki: University of Helsinki, 2006.

Gellner, Ernest. *Nations and Nationalism*. Oxford: Blackwell, 1983.

Grandien, Bo. 'Fornnordiskt i konsten'. In *Natur och nationalitet: nordisk bildkonst 1800–1850 och dess europeiska bakgrund*, eds. Jörgen Weibull & Per Jonas Nordhagen. Höganäs: Wiken i samarbete med Clara Lachmanns fond, 1992: 110–126.

Green, Carina. 'Managing Laponia: A World Heritage Site as Arena for Sámi Ethno-Politics in Sweden'. Diss. Uppsala: Uppsala University, 2009.

Hall, Patrik. 'The Social Construction of Nationalism: Sweden as an Example'. Diss. Lund: Univ. Press, 1998.

Hall, Patrik. *Den svenskaste historien: Nationalism i Sverige under sex sekler*. Stockholm: Carlsson, 2000.

Hedberg, Bengt. *Naturskydd i Sverige*. Stockholm: Svenska turistföreningen, 1987.

Heikkila, Lydia. 'Reindeer Talk – Sámi Reindeer Herding and Nature Management'. Diss. Rovaniemi: University of Lapland, 2006.

Hermanson, Ann-Sofie. 'Miljövårdens institutionalisering i Finland: idé, rörelse, administration'. Diss. Åbo: Åbo akademi, 2006.

Hiltuen, Mauno. 'En värld mellan världar: Befolkningen, näringslivet och markförvaltningen i Enontekis 1550–1808'. In *Yhteenveto ja tiivistelmä Lapinmaan maaoikeudet- tutkimuksesta (Julkaisu 2006:8 Lapinmaan maaoikeudet)*, ed. Jouko Vahtola. Helsinki: Oikeusministeriö, 2006: 102–120.

Hobsbawm, Eric J. *Nations and Nationalism since 1780: Programme, Myth, Reality* (2nd edn). Cambridge: Cambridge Univ. Press, 1992.

Högström, Pehr. *Beskrifning öfwer de til Sweriges krona lydande lapmarker*, Facs.-utg. Umeå: Två förläggare, 1980 [1747].

Hörnberg, G., Josefsson, T., Bergman, I., Liedgren, L., & L. Östlund. 'Indications of Shifting Cultivation West of the Lapland Border: Multifaceted Land Use in Northernmost Sweden since AD 800'. *The Holocene* 25 (2015): 989–1001.

Itkonen, T. I. *Mamme lappalaisen ja suomalaisen asutuksen vaihtea*. SI, 1947.

Johansson, Alf W. 'Nationalism'. In *Flaggor: från fälttåg till folkfest*, ed. Leif Jonsson. Lidköping: Läckö Institutet, 1993: 19–31.

Josefsson, T., Ramqvist, P. & G. Hörnberg. 'The History of Early Cereal Cultivation in Northernmost Fennoscandia as Indicated by Palynological Research'. *Vegetation History and Archaeobotany* 23 (2014): 821–840.

Jutikkala, Eino & Kauko Pirinen. *Finlands Historia* (3rd edn). Stockholm: Natur och kultur, 1973.

Kjellström, Rolf, ed. *Sameforskning i dag och i morgon: rapport från symposium rörande den samiska kulturen 19–20 november 1973 i Nordiska museet*. Stockholm: Nordiska museet, 1974.

*Kommittén för kolonisation av statens skogsmark till jordbruk* (A. Järnefelt a.o.). Helsingfors 4 februari 1888.

Kortesalmi, Juhani J. *Pohjois-Vienan poronhoito*. Helsinki: Suomen muinasmuistoyhdistys, 1996.

Læstadius, Lars Levi. *Om uppodlingar i Lappmarken på det allmännas bekostnad*. Faks.-uppl. Luleå: Tornedalica, 1981 [1824].

Lähteenmäki, Maria. *The Peoples of Lapland: Boundary Demarcations and Interaction in the North Calotte from 1808 to 1889*. Helsinki: Finnish Academy of Science and Letters, 2006.

Lantto, Patrik. 'Tiden börjar på nytt: en analys av samernas etnopolitiska mobilisering i Sverige 1900–1950'. Diss. Umeå: Umeå Univ., 2000.

Lantto, Patrik & Ulf Mörkenstam. 'Sami Rights and Sámi Challenges: The Modernization Process and the Swedish Sámi Movement, 1886–2006'. *Scandinavian Journal of History* 33, no. 1 (2008): 26–51.

Larsson, Bo, ed. *Svedjebruk och röjningsbränning i Norden*. Stockholm: Nordiska museet, 1995.

Lehtola, Veli-Pekka. *Samelaiset Suomaliaset kohtaamisia 1896–1953*. Helsinki: Suomalaisen Kirjallisuuden Seura, 2012.

Lehtola, Veli-Pekka. 'Organiserad samepolitik i Finland efter andra världskriget'. In *Befolkning och bosättning i norr: etnicitet, identitet och gränser i historiens sken*, eds. Peter Sköld & Patrik Lantto. Umeå: Umeå universitet, 2004: 299–304.
Lehtola, Veli-Pekka. *Saamelaisten parlamentti: Suomen saamelaisvaltuuskunta 1973–1995 ja Saamelaiskäräjät 1996–2003*. Inari: Saamelaiskäräjät, 2005.
Leinberg, K. G. *Finlands territoriala församlingars ålder, utbildning och utgrening intill 1885 års utgång*. Helsingfors: Svenska litteratursällskapet i Finland, 1886.
Lindkvist, Thomas & Kurt Ågren. *Sveriges medeltid*. Solna: Almqvist & Wiksell, 1993 [1985].
Linjakumpu, Aini & Leena Suopajärvi. *Sellainen seutu ja sellainen maa: Erot, vastarinta ja uuden politiikan vaatimus Lapissa*. Rovaniemi: Lapin Yliopistopainu, 2003.
Lönnroth, Erik. *Från svensk medeltid* (3rd edn). Stockholm: Bonnier, 1964.
Loomba, Ania. *Colonialism/postcolonialism*. London: Routledge, 1998.
Lundgren, Lars J. *Staten och naturen: naturskyddspolitik i Sverige 1869–1935. D. 1, 1869–1919*. Brottby: Kassandra, 2009.
Lundmark, Lennart. 'Uppbörd, utarmning, utveckling: det samiska fångstsamhällets övergång till rennomadism i Lule lappmark'. Diss. Umeå: Univ. Lund, 1982.
Lundström, Inga, ed. *Historisk rätt?: kultur, politik och juridik i norr* (1st uppl). Stockholm: Riksantikvarieämbetet, 2007.
Mels, Tom. 'Wild Landscapes: The Cultural Nature of Swedish National Parks'. Diss. Lund: Univ. Press, 1999.
Miller, Robert J., Jacinta Ruru, Larissa Behrendt and Tracey Lindberg. *Discovering Indigenous Lands. The Doctrine of Discovery in the English Colonies*. New York: Oxford University Press, 2010.
Müller-Wille, Ludger. 'Lappen und Finnen in Utsjoki (Ohcijohka), Finnland: eine Studie zur Identität ethnischer Gruppen im Kulturkontakt'. Diss. Münster: Geographische Kommission für WestfalenWestfälische Wilhelms-Universität, 1974.
*Nationalparkskommitténs betänkande*. Helsingfors, 1976.
Newcomb, Steven T. *Pagans in the Promised Land: Decoding the Doctrine of Christian Discovery*. Golden, CO: Fulcrum Pub, 2008.
Niemi, Einar. 'Sami History and the Frontier Myth. A Perspective on Northern Sámi Spatial and Rights History'. In *Sámi Culture in a New Era: The Norwegian Sámi Experience*, ed. Harald Gaski. Karasjok: Davvi Girji OS, 1997.
Nilsson Dahlström, Åsa. 'Negotiating Wilderness in a Cultural Landscape: Predators and Saami Reindeer Herding in the Laponian World Heritage Area'. Diss. Uppsala: Uppsala University, 2003.
Nordin, Gabriella. 'Äktenskap i Sápmi: giftermålsmönster och etnisk komplexitet i kolonisationens tidevarv, 1722–1895'. Diss. Umeå: Umeå universitet, 2009.
Nyyssönen, Jukka. ' "Everybody Recognized that We Were Not White": Sámi Identity Politics in Finland, 1945–1990'. Diss. Tromsø: University of Tromsø, 2007.
Olwig, Kenneth. 'The Landscape of Justice Contra that of Custom'. In *Landscape, Law and Customary Rights*, eds. Michael Jones & Audhild Schanke. Dideut No 3 2004, s. 39–63. Kautokeino: Nordisk Samisk Institutt, 2004.
Oommen, T. K. 'Introduction: Conceptualizing the Linkage between Citizenship and National Identity'. In *Citizenship and National Identity from Colonialism to Globalisation*, 27–51. New Delhi and London: Sage Publications, 1997.
Ordinance 1983/229. *Förordningen för Urho Kekkonens nationalpark*.
Päiviö, Nils-Johan. 'Från skattemannarätt till nyttjanderätt: en rättshistorisk studie av utvecklingen av samernas rättigheter från slutet 1500-talet till 1886 års renbeteslag'. Diss. Uppsala: Uppsala universitet, 2011.
Palmgren, Rolf. *Naturskydd och kultur 1*. Helsingfors: Schildt, 1920.
Paulaharju, Samuli. *Ödebygdsfolk: från nordsveriges finskbygder*. Stockholm, Natur och kultur, 1966.

Perttula, Minnu. *Suomen kansallispuistojärjestelmän kehittyminen 1960–1990-luvuilla ja U.S. National Park Servicen vaikutukset puistojen hoitoon.* Sarja A 155. Vanta: Metsähallitus, 2006.
Raitio, Kaisa. 'Konflikten mellan rennäring och skogsbruk i Enare'. In *Omstridd natur: Trender och utmaningar i nordisk naturförvaltning*, eds. Camilla Sandström, Sissel Hovik & Eva Irene Falleth. Umeå: Borea bokförlag, 2008: 227–247.
Reimerson, Elsa. 'Nature, Culture, Rights: Exploring Space for Indigenous Agency in Protected Area Discourses'. Diss. Umeå: Umeå University, 2015.
Ruotsala, Helena. *Muuttuvat palkiset.* Helsinki: Suomen muinasmuistoyhdistys, 2002.
Said, Edward W. *Orientalism.* London: Penguin, 2003 [1979].
Sillanpää, Lennard. *Political and Administrative Responses to Sámi self-determination.* Helsinki: Finnish Society of Science and Letters, 1994.
Sillanpää, Lennard. 'Government Responses to Saami Self-determination'. In *Conflict and Cooperation in the North*, eds. Kristina Karppi & Johan Eriksson. Umeå: Umeå University, 2002: 83–110.
Smith, Anthony D. *The Ethnic Origins of Nations.* Oxford: Basil Blackwell, 1986.
Smith, Anthony D. *National Identity.* London: Penguin, 1991.
SOU 1962:36. *Naturen och samhället.* Stockholm: Jordbruksdepartementet, 1962 (Sweden).
Spira, Thomas. 'Ethnicity and Nationality: The Twin Matrices of Nationalism'. In *Ethnonationalism in the Contemporary World: Walker Connor and the Study of Nationalism*, ed. Daniele Conversi. London: Routledge, 2004: 248–264.
Suopajärvi, Leena. 'Lapin luonnon modernisoituminen toisen maailmaansodan jälkeen. Traditionaalisesti yhteiskunnasta refleksiiviseen moderniin'. In *Sellainen seutu ja sellainen maa: erot, vastarinta ja uuden politiikan vaatimus Lapissa*, eds. Aini Linjakumpu & Leena Suopajärvi. Rovaniemi: Lapin yliopisti, 2003: 138–145.
Tarkiainen, Kari. *Sveriges österland: Från forntiden till Gustav Vasa.* Helsingfors: Svenska litteratursällskapet i Finland, 2008.
Tegengren, Helmer. *En utdöd lappkultur i Kemi lappmark: Studier i Nordfinlands kolonisationshistoria.* Åbo: Åbo Akademi, 1952.
Tham, Richard. *Lappland och Tornedalen i konsten: landskapsvyer 1799–1910.* Luleå: Norrbottens museum, 1989.
Thuen, Trond. 'Acculturation and Ethnic Survival?'. *Acta Borealia* 1–2 (1985) Oslo: 29–45.
Tilly, Charles. *Coercion, Capital and European States AD 990–1992.* Oxford: Blackwell, 1992.
Tunón, Håkan, ed. *Uppsala mitt i Sápmi: rapport från ett symposium arrangerat av Föreningen för samiskrelaterad forskning i Uppsala, Upplandsmuseet 4–5 maj 2011.* Uppsala: Naptek, 2012. http://www.slu.se/Global/externwebben/centrumbildningar-projekt/centrum-for-biologisk-mangfald/Dokument/publikationer-cbm/cbm-skriftserie/skrift55.pdf.
Tuulentie, Seija. 'For and against the Rights of the Sámi People: The Argumentation of the Finnish Majority in the Debate on the Sámi Rights'. In *Indigenous Peoples: Resource Managements and Global Rights*, eds. Svein Jentoft, Henry Minde & Ragnar Nilsen, 275–295. Umeå and Delft: Eburon, 2003.
Zachrisson, Inger, ed. *Möten i gränsland: samer och germaner i Mellanskandinavien.* Stockholm: Statens historiska museum, 1997.

# 3 Rights of the naturised

*Tore Andersson Hjulman*

## Introduction

The notion of pristine nature is not only ideologically, but also on a very practical level historically, linked to that of indigenous peoples. It has very often been incarnated in precisely those landscapes that have been colonised and cultivated by people who have been excluded from 'civilised society' by the European colonial powers. In a colonial context the representation comprised a legitimising function; with the support of a principle derived from Roman law – *ferae bestia* – which was the alleged lack of a particular type of exploitation of 'nature' to justify the adoption of colonial forms of governance. The degree of intervention that could be justified was, therefore, determined by the geographic placement of a people on the intended development ladder, which gained a central role in the modern representational world.[1]

In addition to comprising the people at the bottom of this ladder, the concept of 'primordial nature' came to be the object of strong emotive manifestation and symbolism that were borne by preservation movements that began to sprout particularly during the second half of the nineteenth century. For these the colonised world, unsurprisingly, constituted an important arena, not least in respect of the establishment of national parks. The exchange between colonial ideology, domination and nature preservation interests is an area of research that has already yielded good returns through studies based on several different contexts.[2] Together they accumulate into a history that appears with a greater depth through being genuinely global in character.

One of the phenomena, which has been highlighted for its manifestly cross-national history, is the forced displacement that indigenous peoples living in the national parks were subjected to. At the same time as the connections to the colonial conditions in a good many cases have been well documented, at the core of these events lies a level of contradiction that I maintain is worth highlighting with renewed focus. The re-identification of the national parks' inhabitants as a threat to the preserved nature can actually be understood as being an attempt to sever the link between 'primordial nature' and 'indigenous people', which has constituted the basis for the modern natural preservation movement. In several cases the requirement of forced movement implies a remarkable change in established relations between preservationists and the indigenous people. People and cultivation that were previously seen as more or less assets to the national parks started to be considered as diametrically opposed to the aims of preservation. In these pages I want to highlight this type

1 Fitzmaurice, 'The genealogy of Terra Nullius', 1–15.
2 See e.g. W.M. Adams, 'Nature and the colonial mind'.

of process, founded on a case study on the establishment of a Swedish national park. The purpose of this chapter is to contribute to an understanding of how the relations between preservationists and the indigenous population, who have since time immemorial cultivated an intended national park area, have changed, and the contributory factors to this.

## A Swedish case of national park establishment

Empirical focus for this study is the initiatives and events that led to the creation of the Muddus National Park in northern Sweden in 1942. Major actors that both collaborated with and opposed each other were the Royal Swedish Academy of Sciences, the County Administrative Board of Norrbotten, the state organisation that monitored reindeer husbandry (Lappväsendet) and individual preservationists. These actors also include those families that belonged to the indigenous Sámi people and who populated and lived off reindeer husbandry within the boundaries of the intended national park area.

An overwhelming proportion of the Swedish national parks have been set aside within the Sámi reindeer herding area; i.e. seven of the 13 parks that had been formed before Muddus and these seven represented more than 99 per cent of the land area.[3] It appears to have been primarily due to so many parts of the reindeer herding area having been considered to be in state hands since Sámi land ownership largely ceased to gain state recognition in the nineteenth century. Consequently expropriations became unnecessary.[4] This end of the country had by then already gained a prominence in the minds of preservationists as a 'true wilderness' and to this contributed the exotification of the Sámi people.[5]

With the creation of the first Swedish national parks in 1909, the preservationists had to explicitly relate to the Sámi presence because of several different reasons. Relevant conditions in this respect were that the Swedish preservation organisation was heavily influenced by the German Heimat movement and that it was dominated by scientists that were partly motivated by the opportunity to protect nature for research purposes. There was a strong emphasis that the protection of nature should encompass 'pristine' and 'untouched' nature.[6] The purpose of the national parks was to allow 'natural life to develop completely undisturbed by cultural influences'.[7] Based on this clear distinction between nature and culture, the possibility of also including the idea of a Sámi 'cultural landscape' within the borders of the intended 'natural landscape' was undoubtedly hampered.

Another condition of importance was that the Sámi people within the reindeer herding area held specific exploitation rights that were codified in the Reindeer Act of 1898. To an extent reindeer husbandry was also protected by the state for reasons of national economy.[8] The Swedish preservationist movement was weak, and parliamentary support is considered to have been dependent on the parliamentary bills put forward not being in conflict with

3 Calculations based on data from Lundgren, *Staten och naturen* D.1, and Högdahl, 'Description of Swedish conservation map', 132.
4 Lundgren, *Staten och naturen* D.1, 301 et seq; Lundmark, '*Lappen är ombytlig, ostadig och obekväm*'; Mörkenstam, *Om 'Lapparnes privilegier'*, chs. 4–5.
5 Elenius, 'Selma Lagerlöf och Norrland', 15–41.
6 Lundgren, *Staten och naturen* D.1.
7 Committee report, *Betänkande rörande åtgärder*, 47 (translated from Swedish).
8 Torp, 'Rennäringens rättigheter', 155–192.

other interests.[9] The expert group that prepared the national parks bill and who were also leading lights within the preservationist movement were careful to point out that this was not the case. They indicated that the Sámi people's use of the land could very well be integrated with the preservation of nature:

> The Lapp people's rights practice have so far not had any noticeable effect on natural life, and the Lapp people are so intimately interwoven with nature within their territory that it, so to speak, complements it. It would without doubt be unsuitable to adopt anything that might take away from a Lapp national park the specific interest conferred upon it through the presence of the Lapp people.[10]

In the identification of the Sámi people's lifestyle as being interwoven with nature the ideological alliance between preservation and colonial power is made clear. The approach is linked to the notion that the Sámi people were at a lower level of cultural development, which also characterised the state policy towards the ethnic group.[11] Based on this notion, which was coupled with an assumption that Sámi culture was threatened by degeneration and destruction when it came in too close contact with the surrounding Swedish culture, the state had since the early twentieth century been acting on a policy of segregation in parallel with the assimilation policy. This segregation policy was primarily aimed at the nomadised Sámi people pursuing reindeer husbandry in the mountain regions. The goal was to conserve what was seen as a special, authentic and economical sound driving force of Sámi culture through limiting contact with Swedish society.[12]

The responsibility for administration of national parks in Sweden lay with the Royal Swedish Academy (KVA), and in practice a specific committee, the Nature Preservation Committee (NPC) (Naturskyddskommittén), which handled day-to-day affairs. Its duties included demarcating the parks' boundaries, erecting notices and preparing vegetation maps of the areas concerned. The authority was additionally responsible for taking decisions on possible exemptions to the regulations concerning research, preservation and other specific purposes. If permits were granted for hunting, fishing or erection of buildings it had the right to charge for the same.[13]

In order to track the changes in relations between preservationists and the Sámi people, I started by consulting the NPC's meeting minutes. When problematisations concerning relations to the Sámi people started to appear at the end of the 1920s and the start of the 1930s, they can be ascribed to three separate contexts of which the creation of Muddus National Park is one. I have also been able to find correspondence between the NPC and the actors concerned, which has been preserved, and to follow the political processes that were initiated through cabinet Acts and parliamentary proceedings. In order to further and deepen my understanding of the events I have additionally sought various other sources that have provided broader knowledge concerning the actors involved and their roles. The hitherto most eloquent account of the foreplay to the establishment of the national park is

9 Lundgren, *Staten och naturen* D.1, 301 et seq.
10 Committee report, *Betänkande rörande åtgärder*, 47 (translated from Swedish).
11 Concerning cultural-hierarchical opinion in Sámi policy, see e.g. Lantto, *Lappväsendet: tillämpningen*, 25; Mörkenstam, *Om 'Lapparnes privilegier'*, 108; Lundmark, *'Lappen är ombytlig, ostadig och obekväm'*, 17.
12 Mörkenstam, *Om 'Lapparnes privilegier'*; Lantto, *Lappväsendet: tillämpningen*.
13 Lundgren, *Staten och naturen* D.1, 293 et seq Lundgren describes the KVA as 'conservation's main player' after 1909.

probably in *The State and Nature* (*Staten och naturen*) (2011) by Lars J. Lundgren. How the relation between preservationists and the Sámi people developed is however something that is touched upon only sporadically and sparsely.

## A non-essentialist point of origin

The fact that populations whose identification as indigenous peoples have underpinned the establishment of national parks has in many cases been the subject of forced-displacement and has been attributed various explanations in the literature. By means of a short introduction to my own thesis there is reason already at this stage to take up two types of shortcomings that I maintain occur among these explanatory models. In the one case I understand there to be a tangible risk of them becoming anachronistic, to the extent that they presume that those who have labelled a certain people as indigenous *all the time* have been 'wrong', but at a given point in time have been obliged to correct themselves when 'confronted with reality' or introduced stricter preservation measures. The point of origin is, in other words, a presumption that in actual fact was the result of the process to be explained.[14] In the other case they confirm a colonial description of reality by presuming that the process of change has primarily taken place amongst the indigenous people themselves, that is to say that it has *become* a threat to the protected nature after not having been so.[15] In both cases it is a question of an essentialist concept of nature wherein a people's interwovenness with nature can either be true or false depending on the circumstances.

In order to avoid these problems there are good reasons to seek inspiration in post-constructionist theory and the criticism directed at how the distinction between the natural and the social is taken for granted also when reality in most other aspects is assumed to be made intelligible only in historically specific contexts of human interaction.[16] Nature will consequently not be taken for granted as something that exists regardless of the terminology and categorisation insisting on this existence. By this means it allows the relation of someone or something to nature to be understood as a positive action, as *naturising*.

*Naturising* describes the exclusion of subjects from an envisaged civilisatory community through conceptual incorporation in the nature category. This concerns what happened to the indigenous peoples who were colonised with regard to their supposed primitive level of development. It also concerns what happened to the Sámi people when the government's experts described them as 'intimately interwoven' with nature in connection with the first national parks being established in Sweden. Naturising always occurs in a set context and always implies that something else is denaturised simultaneously. It is thus in the relation between that which is naturised and denaturised respectively that the function of the understanding of nature arises. For the same reason the phenomenon is not as uniform, for example, in the meaning that the implications of naturising should always remain constant. The fact that a populace is naturised in relation to another group does not, automatically blur the distinction between this group of the population in the capacity of humans and a naturised animal species. This can be understood by the analogy with, for example, a particular sample of people identified as men can be feminised without blurring the distinction

14 This type of hypothesis could arguably be ascribed to, inter alia, Neumann, 'Ways of seeing Africa', 149–169.

15 This explanation model has, for example, been furthered by those who argued for forced-displacement within the Swedish conservationist movement, see note 59.

16 Castree, *Making Sense of Nature*, 10.

between these individuals and the group identified as women. The incorporation of something or someone in the nature category is always relative and comparative.

The concept of naturising occurs sparingly in the scientific literature, but examples can be found. The cultural geographer Shirley Brooks describes how tourism interests in South Africa during the 1930s drove a 'process of naturalisation'[17] of the areas earlier used by the indigenous population and as a game reserve. This occurred through a systematic execution of spatial and social control, implicated by romanticising representations of African wildernesses, which in the end caused enforced-displacement of the indigenous population. A theoretical discussion and specification is missing here, but the concept seems to emanate from 'natural spaces', which alludes to the dichotomic distribution of space in nature and culture respectively. Even if the process of naturising is only set in direct relation to the landscape as such, there is an underlying assumption that it also had a bearing on things that were present in this landscape, including indigenous peoples. The author emphasises the importance of conceptions of non-urban Africans as exotic elements against the backdrop of nature.[18] Thus there is a high degree of agreement between Brooks and my own conceptual usage, even if I have chosen the term *naturising* instead of *naturalising* to avoid confusion with alternative meanings of the latter term.

## New landscapes and renewed authorities

During the 1920s, just over a decade after the creation of the first national parks in Sweden, the Swedish Society for Nature Preservation (SNP) (Svenska Naturskyddsföreningen) went looking for new areas as potential objects for further national parks. More specifically, the aim was to find something that could be identified as northern Swedish primeval forest; a type of landscape that until then had been very poorly represented within the existing national parks as they had in the main been assigned to mountain regions. Edvard Wibeck, a preservationist senior research fellow, was given the task of presenting proposals for areas worthy of protection, which he did formally in connection with one of SNP's board meetings in February 1927. Wibeck was born in 1877 in southern Sweden but had worked as a forester in the area around Muddus. As a researcher he represented, inter alia, the department for rejuvenation research in the Swedish north at the State Forestry Research Facility and as an active preservationist he was a board member of SNP from 1927 to 1943 and also editor for its magazine for many years.[19]

The two areas that Wibeck identified as potential national park areas were Muddus and Sjaunja.[20] Of the two, it seems to have been Muddus that he was particularly interested in. The area comprised around 60 square kilometres in the municipalities of present-day Gällivare and Jokkmokk.[21] At the centre of the area are significant swamplands and lake Muttosjávrre, which receives a tributary from the Muttosjåhkå River and which is dewatered flowing through Muttosädno, watercourses that have partially eroded into deep canyon

17 Brooks, 'Images of "Wild Africa": Nature', 235.

18 Ibid., 227, 236.

19 *Nordisk familjebok*: http://runeberg.org/vemardet/1969/1039.html (accessed 26 February 2016); *Vem är det? Svensk biografisk handbok*: http://runeberg.org/vemardet/1969/1039.html (accessed 26 February 2016).

20 The Sámi names are *Muttos* and *Sjávnja* but hereinafter the name *Muddus* will be used for the first of the areas as the national park proposition went under this name.

21 Lundgren, *Staten och naturen* D.2, 300 et seq.

valleys.[22] Wibeck understood the difficulties in logging timber along the Muttusädno River, which meant that no significant deforestation had taken place.[23]

On the other hand, the area had been cultivated and used in many other ways by man. For reindeer husbandry it had served as winter grazing land and the woodlands were rich in traces of bark removal, demarcation lines and tree stumps. Even the region's permanent population had kept reindeer in Muddus and carried out a degree of bog cultivation. Today there are 82 registered prehistoric sites, nine of which are prehistoric dwelling foundations, and as recently as the end of the nineteenth century there was a resident population in the area. The emergence of certain types of forest, such as lichen heaths, have been directly connected by ecologists to human use.[24]

When Wibeck in 1927 presented the Muddus area as a national park proposal, its remoteness from the order of civilisation was, however, a fundamental starting point. This was despite the fact that he himself would at a later juncture tone down the claim of untouched naturalness. As far as SNP's membership was concerned Wibeck maintained that Muddus was part of the least explored nature in the country.[25] At the same time he saw a development in which civilisation moved its dwellings ever closer, ever further out into the very nature that consequently stood to lose its earlier qualities:

> One should not, however, believe that these remote parts of the country are completely forgotten and abandoned by man. For every year that passes, our state and private forestry sector lays claim to ever-greater areas of this region's ancient natural forests. Small cottages housing lumberjacks and loggers grow up like mushrooms along the lakesides and riversides ever-further up the former wilderness; during the winter months axes fell loads of timber along more and more areas up there and in the spring and summer logging work continues along the rivers.[26]

If it had been the case, as Wibeck later claimed, that he had already begun to question the indigenous Sámi people's identity, this had not infiltrated the wilderness feelings he harboured for those areas that the Sámi people had populated since time immemorial. The perception of Sámi as a threath was instead something that crept in along the backwaters of the more comprehensive picture of a civilisational 'frontier' that advanced along virgin ground that had already staked its claim. In a first wave this happened through the scientific examinations that were adopted to clarify if the area was suitable material for a national park.

Botanical and forestry examinations conducted by Henrik Hesselman and Erik Almquist were ready in 1931. The results were to all intents and purposes negative. Felling was judged to have blighted the area's virgin primeval forest status and Hesselman felt that the area in this respect, therefore, could not meet the purpose of preservation under law. He also indicated that the ground cover and rejuvenation had been hard hit by the herds of reindeer

22 *Bevarandeplan Natura 2000*, 6. http://www.lansstyrelsen.se/norrbotten/SiteCollectionDocuments/Sv/djur-och-natur/skyddad-natur/Nationalparker/Bevarandeplan_MuddusNP.pdf [hämtat 2015-09-16]. Names from the Sámi parliament's website, https://www.sametinget.se/1670 (accessed 16 September 2015).

23 Wibeck, 'Muddus', 38.

24 Engelmark, *Muttos = Muddus nationalpark*, 74, 137–144.

25 Wibeck, 'Muddus', 36 (translated from Swedish).

26 Ibid., 37.

that had been seasonally driven along the banks of the Lule River. For his part Almquist also judged that the flora was generally of a trivial nature and uninteresting.[27]

Wibeck had already beforehand feared that the deforestation that had taken place in Muddus would be used as an objection to a more extensive reservation area. He alluded to both 'prehistoric deforestation' and to felling areas that had come about through timber being transported on the relatively recently-laid Porjus railway.[28] By means of a response to the presumed objections Wibeck implemented a means of reasoning that distanced himself from the previously cherished conceptions of a natural state and pristinity. He now meant that the most important matter from a nature preservation point of view was that human influence did not imply that any vegetation had disappeared 'or at all any *fully* indipensable values'.[29] Focus was thus somewhat shifted from the extent of human interventions to the specific values that was still possible to preserve.[30]

It is not taken as given that it was this way of reasoning that would be the guiding light in the case of evaluating Muddus. Not least the botanist Hesselman, who in 1933 became a member of the NPC, stands out as being orthodox in his opinion that only untouched and pristine nature ought to be made the object of nature preservation.[31] It is therefore especially important to note that even his standpoint in this respect actually came to change. Together with Wibeck, in the summer of 1932, he announced that the area was 'exceptionally deserving' of being set aside as a national park. The fauna and the peculiar landscape contours, which were highlighted as motifs, were apparently able to compensate for the lack of primeval forest and interesting flora. Their conclusion was based on statements made by the foresters in 26 of the territories that were considered to lie furthest away and that consequently most likely were expected to comprise of forest areas worthy of preservation:[32]

> The received circular responses have shown that older and newer logging activities have already managed to pass above the north Swedish pine region, that in the event of setting aside of a *larger* national park area in this zone, which to all intents and purposes would be compelled to express less rigorous opinions, than those in themselves would have been desirable.[33]

The foresters supplied too much information about how the forest had been used for anywhere in the north Swedish forest landscape to be entitled to nature preservation in terms of concepts such as *untouched* and *pristine*. The fact that this type of problem arose right then would on a more comprehensive level be put in connection with the preservationists' view being redirected from mountain to forestry environments. Previously only minor forested areas had been in question, but here was a pronounced intention to protect a relatively major area.[34] The shift meant that it became a question of a landscape that within

27 The Nature Preservation Committee's minutes 12/9 1931, § 1, NK.

28 Wibeck, 'Nu eller aldrig', 69. Refer also to Lundgren, *Staten och naturen* D.2, 303.

29 Wibeck, 'Nu eller aldrig', 69. Cursive type in original (translated from Swedish).

30 The focus on originality, however, continued to be prominent well into the future. Lundgren notes the principal difference ('the forest's biological condition rather than its age') in relation to the setting aside of Fiby ancient forest as a nature reserve in 1965. Lundgren, *Staten och naturen* D.2, 313, 334.

31 Lundgren, *Staten och naturen* D.2, 311.

32 Report by Wibeck and Hesselman to KVA, 1/7 1932, SNFA, RA. See also Lundgren, *Staten och naturen* D.2, 7.

33 Ibid., 8. Cursive text is underlined in the original (translated from Swedish).

34 Lundgren, *Staten och naturen* D.2, 300 et seq.

a Swedish conscience generally constituted a more well-known environment for traditional and industrial use, and foremost that the preservationists became dependent on an institutionalised network of practitioners (foresters). In other words, the power of definition for nature was transferred to a new category of people whose perception of reality had previously not had any great sphere of influence in connection with the establishment of national parks. The Sámi people's considerations were still not given credence but possibly the distance to the guideline talks concerning nature preservation policy were shortened somewhat through the foresters' possible somewhat stronger local roots. The dynamic between different groups' access to the powers of definition, and not least the tensions between theorists and pragmatists, is an important factor for Swedish preservationism, which is also strengthened on the basis of previous research.[35] In this case the scene changes seem to have been driven by the lack of any strong national park proposition and by the starting position consisting of an intention to protect a certain 'type of nature'.

The attention that was directed early in the process towards the Sámi land use chafed against the nature preservation legislation's exceptions to this practice. The reindeer herds that were driven along the banks of the Lule River were pointed out as having caused damage to the ground cover. The impressions on the ground were interpreted as being damage to nature. What did it mean in terms of the attitude towards the tracks that the reindeer herds continued to leave also when they crossed the border upstream to the Stora Sjöfallet National Park? The tracks were mentioned in connection with the dedication of that national park in 1909, but then as part of nature. The preservationist Einar Lönnberg had compared the reindeer herds' tracks with those of the Arctic fox: 'marks of the Arctic fox are to be seen there, as can those of the Gällivare Lapps' reindeer that have passed here'.[36]

Also the changed opinion about the starting points of preservationism that was forced out enabled ideological implications that were not immediately perspicuous. The extrapolation of a move away from concepts such as *natural state* and *pristine* probably encompassed the potential to expand the negotiation margin for both the Sámi identity and the distinction between nature and culture in general. Nature could now be regarded as worthy of protection even if its conceptual boundaries narrowed and its material manifestations consequently to an extent were considered to be corroded by cultural tracks. Thus opened an ideological track that with greater generosity could embrace the Sámi as a civilised people without exacting any doubts about the intrinsic value of the Lapland national parks.[37]

## Reindeer herdsmen Nilsson Kemi relocate to Muddus

The next phase in how the case of Muddus brought to the fore the relations between preservationists and the Sámi people took place during the early spring of 1932. Newly resettled Sámi people erected a reindeer pen in the Muddus area, which a few months later came to the attention of the NPC by means of the Swedish National Forest Enterprise (Swe. *Domänstyrelsen*).[38] In the construction of the pen, which measured just under five

35 Ibid: 342–68; Lundgren *Staten och naturen* D.1, 408 et seq.

36 Lönnberg, 'De båda stora lappländska nationalparkerna', 37 (translated from Swedish).

37 The focus on originality, however, continued to be prominent well into the future, see e.g. Lundgren, *Staten och naturen* D.2, 313.

38 For this the county administration board allocated them an interest-free loan of SEK 1200 from Carolina Mannerstråle's fund. It is recorded that the Lapp Sheriff Ragnar Pappilla and the Nilsson Kemi families in

and a half kilometres long, some 647 pine trees and 1,246 spruce trees had been felled, and 804 dead windfall trees had been used. The committee immediately sent the matter on to Wibeck and Hesselman, whose task it was to work out a proposal as to how to set aside Muddus as a national park.[39] In their statement they did not express their concern only in terms of the reindeer enclosure, but moreover the Sámi population that had given rise to it. The group of Sámi concerned had been forcibly relocated there by the power of the state for reasons that I shall return to. The two preservationists gave great credence to the fact this now amounted to a permanent settlement by the reindeer herders there. They stated that this would in all likelihood imply that the larger predators in the area would be eradicated. This meant both bears and wolverines, and possibly also martens. One matter that is noteworthy is that Wibeck and Hesselman had motivated the creation of a national park by highlighting the fauna concerned. They now understood that the animal life was threatened in its entirety:

> Even for the rest of the animal world, not least for shy and sensitive animals such as the whooper swan, a Lapp invasion into previously completely void areas would imply a change for the worse.[40]

They do not state what they base their conclusions on concerning the repercussions of the difference between fixed and non-fixed abode, but seem to intend to let the distinction become an absolute frontier guard for the untouched nature. In doing so, they consequently alluded to, consciously or unconsciously, the traditional association between settled life and civilisation. The Sámi people who had moved in belonged to the group of Forest Sámi – a category that in relation to the strong conception of Saminess which had, inter alia, been integrated in Swedish Sámi policy, were clearly marginalised. It had frequently been possible to dismiss them as not being 'proper' Sámi people, and up to 1917 there was a discussion about whether forest reindeer husbandry should be allowed at all. The Forest Sámi lived too closely to the Swedish farmers, both physically – through competing for natural resources – and culturally – inter alia through frequently combining reindeer husbandry and agriculture. The distance to the Swedish civilisation was too small for it to be able to fit in to the identity schedule that called for a clear demarcation between that which was Swedish and what was Sámi. Even if the preservationists did not explicitly use the label 'Forest Sámi', or 'Forest Lapps', it is natural to understand their attitude against this background. The fact that fixed abodes had previously been found within the Muddus area was not commented on. Their recommendation to the committee was to prevail upon the Ministry of Public Administration to ensure that the Sámi people were allocated another area, that is, subject them to yet another forced relocation.[41]

The migrant reindeer herders had previously belonged to Talma Lapp village north of Torneträsk. In the Lapp Sheriff's documentation the brothers Johan Nilsson Kemi (b. 1893)

---

some way agreed on the length and position. Letter to the county administrative board 4/4 1932, item 671, vol. Outgoing communications B1:2, LNA, LAH; Excerpt from minutes held before the county administrative board of Norrbotten County and the county secretariat in Luleå, 6/4 1932, item 237, vol. Letter concept in Lapp matters A 2 C:5, NLA, LAH.

39 The NPC's minutes, 10/6 1932, §1, NK; List of documents concerning Muddus, appended to Wibeck and Hesselman's proposal for setting aside of the Muddus area as a national park, December 1937, vol. Incl. letters and written communications 1937–1938 (2), NK.

40 Communication from Wibeck and Hesselman to the NPC (copy), 1/7 1932, vol. Fla:15, SNFA, RA (translated from Swedish).

41 Ibid.

and Nikolaus Nilsson Kemi (b. 1901) are mentioned by name, but these two also brought their family members with them.[42]

The forced relocation to Muddus involved many turns and finally became the subject of a government ruling. Already in 1927 the county administration board had instructed the brothers, under the threat of penalty of a fine, to move their reindeer husbandry that same year to the area that encompassed Muddus. The reason was the Reindeer Grazing Convention that the state had negotiated with the Norwegian state concerning the Swedish reindeer herders' access to the summer grazing areas across the border in Norway. The number of reindeer allowed to cross was limited and consequently the reindeer, especially in the northernmost Lapp villages, became too many in number in relation to the grazing areas available. In order to reduce the numbers of reindeer in the Lapp villages concerned, forced relocation had been in effect for all of the 1920s.[43] As the reason for the Nilsson Kemi brothers having to move, the Lapp Sheriff stated that contrary to the village by-laws they had allowed their reindeer to graze year-round on winter pastures and adjacent Lapp village land.[44] They themselves attest in an interpellation that their father ceased to pursue mountain reindeer husbandry, that is longer movements with the reindeer during the summer, around 25 years previously, and that they primarily wished to pursue forest reindeer husbandry. Rather than move to Muddus they explained that they were willing to make the transition to mountain reindeer husbandry, and that they were located in Muddus very much against their will and at significant personal loss, which is also borne out by their repeated attempts to avoid the decree.[45] In another communication they write, among other matters, that:

> even as well as the mountains, lakes and streams on whose shores we were born, grew up and lived until now, are so firmly attached to our minds, as we are forced to leave under duress, our hearts feel as heavy as if we were being exiled to Siberia.[46]

The Nilsson Kemi families' fight with the authorities can be followed at quite a detailed level through the material preserved in the Lapp Sheriff's archives and in the cabinet Acts that were drawn up in connection with government rulings in their case. Johan Nilsson Kemi travelled personally to Stockholm in 1929 to put his own case and attempt to bring about a correction to the regional authorities' decision. Their case was reported in both the local and national press.[47] It appears against the background of what can be proven concerning their earlier actions, possibly and even likely that the Nilsson Kemi brothers also attempted to influence the sequence of events more than can be surmised from the empirical evidence available.

42 In 1968 the ethnographer Ernst Manker described the families as comprising a total of eight persons. They moved seasonally between three different locations with so-called 'fork-poled huts'. The reindeer, which were kept relatively tame, were driven between the locations in packs when the ground was clear, and were milked during limited periods in the summer and autumn. Manker, *Skogslapparna i Sverige*, 74.

43 Lantto, *Tiden börjar på nytt*, 88 et seq.

44 Statement by Johan Olof Holm to the County Administrative Board, 19/2 1929, Socialdepartementets konseljakter 26/4 1929, no. 29, RA.

45 Communication from Johan Nilsson Kemi and Nikolaus Nilsson Kemi to His Majesty, 4/4 1929, Socialdepartementets konseljakter 26/4 1929, no. 29, RA.

46 Communication from Johan Nilsson Kemi and Nikolaus Nilsson Kemi to His Majesty, 30/12 1928, Socialdepartementets konseljakter 26/4 1929, no. 29, RA.

47 Dagens Nyheter, 'Two Vittangi Lapps pray for their reindeer pasture, seek the King's mercy', in *Dagens Nyheter* 7/1 1929; Haparandabladet, 'The dreadful mess of the Kemi brothers' reindeer herd', in *Haparandabladet*, 14/3 1931.

## Ideological exchange

The committee decided, based on Wibeck and Hesselman's recommendation, to contact the county administration board in Norrbotten with a view to bringing about a new forced relocation of the Nilsson Kemi family. They also wanted to ensure that no further migration would occur. These measures were regarded by the committee as 'unavoidably necessary'.[48] Lundgren notes that the necessity in accordance with the committee's minutes arose through the national park creation being threatened by 'the Lapps' damage to forestry and nature in general', despite the forestry aspect to all intents and purposes having been toned down at this juncture.[49] Both the motivation for a national park and Wibeck's and Hesselman's recommendation focussed on animal life. My interpretation is that this was the result of an amalgamation of the different cases that involved the Sámi. The formulation may have been an indication that the Muddus case at a basic level was connected to other problems that the NPC were party to. In addition to the establishment of Muddus came the impulses that renewed the committee's interest in the Sámi people from another two directions. Even if the problems that were addressed were not identical, they shared a number of common denominators and it consequently appears not unlikely that at a central level they partly came to reinforce one another and create a common problem image to some extent.

After studying the NPC's wishes, the county administration board requested a statement from the Lapp Sheriff Ragnar Pappila. His response was very sharply worded. Was the NPC trying on the quiet to create a precedent to introduce a new and foreign national park institution in Swedish law? Even if Muddus was to become a national park there was, as the National Park Act was written, no support whatsoever for restricting the Sámi peoples' right to reindeer pasture, hunting and fishing, he indicated. A matter of interest in this connection is the fact that Pappila seems to have had a clear insight into the principal tenor of the committee's change of step:

> A questionable bias seems . . . to be inherent in a nature preservation movement . . . that ignores the human group, which since ancient times lives and resides in a country belonging to the country's 'nature' as much as the roving wild animals that dwell there, notwithstanding the fact that its exploration fails to fall under the jurisdiction of zoology and forestry science.[50]

Taken out of context, the quote could be taken as an expression, even from a contemporary perspective, of a very progressive idea of the relationship between nature and culture – one where the boundaries blur and nature is relativised.[51] If we stay within the context it instead appears as a very explicit defence of the then Sámi policy's basic cornerstones. Implicitly it is not the distinction between nature and human groups with a historical local connection in general that is being criticised. It is not the Sámi peoples' connection to a

48 The NPC's minutes 23/5 1932, § 4, NK (translated from Swedish).

49 Lundgren *Staten och naturen* D.2, 308 (translated from Swedish).

50 Statement addressed to the county administration board, 22/2 1933, NLA, vol. Lapp cases part 1, letters received 1932 (DIb:10) (translated from Swedish).

51 Compare, for example, the concept of *anthropocene*.

population several hundred years back in time that makes Pappila regard them as a part of Nature, but rather that they to all intents and purposes are assumed to *comprise* this people. In other words, that they are denied contemporaneousness, are denied a chronological distinction from earlier generations within a global image that accounts for time in stages of development.[52] The Lapp Sheriff immediately attributed to a very ideological argumentation and this strong reaction indicates how the committee's new attitude struck the heart of the Sámi policy. By virtue of their joint heritage two seemingly different policies were in communication.

Neither did Pappila make the same judgment as Wibeck and Hesselman concerning which consequences the reindeer husbandry would have on the fauna. He maintained that forest reindeer husbandry had been pursued in Muddus since time immemorial. In addition he pointed out that the bear population had become significantly greater in number in the pre-existing national parks despite the fact that mountain reindeer husbandry had been pursued in these areas. Experience showed, he considered, that the larger predatory animals were attracted to the areas where there were reindeer as they represented important prey. The reintroduction of forest reindeer husbandry had, to his mind, already boosted the eagle population in Muddus.[53]

Both the Lapp Sheriff's and the county administration board's responses were reproduced in full in the local newspaper *Norrbottens-Kuriren*.[54] The county administration board agreed with the Lapp Sheriff and chose not to meet with the wishes of the Nature Preservation Committee. Pappila's statement was supplemented by the county administration board's county secretariat, that the intended national park area had been utilised as summer pasture for a couple of thousand reindeer as recently as 1918. This was to be compared to the Nilsson Kemi brothers' 350 reindeer. Just as Pappila had done, they emphasised that they considered 'the Lapps with their dwellings, possessions and reindeer (. . .) not to constitute a disturbance even in a national park'. They also commented on Nilsson Kemi as representing a very good, old-fashioned form of reindeer husbandry with reindeer in hand, all year round, milking of reindeer, and so forth.[55] Their skill was also maintained by Pappila.[56] The distinction between old-fashioned and degenerated reindeer husbandry, between good and bad Sámi, resonated strongly within the Sámi policy. It appears as if the county administration board at this juncture wanted to take the initiative and send a clear signal that this differentiation would not work. At the same time, the differentiation between permanent and seasonal utilisation was disarmed, which Wibeck and Hesselman had tried to establish. The message was still that even if the two families in Muddus did not move the same distances as the mountain Sámi, they still stood outside civilisation. The NPC subsequently found it more difficult to claim that in an unforeseen manner it was only a certain group of Sámi that caused the problem. In this context a juxtaposition had taken place in the preservationists' calling into question the identity of the indigenous population.

52 Fabian, *Time and the Other: How Anthropology Makes its Object*.
53 Ibid.
54 27/5 1933.
55 Communication from the county administration board to the NPC, 19/5 1933, NLA, vol. Lapp cases part 1, letters received 1932 (DIb:10) (translated from Swedish).
56 Statement by Ragnar Pappila addressed to the county administration board, 22/2 1933, NLA, vol. Lapp cases part 1, letters received 1932 (DIb:10).

The same distinction that the county administration board had made had the exact opposite meaning for Edvard Wibeck. It was precisely Nilsson Kemi's intensive reindeer husbandry with active herding and watch-keeping within the Muddus area that in his view posed a threat to the fauna there. He was of the opinion that the county administration board created a confusion of ideas by not differentiating between the presence of reindeer and the Sámi people's permanent dwellings within the area. It was not the reindeers that were the problem, but the people. According to Wibeck the Sámi people had a very hostile attitude towards the predatory animals as the reindeer were their prey, and the furs of the predators additionally represented an economic value. If Pappila evoked an image of harmony between Sámi and predatory animals, Wibeck's was one of absolute conflict. In the event that bears had increased in number in the existing national parks, this should be put in context with the fact that restrictions on hunting also applied to the Sámi people. There was no question regarding increased numbers of wolves and wolverines and how the eagles had managed to flourish in Muddus was impossible to know, he noted.[57]

It is also in this context that Wibeck, in response to Pappila's and the county administration board's principal arguments, becomes more vocal concerning the changed point of view of the nature preservation movement. He states that the view of the Sámi people as an indigenous people with special attachment to nature is antiquated. According to Wibeck the attitude of preservationists had started to change just shortly after the establishment of the national parks in 1909:

> That our contemporary Lapps, who in terms of book-based learning is not behind the resident population, have radio and modern hunting weapons and an often incontemptible mercantile enterprising, no longer ought to or should be regarded as an 'primitive people' whose existence in all cases is desirable and ought to be privileged within the national parks, is well now quite obvious to anyone who really wants to see the issue with objectivity.
>
> The Lapps, and obviously not least those in the Muddus area, represent a *culture* form, which to the same extent as the agricultural settler's seeks to transform and adapt the surrounding nature for their own special, human purposes.[58]

Wibeck's association between Sámi as a threat to nature and a considered advancement in technological or cultural terms is complicated by the examples that he later on provides in this respect. Amongst other matters he took up customs that had been normal among Sámi reindeer herders for a long time, such as them felling lichen trees where there was bad reindeer pasture.[59]

## In the waiting for a decision

Wibeck made the assumption that there was no time to try to reform the, as he saw it, antiquated National Park Act and instead recommended the NPC to avail itself of the special

57 Statement by Edvard Wibeck to the NPC, 2/6 1933, vol. F 5:5 SNFA.

58 Ibid., cursive text is underlined in the original.

59 Draft to response by Mr O.W. Lövgren and others' proposal no. 254 (transcript), 6/3 1942, vol. Incl. letters and written communications (2) 1941–1942, NK.

provisions in the Reindeer Grazing Act.[60] The committee seems, however, to have waited in making any further direct attempts to relocate the Nilsson Kemi families. A contributory factor to this may be the dismissive attitude that the government had demonstrated as recently as in November 1932 when it ruled not to comply with the committee's earlier request for a judicial review.[61] The only decision the committee arrived at based on discussions concerning the various communications with the county administration board, the Lapp Sheriff and Wibeck was for continued measures to be taken with a view to setting aside Muddus as a national park.[62] Wibeck did however continue to prepare the ground for a dislocation of the reindeer herders by inquiring about suitable areas to direct them to and whether any bounty fees had been paid for the killing of predators.[63] He also continued to openly argue that the Sámi people's right to live within the intended park area would constitute a threat to 'the entire basic concept of the national parks'.[64]

Some time thereafter the county administration board announced it had no intention within the foreseeable future of moving more Sámi people to Muddus, which possibly reduced the pressure to act.[65] The Nilsson Kemi families themselves stated that conditions would not allow for sharing the district with more reindeer herders.[66] The ensuing years seem to have been very difficult in Muddus with serious problems in reindeer husbandry. In December 1936 the researcher and preservationist Tore Arnborg reported that the reindeer herder families the previous winter had lost a large number of their reindeer and that due to the poor condition of the pasture areas stated that they were themselves considering moving to another area.[67] In the early spring of 1937 both Johan and Nikolaus Nilsson Kemi were sentenced to forced labour for reindeer rustling, and, possibly in connection with this, they came into conflict with other reindeer herders in the district. The neighbours demanded that the county administration board move the brothers away from Muddus, and claimed that the reason for the first forced movement had actually been due to their dishonesty. They also stated that the area had since ancient times belonged to the Sörkaitum mountain Sámi people and 'real' Jokkmokk mountain Sámi people to be used when the grazing conditions in the mountains so required. In this instance the brothers had no intention of moving and threatened rather to stop their reindeer herding if this was to be the case. The county administration board rejected the neighbours' demands.[68]

60 Section 5 of the Swedish Lapps' Right to Reindeer Grazing Act 1928: 'Should the King find an area or district, wherein the Lapps have a right to live with their reindeer, strictly necessary for a specific purpose of greater importance, such an area may be exempted from the Lapps' utilisation.' Ibid.

61 The request had been made based on Erik Bergström's intervention. Refer to the cabinet minister's minutes for the Department of Agriculture's cases 24/11 1932, No. 36, RA.

62 Meeting minutes 3/6 1933, NK.

63 Letter from Otto Lindgren to Edvard Wibeck, 28/4 1934, vol. F 5:5 SNFA; Letter from [illegible signature] to Edvard Wibeck, 15/2 1935, vol. F 5:5 SNA, RA.

64 Wibeck, 'Muddus'. In Årsbok 1934, Gunnar Ullenius red., 170 et seq.

65 Communication from the county administration board in Norrbotten county to the NPC, 30/12 1933, vol. F 5:5 SNFA.

66 To the county administration board in Norrbotten county concerning the NPC's case concerning setting aside the so-called Muddusjaure area in Gällivare parish as a national park, County Secretariat 10/96, 28/12 1933, vol B1:3, NLA, outgoing communications, LA.

67 Communication to the NPC, 5/12 1936, vol. F 5:5 SNFA.

68 Communication from Frans Persson, Wilhelm Nordvall et al. to the county administration board, undated, L71/80, NLA, vol. Lapp case part 1, letters received 1937 (21), LA; Communication from Edvin Kangas, Erik Hedbäck et al. to the county administration board concerning the Kemi brothers' removal from the Muddus area, County Secretariat no. L. D. 71/80 1937, 13/3 1937, NLA, vol. Lapp cases part 1, letters received 1937 (21), LA.

The Nilsson Kemi brothers on their release were able to strengthen their financial situation by taking over the management of others' reindeers (Swe. *skötesrenar*). The Lapp civil officials anticipated that several reindeer husbandry groups in Gellivare forest Lapp village would transfer the care of their reindeer to the brothers.[69] In the same winter of 1937, Edvard Wibeck presented a proposal for the formation of Muddus national park and consequently the matter of Sámi rights and land utilisation came up on the agenda again. Of the three points that were discussed during the NPC meeting held to discuss Wibeck's proposal, two were directly connected to the Sámi people. The first point was about how the committee could call for a complete ban on hunting within the Muddus national park. The discussion did not, however, concern only Muddus but the members were apparently rather more inclined to try and achieve a general prohibition in all national parks.[70] This strengthens the hypothesis that it was not only Muddus national park's specific motives to protect the fauna that had given rise to the question, but that several different problematics had been intertwined into a common problem image at a central level. The proposal for establishing Muddus national park that was submitted to the government contained a clause for the total prohibition on hunting and fishing, even for transient Sámi peoples, within the protected area.[71]

The second point that the committee took up to discussion was the possibility of bringing about a forced removal of the Nilsson Kemi family from the national park area. The committee once more adopted the standpoint that this would be a necessary precondition for being able to maintain an effective nature preservation status. An investigation was subsequently requested of His Majesty.[72] The removal seems subsequently to have been intertwined with the notion of introducing a 'wild' forest reindeer herd.[73] The difference between bred and domesticated and non-domesticated reindeer had never been unknown, but set against the background of preservation this possibly represented one of the most significant symbolic expressions of the Sámi people's denaturising: a hope of being able to replace the Sámi culture reindeer with natural reindeer.

## Parliamentary process

The rights of the Sámi people came to represent one of the questions that were highlighted during the national park case's parliamentary process. The responsible minister, however, tried to avoid this happening by rejecting outright the proposal for a new forced displacement and maintained that the exemption stipulated in the National Parks Act would continue to apply.[74] The major obstacles did accordingly concern other aspects entirely, such as the economic value of the forests and how the scientific use could be understood. The preservationists could yet hopefully note that the Agricultural Committee, which had been positive to the proposition, once again opened the door to forced displacement of the Sámi families. The committee was of the view that such a displacement should not take place immediately, but that the question ought to be taken up for consideration in the event that a similar area could be identified and presented.[75] This subsequently became a direct target for those who opposed the national park proposal.

69 Ibid:
70 The NPC's minutes 8/1 1938, Section 1, NK.
71 Proposition No. 48, 1942, 2.
72 The NPC's minutes 8/1 1938, Section 1, NK.
73 The NPC's minutes 26/3 1941, 13/11 1941, NK.
74 It did, however, imply a prohibition on the hunting of bear, lynx, elk and eagles. Proposition no. 62, 1941.
75 Agricultural Committee statement no. 19, 1941. The NPC's minutes 26/3 1941, NK.

In the second chamber the member for Norrbotten, Oscar Lövgren, directed strong criticism against the proposition and seems to have surprised many of the supporters by gaining a majority for a negative result. However, the government gave the Royal Swedish Academy of Science and the Domain Board the task of returning a new suggestion, which was put forward in the form of a new proposition the year after. By now the ministry had adopted the agriculture committee's earlier opinion to reconsider the issue of forced relocation at a later stage. There had, however, been a shift in semantics. Now the matter was to 'offer [the Sámi people an] other equivalent domicile'.[76] Even Wibeck made the point that it was not a matter of any banishment.[77] The new suggestion meant that the area that was to be set aside was reduced by around 20 per cent, which was a response to the more influential objections concerning the costs involved.[78] The preservationists possibly also adopted a somewhat more conservative attitude towards reindeer husbandry by giving up plans for a wild forest reindeer herd in the area.[79]

Consequently two chamber debates were conducted concerning the national parks matter, 1941 and 1942. Resistance was lower in the first chamber. During the first reading it was not noticeable at all, and the only person who stood to speak was the member Tamm. He did not only recommend approving the proposition, but also strongly impressed upon the chamber the necessity of preventing Sámi settlements. He explained that the Sámi people had not yet felled the lichen tree forests in the Muddus area, and made it clear that this in itself was the reason for the area's suitability as a national park. To this he added his knowledge of the sentences the newly arrived Sámi people had been handed down for reindeer thieving and emphasised that they could 'hardly be considered as belonging to the more desirable elements'. Due to the difficulties in setting up an effective control function, they would continue to pose a constant threat to the wildlife in the park. Even the plans for introducing wild reindeer was used in the address as an argument against allowing the Sámi people's settlement in the area.[80] Tamm was obviously well-informed even if his statements differed from the NPC's official line. It cannot be discounted that it to an extent reflected the argument that had been put about by preservationists in more informal contexts. Following the defeat in the second chamber the preservationists' lobbying activities intensified. The committee ruled, inter alia, that through a process of 'suitable unions' arrange a meeting with lectures and discussions to 'arouse the parliamentarians' . . . interest and understanding of the cause'.[81]

When the case of the national parks was returned to the plenary sitting in the second chamber the committee there had chosen to table a proposal in accordance with the original proposition. Following a drawn-out debate the chamber voted along the chamber's line, but with deeply divided opinions among the members. Certain of the speakers themselves noted a dividing line between north and south. Karl Magnusson, elected member for Skaraborg County, was of the opinion that the population in the northern region had not understood the importance of the national parks, but in reality it was they who stood to gain

76 Proposition No. 48, 1942, 8 (translated from Swedish).

77 Yet he still ascribes reindeer herders a completely passive role, in terms of that they will be 'moved'. 'Draft response to Mr O.W. Lövgren and others' motion no. 254' (transcript), 5, 16/3 1942, vol. Incoming letters and written communications, NK.

78 Ibid., 7.

79 Within the Nature Preservation Committee itself there was disagreement as to whether it was at all possible. The NPC minutes 13/11 1941, NK.

80 FK 21: 63 d (translated from Swedish).

81 Minutes 18/10 1941, Section 1, NK (translated from Swedish).

the most. To this Karl Mäler responded bitterly that the attempt to 'educate us northerners . . . was akin to forcing . . . in open doors'.[82]

With hindsight Mäler's opinion ought to be granted a degree of recognition; the look given by Magnusson can doubtlessly be described as being strongly coloured by colonial thinking. One of his arguments concerning the preconditions for preservation by preserving set natural values demonstrates a good insight into the preservationist mindset. Forms of vegetation were somewhat changeable, he indicated. As opposed to a granite boulder vegetation was not something that could be preserved in an untouched condition. By way of example he took up the partially preservation-protected Dalby pasture. In this scenario the domestic level of felling hundreds of years had meant the trees had been thinned out, he stated. Left to its own devices nature would have quickly taken things to another level. According to Magnusson, however, this only applied to southern and mid-Sweden. 'Concerning the Muddus area there is no reason to make a similar claim' he explained. There, through the limitations imposed by the climate, only one type of vegetation could exist and no other. Consequently nature there could also be made an object for 'complete preservation'.[83]

The local populace that was partly ignored and partly pronounced as ignorant with Magnusson's analysis were given a lot more attention when Löfgren again took the rostrum. He spoke of the sawmill workers, the hunters, berry pickers, fishermen and the Sámi. He said he did not doubt that the Domain Board would find another suitable location for the Sámi people. But could the Swedish parliament just force these Sámi people to move, he asked? Could a line simply be struck through their legal rights? By way of comparison he took up the damming of Sourva and the monetary settlements that were then paid out to the reindeer herders who lost their grazing pastures. Now a group of Sámi people were to be robbed of 50 square kilometres of reindeer pasture land, and how large was that compensation going to be? Was it at all justifiable to take reindeer pasture land from one part of the population that already were very hard done by? Löfgren said that all the timber and fishing assets in the area were important even to the local population in general, including other Sámi peoples in the area. As support for his critical objections he referred to a communication from one of the Sámi policy movement's representatives, Gustav Park, who was said to be in agreement with them all.[84] The minister responded only curtly to this part of the criticism and mainly referred to the fact that the existing legislature guaranteed that Sámi rights would not be breached. He did, however, supplement this response with a comment of a more moral nature: the two Sámi families that were the case in point only had a short history in the area. There was no connection to ancestors that had settled the area since time immemorial. They had been moved to the park as recently as 1931. The minister left the public to make what they would of that fact.[85]

No new forced relocation occurred. The NPC did however install a guardian whose task it became to put up a cottage by the shore of Muttosjávrre and who, in Wibeck's words, was to 'keep an eye on the Lapps' otherwise completely uncontrolled felling'.[86] The guardian,

82 AK 12: 91 d (translated from Swedish).

83 AK 12: 89 d.

84 Ibid., 96 et seq.

85 Ibid., 102.

86 'PM concerning the need for permanent monitoring in Muddus national park and employment of guardian', no. 392, vol. Incoming letters and communications 1941–1942 (2), NK (translated from Swedish).

Sigurd Lundgren, himself underscored the importance of carefully monitoring even the transition of the mountain Sámi peoples in the autumn and spring.[87]

## Conclusions

The process that preceded the establishment of Muddus national park occurred at about the same time as other major conflicts and interactions between preservationists and Sámi and therefore only forms part of that greater whole of events. As an origin of the reconsideration of the boundary between nature and culture that took place within the preservation movement, it was, however, as far as can be determined, the result of a completely independent logic. In particular it seems to have been the local shift of focus from mountain to forest landscape that caused unforeseen consequences. This meant that foresters as a new category gained a decisive influence on the perception of what was nature and what was culture. The image of a civilisation as forming a clear frontline that digs itself ever deeper into a virgin wilderness, as described by Edvard Wibeck, was replaced by an impression that there was no northern forest that was through-and-through nature. One of several causes indicated was the Sámi reindeer husbandry that had previously most often represented the absence of civilisation.

Because of this the preservationists ended up in a situation that called for a quite remarkable change in the understanding of what a nature worthy of protection should encompass if it was at all going to be possible to realise the hopes for new national parks. It is interesting to note how the changed relationships between the preservationists and the Sámi people in this case took place in combination with certain preservationist ideas being placed in the foreground at the expense of others. At the same time as the Sámi peoples' place in nature became less obvious, the preservationists' focus tended to move from what was 'untouched' to the presence of positive characteristics. The more narrow focus on wild life became another reason for the preservationists to perceive the Sámi as a threat.

Something that suggests this change ought to be described as a shift, rather than a move along one and the same line, are the paradoxes that arose as a consequence. The naturising of the Sámi people was at least in two different ways a premise for how Swedish nature preservation was founded. Partly by 'creating' landscapes that could be seen to equate to the preservationists' conception of nature worthy of protection, that is based on the previously held notion of untouched nature. Partly through enabling the introduction of preservation legislature in these landscapes despite them being affected by Sámi rights and interests. This process of naturising can be tied to a colonial power's exercising its might, but yet the process of denaturising became a clear and present threat to the Sámi rights as these consequently ended in conflict with the interests of preservationists. This doubleness meant that the Sámi people in order to protect their interests had partly to trust in an argument that was simultaneously used to legitimise a paternalistic segregation policy.

### Archive abbreviations

AK: Second chamber in the Parliament.
FK: First chamber in the Parliament.
LA: Landsarkivet in Härnösand.
LNA: Lappfogden i Norrbottens norra distrikts archive at Landsarkivet in Härnösand.

87 Letter from Sigurd Lundgren to the NPC, 9/5 1944, no. 112, vol. Incoming letters and com. 1944, NK

NLA: Norrbottens läns landskanslis archive at Landsarkivet in Härnösand.
NK: archive of the Nature Preservation Committee at the Royal Swedish Academy of Sciences.
RA: the Swedish National Archives.
SNFA: archive of the Swedish Association of Nature Preservation at RA.

## Bibliography


Adams, William. M. 'Nature and the Colonial Mind'. In *Decolonizing Nature: Strategies for Conservation in a Post-Colonial Era*, ed. W. M Adams. London: Earthscan Publications, 2003: 16–50.

Anonymous. Haparandabladet. 'Det bedrövliga trasslet med bröderna Kemis renhjord', in *Haparandabladet*, 16/3 (1931).

*Bevarandeplan Natura 2000*. Länsstyrelsen i Norrbottens län, 2007. http://www.lansstyrelsen.se/norrbotten/SiteCollectionDocuments/Sv/djur-och-natur/skyddad-natur/Nationalparker/Bevarandeplan_MuddusNP.pdf (accessed 16 September 2015).

Binnema, Theodore & Melanie Niemi. ' "Let the Line Be Drawn Now": Wilderness, Conservation, and the Exclusion of Aboriginal People from Banff National Park in Canada'. *Environmental History* 11 (2006): 724–750.

Brooks, Shirley. 'Images of "Wild Africa": Nature, Tourism and the (Re)creation of Hluhluwe Game Reserve, 1930–1945'. *Journal of Historical Geography* 31, no. 2 (2005): 220–240.

Castree, Noel. *Making Sense of Nature*. London: Routledge, 2014.

Committee Report. *Betänkande rörande åtgärder för skydd för vårt lands natur och naturminnesmärken* (Sweden).

Dagens, Nyheter. 'Two Vittangi Lapps Pray for Their Reindeer Pastures, Seek the King's Mercy'. *Dagens Nyheter* 7/1 (1929): 1.

Elenius, Lars. 'Selma Lagerlöf och Norrland: Nationella idealbilder i Nils Holgerssons underbara resa'. In *Sekelskiftets utmaningar*, ed. Ann-Katrin Hatje, 15–41. Stockholm: Carlsson, 2002.

Engelmark, Ola. *Muttos = Muddus Nationalpark: obändig mångfald, kulturarv och skogshistoria*. Karlstad: Votum, 2014.

Fabian, Johannes. *Time and the Other: How Anthropology Makes Its Object*. New York: Columbia University Press, 1983.

Fitzmaurice, Andrew. 'The Genealogy of Terra Nullius'. *Australian Historical Studies* 38, no. 129 (2007): 1–15.

Högdahl, Thor. 'Beskrivning till naturskyddskarta i Sverige'. *Sveriges r: Svenska naturskyddsföreningens årsbok 1* (1924): 132–145.

Lantto, Patrik. *Lappväsendet: tillämpningen av svensk samepolitik 1885–1971*. Umeå: Umeå universitet, 2012.

Lönnberg, Einar. 'De båda stora lappländska nationalparkerna: Stora Sjöfallet och Sarjek'. *Sveriges Natur: Svenska naturskyddsföreningens årsbok* 1 (1910) 33–48.

Lundgren, Lars J. *Staten och naturen: Naturskyddspolitik i Sverige 1869–1935. D. 1, 1869–1919*. Brottby: Kassandra, 2009.

Lundgren, Lars J. *Staten och naturen: Naturskyddspolitik i Sverige 1869–1935. D. 2, 1919–1935*. Brottby: Kassandra, 2011.

Lundmark, Lennart. *'Lappen är ombytlig, ostadig och obekväm': svenska statens samepolitik i rasismens tidevarv*. Bjurholm: Norrlands universitetsförl, 2002.

Manker, Ernst. *Skogslapparna i Sverige*. Stockholm: A & W, 1968.

Mörkenstam, Ulf. *Om 'Lapparnes privilegier': föreställningar om samiskhet i svensk samepolitik 1883–1997*. Stockholm: University of Stockholm, 1999.

Neumann, Roderick. 'Ways of Seeing Africa: Colonial Recasting of African Society and Landscape in Serengeti National Park'. *Cultural Geographies* 2, no. 2 (1995): 149–169.

*Nordisk familjebok*, 1926. http://runeberg.org/vemardet/1969/1039.html (accessed 26 February 2016).

Sámi Parliament's Website. https://www.sametinget.se/1670 (accessed 16 September 2015).

Torp, Eivind. 'Rennäringens rättigheter i nationalparker och naturreservat'. *Förvaltningsrättslig tidskrift* 2 (2005): 155–192.

*Vem är det? Svensk biografisk handbok*, 1969. http://runeberg.org/vemardet/1969/1039.html (accessed 26 February 2016).

Wibeck, Edvard. 'Kring Muddussjön och Muddusälven'. *Sveriges Natur: Svenska naturskyddsföreningens årsbok* 1 (1927), 36–63.

Wibeck, Edvard. 'Nu eller aldrig! Några upplysningar och reflektioner om vår för närvarande viktigaste naturskyddsfråga'. *Sveriges Natur: Svenska naturskyddsföreningens årsbok* 1 (1931), 57–70.

Wibeck, Edvard. 'En sommarvandring till Muddus'. In *Årsbok 1934*, red. Gunnar Ullenius. Luleå: Norrbottens läns hembygdsförening, 1934: 128–173.

# 4 Protecting sacred sites, maintaining cultural heritage, and sharing power

## Co-management of the S*G*ang Gwaay UNESCO World Heritage site in Canada

*Thora Herrmann, Leena Heinämäki and Cindy Morin*

## Introduction

The S*G*ang Gwaay World Heritage site is located in the extreme south of the Haida Gwaii archipelago, which means 'islands of the People' in the Haida language (formerly, the Queen Charlotte Islands). It is home to the Haida First Nation and is located 120 kilometres off the coast of British Columbia, Canada, near the Alaskan border (Figure 4.2). S*G*ang Gwaay, which means 'wailing island', shelters an old Haida village, where ten large cedar longhouses and 32 carved totem and mortuary poles of about six metres in height remain from the traditional daily life of the native Haida (Figure 4.1).

Totem poles serve to represent and commemorate ancestry, history and people.[1] The poles were created out of 400-year-old cedar trees. The village was once adorned with frontal poles for homes, memorial poles commemorating people or important events and mortuary poles, which were erected to honour the dead. The poles on S*G*ang Gwaay were raised prior to the inhabitants' relocation which took place around 1890. The crests that have been carved on the poles represent both natural and supernatural animals, natural phenomena (such as clouds or rainbows) and celestial bodies (such as the moon and stars).[2] Each clan or moiety earned or inherited the crests depicted on the poles. Most of the remaining poles are mortuary poles and indicate that a chief or person of high esteem is buried in that place. Totem poles serve as illustrations of family lineage. The carved mortuary totem poles express aspects of Haida spirituality, especially their admiration of and respect for their chiefs and ancestors.

On 24 July 1787, George Dixon was the first to officially mention the village of S*G*ang Gwaay; he then demanded that the island on which the village is located be named Queen Charlotte. The first contact with Europeans was peaceful and centred on trade, but relations rapidly degenerated. Diseases of European origin, such as smallpox, wiped out almost the entire population of this region of the archipelago. The population of S*G*ang Gwaay was estimated at more than 300 people in 1841, but fewer than 30 inhabitants remained in 1884, and the few survivors of smallpox were forced to leave. The island of S*G*ang Gwaay where the ancestors of the Haida Nation lived is considered a sacred place by the Haida and is preserved as such by the Nation; it is considered more than a historical village site, since the remains of many Haida ancestors and their spirits still reside there.[3]

1 Aldona and Glass, *The Totem Pole: An Intercultural History.*

2 Horwood, *Haida Gwaii: The Queen Charlotte Islands.*

3 Pers. communication: Camille Collinson, Cultural Resource Management Advisor & Treaty Negotiations Advisor, Gwaii Haanas National Park Reserve, National Marine Conservation Area Reserve & Haida Heritage Site, Aboriginal Affairs Secretariat, Parks Canada, Government of Canada, Queen Charlotte, BC, V0T 1S0, Canada (August 2015).

*Figure 4.1* Totem poles on the SGang Gwaay UNESCO World Heritage site
Photo credit: Cindy Morin

The SGang Gwaay Haida Heritage Site and UNESCO World Heritage site are managed within the Gwaii Haanas National Park Reserve, the National Marine Conservation Area Reserve and the Haida Heritage site under the Gwaii Haanas Agreement (1993), the Gwaii Haanas Marine Agreement (2010), the National Parks Act (2000) and the National Marine Conservation Areas Act (2002).

Inscribed on the list of UNESCO[4] World Heritage sites since 1981, this site and surrounding cultural landscapes reflect the Haida identity and worldview. In 1972, UNESCO adopted the Convention Concerning the Protection of the World Cultural and Natural Heritage, in order to identify cultural and natural heritage worldwide considered to be of 'outstanding universal value'[5] and to provide international protection for and preservation of World Heritage sites. As of June 2014, 191 states have ratified the World Heritage Convention. Currently, the World Heritage List comprises 1,031 properties, including 802 cultural, 197 natural, and 32 mixed properties in 163 states parties.[6] According to UNESCO, World Heritage sites 'belong to all the peoples of the world, irrespective of the territory on which they are located'.[7]

However, in what ways and to what extent does the notion of world heritage encourage aboriginal governance and the self determination of a First Nation community linked to a World Heritage site? The long-term sustainability of social–ecological systems necessitates management strategies that go beyond the boundaries of government-managed protected

4 United Nations Educational, Scientific and Cultural Organization.
5 UNESCO, *World Heritage Information Kit*.
6 UNESCO: http://whc.unesco.org/en/list/.
7 UNESCO: http://whc.unesco.org/en/about/.

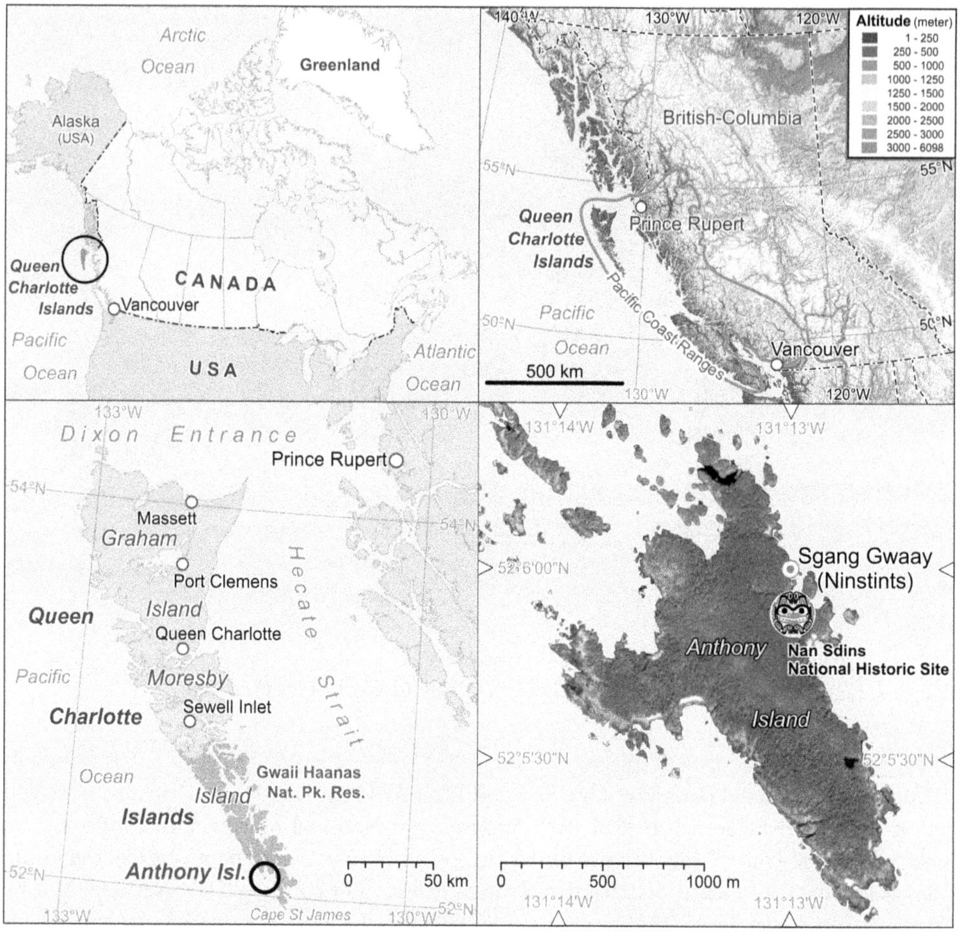


*Figure 4.2* Location of the SGang Gwaay UNESCO World Heritage site
Cartography: Marc Girard, Université de Montréal, 2015

areas. In what contexts and by whom have the heritage sites located on indigenous lands been designated? But above all, what place is left for indigenous peoples with rights of ownership, access to or use of these sites in the activities related to heritage management? Some crucial questions remain: Are indigenous peoples involved in the designation, management and protection of their heritage sites and, if so, at what level? Do governance, policy and management practices draw upon and integrate both indigenous conservation practices and state conservation practices when safeguarding cultural sites? Is engagement with indigenous communities in World Heritage site management in line with the distinct rights of indigenous peoples, in particular the right of self-determination, as recently affirmed in the United Nations Declaration on the Rights of Indigenous Peoples? Based on analysis of the SGang Gwaay site in Canada, we argue that aboriginal governance, ownership and control, self-determination, power sharing and community participation have significant implications for the role of indigenous peoples in protecting and governing cultural heritage and associated cultural landscapes. In this chapter, we will take a closer look at the local indigenous population's participation in managing and conserving this site. We will illustrate possible ways of collaborating with indigenous peoples and of enhancing these partnerships. The cooperative management of SGang Gwaay has broadened the concept of cultural heritage and cultural landscapes, creating an opportunity to develop new collaboration and conservation approaches. Lessons learned provide practitioners with a possibility to reconsider the ways in which they collaborate with indigenous peoples.

## Indigenous peoples' cultural landscapes and sacred sites

Landscapes are hybrids of natural and cultural elements. The cultural values of natural ecosystems embody far more than tangible services; they are often of a non-material or intangible nature, derived from human interaction with ecosystems, and are part of indigenous peoples' traditional knowledge, belief systems, spiritual values and worldviews. These cultural values play an important role in understanding and conserving natural places. Intangible values can therefore help to reduce or prevent human disturbances of ecosystems. For example, spiritual values attributed to sacred places in nature often entail restricted access and use, which help safeguard these ecosystems.[8]

Continuous, long-term spiritual or cosmological associations with specific sacred places characterise many cultural landscapes of importance to indigenous peoples. These sites, which can be markers of indigenous cultural identity and traditional values, can play a key role in ways of life.[9] Nicholas Saunders explained that 'sacred landscapes are a manifestation of worldviews, which populate a geographical area with a distinctive array of mythical, religious, or spiritual beings or essences'.[10] With management tools based on customary access and regulations regarding use, these landscapes often remain in their natural or near-natural state. In this respect, Schaaf highlighted that '[o]ne of the most salient forms of culture-based conservation has been the identification and protection of sacred natural sites, which often harbour valuable biodiversity and protect key ecosystems'.[11]

Landscape is also, therefore, a cultural construct. In *Landscape and Memory,* Simon Schama contended that 'landscapes are culture before they are nature – constructs of the imagination projected onto wood and water and rock'.[12] As Rössler aptly stated:

> Cultural landscapes are at the interface between nature and culture, tangible and intangible heritage, biological and cultural diversity – they represent a closely woven net of relationships, the essence of culture and people's identity. Cultural landscapes are a focus of protected areas in a larger ecosystem context, and they are a symbol of the growing recognition of the fundamental links between local communities and their heritage, humankind and its natural environment.[13]

As stated by Tobin, indigenous peoples' worldviews or cosmovisions and distinct epistemologies underlie their legal systems, customs and traditions, and are rooted in land,

8 Verschuuren et al., *Sacred Natural Sites Conserving Nature & Culture.*
9 Carmichael et al., *Sacred Sites, Sacred Places*, 1–8.
10 Saunders, 'At the mouth of the obsidian', 172.
11 Schaaf, 'Foreword'.
12 Schama, *Landscape and Memory*, 6–7.
13 Rössler, 'World heritage cultural landscapes', 334.

spirituality and culture.[14] The infusion of law with spirituality is described as 'an inevitable consequence of indigenous cosmovision, which sees the natural world as "sacred; it is in essence" a divine legal tradition'.[15]

The landmark Canadian Supreme Court case *Delgamuukw v British Columbia*,[16] initiated by the Gitskan and Wet'suet'en peoples, includes the statement that '[t]he land, the plants, the animals and the people all have spirit – they all must be shown respect. That is the basis of our law' as evidence of the strength of the indigenous concept of sovereignty and its spiritual basis.[17] According to Tobin, this statement makes the spiritual nature of the indigenous concept of sovereignty clear; this spirituality is infused in indigenous law, relations with the land, biological diversity and culture. This spiritual link and the sense of belonging, responsibility and stewardship it confers distinguishes indigenous notions of sovereignty from Western ones.[18] Indigenous peoples claim self-determination to maintain and safeguard their cultural heritage.[19]

## UNESCO World Heritage Convention and indigenous peoples: How to turn challenges into opportunities?

The Convention Concerning the Protection of the World Cultural and Natural Heritage (World Heritage Convention), an international treaty adopted by UNESCO's General Conference in 1972,[20] is one of the most widely ratified international legal instruments. Its main purpose is to identify and collectively protect that part of the world's cultural and natural heritage considered to be of 'outstanding universal value'.[21] The Convention concerns only tangible, immovable heritage (that is 'sites'). These can be cultural sites (such as sacred sites, monuments or buildings), natural sites (such as biodiversity hotspots or outstanding geological formations), or mixed cultural/natural sites.[22]

The World Heritage Committee, an intergovernmental committee representing 21 states parties to the Convention, governs implementation of the World Heritage Convention. The Committee maintains a list of sites considered to have outstanding universal value (the World Heritage List) and ensures that World Heritage sites are adequately protected and safeguarded for future generations. The Committee can only inscribe sites on the World Heritage List following a formal nomination by the state party in whose territory they are situated.[23]

A significant number of the properties designated as World Heritage sites are situated in the territories of indigenous peoples or are areas where indigenous peoples have rights of ownership, access and use. The vast majority are inscribed as natural sites with no reference to indigenous culture or the presence of indigenous peoples in the justification for inscription.

14 Tobin, *Indigenous Peoples*, 29.
15 Glenn, *Legal Traditions of the World*, 68.
16 *Delgamuukw v British Colombia* (1997) 3 SCR 1010.
17 Turner, 'Liberalism's last stand', 141.
18 Tobin, ibid., 38.
19 Human Rights Council Expert Mechanism on the Rights of Indigenous Peoples, A/HRC/EMRIP/2015/2.
20 UNESCO, Convention Concerning the Protection of the World Cultural and Natural Heritage.
21 Cleere, 'The concept of', 227–233.
22 http://whc.unesco.org/en/about/; http://www.iwgia.org/human-rights/un-mechanisms-and-processes/world-heritage-convention (accessed 21 October 2015).
23 UNESCO World Heritage Committee: http://whc.unesco.org/en/committee (accessed 21 October 2015).

In 1992, the Committee created the cultural landscapes category. In 2003, it merged the selection criteria for cultural and natural heritage into a single set of criteria in order to 'better reflect the continuum between nature and culture'.[24] Three different categories of cultural landscapes were included:[25]

1 Clearly defined landscapes designed and created intentionally by man;
2 Organically evolved landscapes, which can be either relict landscapes or continuing landscapes;
3 Associative cultural landscapes, *justifiable by virtue of the powerful religious, artistic or cultural associations of the natural element rather than material cultural evidence, which may be insignificant or even absent.* (italics added)

The associative cultural landscapes category has been crucial in the recognition of intangible values for indigenous people. S*G*ang Gwaay is inscribed on the World Heritage List under the third category,[26] on the grounds that 'the site commemorates the living culture of the Haida people and their relationship to the land and sea, and offers a visual key to their oral traditions'. This description of S*G*ang Gwaay on the World Heritage List reflects the complexity of cultural heritage as a manifestation of both tangible (the mortuary or memorial poles and the ten cedar longhouses that are valued in part for their artistic expression) and intangible elements (Haida oral history and identity).

The World Heritage Convention differentiates between cultural heritage and natural heritage, defining them in Articles 1 and 2 respectively. As a consequence, the Committee maintains a distinction between cultural and natural properties, with the classification depending on the criteria under which a site has been inscribed on the World Heritage List. This distinction has been criticised as over-simplified and, in response to such criticisms, the Committee has taken various steps towards recognising the impossibility of strictly separating cultural and natural values in the specific context of many World Heritage sites.[27] However, as Disko pointed out, despite the fact that the Committee has combined the criteria, it has somewhat contradictorily continued to uphold the distinction between cultural and natural properties.[28]

This distinction is particularly problematic in the context of World Heritage sites located in the territories of indigenous peoples, because as Daes, the United Nations Special Rapporteur on Protection of the Heritage of the Indigenous People, noted, '[H]eritage for indigenous peoples includes all expressions of the relationship between the people, their land and the other living beings and spirits which share the land . . . All of the aspects of heritage are interrelated and cannot be separated from the traditional territory of the people concerned.'[29] Indigenous peoples hold a holistic view of the landscape, asserting that a

24 UNESCO World Heritage Committee, Twenty-second session.
25 UNESCO, *Operational Guidelines for the Implementation of the World Heritage Convention*.
26 A World Heritage site selected on the basis of UNESCO selection criterion (iii) is characterised as bearing 'a unique or at least exceptional testimony to a cultural tradition or to a civilization which is living or which has disappeared' see http://whc.unesco.org/en/criteria/; see also http://whc.unesco.org/en/list/157/ (accessed 21 October 2015).
27 Disko, 'World Heritage and cultural diversity', 168.
28 Ibid.
29 UNCHR, Study on the Protection of the Cultural and Intellectual Property of Indigenous Peoples, paras. 31 & 164.

region's natural and cultural values are inseparably interwoven into the social, cultural, economic and legal framework, as well as traditional customary norms.[30]

Failure to take indigenous peoples' own values into account can have major implications. Inscribing and protecting a site as a natural site without recognising the presence and role of its indigenous inhabitants can cause all kinds of restrictions to be placed on their land-use practices and undermine their ways of living. It can lead to a loss of control over their lands and can have significant consequences for their ability to maintain and strengthen their cultural traditions and develop their societies in accordance with their own aspirations and needs.[31] In some cases, indigenous peoples have been forcibly removed or put under pressure to leave following the creation of protected areas, often without any consultation.[32]

The relocation of indigenous peoples seriously violates international human rights and contradicts the World Heritage Committee's new operational guidelines, which encourage the states parties to ensure the participation of local communities.[33] The guidelines also embrace 'a partnership approach' to nomination, management and monitoring, which contributes to the protection of World Heritage properties and the implementation of the Convention.[34] Additionally, at its 35th session in 2011, the Committee adopted a resolution that encourages states parties to involve indigenous people and local communities in decision-making, monitoring and evaluating conservation of the properties and their outstanding universal value. Benefits to the local community are therefore linked to protection outcomes[35] and respect for indigenous rights when nominating, managing and reporting on World Heritage sites in indigenous peoples' territories.[36]

Respecting the cultural integrity of indigenous peoples includes protecting cultural and sacred sites, as well as ensuring the effective participation of indigenous peoples in the decision-making process concerning the use and management of their traditional territories with their free, prior and informed consent.[37] Implementation of the World Heritage Convention requires that the rights of indigenous peoples be respected; therefore, the World Heritage Committee is bound to encourage the states parties to enhance the effective and meaningful participation of indigenous peoples in the Convention's nomination, management and reporting procedures. Being subject to international law and a specialised agency of the United Nations, UNESCO has clear obligations concerning human rights.[38] UNESCO adopted the Strategy on Human Rights in 2003, declaring as its objective the integration of a human rights-based approach into all its programmes and activities.[39] The Charter of the United Nations states respect for human rights and the fundamental freedoms of all as a major objective for the entire United Nations system. Article I of the UNESCO Constitution affirms this commitment. International conventions adopted by United Nations organisations must not operate in conflict with internationally recognised

30 UNESCO, World Heritage Committee, Twenty-fifth Session, WHC-2001/CONF. 208/13, 99.
31 Disko, above note 27, 169. See also, Viikari, 'World Heritage Convention', 184.
32 Stankley, *Conservation through Cultural Survival.*
33 Paras. 12 & 26.5.
34 Para. 39.
35 UNESCO, World Heritage Committee Decision, 35 COM 12 E, para. 15 e.
36 Ibid., para. 15 f.
37 Heinämäki and Herrmann, 'The recognition of sacred natural sites', 206–231; *Poma Poma v Peru*, Human Rights Committee, Communication No. 1457/2006.
38 Chittharanjan, *Principles of the Institutional Law.*
39 UNESCO, Strategy on Human Rights, paras. 10–14; UNESCO, Medium-Term Strategy for 2008–2013, paras. 6, 69.

human rights. A continuous effort must be made to create synergy between environmental and human rights treaties, specifically in the case of indigenous peoples, where cultural and environmental integrity are inherently linked.

Indigenous peoples have made strong efforts to gain recognition of this fundamental link in the World Heritage Convention machinery. In December 2000, a World Heritage Indigenous Peoples' Forum was held in conjunction with the 24th session of the World Heritage Committee in Cairns, Australia. Pursuant to the provisions of 10(3) of the World Heritage Convention, the Forum recommended the creation of a World Heritage Indigenous Peoples Council of Experts (WHIPCOE).[40]

The aim for the proposed body was to provide competencies and expertise that would complement other expert groups and support the World Heritage Committee's objectives by providing expert indigenous advice on the holistic knowledge, traditions and cultural values of indigenous peoples related to implementation of the World Heritage Convention and its operational guidelines.[41]

Though the World Heritage Convention allows the Committee to create 'such consultative bodies as it deems necessary for the performance of its function'[42] when the Committee met in December 2001 in Helsinki, it did not support the establishment of WHIPCOE. However, the Committee did recognise that these issues were important and needed to be discussed. It suggested that indigenous communities should work together and encouraged research in the field with the aim of exchanging views on the subject.[43]

More than a decade later, many issues concerning the World Heritage Convention regarding indigenous peoples remain unresolved. In his 2012 and 2013 reports United Nations Special Rapporteur, James Anaya, expressed the concern of indigenous peoples over their lack of participation in the nomination, declaration and management of World Heritage sites, and about the negative impact these sites have had on their substantive rights, especially their rights to lands and resources.[44] Concerns related to indigenous rights and traditional ways of life have been raised by two other United Nations bodies on indigenous peoples, the United Nations Permanent Forum on Indigenous Issues[45] and the Human Rights Council's Expert Mechanism on the Rights of Indigenous Peoples.[46] The Expert Mechanism's 2015 study on cultural heritage noted that indigenous peoples should be consulted and allowed to participate actively throughout the process of identifying, evaluating, classifying, interpreting, preserving, safeguarding, monitoring, stewarding and developing their cultural and natural heritage.[47] Referring to the United Nations Declaration on the Rights of Indigenous Peoples, the Expert Mechanism declared that 'no inscription on lists of the United Nations Educational, Scientific and Cultural Organization (UNESCO) relating to the cultural or natural heritage of indigenous peoples or national lists or registers should be requested or granted without the free, prior and informed consent of the indigenous peoples concerned'.[48]

40 UNESCO, World Heritage Committee, Twenty-fifth session, Progress Report on the Proposed World Heritage Indigenous Peoples Council of Experts (WHIPCOE).
41 Ibid.
42 Article 10(3).
43 Titchen, 'On the construction of', 235–42.
44 Anaya, UN Doc. A/67/301; Anaya, UN Doc. A/68/317.
45 UNPFII, E/2010/43-E/C.19/2010/15, para. 131; UNPFII, Statement at the 34th Session of the UNESCO World Heritage Committee; UNPFII, E/2011/43-E/C.19/2011/14, paras. 40–42; UNPFII, E/2013/43-E/C.19/2013/25, para. 23.
46 EMRIP, A/HRC/18/42, Annex, para. 38; EMRIP, A/HRC/21/52, at 7 (Proposal 9).
47 UN Human Rights Council, A/HRC/EMPRIP/2015/2, para. 10.
48 Ibid, para. 12.

As Sarah Titchen has maintained, there is tremendous potential for World Heritage conservation to truly contribute to the cultural survival of indigenous peoples. It can also contribute to the meaningful protection of lands and waters important to indigenous peoples, using their traditional knowledge as the foundation for an environmentally sustainable future.[49] Recent developments in the international legal status of indigenous peoples culminated in the United Nations Declaration on the Rights of Indigenous Peoples. The right to self-determination, as well as free, prior and informed consent and its implications for general human rights law, will necessarily be reflected in the operation of the World Heritage Convention. Endorsing a human rights approach is the only legal and sustainable way in which to implement the World Heritage Convention.[50]

## Aboriginal–state relations in the co-management regime of S*G*ang Gwaay UNESCO World Heritage site

The following section will discuss the evolution of relations between the Haida First Nation and various governmental institutions throughout the decades up to the present through a brief history of S*G*ang Gwaay management. We aim to point out where conflicts originated and the consensual approaches that have been adopted, while emphasising the different points of view the two groups of actors in heritage management have regarding this sacred site, as well as the concept of heritage in general.

### *Introduction*

Interest in the heritage left by the Haida at S*G*ang Gwaay began at the turn of the twentieth century when Charles Newcombe, a doctor, botanist and anthropologist, photographed what remained of the village in 1897 and 1913. He also drew plans and sketches of the village. Throughout the 1930s, totem poles were sent to Prince Rupert, on the British Columbia mainland.[51] In 1947, anthropologist Marius Barbeau undertook an expedition for the former National Museum of Man to determine what could be saved from the many sculptures left on the island. In 1957, Wilson Duff, curator of the anthropology section at the Royal British Columbia Museum, bought some totem poles from Haida descendants so that they could be recovered and preserved in provincial museums.[52] In 1958, the village was declared a provincial park. The province of British Columbia added other designations: islets and beaches on the island were proclaimed ecological reserves in 1979, and the island was designated a provincial site of archaeology and heritage in 1980. A long-term development plan was created, and the Historic Sites and Monuments Board of Canada recognised the village as a national historic site, with a plan to have UNESCO later designate it a World Heritage site. Nomination of the village was based on the fact that it 'is the most complete example of a totem village in Canada for commemoration' and that it 'still offers visitors a better glimpse of Haida monumental sculptures in their original setting than any other village on the Queen Charlotte Islands'.[53]

49 Titchen, above note 43.

50 Gilbert, 'Indigenous peoples' heritage', 55–64.

51 Various sources offer different chronologies and numbers of totem poles removed.

52 It is still possible to look at some totem poles removed from S*G*ang Gwaay at the *Royal British Columbia Museum* in Victoria and the Museum of Anthropology of the British Columbia University in Vancouver. See also: Duff and Kew, *Anthony Island, a Home of the Haidas*.

53 MacDonald, *The Haida Village of Ninstints*; MacDonald, *Ninstints; Haida World Heritage Site*.

On 27 November 1981, in Sydney, Australia, SGang Gwaay was proclaimed a World Heritage site, important for human history according to the third category of criteria, establishing that the area 'bear[s] a unique or at least exceptional testimony to a cultural tradition or to a civilization which is living or which has disappeared'.[54]

According to a Haida elder[55] who knew of this process, the sites' descendants were not consulted. The first action taken to conserve this sacred native heritage site was initiated by non-native professionals, without the approval of the Haida Nation still living in the archipelago.

In 1985, after major conflicts with forestation companies, the Council of the Haida Nation, formed in 1974, finally designated South Moresby Island a Haida Heritage site, adding their name and taking back their sacred, cultural and natural heritage. In 1988, the governments of Canada and British Columbia signed the Memorandum of Agreement on South Moresby and committed to protecting the land by designating it a National Park Reserve. Between 1988 and 1992, the Canadian government and the Council of the Haida Nation jointly managed the area. During that time, the two parties worked out details of an agreement that would protect Gwaii Haanas and respect the interests of both. In 1993, they signed the Gwaii Haanas Agreement, which established cooperative management of Gwaii Haanas by the Haida Nation and the government of Canada as a National Park Reserve.

The Haida are a sovereign nation and hold aboriginal title to their territory. The Haida have never signed treaties with Canada or the British government, yet Canada has asserted sovereignty and legislative jurisdiction over the Haida and their lands since the province of British Columbia joined the Canadian confederation in 1871.[56] The Haida Nation, in contrast,

> [s]ees the Archipelago as Haida Lands, subject to the collective and individual rights of the Haida citizens, the sovereignty of the Hereditary Chiefs, and jurisdiction of the Council of the Haida Nation. The Haida Nation owns these lands and waters by virtue of heredity, subject to the laws of the Constitution of the Haida Nation, and the legislative jurisdiction of the Haida House of Assembly
>
> (Gwaii Haanas Agreement, 1993).

This statement is a clear delineation of customary laws and authority. Nevertheless, there is a longstanding disagreement in respect to sovereignty, title and ownership of Haida Gwaii, recognised in the Kunst'aa Guu–Kunst'aayah Reconciliation Protocol in 2009, which outlined a process to reconcile Haida and Crown titles. Operating under their respective authorities and jurisdiction, the parties agreed to focus on joint decision-making regarding lands and natural resources on Haida Gwaii and on other collaborative arrangements (including socio-economic matters pertaining to children and families). Acknowledging their 'differing views with regard to sovereignty, title, ownership and jurisdiction over Haida Gwaii' (Kunst'aa Guu–Kunst'aayah Reconciliation Protocol 2009), both parties have been managing and controlling Haida heritage cooperatively for years. The name Haida Gwaii was restored to the islands in June 2010.

54 The criteria are set out on the UNESCO World Heritage Site web site at http://whc.unesco.org/en/criteria/.

55 To read the entire interview with Barbara Wilson carried out in 2005, see Morin, *Étude de deux cas sur la patrimonialisation*.

56 Wilson et al., *An Analysis of International Law*.

The Government of Canada and the Haida Nation agree on the need to protect Gwaii Haanas. In 1993, after six years of negotiations, an unprecedented understanding was reached between the government of Canada and the Council of the Haida Nation. It referred to the Gwaii Haanas–South Moresby Agreement, in which both parties agreed on the importance of protecting the purposeful party of the archipelago as a unique cultural[57] and natural treasure in the world, in spite of conflicts surrounding possession rights to these lands. Since then, both parties have worked together on the Archipelago Management Board (AMB)[58] to manage the Gwaii Haanas National Park Reserve.

## *From conflict to consensus*

The Archipelago Management Board is a means by which the government of Canada and the Council of the Haida Nation can work cooperatively. The six-member board provides the government of Canada and the Council of the Haida Nation with equal representation.[59] The board's function is 'to examine all initiatives and undertakings relating to the planning, operation and management of the archipelago'.[60] The Archipelago Management Board looks into management plans, cultural and traditional activities, identification of sites of spiritual and/or cultural importance, communication with other organisations and guidelines for the maintenance, protection and use of the archipelago. It also makes decisions concerning annual working plans, staffing needs, budgets and expenses. Ultimately the board ensures that the Haida can take advantage of job opportunities and benefit from economic possibilities linked to the management of the Gwaii Haanas.

Under this cooperative management board, the six members make all decisions together in consensus. In Article 5.1., the Gwaii Haanas Agreement states that '[d]eliberations of the AMB on any particular proposal or initiative will strive in a constructive and cooperative manner to achieve a consensus decision of the members'[61] and reiterates it in Article 5.1 of the Gwaii Haanas Marine Agreement.[62] Article 5.3 of the Agreement states that:

> [i]n the event of a clear and final disagreement of AMB members on a matter, related decisions and any actions arising will be held in abeyance, and will be referred to the Council of the Haida Nation and to the Government of Canada to attempt to reach agreement on the matter in good faith.

57 The Gwaii Haanas National Park Reserve protects several sites of patrimonial importance including SGang Gwaay, which is therefore managed inside the park by the Archipelago Management Board.

58 Archipelago Management Board, Gwaii Haanas, National Park Reserve and Haida Heritage Site, *Management Plan for the Terrestrial Area.*

59 At the beginning the board consisted of four members. When the Gwaii Haanas Marine Agreement was signed on 16 January 2010, the number was increased to six as the cooperative management partnership was expanded to include representation from Fisheries and Oceans Canada. The equal representation has been maintained.

60 Minister of Environment of Canada and Council of The Haida Nation, *Gwaii Haanas Agreement.*

61 Canada, *Gwaii Haanas Agreement between the Government of Canada and the Council for the Haida Nations.* Article 5.1.

62 The *Gwaii Haanas Marine Agreement* was signed in 2010, representing the common desire of Canada and the Council of the Haida Nation to respect and manage the Gwaii Haanas Marine Area in an ecologically sustainable manner. The duties of the Archipelago Management Board were expanded to include management of the marine area. The membership of the board was increased to three representatives of each party. See here: *Gwaii Haanas Marine Agreement.* 2010.

Both parties are therefore in constant negotiations, and the model is clearly functional. When there are conflicts within the Archipelago Management Board, Haida members consult with other specialists, elders, or even the entire Haida community. The community is consulted when a matter arises that is not advantageous to the Haida, since they can refuse to support any decision if the conditions are not in their best interest. The cooperative management model has grown into a functional relationship based on respect, harmony and communication between the two communities. However, one must not forget the different views on sovereignty held by the Haida people and the government of Canada, and as Wilson et al. noted, 'Although Parks Canada construes these agreements as cooperative management, they are in actual fact a type of co-governance arrangement as neither party has relinquished claims to sovereignty.'[63]

The S*G*ang Gwaay World Heritage site is managed under the Gwaii Haanas Agreement,[64] the Canada National Parks Act and the Canada National Marine Conservation Areas Act. The hereditary leaders of the Haida Nation have been consulted on site management, and these consultations have laid the foundation for the long-term strategy to protect S*G*ang Gwaay. In 1997, Haida hereditary leaders were asked what they considered to be of greatest significance at this site:

> They identified the site as a burial place and a place of artistic magnificence expressing the history of their culture. This history does not end in the past, but is vital and ongoing. Haida life is connected to the land and ocean. The poles are an outstanding expression of their magnificent art and oral history. The carved figures express both the oral and visual culture of the Haida. This is a place of spiritual significance.[65]

Furthermore, Haida hereditary leaders indicated a series of priorities that they would like to see incorporated into S*G*ang Gwaay management, including changing the site's name from the former gazetted name, Anthony Island, to its proper Haida name, S*G*ang Gwaay; educating visitors to the site about Haida history; ensuring that any interpretation reflects the Haida's living culture and their relationship to the land and sea and making sure that any plans for changes, especially for physical structures, are brought to the hereditary leaders.[66]

## *Haida values and views versus Western views on tangible heritage conservation*

The Agreement also says that the Archipelago Management Board must consider scientific, traditional and local knowledge that presents opportunities and challenges to both parties. The biggest challenges appear particularly in terms of the future of the site's tangible cultural heritage and long-term management. How should the mortuary and memorial poles be conserved?

63 Wilson et al., above note 56, p. 79.

64 Above note 60.

65 Nan Sdins DRAFT commemorative Integrity Statement (never signed off). See also. Anonymous, *Nan Sdins National Historic Site*, 2002; Anonymous, *Nan Sdins National Historic Site*, 2000.

66 Pers. communication: Camille Collinson, Cultural Resource Management Advisor & Treaty Negotiations Advisor, Gwaii Haanas National Park Reserve, National Marine Conservation Area Reserve & Haida Heritage Site, Aboriginal Affairs Secretariat, Parks Canada, Government of Canada, (August 2015).

Obviously, for a scientist from Parks Canada, and from the perspective of Western conservational practices, the poles should be preserved using appropriate technology and taking effective measures to maintain them. The Haida Nation, however, supports an approach based on the traditional Haida worldview. Mortuary poles contain the remains of the deceased in grave boxes, and thus exemplify traditional burial practices. Haida cultural tradition and customary rules dictate that no one should prevent nature from doing its work, and therefore the wood should go back to the earth. In other words, they accept the fact that the village's tangible cultural artefacts will decompose naturally, return naturally to the earth, and ultimately disappear.[67] In this way, the circle of life, linking the Haida people to the Earth and all living beings, can continue. As stated in the Kimberley Declaration, 'We are the land, the land is us.'[68]

How can the two parties reach a consensus on this issue? Both the Haida Nation (as the traditional owners) and Parks Canada (as the agency representing the state) have agreed on certain measures aimed at postponing the process of natural deterioration. For examples, mosses and other vegetation that take root on the totem poles and other cultural items are removed every year, some poles have been straightened or strengthened to prevent them from falling (Figure 4.3) and deer are hunted every year on the island.[69] However, the wood engravings have not been reworked (Figure 4.4) and the use of chemicals is not authorised. There is, therefore, a real reconciliation of the opposing positions on the issue of conservation. This conservation approach respects both tangible and intangible heritage so as to enhance the continuity between the Haida people and their surrounding environment.

### *Two opposing views on the notion of 'heritage'*

Another challenge concerns comprehension of the notion of 'heritage', which differs between Western scientists and the Haida. The former have developed a system of recognition that divides, categorises, classifies and separates different types of heritage according to their level of recognition (local, national, international) and the type of heritage (historical, natural, immaterial).

The Western system is quite different from the holistic indigenous vision. For the Haida, it is not sufficient to protect only the totem poles, the villages or even the island. For them, it is also important that the neighbouring rocks, the sea, the island's fauna and flora and the entire archipelago, as well as the air transporting the birds, are protected. For the Haida, all these elements create a whole that should never be divided. For instance, if the sea is threatened, the totem poles are equally threatened, because the Haida concept of heritage is based on all these elements together. In this sense, it is a positive step that SGang Gwaay has been recognised as a heritage site, but it is even better that it is part of a National Park Reserve and, since 2010, a National Marine Conservation Area Reserve. The protected area comprising the site has been enlarged, and the protected types of heritage have been diversified in accordance with the Haida's wishes, but these changes also had to be in line with Western criteria and categories.

67 Gajda, *Skung Gwaii Site Plan*, 28 p.

68 The Kimberley Declaration.

69 Many plants take root in the dead wood causing irreversible damage to the carved drawings. Once the pole falls to the ground, the humidity of the grass speeds up the process of deterioration. In addition, deer damage the poles by scratching their heads or their bodies on the wood to mark their territory.

*Figure 4.3* Sustained totem pole
Photo credit: Cindy Morin

*Figure 4.4* Fallen totem pole left without intervention
Photo credit: Cindy Morin

### *Managing SGang Gwaay–Haida values and customary rules*

According to Haida tradition, Haida watchmen were posted at strategic positions around the villages to raise the alarm when an enemy was approaching:

> Legend says that the role of the watchmen was to alert its owner to the approach of an enemy or any other happenings he should be aware of. It is symbolized by three human figures wearing high hats and is often found perched on top of Haida poles. This is the symbol adopted by the Haida to represent the Haida Gwaii Watchmen Program
>
> (Coastal Guardian Watchmen Network, n.d.).[70]

Today, the Haida ensure the security of some old villages through the Watchmen Program. In this programme, Haida watchmen serve as guardians, ensuring that potentially negative visitor impact is minimised and that the inflow quotas are respected.

The watchmen are also encouraged to act as interpreters of Haida culture by sharing their history and first-hand knowledge of the land and sea with visitors. Throughout the tourist season, Haida Gwaii watchmen live in wooden houses located close to five important sites, including S*G*ang Gwaay, within the national park.[71] The Archipelago Management Board established a quota of 3,300 user nights and allowed no more than 12 people on shore at a single site at any one time, thus allowing the watchmen to supervise all visitors to each site. In 2007, Moresby Explorers Ltd., a non-Haida tour operator who had been taking tourists into the park since 1988, challenged the Gwaii Haanas's management arrangement in court. The court ruled that the management and quota system was legal and an innovative solution for protecting the area, and the company had to remove their floating lodge from the park.[72] Today, Haida-owned and operated companies such as Haida Style Expeditions offer day tours to Gwaii Haanas.

A final general and positive point is that sacred, spiritual, cultural and natural values are respected in the management and development of this site. S*G*ang Gwaay has not been the object of denaturalisation or desacralisation by the tourist industry. The spirit and the state of the site are primordial for both parties and remain mostly untouched, even though this site has attained a certain international reputation and could easily become subjected to much more exploitation than is currently the situation.

S*G*ang Gwaay is an excellent example of mixed intangible and tangible heritage and demonstrates how important it is to take intangible elements of indigenous culture into account at World Heritage sites. It was not until 2003, however, that the UNESCO Convention for the Safeguarding of the Intangible Cultural Heritage recognised the important intangible values associated with World Heritage sites. This convention defines intangible heritage as 'the practices, representations, expressions, knowledge, skills – as well as the instruments, objects, artefacts and cultural spaces associated therewith – that communities, groups and, in some cases, individuals recognize as part of their cultural heritage' (Article 2, para. 1). The 2003 UNESCO Convention was strengthened by the UNESCO Convention

70 http://coastalguardianwatchmen.ca/haida-gwaii-watchmen-program.

71 The other sites are *K'uuna llnagaay* (Skedans), *T'aanuu llnagaay* (Tanu), *Hlk'yah GaawGa* (baie Windy) et *Gandll K'in Gwaayaay* (île Hotspring). The first two are not part of the National Park Reserve but are located near the Haida Heritage Site.

72 'Athlii Gwaii: 25 Years Down the Road', cited in: Susemihl, Cultural World Heritage and Indigenous Empowerment The Sites of S*G*ang Gwaay and Head-Smashed-In Buffalo Jump, 63.

on the Protection and Promotion of the Diversity of Cultural Expressions in 2005. Though Canada ratified the 2005 UNESCO Convention and is also legally bound by the 1972 Convention on World Heritage, it has so far failed to ratify the 2003 Convention on Intangible Cultural Heritage. The latter convention is of major importance for preventing indigenous cultures from disappearing. Ratification would be proof of government support for those nations, or at least a small step towards it, following the evidence of the Truth and Reconciliation Commission and apologies from Canadian Prime Minister Stephen Harper in 2008.[73] Although Canada has recognised the damage caused by its assimilation policies, there is still a long way to go in repairing these relationships.

## Conclusion: Rethinking co-management – towards community-led cultural heritage management

In conclusion, S*G*ang Gwaay is an example of a negotiated co-governance and cooperative management system for a World Heritage site. The Haida are involved as full members in all the decision-making processes concerning the management of the Gwaii Haanas National Park Reserve, the National Marine Conservation Area Reserve, and the Haida Heritage site. Two completely different mentalities work together to the benefit of a natural, cultural and spiritual heritage acknowledged by the government of Canada and the Haida Nation. This unprecedented collaboration seems to work well. S*G*ang Gwaay has more integrated involvement in decision-making than other Canadian examples of co-management and has been identified as an example of best practices for aboriginal co-management of World Heritage sites.[74] Additionally, Gwaii Haanas is an example of how co-management can work despite prevailing issues concerning self-determination, sovereignty and land ownership. The Council of the Haida Nation and Parks Canada – at least within the silo of the Gwaii Haanas area – have a mutually respectful relationship.

Why did the Gwaii Haanas Agreement set a precedent? It is often referred to as an agreement before its time. When Parks Canada, on behalf of the government of Canada, and the Haida Nation entered into this agreement, their relationship extended beyond what was expected in the way of aboriginal consultation in Canada at the time.

What lessons can be drawn from this case for developing conservation practices that respect both the tangible and the intangible values of World Heritage sites? There is a need to develop safeguarding policies that go beyond the original focus on tangible heritage and create an equal footing between all the groups with an interest in the site, in order to protect both tangible and intangible heritage as they apply to a designated heritage site. This includes governance frameworks, values-based planning and management of cultural heritage sites. Traditional knowledge, customary rules, indigenous worldviews and traditional values, traditional skills and practices and traditional management approaches must be recognised as being equally as valuable as science-based conservation approaches. Agreed-upon values, rather than top-down prearranged practices, can then become the basis for decision-making when dealing with cultural landscapes. Moving towards such a value-based approach means acknowledging that caring for a cultural site requires conservation practitioners and scientists to rethink their roles and practices. It means listening to, working with, and empowering communities.

73 Prime Minister of Canada Stephen Harper. 'Prime Minister Harper offers full apology on behalf of Canadians for the Indian Residential Schools system', [speech] Ottawa, 11 June 2008.

74 UNESCO, World Heritage Centre, Sharing best practices in World Heritage management.

The relationship between the Haida Nation and Parks Canada took many years to develop into what it is today. The beginning of the working relationship was extremely challenging, and what has been achieved is based on the successful development of this cooperative management relationship. The partnership was built not only on consultation, but also on engaging the Haida in a meaningful way from the beginning. Engagement is not the same as consultation; it is more meaningful.[75]

## Bibliography


*Aldona*, Joanitis & Aaron Glass. *The Totem Pole: An Intercultural History*. Douglas and McIntyre, University of Washington Press 2010.

Anaya, James. *Report of the Special Rapporteur on the Rights of Indigenous Peoples*. UN Doc. A/67/301, 2012.

Anaya, James. *Report of the Special Rapporteur on the Rights of Indigenous Peoples*. UN Doc. A/68/317, 2013.

Anonymous. *Nan Sdins National Historic Site, Commemorative Integrity Statement*. November 2000, British Columbia, Queen Charlotte City, Gwaii Haanas Archives, No. 4325.

Anonymous. *Nan Sdins National Historic Site, Commemorative Integrity Statement*. Parks Canada, November 2002, 22 p.

Archipelago Management Board, Gwaii Haanas, National Park Reserve and Haida Heritage Site. *Management Plan for the Terrestrial Area*, 2001, 37 p.

'*Athlii Gwaii: 25 Years Down the Road*'. Haida Laas – News of the Haida Nation, Nov. 2010. http://www.haidanation.ca/Pages/haida_laas/pdfs/journals/jl_nov.10.pdf (accessed 8 July 2015).

Canada. *Gwaii Haanas Agreement between the Government of Canada and the Council for the Haida Nations*. Environment Canada, Ottawa, Ontario, 1993. See Article 5.1.

Canada, Parks Canada. *Canada World Heritage Sites, SGang Gwaay, British Columbia*, website consulted in 2005–2009. http://www.pc.gc.ca/progs/spm-whs/itm2-/site5_e.asp (last updated: 25 October 2006).

Canada, Parks Canada. *Parks Canada Guiding Principles and Operational Policies*. Ottawa, 1994, 127 p.

Canada, Parks Canada. *National Historic Sites of Canada, System Plan*. Ottawa, 2000, 118 p.

Carmichael, David, Hubert, Jane, Reeves, Brian & Audhild Schanche, eds. *Introduction to Sacred Sites, Sacred Places*. Abingdon and New York: Routledge, 1994, 1–8.

Chittharanjan Felix Amerasighe. *Principles of the Institutional Law of International Organizations*. Cambridge: Cambridge University Press, 1996.

Cleere, Henry. 'The Concept of "Outstanding Universal Value" in the World Heritage Convention'. *Conservation and Management of Archaeological Sites* 1, no. 4 (1 January 1996): 227–233.

*Delgamuukw v British Colombia*, 1997. 3 SCR 1010.

Disko, Stefan. 'World Heritage Sites in Indigenous Peoples' Territories: Ways of Ensuring Respect for Indigenous Cultures, Values and Human Rights'. In *World Heritage and Cultural Diversity*, eds. Dieter Offenhäusser, Walter Zimmerli & Marie-Theres Albert, 168. Cottbus: DRUCKZONE GmbH & Co. KG, 2010.

Duff, Wilson & Michael Kew. *Anthony Island, a Home of the Haidas*, Victoria: Royal BC Museum, 1958, 28 p.


75 Pers. communication: Camille Collinson, Cultural Resource Management Advisor & Treaty Negotiations Advisor, Gwaii Haanas National Park Reserve, National Marine Conservation Area Reserve & Haida Heritage Site, Aboriginal Affairs Secretariat, Parks Canada, Government of Canada (August 2015).

EMRIP 2011. *Final Report of the Study on Indigenous Peoples and the Right to Participate in Decision-making*. UN.Doc.A/HRC/18/42, Annex, para. 38.

EMRIP 2012. *Report of the Expert Mechanism on the Rights of Indigenous Peoples on its Fifth Session*, UN.Doc.A/HRC/21/52, at 7 (Proposal 9: World Heritage Committee).

Gajda, Anna. *Skung Gwaii Site Plan*. Gwaii Haanas Resource Conservation (Strategic Planning Series), April 1998, 28 p.

Gilbert, Jérémie. 'Indigenous Peoples' Heritage and Human Rights'. In *World Heritage Sites and Indigenous Peoples' Rights*, eds. Stefan Disko & Helen Tugendhat, 55–64. Copenhagen: IWGIA – Document 129, 2014.

Gladstone, Ernie. *Report on the State of Conservation of SGuang Gwaii (Anthony Island), in Parks Canada Agency*. Periodic Report on the Application of the World Heritage Convention, 2004, website consulted in 2005–2009. http://www.pc.gc.ca/docs/rspm-whsr/rapports-reports/r9_e.asp (last updated 23 September 2004).

Glenn, H. P. *Legal Traditions of the World*. Oxford: Oxford University Press, 2000, 68.

*Gwaii Haanas Marine Agreement*. 2010. Her Majesty the Queen in Right of Canada, as represented by the Minister of the Environment for the purposes of the Parks Canada Agency and the Minister of Fisheries and Oceans ('Government of Canada') and The Haida Nation as represented by the Council of the Haida Nation ('Council of the Haida Nation'), Vancouver.

Heinämäki, Leena & Thora Martina Herrmann. 'The Recognition of Sacred Natural Sites of Arctic Indigenous Peoples as Part of their Cultural Integrity'. *Arctic Review on Law and Politics* 4, no. 2 (2013): 206–231.

Horwood, Dennis. *Haida Gwaii: The Queen Charlotte Islands*. Nanoose Bay: Heritage House Publishing, 2006.

Human Rights Council Expert Mechanism on the Rights of Indigenous Peoples. *Study and Advice on the Promotion and Protection of the Rights of Indigenous Peoples with Respect to their Cultural Heritage*. A/HRC/EMRIP/2015/2.

*The Kimberley Declaration*. The Voice of Indigenous Peoples, International Indigenous Peoples Summit on Sustainable Development, 20–23 August 2002. http://www.ipcb.org/resolutions/htmls/kim_dec.html (accessed 8 July 2015).

Lair, Rick, Nika Brown & Nan Sdins. *Cultural Resource Conservation Monitoring & Maintenance Manual*. Text & Forms – 1999 Records, Observations & Recommendations, Gwaii Haanas, August 1999, 22 p.

MacDonald, George F. *The Haida Village of Ninstints, Queen Charlotte Island*. Report and Recommendations to the National Historic Sites and Monuments Board of Canada, 1980, British Columbia, Queen Charlotte City, Gwaii Haanas Archives, No. 3120.

MacDonald, George F. *Ninstints; Haida World Heritage Site*. Hull: Canadian Museum of Civilizations, 1992, 60 p.

Minister of Environment of Canada and Council of The Haida Nation. *Gwaii Haanas Agreement, Gwaai Haanas Agreement*, 1993. http://www.pc.gc.ca/pn-np/bc/gwaiihaanas/plan/plan2a_e.asp.

Morin, Cindy. 'Étude de deux cas sur la patrimonialisation de sites sacrés amérindiens au Canada: SGang Gwaay en British Columbia et Áísína'pi en Alberta'. Master thesis, Departement of history of art, Université du Québec à Montréal, 2007, 207 p.

Morin, Cindy. La gestion du patrimoine *in situ* amérindien au Canada comme lieu de rencontre entre les Autochtones et l'État, in Alain Beaulieu and Maxime Gohier (dir.), *Les Autochtones et l'État, Actes du colloque étudiant 2006*, Chaire de recherche du Canada sur la question territoriale autochtone, 2008, 213–238.

*Poma Poma v Peru*. Human Rights Committee, Communication No. 1457/2006, Doc. CCPR/C/95/D/1457/2006 of 27 March 2009.

Prime Minister of Canada Stephen Harper. '*Prime Minister Harper Offers Full Apology on Behalf of Canadians for the Indian Residential Schools System*', [speech] Ottawa, 11 June 2008. https://www.aadnc-aandc.gc.ca/eng/1100100015644/1100100015649 (accessed 23 March 2016).

Rössler, Mechtild. 'World Heritage Cultural Landscapes: A UNESCO Flagship Programme 1992–2006'. *Landscape Research* 31, no. 4 (2006): 334.
Saunders, Nicholas J. 'At the Mouth of the Obsidian Cave: Deity and Place in Aztec Religion'. In *Sacred Sites, Sacred Places*, eds. David Carmichael, Jan Hubert, Brian Reeves & Audhild Shanche, 172. Abingdon and New York: Routledge, 1994.
Schaaf. 'Foreword'. In *Sacred Natural Sites: Guidelines for Protected Area Managers*, eds. Robert Wild & Christopher McLeod, ix. Gland, Switzerland: IUCN, 2008.
Schama, Simon. *Landscape and Memory*. New York: Vintage, 1995, 6–7.
Simonsen, Bjorn. *Anthony Island Park, Planning and Management Activities, 1975–1985, A Summary Report*. Victoria, March 1986, British Columbia, Queen Charlotte City, Gwaii Haanas Archives, No. 5565.
Stankley, Stevens. *Conservation through Cultural Survival: Indigenous Peoples and Protected Areas*. Washington, DC: Island Press, 1997.
Susemihl, Genvième. 'Cultural World Heritage and Indigenous Empowerment the Sites of SGang Gwaay and Head-Smashed-In Buffalo Jump'. *Zeitschrift fur Kanada-Studien* 33, no. 1 (2013): 51–77.
Titchen, Sarah. 'On the Construction of "Outstanding Universal Value": Some Comments on the Implementation of the 1972 UNESCO World Heritage Convention'. *Conservation and Management of Archaeological Sites* 1, no. 4 (1 January 1996): 235–242.
Tobin, Brenda. *Indigenous Peoples, Customary Laws and Human Rights – Why Living Law Matters*, London and New York: Routledge, 2014, 29.
Turner, D. 'Liberalism's Last Stand: Aboriginal Sovereignty and Minority Rights'. In *Aboriginal Rights and Self-Government: The Canadian and Mexican Experience in North American Perspective*, eds. C. Cook & J. D. Lindau, 141. Montreal: McGill-Queens University Press, 2000.
UN Commission on Human Rights. *Study on the Protection of the Cultural and Intellectual Property of Indigenous Peoples*. Erica-Irene Daes, Doc. E/CN/4/Sub.2/1993/28, paras. 31 and 164.
UN Human Rights Council, Expert Mechanism on the Rights of Indigenous Peoples. *Study and Advice on the Promotion and Protection of the Rights of Indigenous Peoples with Respect to their Cultural Heritage*. A/HRC/EMPRIP/2015/2, para. 10.
UNESCO. *Convention Concerning the Protection of the World Cultural and Natural Heritage*. 16 November 1972, 11 I.L.M. 1358.
UNESCO World Heritage Committee. *Twenty-second session*. Kyoto, Japan, 30 November–5 December, Report. Doc. WHC-98/CONF. 203/18, 1998, para. IX; and Decision 6 EXT. COM 5.1, 2003.
UNESCO. *Review of Aboriginal Involvement in the Management of the Wet Tropics World Heritage Area* (Vol. 1), Cairns, Australia, Wet Tropics Management Authority, WTMA, 12; World Heritage Indigenous Peoples Forum, 2000, Submission to the World Heritage Committee from a Forum of Indigenous Peoples Assembled in Cairns, Australia, 24 November 2000. WHC-2001/CONF. 208/13, 99.
UNESCO. *Convention Concerning the Protection of the World Cultural and Natural Heritage, World Heritage Committee, Twenty-fifth Session*, Helsinki, Finland, 11–16 December 2001. Item 14 of the Provisional Agenda: Progress Report on the Proposed World Heritage Indigenous Peoples Council of Experts (WHIPCOE), 3. http://whc.unesco.org/uploads/activities/documents/activity-496-4.pdf (accessed 21 October 2015).
UNESCO. *Strategy on Human Rights*, adopted by the General Conference on 16 October 2003. UNESCO Doc. 32 C/57, paras. 10–14.
UNESCO. *Medium-Term Strategy for 2008–2013*, adopted by the General Conference on 2 November 2007. UNESCO Doc. 34 C/4, paras. 6, 69.
UNESCO. *Operational Guidelines for the Implementation of the World Heritage Convention*, Paris, 2008. http://whc.unesco.org/archive/opguide08-en.pdf#annex3 (accessed 21 October 2015).

UNESCO, *World Heritage Information Kit.* Paris: UNESCO World Heritage Centre, 2008.
UNESCO World Heritage Centre. *Sharing Best Practices in World Heritage Management.* http://whc.unesco.org/en/recognition-of-best-practices/ and also http://whc.unesco.org/en/list/157/bestpractice (accessed 5 November 2015).
UNESCO World Heritage Committee Decision. 35 COM 12 E, Para 15 e. http://whc.unesco.org/en/decisions/4406 (accessed 21 October 2015).
UNESCO World Heritage Committee. http://whc.unesco.org/en/committee (accessed 21 October 2015).
UNESCO World Heritage List. http://whc.unesco.org/en/list/ (accessed 8 July 2015).
UNESCO World Heritage Centre. http://whc.unesco.org/en/about/.
UNPFII, 2010. *Permanent Forum on Indigenous Issues: Report on the ninth session.* UN Doc. E/2010/43-E/C.19/2010/15, para. 131.
UNPFII, 2010. *Statement of the United Nations Permanent Forum on Indigenous Issues at the 34th Session of the UNESCO World Heritage Committee* by Victoria Tauli-Corpuz.
UNPFII, 2011. *Permanent Forum on Indigenous Issues: Report on the Tenth Session.* UN Doc. E/2011/43-E/C.19/2011/14, paras. 40–42.
UNPFII, 2013. *Permanent Forum on Indigenous Issues: Report on the Twelfth Session.* UN Doc. E/2013/43-E/C.19/2013/25, para. 23.
Verschuuren, Bas, Wild, Robert, A. McNeely, Jeffrey & Gonzalo Oviedo. *Sacred Natural Sites Conserving Nature & Culture.* London and Washington D.C.: Earthscan, 2010.
Viikari, Lotta. 'World Heritage Convention, Climate Change and the Arctic'. In *Climate Governance in the Arctic*, eds. Timo Koivurova, Carina H. Keskitalo & Nigel Bankes, 171–205. Springer Netherlands, Springer Science+Business Media B.V., 2009.
Wild, Robert & Christopher McLeod, eds. *Sacred Natural Sites: Guidelines for Protected Area Managers.* Gland, Switzerland: IUCN, 2008, ix.
Wilson, Peigi, Larry McDermott, Nathalie Johnston & Meagan Hamilton. *An Analysis of International Law, National Legislation, Judgements, and Institutions as they Interrelate with Territories and Areas Conserved by Indigenous Peoples and Local Communities: Report No. 8: Canada, 2012.* Natural Justice and Kalpavriksh: India, 2012.

# 5 Land rights as the prerequisite for Sámi culture

## Skolt Sámi's changing relation to nature in Finland

*Panu Itkonen*

## Introduction

This article explores Skolt Sámi culture's relation to environment in Sevettijärvi in northern Finland. It approaches culture through nature-related forms of livelihood, reindeer herding in particular. Environmental rights and nature conservation form the basis for the analysis. The position of the Skolt Sámis in different time periods is examined with the main interest lying in cultural changes after the Second World War. The article contributes to the discussion about land rights with reference to the Sámi people, especially the Skolt Sámi, and to the protection of Skolt Sámi culture. Nature is seen as the basis of culture, and the role of nature conservation in the protection of Skolt Sámi culture is evaluated.

The theoretical starting point is legal anthropology, which focuses on the use of rules at the grass root level.[1] In the field of anthropology of law, Leopold Pospisil has studied interrelations between laws and such cultural features as terrain types and land tenure.[2] In my view these can be used in analyses of current rights and in options for future rights of the Sámi people. Landscape can be seen as a relational concept, where people's relations to territory, animals, and plants are taken into consideration; moreover, in these relations, action is central, i.e. what people actually do in their environment.[3] Land rights have often been seen as part of the human rights of indigenous peoples. Representatives of minorities have the right to protect their rights and their culture,[4] while the representatives of the national majority ought to utilise specific knowledge in order to better understand the justification for the protection of certain minorities.[5]

Sámi rights to land and water constitute the basis of Sámi culture in northern Europe,[6] in the same way as the rights of other indigenous peoples do in other parts of the world. Land and water are crucial elements for instance in such traditional forms of livelihood as reindeer herding and fishing. The rights of the Sámi to use the natural environment in the Nordic countries have been officially recognised,[7] whereas the ownership rights to most northern lands and waters are held by the states with a minor portion held by individuals.

The northernmost part of Finland forms an administrative area called the Sámi homeland, i.e. the Sámi district, but the question of Sámi territorial rights has not been settled

1 Moore , 'Introduction', 11.
2 Pospisil, *Anthropology of Law*, 295–297, 316, 346.
3 See Ingold, 'Anthropology beyond humanity', 18, 21.
4 Eriksen, 'Multiculturalism, individualism, and human rights', 51.
5 Toivanen, 'Das Paradox der Minderheitenrechte in Europa', 204.
6 Allard, 'The Nordic countries' law on Sámi territorial rights', 1.
7 Ibid. 2.

by legislative means. The immemorial usage of land and water has been used to successfully promote Sámi interests in Norway, but has been utilised less in Finland and Sweden.[8] Finland's Nature Conservation Act (1996) and the European Union Directive concerning the conservation of natural habitats and of wild fauna and flora (1992) form the basis of nature conservation in Finland. The Forest Care and Park Services of the state of Finland have published a plan for the use of natural resources in northernmost Finland, which includes attempts to combine the sustainable use of the natural environment with Sámi culture and its nature-related forms of livelihood.[9]

In Finland, the Sámi people's rights regarding nature and natural resources are regulated through a variety of laws that concern such traditional forms of livelihood as reindeer herding, fishing, hunting, and gathering. In many nature-related activities, the Sámi are in a position similar to that of other local people, who for the most part belong to the majority population, the Finns. Some aspects of Sámi people's rights to use nature have been given stronger protection than other people's rights, justified by the need to protect Sámi culture. There is a specific Skolt Act (1955/1995) for the protection of the Skolt Sámi culture in the so-called Skolt Sámi district, in the northeastern part of Lapland that lies in Finland. This Act gives the Skolt Sámi some privileges in the surrounding natural environment, such as the right to have a fishing cottage in the wilderness and the right to take firewood. The Act also directs state funding for investment in housing and reindeer herding. The Act helped the Skolt Sámi to adapt to Finnish society after the Second World War.

In order to clarify and strengthen the position of the Sámi people, the Sámi Parliament of Finland has worked for the ratification of the Indigenous and Tribal Peoples Convention 169, adopted by the International Labor Organization, ILO (1989). This ILO 169 treaty deals especially with the rights of indigenous peoples, and has been seen as part of a development that gave rise to new customary law.[10] According to the ILO 169 Convention, Article 14.2, land falls into two categories for indigenous people and governments have to recognise their rights to both. Thus, A) governments shall recognise indigenous people's rights of ownership and possession over the lands which they traditionally occupy, and B) governments shall protect indigenous people's right to use lands not exclusively occupied by them, but to which they have traditionally had access for their subsistence and traditional activities.[11] The concept of land can be interpreted so as to include waters. In relation to the land rights of the Skolt Sámi and other Sámi people, one interesting point is whether the land in question belongs to category A or B.

## Historical background

In the Tarto Treaty in 1920 the Soviet Union and Finland divided most of the Skolt Sámi lands between them. At this time a small number of Skolt Sámi lived in Norway. On the Finnish side, in the Petsamo area, three *sijds* continued with their lives, namely the *Suenjel*, *Peaccam*, and *Paacjok*. The sijds were old Skolt Sámi villages that managed their natural environments. The Suenjel people were allowed to continue their semi-pastoral way of life where they combined several forms of livelihood the most important being fishing and reindeer herding. The two other Skolt Sámi villages had to adjust more to the arrival of Finnish

8 Ibid. 19, 21–22.
9 Metsähallitus, *Ylä-Lapin luonnonvarasuunnitelma*, 126–130.
10 Ludescher, 'Indigenous people's territories and natural resources', 156–157.
11 Ibid., 160–161.

settlements and industry. On the Soviet side, the Skolts suffered from the collectivisation of reindeer herding, and were forced to leave their old grazing grounds.[12]

The greater part of the traditional Suenjel area belonged to Finland from 1921 to 1944. Suenjel was a country rich in lakes, forests and hills. There were only tracks leading to Suenjel in 1938 but no roads. The Skolts spent summers and autumns in their separate family areas round the lakes.[13] There were 30 family areas officially listed in Suenjel in 1938, each usually occupied by one family household, but sometimes by two and in one case by six households. Family areas measured approximately 140 km$^2$, that is nearly 12 km x 12 km. The households spent around seven to eight months of the year spread out among these family areas, starting in April–May when the reindeer were moved to their calving grounds. After calving the reindeer were left free until autumn. During the seven summer and autumn months, the families usually stayed in two or three different fishing camps. The main food for the summer and autumn period was fish. In 1938 the average size of the herds in Suenjel was 101 reindeer per household.[14]

The outbreak of the Second World War broke the peace of the three Skolt Sámi villages in Finland, and the men of the villages had to serve in the Finnish army. As a result of the war, the former Finnish Skolt Sámi territory in Petsamo became part of the Soviet Union.[15] At the end of the war the Petsamo Skolt Sámi were evacuated to Finland. They had altogether a hundred reindeer left. The members of the former Suenjel together with a few families from the other villages moved to the Sevettijärvi area, on the northern side of Lake Inari, where the state had built 51 houses for them. Most members of the former Peaccam and Paacjok were placed on the southern side of the lake.[16] A special law, the Skolt Act, was established in 1955 to regulate Skolt Sámi rights, including housing. When the Skolt Sámi of Sevettijärvi celebrated the first 60 years in their new environment in 2009, the president of Finland, Tarja Halonen, took part in the celebration. This symbolises the state's concern for this small ethnic group.

## Traditional forms of livelihood in relation to land rights

The Skolt Sámi moved to their new homes after the Second World War, and their traditional forms of livelihood were reorganised. Each family got its own reindeer, fishing places, and some possibilities for hunting. They usually owned small land properties around their houses, and some of them owned fairly small forest areas for purposes of forestry. Today their way of life is no longer self-sufficient in the old sense. Factory-produced goods have replaced hand-made, and part of their income derives from outside jobs.

The Skolt Sámi have certain rights that make it possible for them to utilise the natural environment, but there is a great deal of variety in how these rights are actually realised, in other words, what are the exact rights of people in relation to nature. These rights to nature are now mostly *shared* with other locals and visitors. Reindeer can roam free on all lands, state owned, or private, in the reindeer herding district of Northern Finland and the Sámi share the right to own reindeer with other people who live in the area, i.e. mostly with

12 Linkola and Linkola, *Kolttasaamelaiset*, 10–11, 21; Tanner, *Ihmismaantieteellisiä tutkimuksia Petsamon seudulla*, 70; Nickul, *Eräs Petsamokysymys*, 10; Nickul, *The Skolt Lapp Community Suenjelsijd*, 60.
13 Nickul, *The Skolt Lapp Community Suenjelsijd*, 13–14.
14 Ibid., 21–22, 61–62.
15 Linkola et al., *Kolttasaamelaiset*, 17.
16 Ibid., 18; Sverloff, *Suonjelin saamelaisten perintö*, 13–14.

Finns. In Sevettijärvi today more than 90 per cent of the reindeer belong to the Skolt Sámi, but this number can change at any time. The fishing rights of the Skolt Sámi are quite similar to the rights of other local inhabitants, but their rights to own fishing cottages give them an advantage by making it easier to fish in distant waters.

In the Sevettijärvi area there are also many non-local owners of holiday cottages, mostly located closer to the main road than the fishing huts of the Skolt Sámi. The non-local owners have fewer rights than permanent inhabitants, for example regarding the number of fishing nets that can be used. Visiting tourists can buy fishing permits from the Forest Care and Park Services of the state. The hunting rights of the Sevettijärvi Skolt Sámi are also similar to those of other local people and tourists can buy hunting permits from the Forest Care and Park Services. With regard to the gathering of berries and mushrooms, everyone has similar rights.

Skolt Sámi reindeer herding in Sevettijärvi was initially organised in the form of two large reindeer herding cooperatives, where there were many other local reindeer herders, mainly Inari Sámi and Finns. In a competitive situation the Skolt Sámi proved that they were skilful enough to survive. Later on, starting in the 1970s, the Skolt Sámi founded new reindeer herding cooperatives, which were separate from the earlier larger cooperatives (see Figure 5.1). In this way they could keep more of the power in their own hands regarding reindeer issues.

Novel aspects of Sevettijärvi reindeer herding are the use of machines, state subsidies, separation sites, and slaughterhouses, to mention just a few. Reindeer roam free most of the time but in winter are herded into specific, fairly large areas. The snowmobile revolution in the middle of the 1960s accelerated changes in reindeer herding, and several families gave up the livelihood because of the increased costs.

In 1995, Finland became a member of the European Union, and a new phase began in the state policy concerning reindeer herding. From that date, through its policy of subsidies, the state has reinforced the centralisation of reindeer ownership, in other words forced a reduction in the community of reindeer herders. Owners of small individual reindeer herds, with fewer than 80 reindeer, have been excluded from subsidies. The largest number of individually owned reindeer allowed is 500. The division into owners and non-owners of reindeer has strengthened features of a local class society in Sevettijärvi. Similar processes have taken place globally, for example among cattle herders of Africa.[17]

The Skolt Sámi community of Sevettijärvi used to be based on a broad ownership of reindeer, with many reindeer owners, and in the community of reindeer herders in 2002 households still had various combinations of livelihoods.[18] The total number of Skolt Sámi in 2002 was 220 in Sevettijärvi,[19] around 25 per cent belonging to reindeer herding households. The average number of reindeer per household was 138 among the active reindeer herders at that point. There were 41 active Skolt Sámi reindeer herding households in 2002 but by 2015 this number had declined by 25 per cent.

One consequence of the centralisation policy is that reindeer ownership has been concentrated strongly to certain families. Today the most important factor in this situation is the small number of young people in the households who are potential herders. As only a few of these households include youngsters, the strong centralisation of reindeer ownership seems likely to continue in the near future, meaning that ever fewer Skolt Sámi people can benefit from the

17 See Rigby, *Cattle, Capitalism, and Class*, 8.
18 Itkonen, *Skolt Sámi Cooperation*, 252.
19 Ibid., 21; Feodoroff, *Näätämön koltta-alue*, 2.

*Figure 5.1* The location of the two Sevettijärvi reindeer herding cooperatives, Näätämö and Vätsäri, on the map of the reindeer herding district of Finland

natural environment through herding reindeer. Most of the Sevettijärvi Skolt Sámi fish, but the function of fishing has changed from being vital to the old Suenjel and an additional source of income in the first decades of Sevettijärvi solely into a cultural tradition, i.e. where only part of the food for the household is obtained directly from nature. Modern businesses and wage labour have replaced fishing as additional sources of income for the Skolt Sámi.

Even though the Skolt Sámi of Sevettijärvi, in principle, have fairly equal rights to fishing, their actual fishing possibilities and equipment vary. Households belong to different categories according to ownership and use of fishing gear such as boats, fishing cottages, snowmobiles, all-terrain vehicles, nets, and other equipment. In a few places they have also had to compete with each other, other local people, and visitors for fishing opportunities. The households have an average of 30 nets, from one to six boats, mostly factory made, the average number being around two per household. Between 1974 and 2003 the value of tools, equipment, and buildings connected with fishing nearly doubled. Moreover, the average distances to fishing places had increased. In other words, costs in connection with fishing had risen considerably, while in the same period, the average catch per individual remained almost unchanged.[20] In 2003, the Skolts spent a lot of time fishing, even though its overall economic profitability had slightly declined.

In Sevettijärvi, in the 1950s, ptarmigan trapping provided important additional income for several Skolt Sámi households. In the 1950s and 1960s several Skolt families sold fish, ptarmigan, and berries. Part of the economic potential of fishing, hunting, and gathering has been lost since then, as the Skolts have begun to use these products only for their own households and no longer market them to meet other peoples' needs.

Recently other people have taken up ptarmigan trapping, and it has been centralised so that it is economically beneficial for only a few people. In addition, visiting leisure hunters hunt ptarmigan with shotguns in the Sevettijärvi area. Their movements and their dogs have occasionally been accused of disturbing the Skolt Sámi reindeer. Local people, including Skolt Sámi, Finns and other locals, also hunt ptarmigan in this way. The major ethnic groups of Sevettijärvi, namely Skolt Sámi and Finns, have united forces for moose hunting.

In today's Sevettijärvi, the division of people in relation to the gathering of berries is similar to that for fishing, but on a smaller scale, in the sense that there can be competition among all berry pickers over some spots, and the ownership of equipment varies so that distant places cannot be reached by all. Nevertheless, various households still have, to some extent, unique knowledge about their traditional gathering places. Cloudberry (*Rubus chamaemorus*) is the most popular berry among gatherers. One factor in relation to the divisions concerning berry gathering is the level of interest. Some people are not interested in gathering and do not take part in it. In their first decades in Sevettijärvi, many households continued their traditional sheep-rearing, but at the beginning of the twenty-first century the last sheep were given up. The last cow in Sevettijärvi had disappeared a lot earlier.

## Changing economic development and social networks

Some new, additional nature-related forms of livelihood have been developed during last 50 years among the Skolt Sámi reindeer herders of Sevettijärvi. Tourist accommodation has been one of the most successful. Current restaurant services can also be seen as activities related to nature, as they use reindeer meat. Local meat manufacturing and nature guide services have suffered lately as additional means of livelihood for the Skolt Sámi, because many of those involved have withdrawn from professional activities.

In the Sevettijärvi reindeer herding community at the beginning of the twenty-first century, there were numerous entrepreneurial activities, such as tourist accommodation, restaurant services, meat manufacturing, tourist services, nature guiding, and handicrafts. Wage labour was common in the households of the Skolt Sámi reindeer herders in such fields as teaching in elementary school, cleaning, state Forest Care and Park Services, nursing,

20 Sutela and Niva, *Sevettijärven kolttien kalastusolot*, 4, 6–7, 13–15, 17.

building work, technical work as janitors, and work as political trustees. Approximately 30 different additional forms of livelihood were registered in 2002. At this point, there were individually owned reindeer herds of various sizes, with occasionally only one outside helper in reindeer activities. This branch can be characterised by ***multiplicity***.[21] The professional community was still fairly big, and the forms of cooperation and reciprocity were rich in the community. In their additional forms of livelihood, reindeer herders had many contacts with people who were outside the community.

One consequence of the centralisation of reindeer ownership is the declining economic potential of the Skolt Sámi social organisation. Moreover, the weakening economic base of the community constitutes a loss for the Skolt Sámi culture. The old tradition of combining reindeer herding with other forms of livelihood is weakening. As the number of reindeer herders has declined, the number of additional businesses among them has also declined. The Skolt Sámi have lost some of the economic advantage brought by reindeer ownership combined with other forms of livelihood. So far the additional businesses have been developed mainly by small and medium-sized reindeer owners in Sevettijärvi. Big reindeer owners have less need for such development efforts.

There were multiple forms of cooperation and reciprocity in Sevettijärvi in 2002; altogether 19 positive forms of reciprocity could be found in connection with cooperation. Some forms of cooperation and reciprocity have declined, for example cooperation between adults from different households of the same reindeer herding cooperative. This was still common in Sevettijärvi reindeer separations in 2002 between medium-sized and small reindeer owners and can be characterised as cooperation based on equality. As this kind of cooperation has diminished in reindeer separation, another kind has increased – the hierarchical work groups, organised by single households. The bigger reindeer owners usually have more hierarchical patterns in work groups that they lead.

From different forms of cooperation and reciprocity in reindeer separation it is possible to establish a link to different organisations of additional forms of livelihood as follows. Between partners from work groups and herding groups that were based on equality, two specific cases of cooperation emerged in additional forms of livelihood. Firstly, the combination of three medium-sized reindeer owners developed and operated together a local meat manufacturing business. Secondly, the combination of two medium-sized reindeer owners were able to get a waged job where a work pair was required. Some other work groups in reindeer separation have been based on hierarchical forms of cooperation that have developed additional businesses. Their efforts have largely been based on cooperation and reciprocity within nuclear families.

By 2015, the number of small reindeer owners with fewer than 80 reindeer has decreased strongly, and the number of Skolt Sámi working in the Sevettijärvi reindeer herding community has diminished considerably. The reindeer herders still carry out the slaughtering activities, but some outsiders help at times. Local meat manufacturing has declined somewhat. The opportunities for reindeer herders to develop additional sources of livelihood have declined, because of the lack of people in their community and because the general atmosphere stresses competition between reindeer herders. In the mainstream ideology of reindeer herding, a better economic position is reached mainly through an increase in the number of individually owned reindeer.

21 Itkonen, 'Skolt Sámi reciprocity', 76.

## Nature conservation in relation to Skolt Sámi culture

The first four National Parks were established in Finland in 1938, one in the Petsamo area after 60 years of public debate about the issue. The nature conservation ideology was combined with cultural and national values, following the example of the world's first National Park, Yellowstone, in the US founded in 1872.[22] The Skolt Sámi language is related to Finnish, and the protection of Skolt Sámi culture was thus seen as part of the national project, which could also be combined with ideas of nature conservation.

The Ministry of Home Affairs took the initiative in 1932 to establish a special Skolt Territory, i.e. Suenjel, to protect Skolt Sámi culture. This was supported by scientists both native and foreign.[23] In practice, the Skolt Sámi rights to their environment were exclusive to Suenjel at that time. The land was owned by the state, and the Skolt Sámi had usufruct rights to it. The Skolt Sámi followed their traditional forms of livelihood, which had to be sustainable in relation to nature. Pearl-fishing and squirrel hunting were prohibited in 1938 in Suenjel, whereas several other animals were hunted and trapped, for example bear, wolf, elk, lynx, wolverine, fox, and ptarmigan.[24]

In 1956 the role of nature conservation was strengthened through the foundation of seven new National Parks in Finland. At this stage, three of them were located in Lapland. These areas still had low profiles, and they were not yet promoted, for example, for their hiking possibilities as they are today.[25] The Sevettijärvi area did not belong to any National Park. However, reindeer herding was fairly sustainable, with no motor vehicles in the vicinity.

The Sevettijärvi area comprises the grazing grounds of the Näätämö and Vätsäri reindeer herding cooperatives that are abutting, each one being about 60 kilometres long and 25 kilometres wide. This area partly includes the same land and water as the old Skolt Sámi *Neiden* village. The natural environment of the Sevettijärvi area is a combination of high land with no trees, swamps, and forests made up mainly of pine and birch on lower land. There are numerous lakes throughout the area. The Näätämö River, flowing into the Arctic Ocean, is a popular site for salmon fishing, visited by local people as well as tourists. The permanent housing is located along the road which runs through the centre of the area from southwest to northeast.

The Wilderness Act was passed in 1991 in Finland. Considerable sections of the Sevettijärvi area became parts of two Wilderness Areas, *Kaldoaivi* and *Vätsäri*.[26] This was a step forward for Skolt Sámi culture, in that traditional cultural activities were allowed in the Wilderness Areas, but many other things were prohibited, such as the construction of permanent housing. The Skolt Sámi fishing cottages were allowed in the Wilderness Areas, and many were built after the Act came into force.[27] Today there are 12 Wilderness Areas in Lapland, managed by the state Forest Care and Park Services.

Most of the land and water in the Sevettijärvi area is owned by the state. The area is divided into two different nature conservation categories.[28] The Wilderness Reserve Area,

22 www.luontoon.fi/kansallispuistojemmehistoriaa.
23 Ibid. 15.
24 Ibid. 67, 69.
25 www.luontoon.fi/kansallispuistojemmehistoriaa.
26 www.luontoon.fi/erämaa-alueet.
27 Sutela and Niva, *Sevettijärven kolttien kalastusolot*, 9–10.
28 www.metsa.fi/web/en/landuse/northernlapland.

i.e. the Wilderness Area, starts 5–15 kilometres from people's permanent housing and stretches to the outer edges of the Sevettijärvi area. The aim in this area is, on the one hand, to preserve its wilderness character and on the other, to protect the Sámi culture and nature-related forms of livelihood, but also to develop multiple uses for nature. In this area, buildings can only be constructed in special circumstances and forestry is not usually practised at all. There is fishing, hunting, and berry gathering in this area, but motorised traffic is restricted. Reindeer herders are allowed to use off-road vehicles in the Sevettijärvi area to a certain extent, in order to make it possible for them to carry out their work.

The second protection category Regeneration Protection Forest comprises land within a 5–15 kilometre range from the permanent housing of Sevettijärvi. New housing can be built, and permanent housing and holiday cottages are located in this area. Forestry is allowed, but, according to the regulations, forest is more sensitive in this area than in more southern areas. The state has not engaged widely in forestry in the Sevettijärvi Regeneration Protection Forests during recent decades. These kinds of forests are more protected than the so-called Managed Forests, where the state's Forest Care and Park Services can engage in larger-scale commercial forestry. The Managed Forests are located in more southern parts of Inari municipality and in the rest of the country. The protection of forest nature can be seen as a positive thing from the perspective of reindeer herding as the nature conservation requirements have not prevented some of the Sevettijärvi reindeer herders from using their small privately owned forests for commercial purposes.

The condition of reindeer pastures has been the reason for limitation of the overall numbers of reindeer: 3,600 in the Näätämö reindeer herding cooperative, and 3,000 in Vätsäri. Reindeer eat lichen in the winter period. The herders also give reindeer some additional nutrition, mainly hay, during the winter months. Studies of Sevettijärvi lichen pastures show that the current intensity of reindeer herding has not endangered them to any great extent. Nevertheless, the condition of the pastures is monitored in order to meet future requirements for sustainable reindeer herding and to take into consideration other forms of land use.[29]

One influential part of nature conservation from the point of Sevettijärvi reindeer herders is predator preservation. Since 1996, the state's predator policy has supported the growth of predator populations, i.e. wolfs, bears, wolverines, and lynxes. The number of predators in the reindeer herding district doubled between 1995 and 2012.[30] The number of eagles has also grown. There has been a simultaneous increase in predator damage in the same time period, 66 per cent in the whole reindeer herding district and 83 per cent in Sevettijärvi. In this way the predators have taken an ever-growing share of the natural environment. The state pays compensation for predator damage, but many of the reindeer killed are not found. Compensation for damage caused by eagles is paid in relation to the number of eagle nests. In southern parts of the reindeer herding district, the rapid growth in the predator population has seriously endangered the future of reindeer herding. Little by little the predator problem has spread towards the northern parts of the district where the Sámi people have their reindeer.

Another factor that influences nature is traffic, i.e. motor vehicles in the wilderness. The state Forest Care and Park Services administer off-road traffic issues, taking into account the requirements of both nature conservation and Sámi culture. The tourists' snowmobiles

29 Kumpula et al., *Poronhoitoalueen pohjoisimman osan*, 26–29, 34.
30 *Poromies* 1996 and *Poromies* 2013.

are supposed to stay on the main routes whereas local people can drive around more freely. The use of all-terrain vehicles is strictly restricted, but those required in reindeer herding are excepted from this rule. However, there are not so many limitations on the use of such motor vehicles as motor boats, helicopters, or planes in the Sevettijärvi Wilderness Areas.

## Conclusion

In the old Suenjel, the Skolt Sámi households had a symmetrical relation to nature. They all had several kinds of nature-related forms of livelihood, namely reindeer herding, fishing, hunting, and gathering. All households had their own share of the environment, which was sufficient for them to survive. After the Second World War, the principle of symmetry was applied to conditions in Sevettijärvi. Every household owned reindeer and was able to fish, hunt and gather berries etc.

In today's Skolt Sámi community of Sevettijärvi, some symmetry can be found in fishing, even though it is no longer a vital condition as it was in Suenjel. The other fairly widespread, and therefore symmetrical, old tradition among Sevettijärvi Skolt Sámi is the gathering of cloudberries. On the other hand, symmetry is not a quality that can be linked to many cultural changes among the Sevettijärvi Skolt Sámi; quite the opposite. Most changes can be characterised by the concept of ***division,*** based on increased competition and the centralisation of materialised rights. These processes mean that the personal ***share of environment*** and ***culture*** has become remarkably centralised during the decades in Sevettijärvi.

All Skolt Sámi households in Sevettijärvi still practised reindeer herding in 1958. Since then the share of environment based on reindeer ownership has been increasingly centralised into the hands of a few reindeer owners. This is worth noting, because reindeer herding is the most important form of production and this means that actual reindeer herding rights today are beyond the reach of more than 75 per cent of the Sevettjärvi Skolt Sámi. There are also factors that have caused division in other nature-related forms of livelihood, for instance differences in equipment. Simultaneously, some other parts of culture have been centralised, namely membership in the reindeer herding community and its reciprocity networks that strengthen the coherence of the community. When people have lost their share of the environment, they have also lost the corresponding share of the culture.

Reindeer ownership has often played a part in the other entrepreneurial activities of Skolt Sámi households. In the past, economic development was rather strong in Sevettijärvi in connection with reindeer ownership, but it declined as ownership was centralised, and the idea of combining different forms of livelihood with reindeer herding weakened. The roles of legislation and the state have been twofold in this process. Partly they have supported the Skolt Sámi people's relation to nature, for instance through the Skolt Act. Partly the state has weakened the Skolt Sámi's connection to nature. This has happened indirectly, through legislation and state interventions, such as the policy of subsidies with regard to reindeer herding and the predator policy. The fact that the Skolt Sámi have had to share many of their nature-related rights with other people has meant competition over natural resources. So far the Skolt Sámi of Sevettijärvi have succeeded fairly well in this competition, but some aspects of it may be seen as threats to their culture in the long run.

Pospisil combined laws with two issues, terrain types and land tenure, in his analysis of environment. I would like to add one more topic, namely land use. Who uses the land and how? This is an important dimension when environmental law is implemented. I argue that the land rights of the Skolt Sámi of Sevettijärvi need to be protected better than today, if the aim is to preserve the Skolt Sámi culture. For example, Skolt Sámi reindeer ownership could be better protected in order to preserve land rights that are realised through reindeer herding. Competition in other nature-related forms of livelihood can also be strong, and they too might need some form of protection.

The discussion about Sámi environmental rights is usually linked to traditional forms of livelihood and not to modern nature-related businesses. For centuries, Sámi people have had the right to utilise their environment and they have varied the ways in which they use natural resources. There may be many reasons for also taking into account the modern version of nature-related livelihoods when discussing the territorial rights of the Skolt Sámi people.

Nature conservation is an essential element in the protection of Sámi culture and is also an important factor in the discussion of land rights, in two different ways. Firstly, nature conservation sets limits for the utilisation of natural resources in all cases; it should be sustainable. In the future, the exploitation of nature may be questioned more than it is today. Modern technology has made nature-related activities easier and more effective than before, but there has not been too much new legislation or public discussion about new restrictions. I suggest that nature conservation should be part of all discussions about the land rights of the Sámi people and other people.

Secondly, nature conservation influences the Skolt Sámi culture, the wider Sámi culture, and other cultures. For example, the level of predator protection is central for reindeer herders. It is therefore important that the extent of nature conservation is adjusted to the demands of cultures in a reasonable way. Nature conservation and the preservation of Sámi culture are today organised mainly by the Forest Care and Park Services. Regulations concerning these matters are spread over several laws, Acts, and statutes. If the ILO 169 Convention were to be ratified in Finland, it would provide for the possibility of bringing some of these regulations closer together. The use of Wilderness Areas and other areas could be more precisely defined in regulations than today. Moreover, it would be possible to fine-tune some forms of environmental administration.

## Bibliography

Allard, Christina. 'The Nordic Countries' Law on Sámi Territorial Rights'. *Arctic Review on Law and Politics* 2 (2011): 159–183.

Eriksen, Thomas Hylland. 'Multiculturalism, Individualism, and Human Rights: Romanticism, the Enlightenment and Lessons from Mauritius'. In *Human Rights, Culture & Context, Anthropological Perspectives*, ed. Richard A. Wilson. London: Pluto Press, 1997: 49–69.

*European Union Directive on the Conservation of Natural Habitats and of Wild Fauna and Flora 1992.*

Feodoroff, Mariia. *Näätämön koltta-alue, a Report.* Inari: Sámi Soster ry., 2002. http://www.metsa.fi/web/en/landuse/northernlapland (2015).

*Finland's Nature Conservation Act 1996.*

*Indigenous and Tribal Peoples Convention 169, adopted by the International Labor Organization (ILO) 1989.*

Ingold, Tim. 'Anthropology beyond Humanity'. *Suomen Antropologi, Journal of the Finnish Anthropological Society* 38, no. 3 (2013): 5–23.

Itkonen, Panu. *Skolt Sámi Cooperation: Forms of Reciprocity in Work Situations of the Sevettijärvi Reindeer Herding Community at the Beginning of the 21st Century and Actions of the State Administration.* Helsinki: Unigrafia, 2012.

Itkonen, Panu. 'Skolt Sámi Reciprocity and Actions of State Administration: The Sevettijärvi Reindeer Herding Community under Outside Influence'. *Suomen Antropologi, Journal of the Finnish Anthropological Society* 2 (2014): 73–82.

Kumpula, Jouko, Colpaert, Alfred, Anttonen, Marja & Mauri Nieminen. *Poronhoitoalueen pohjoisimman osan (13 paliskuntaa) talvilaidunten uusintainventointi vuosina 1999–2003, Kala- ja riistaraportteja nro 303.* Helsinki: Riista- ja kalatalouden tutkimuslaitos, 2004.

Linkola, Anni & Martti Linkola. *Kolttasaamelaiset.* Kuopio: Saamelaismuseo, 2000.

Ludescher, Monica. 'Indigenous People's Territories and Natural Resources: International Standards and Peruvian Legislation'. In *Law and Anthropology, International Yearbook for Legal Anthropology, Volume 11*, eds. René Kuppe & Richard Potz. The Hauge: Martinus Nijhoff Publishers, 2001.

Metsähallitus. *Ylä-Lapin luonnonvarasuunnitelma.*Vantaa: Metsähallituksen metsätalouden julkaisusarja, 2000.

Moore, Sally. 'Introduction'. In *Law as a Process: An Anthropological Approach*, ed. Sally Moore. London: Routledge & Kegan Paul, 1978: 1–31.

Nickul, Karl. *Eräs Petsamokysymys, Suonikylän alueesta olisi tehtävä kolttakulttuurin suojelualue.* Helsinki: Suomen maantietellinen seura, 1935.

Nickul, Karl. *The Skolt Lapp Community Suenjelsijd, during the Year 1938.* Stockholm: Hugo Gebers Förlag, 1948.

Pelto, Pertti J. *Individualism in Skolt Lapp Society.* Helsinki: Suomen muinaismuistoyhdistys, 1962.

Pelto, Pertti J. *The Snowmobile Revolution: Technology and Social Change in the Arctic.* Menlo Park California: Cummings Publishing Company, 1973.

*Poromies* (the magazine *Reindeer Herder*) no. 2 (1996), no. 2 (2003), no. 2 (2013).

Pospisil, Leopold. *Anthropology of Law: A Comparative Theory.* New York: Harper & Row cop., 1971.

*Reindeer Husbandry Act 1990.*

Rigby, Peter. *Cattle, Capitalism, and Class, Ilparukuyo Maasai Transformations.* Philadelphia: Temple University Press, 1992.

*Skolt Act 1955/1995.*

Sutela, Tapio & Teuvo Niva. *Sevettijärven kolttien kalastusolot 1970-luvulta 2000 luvulle, Kala- ja riistaraportteja nro 365.* Helsinki: Riista- ja kalatalouden tutkimuslaitos, 2005.

Sverloff, Matti. *Suonjelin saamelaisten perintö.* Sevettijärvi: Matti Sverloff, 2003.

Tanner, Väinö. *Ihmismaantieteellisiä tutkimuksia Petsamon seudulla.* Helsinki: SKS, 2000.

Toivanen, Reetta. 'Das Paradox der Minderheitenrechte in Europa'. *SWS-Rundschau* 45, no. 2 (2005): 185–207.

www.luontoon.fi/erämaa-alueet (2015).

www.luontoon.fi/kansallispuistojemmehistoriaa (2015).

# 6 Nature conservation in Russia

## The case of indigenous Sámi rights in the Kola peninsula

*Vladislava Vladimirova*

### Introduction

The Sámi are one of the minority peoples of the Russian North, who are settled to the north of Karelia and the border with Fennoscandia. Seidozero Lake is a sacred Sámi site on the Kola peninsula that was converted in 1982 into a *zakaznik*, a kind of nature reserve of local importance.[1] As happened with many other protected areas after *perestroika* in the 1990s, the local government stopped supporting Seidozero Lake and it suffered from uncontrolled 'wild' tourism and poaching. In the 2000s, local people were alarmed that these activities were destroying the area, and after long lobbying by one Sámi organisation, Seidozero's status was reconfirmed in 2003. The municipal administration of Lovozero employed the staff to manage the *zakaznik*, but the Sámi were not given the right to be represented. Nevertheless, for the first time in the history of conservation in the region, the preservation of a traditional Sámi natural environment and lifestyle, and the future development of Sámi culture were emphasised.[2] Apart from the symbolic importance of this innovation for the Sámi community, the move was expected to provide economic opportunities for indigenous people, mostly through the development of private reindeer herding and tourism.

The reasons for and implications of this exceptional status are my focus here. Globally, similar moves have been interpreted as instances of a change in Western-dominated conceptions of nature from pristine wilderness to human landscape that is home to indigenous people. This also reflects the recommendation of the World Heritage Convention expert meeting in Narvik, Norway, in 2007 to increase the number of properties of mixed nature and culture on the List.[3] In this particular case, however, as my analysis shows, it is more a formal change of category that does not bring with it much noticeable epistemological or practical innovation.

This chapter is based on a series of field trips spread over more than ten years, between 2002 and 2014. The major focus of my empirical exploration has been reindeer herding and Sámi politics, including other relevant problems in the local economy and culture.[4] The data concerning Zakaznik Seid"iavvr' relies heavily on repeated interviews with key stakeholders,

1 Zakaznik (from the Russian *zakaz* – order, reserve) is an area where certain economic activities (logging, mining, grazing, hunting) are limited, see Pryde, *Conservation in the Soviet*; Borissoff, 'Soviet system of protected'. It can correspond to IUCN category III (Natural Monument or Feature) or more often to category VI (Protected Area with sustainable use of natural resources). See *Decision of the Executive Committee*, 1982.

2 *Decree from 31 March*, 2003.

3 Marsden, 'The World Heritage Convention', 245.

4 The empirical data I use in the text have been collected over extended field visits and as parts of many different projects. Hence, the contexts of the interviews have also been diverse, given that the focus of the

such as the leader of the ***zakaznik***, representatives of influential Sámi organisations like the Sámi Parliament, the Organisation of the Sámi of Murmansk Region (OOSMO), Sámi *obshchinas*, and the management and herders of Cooperative Tundra.[5] Obshchinas are non-profit subsistence-oriented economic units of Sámi kin or neighbours, provided by law with the possibility of renting land and engaging in traditional economic activities.[6] Interviews with other community members from the village of Lovozero and the members of the Danish NGO INFONOR provide supplementary information. Lack of space and the character of long-term anthropological enquiry make it impossible to provide information about each individual and all recorded data mentioned in the text. Whenever I make a claim that opinions are shared by the majority community, this is confirmed in their repeated reiteration by many informants on a number of occasions.

## Sámi people in the Murmansk Region: History, economy and rights

The Sámi occupy a strategic location close to the most developed industrial centres of Russia, with access to the Northern Sea Route and an ice-free port. Industrial development and strategic military projects during the Cold War, together with the Soviet policies toward indigenous people, caused huge relocations of population and gradual urbanisation.[7] Reindeer herding, one of the traditional subsistence economies, underwent radical transformation from small herds, with predominantly transport functions, to state-managed farms, where herders were employed for monthly remuneration. Land was collectivised and new, scientifically based rationales were applied to herding routines.[8] As a result of displacement of part of the Sámi population, currently only one village, Lovozero, is defined as Sámi, with a population of 800 indigenous people out of 3,000 residents.[9]

Despite the industrial expansion, experts assert that, because of the uneven distribution of production, the Murmansk Region has huge natural areas that are relatively little affected.[10] Nevertheless, extensive extractive production, as well as the nuclear power plant at Lake Imandra, cause considerable pollution and destruction in some areas. In addition to mining, felling forests and constructing dams change ecological and water systems.[11]

Indigenous legislation in Russia has been formally harmonised with international human rights directives.[12] It recognises that indigenous people should receive primary rights over lands where they have traditionally lived. Clear provision of administrative practices to

---

projects differed. Many of the interviews have been recorded and are stored in my personal archive. Others remain in written form in my field diaries.

5 The full name of the cooperative is Agricultural Production Cooperative Enterprise Tundra, here shortened to Cooperative Tundra.

6 The term *obshchina* has been translated into English as clan- or neighbourhood-based communities, but the Russian word of course has richer historical and semantic connotations. It needs to be underlined that *obshchina* does not correspond to any indigenous pre-revolutionary form of social organisation. Rather, it was borrowed from the intellectual and political discourses of nineteenth century social and economic transformation of Russia. The term was revived in the late twentieth century within debates among Russian ethnographers and politicians about transforming indigenous natural resource use and self-government.

7 Kiselev and Kiseleva, *Sovetskie Saamy*; Vakhtin, *Native Peoples of the Russian*.

8 Luk'ianchenko, *Material'naia kul'tura saamov*; Golovin and Druri, 'Nachalo stacionarnogo izucheniia'.

9 Kiselev and Kiseleva, *Sovetskie Saamy*.

10 Kobiakov, *Sokhranenii cennykh*.

11 Hønneland, *Russia and the West*.

12 Donahoe, 'The law as a source'; Kriazhkov, *Korennye malochislennye*.

ensure these rights, however, is lacking. Each administrative region has relative freedom in allotting such lands and resolving competing claims by industrial companies. In addition, different indigenous groups have their own customary regulations and traditional practices that need to be considered when negotiating such rights.[13] In the Murmansk Region, Sámi people have little direct impact on the procedures for allotting land to companies. The only case of public consultation that I have witnessed concerned the Canadian company, Barrick Gold, which tried to launch a big mining project in the grazing lands of the Cooperative Tundra. In this case local residents were informed about the project and were granted the right to communicate their concerns to a representative of the company. The director of the Cooperative complained that the sum that was paid as compensation for the exploration in their pastures went to the municipal administration and was redirected to fill the holes in the municipal education budget.[14] The consultation project was organised, as the company representative admitted, mostly in order to fulfil the requirements of Canadian legislation. This case is an illustration of land allotment procedures and the limited legal means that indigenous people have to influence them.

The social environment does not always support indigenous rights to natural resources as recommended in international legislation and demanded by the indigenous movement. A predominant argument in the Russian context is that all citizens of the Federation must have equal rights, including those governing political representation, and this is realised during general elections. Negative attitudes toward the Sámi have been manifested in connection with the process of social and economic reformation through the organisation of *obshchinas*. Some of the first Sámi *obshchinas* in the early 2000s received substantial support from abroad, and managed to rent land, a procedure that proved difficult and expensive.[15] Most *obshchinas* applied for land in order to develop private reindeer herding.[16] The *obshchina* that was granted pastures in Zakaznik Seid"iavvr', discussed below, tried for a short time to keep reindeer as part of a more complex tourism-oriented economy. The fact that the *obshchina*, when allotted land, did not use it as they had said they would, even though they were granted financial support from abroad, has given rise to contradictory feelings. Many people feel this arrangement is unjust and are therefore not supportive of indigenous rights.

Sámi people are not the only ethnic group that practise reindeer herding and, indeed, the two reindeer herding cooperatives in the region, Tundra and Olenevod, predominantly have herders of Komi and Nenets ancestry. Thus, even though local residents point to reindeer herding as an important identity-forming economy, they do not consider that its future and recovery will result primarily from Sámi *obshchinas*. The social segregation within the indigenous community contributes to such attitudes: the Sámi political elite who lead the struggle for indigenous rights is seen as disconnected from Sámi reindeer herders, who are a marginal minority.[17] Many local residents point out that more than 20 years of successful Sámi political activism and the support it has gained within Russia and from abroad have had little positive influence on reindeer herding, which has remained in a serious crisis since the time of *perestroika*.

13 Novikova, *Ohotniki i neftianiki*; Stammler and Peskov, 'Building a "culture of dialogue" among'; Stammler and Wilson, 'Dialogue for development'.
14 Interview with Viktor Starcev, February 2008.
15 Kalstad, *The Road to the Last Chance*.
16 Vladimirova, *Just Labor*.
17 Konstantinov, *Conversations with Power*; Vladimirova, *Just Labor*; Øverland and Berg-Nordlie, *Bridging Divides*.

## Indigenous people and nature conservation in the Murmansk Region

Protected areas in the Murmansk Region constitute 7.9 per cent of the whole territory. Only half of these areas, however, are under regimes that can ensure their preservation from damaging anthropogenic activities. Conservation in the region is in crisis, according to the conclusions of the representative international project Mapping of High Conservation Value Areas in Northwestern Russia.[18] Even in territories with adequate levels of protection, such as *zakazniks*, where all economic activities are banned and the area is closed to visitors, the authorities have no resources to organise protection in practice. At present, the Murmansk Region has only three state *zapovedniks* and ten *zakazniks* with differing levels of limitation on economic activity. The case of Zakaznik Seid"iavvr' presents a further illustration of these complexities.

### *Russian traditions in conservation*

Conservation has a long history in Russia, even though the state did not become a member of the International Union for Conservation of Nature until the late 1980s, claiming in doing so that it respects and applies the common principles of nature protection and international cooperation. However, Russia has not accepted the IUCN's protected area categories choosing instead to retain its own historical divisions. The Federal Law on Protected Natural Areas, issued on 14 March 1995 stipulates these categories, and also regulates the ownership of the land, the level of protection and the governing state organisation. *Zapovedniks*, national parks, and nature parks have a higher protected status than other areas and are governed directly by the state. However, most protected areas, such as *zakazniks*, nature monuments, and a few others, are largely under the authority of regional administrations.[19]

The *zapovednik*, the category subject to the greatest restriction on human activities, which excludes most kinds of visits, is also the oldest form. The whole academic branch of the study and the very practice of protecting nature take their name from it, *zapovedenie*. In contrast to early conservation projects elsewhere, such as Yellowstone National Park in the US, or those in Sweden, where nature conservation from the very beginning was about providing the basis for tourism, the Russian *zapovedniks* were considered to be fields intended for scientific exploration.[20] Their founders were often scientists and enthusiasts, who argued that *zapovedniks* are examples of pristine nature and habitats of species unaffected by human activities. Such territories needed to be off-limits for agriculture and other human economic activities, in order to preserve their biodiversity and to study the development of biological systems through the organisation of long-term scientific observation.[21]

In the early twentieth century, as a result of the work of an increasing number of scientific societies, *zapovedenie* became a popular movement among the Russian intelligentsia. In 1912 at the Russian Geographical Society, a Nature Protection Committee was established in order to sketch the first proposal for a Law on Nature Protection Territories and mapping all existing *zapovedniks*.[22] All these developments, despite their specific manifestations,

18 Kobiakov, *Sokhranenii cennykh prirodnykh.*

19 Federal Law N33-FZ 1995.

20 Löfgren, 'Längtan till landet Annorlunda'; Mels, *Wild Landscapes*; Reinius, *Protected Attractions*; Sörlin, *Humanekologi.*

21 Reimers and Shtil'mark, *Osobo okhraniaemye prirodnye.*

22 Op cit.

should be seen in the context of a synchronic fast-growing global interest in nature conservation.[23] Informed by such influences, at the beginning of the twentieth century, the pioneers of conservation formulated three ideas: preservation of biodiversity for its economic utility, for its scientific value, and the so-called 'ethical–aesthetic' rationale, which claims that protection should be motivated by nature's right to live and its intrinsic aesthetic value.[24] Subsequently, the scientific and utilitarian rationales outweighed the ethical considerations, while the role of aesthetics became politically controversial in Soviet ideology because it matched bourgeois values.[25] Indigenous reservations were also mentioned in this debate, as a way to preserve the last 'tribal people'. The main value of the indigenous peoples of the North was that they were seen as reflecting earlier stages in the development of civilised peoples, so their preservation was also deemed important for scientific study of the history of mankind. Later, common sense ethics dictated that 'if we strive to rescue animal species, we are even more obliged to protect primitive people, who represent the most noble of all beings living in the wild'.[26] Taking care of these people must have been even more appealing to the state and the majority population because, given the new Soviet state policy regarding development of the northern peripheries, they became increasingly important as they could help the incoming population to survive in their lands. The best policy, then, was to allot territories for indigenous reserves, forbidden for outsiders, where they could continue to pursue traditional hunting and reindeer herding.[27] Taking up the American experience of tribal reservations as a means to 'civilise' indigenous people, research emphasised the harm that civilisation had brought to 'primitive people' and offered instead a model of conservation of indigenous culture in its original state and natural habitat. Finally, the argument goes, the existence of indigenous people is so closely dependent on hunting resources, that to separate the question of their survival from that of nature protection does not make sense. Indigenous reserves will not only present anthropological features but also ensure the conservation of the flora and fauna, on which their existence depends.[28] The idea of indigenous reserves never became dominant among Soviet politicians, but it was further reiterated, especially immediately after the time of *perestroika*, as one possible way to reorganise indigenous economy and community in Russia.[29] The example of Laplandskii Zapovednik, the earliest protected area in the Kola peninsula, which was established in the period of a boom throughout the 1920s and 1930s in Soviet *zapovedenie*, is revealing of the dominant scientific objectives of Soviet conservation and the exclusion of the indigenous population from conservation areas.

## *Laplandskii Zapovednik*

The Kola peninsula was attractive to many nineteenth and early twentieth century exploration expeditions, which investigated its geological abundance, soil structure, landscapes, plant species, and ethnographic variety, according to the official story of the Laplandskii Zapovednik. Foreseeing its industrial development, some scholars in the 1920s who were

23 Dahlström, *Negotiating Wilderness.*
24 Reimers and Shtil'mark 1978, Osobo okhraniaemye prirodnye, 9.
25 Op cit.
26 Solov'ev, 'Tipy organizatsii, sposobstvuiushchikh', 14.
27 Solov'ev, 'Tipy organizatsii, sposobstvuiushchikh', 14–16.
28 Op cit.
29 Murashko, 'Obsuzhdenie Proekta Zakona'.

interested in the then popular idea of preserving natural landscapes, with all their ancient species for future generations of scholars, suggested creating a *zapovednik* in the region of Chuna-tundry and Monche-tundry. The species that the initiative targeted were goose and wild reindeer. In 1928–1929 Professor German Kreps, the most active figure, organised the counting of wild reindeer in the above listed territories and found that only 95 remained. At the same time, a description of all plant species was made. On the basis of these results, on 17 January 1930, the Executive Committee of Leningradskii Region took the decision to establish the Laplandskii Zapovednik on 1,600 sq km of land and to employ three scholars and two guards. In 1935 the Laplandskii Zapovednik was included in the list of state-protected natural areas which permitted the erection of some buildings and stations for nature observation and the employment of new people, which eventually led to the release of the first edition of scholarly publications of the Laplandskii Zapovednik.

In this official historical account, indigenous Sámi people were given little space, physically and symbolically. With regard to the first, the mention of reindeer transportation, used in the years before snow scooters were introduced, leads us to speculate that some reindeer herders must have been employed because of their special knowledge and skills. In symbolic terms, it was stressed in the 1980s, that the name of the territory, as well as the preservation of the original Sámi geographical toponymy within it, indicates that apart from its primary purpose of maintaining nature, it has also preserved a part of its human history, including a few stone monuments and Sámi village remains.[30]

It has proved difficult to find accounts of how the formation of the Laplandskii Zapovednik affected indigenous people living in the three nearest Sámi villages, who continued to use parts of its territory to fish and gather berries even after it was marked off, despite official restrictions. All land in the Soviet Union has already been legally converted into collective ownership in 1918. Sámi people have been brought to a certain degree of sedentarisation by the 1930s, together with the introduction of state-controlled collectivised reindeer herding in the late 1920s. Therefore, the change that the conservation of the Laplandskii Zapovednik might have imposed on the Sámi residents of the nearby villages was not an issue that roused much public interest. The restriction of the area, in order to preserve wild reindeer, was indirectly related to past Sámi residents, who allegedly caused the depletion of the wild reindeer population through extensive hunting.[31]

In the 1970s, the territory of the Laplandskii Zapovednik was increased considerably, on the grounds that the wild reindeer migration needed protection, and was then further elaborated in the mid-1980s with its conversion into a biosphere reserve and inclusion on the UNESCO list. This case is indicative of the main trends and ideas of zapovedeniks in Russia up to the present. Laplandskii Zapovednik is a closed territory, preserved for the conservation of nature in the form of plants and species, and their exploration by scholars and a limited circle of people. The social history of the territory as an indigenous Sámi herding and hunting area has been largely ignored.

Tourism in Laplandskii Zapovednik has been prohibited, and only now is the infrastructure being created that will allow visitors access to the territory. This follows a recent trend in thinking of tourism as fund raising for nature conservation.[32] As my field research also indicates, local people have mixed feelings about tourism as well. On the one hand, they often travel in the natural environment, and Seidozero especially is one of the most popular

30 Semenov-Tian-Shanskii, *Laplandskii zapovednik*, 15.
31 Op cit.
32 Wells and Williams, 'Russia's protected areas', 203.

local destinations. On the other hand, there is a strong argument that tourism damages nature as a result of increased poaching and reduced control.[33] This view is often expressed towards tourists coming from outside the region. A third opinion centres on the fact that places that are under less strict preservation regimes, such as Seid"iavvr', often have no restrictions on fishing and gathering activities, which are open for all local residents, regardless of ethnic and cultural origin. The influx of outsiders and tourists in such cases could cause conflicts with local economic practices.[34] As such contradictions indicate, local goals and concepts about nature protection may be closely entangled with considerations of a more economic character. Such contradictions will be discussed below, where the public debates about Zakaznik Seid"iavvr' are described.

## Zakaznik Seid"iavvr' – A new conception of nature conservation?

Zakaznik Seidozero was established in Soviet times, in the late 1970s and 1980s, which has been described as a golden age in the development of protected areas, perhaps as a result of the growing awareness of the huge ecological damage that Soviet industry and militarisation were causing. In its early days, the *zakaznik* offered protection to some fish, bird and animal species, organised by a full-time guard, living in a cabin by the lake. The decision to set up the *zakaznik* was issued by the Executive Committee of the Murmansk Regional Council of Deputies in 1982.[35] The initiative, not unexpectedly, came from the Polar Scientific Research Institute for Fishing and Oceanography – the oldest academic institution in the north of Russia. This exemplifies the mechanism for establishing a protected area during that period. The initiative, even if following the desires of local people, had to move all the way up the administrative hierarchy and finally be taken by a public organisation that was officially responsible, such as a scientific institute.

Seid"iavvr' was given the status of a State Complex Natural Zakaznik of Regional Importance. Historically, *zakaznik* has had a more concrete meaning than *zapovednik*, and initially indicated a ban on hunting. In some contexts however, as well as for many ordinary people, the words are synonymous.[36] *Zakaznik* is one of the most common types of protected area in Russia and it can meet the IUCN category III criterion, a natural object or feature or, more frequently, the category VI criterion, protected area with sustainable use of natural resources. In the case of Seid"iavvr', with its re-establishment in 2003, a transition seems to have been made from category III to category VI, hence the *zakaznik* was supposed to accommodate more Sámi reindeer herding and other traditional activities. As the description of the case and my analysis below show, this transition proved to be more formal than real.

Zakaznik Seid"iavvr' was founded on 17,400 hectares, which makes it a medium-sized area. It should be recalled here that this is one of 66 protected areas of various sizes and types in the Murmansk Region, 12 of which have federal status, i.e. they are centrally governed. Seid"iavvr' constitutes an exception. First because it is maintained under a more restrictive regime: logging, geological explorations, extractive industry and mining, turf extraction, building houses, roads, pipelines, electricity supply systems and communication infrastructure, are all forbidden, except when constructing

33 Op cit, 202.
34 Konstantinov, *Reindeer-herders*; Vladimirova, 'We are reindeer people'.
35 Decision 1982.
36 Reimers and Shtil'mark, *Osobo okhraniaemye prirodnye*, 12.

the infrastructure of the territory itself. Second because, for the first time, it incorporates not only features of the natural environment or cultural monuments, but also the traditional environment, lifestyle and original culture of the native Sámi people.[37] This is what the word 'complex' in the designation State Complex Natural Zakaznik of Regional Importance refers to.

This practice of establishing protected areas 'from above' instead by a bottom-up initiative does not appear to differ so much in substance from other places, such as Sweden, for example. As Åsa Dahlström and Carina Green describe in their studies of the Laponia World Heritage Area, its nomination was a long and complex process, with the initiative coming from the local and national administrative offices, and definitely not unanimously accepted by local indigenous people.[38] What distinguishes the Russian case, however, is the primary role of scientific organisations and scientists in the process of conservation, a phenomenon that has been analysed in the literature.[39] As the case of Laplandskii Zapovednik above shows, *zapovedniks* indeed had the status of scientific organisations, which stood high in the academic hierarchy, at least in the early days of Soviet history.[40] To further advance their scientific role, in line with the policy of Soviet modernity, the authorities slowly shifted the idea of *zapovedniks* as untouched wild nature reserves to fields for experimentation in the control and transformation of nature, including the study of adaptation and preservation of endangered or valuable species, predator control, use of new natural resources, and for the study of anthropogenic impact on nature in general.[41] In a formulation that harmonises with contemporary nature politics, some of these objectives have been repeated in the decree founding Seid"iavvr', for example 'the working out and introduction of efficient methods of nature preservation and sustenance of ecological balance under conditions of recreational use of the territory'.[42]

What becomes immediately obvious, as also in the case of Laplandskii Zapovednik, is the marginal and insignificant position of indigenous people and culture in relation to nature conservation under the Soviet state. Positivistic science is expected to deal with the laws of nature and society, and lead the way to the best management and engineering of nature, as well as of the people themselves.[43]

The gradual decay in the system of guarding and observing the status of protected areas in the post-*perestroika* period is a common topic of discussion.[44] Many well-organised *zakazniks* were simply deserted and game poachers were allowed to do as they wished, in what is locally called 'wild tourism', involving unorganised tourists from the big cities. 'Wild tourists', as local people describe them, go into natural environments in search of adventure, with a large supply of alcohol, leaving piles of garbage and destruction after them. In this situation, many local people expressed their concern for Seidozero, a place with special attraction and status not only for indigenous people but for all local residents, and even for people far beyond the Kola peninsula.

37 Decree 2003.
38 Beach, 'Ecological man and the Laponia'; Dahlström, *Negotiating Wilderness*; Green, *Managing Laponia*, 102–106.
39 Ostergren and Hollenhorst, 'Convergence in protected area'; Weiner, *A Little Corner of Freedom.*
40 Reimers and Shtil'mark, *Osobo okhraniaemye prirodnye*, 36.
41 Op cit, 38.
42 Decree 2003.
43 Slezkine 1992.
44 Lutz and Caldecott, *Decentralization and Biodiversity*; Sobolev et al., 'Russia's protected areas: A survey'; Wells and Williams, 'Russia's protected areas'.

### *The symbolic meaning of Seidozero*

The attraction of the lake, besides its scenic beauty and the historical heritage of the stone formation Kuiva, resides in its aura of mysticism and adventure with their many nuances. The most predictable layer is, of course, related to Sámi religious beliefs, even though we need to keep in mind that the majority of Russian Sámi were already baptised into Orthodox Christianity in the mid-sixteenth century.[45] First of all, the name of the lake is translated from Sámi as the Sacred Lake. The stone image by the lake is considered to be *seid*, a mythical creator or stone person. One of the versions of the myth tells that in the days when Swedes were still ravaging these territories, one of them was ambushed by Sámi hunters. They demanded that he surrender by putting a *kanga* – a traditional Sámi shoe – on one of his feet. The Swede did what he was told, but the hunters killed him anyway. After this, he became a stone man, a *seid*, and is still sitting there by the lake.[46] Sámi people have been reported to treat the Kuiva, meaning an old man in Sámi, with great respect, by leaving him tobacco, and by women avoiding walking on that side of the lake.[47]

The indigenous legends have contributed to the occult aura of the lake, which has perhaps an even wider circulation and provides food for endless speculations and the production of new stories. The Russian occultist Alexander Barchenko was employed by OGPU, Stalin's notorious organisation responsible for fighting political enemies, to help find assistants with paranormal abilities to work in their cryptographic team. Barchenko organised an expedition to Russian Lapland to study the so-called Arctic Psychosis, a state in which people fall prostrate, follow someone else's will, become prophets, or speak in tongues. Instead, Barchenko found Seidozero and the Kuiva, together with an underground cave, and a pyramid. Comparing these artefacts with Sámi legends, he came to the conclusion that he had found the original land of the oldest world civilisation, Hyperborea.[48] The other participants in the expedition, as well as many scholars after Barchenko, asserted that all the formations are natural. Nevertheless, Barchenko's speculative theory gained popularity. There was even a secret German expedition to Seidozero during the Second World War, whose campsite remains were discovered by geologists in 1955.[49]

The Hyperborean theory gained new life in the 1990s when the philosopher Valerii Demin organised a series of expeditions, including scientists and people represented as experts on anomalous phenomena, such as UFOs, witches, etc. He continues to write actively, and new pilgrims and adventure-seekers keep visiting Seidozero in search of Hyperborea and UFOs.[50] Contemporary folklore perhaps contributes to this mystical image of the lake. Visitors, local and from outside, keep reporting strange phenomena happening at the lake and Sámi people play their role in sustaining such tales by narrating memories of all the restrictions their parents instructed them to observe when visiting the lake: such as never throwing garbage, speaking in a loud voice, or disturbing the water, etc. Some claim that they were advised to avoid going to the lake; others the opposite, that they feel relaxed, or recharged when they are at the location.

45 Ushakov, *Izbrannye proizvedeniya*.
46 Kert, *Saamskie skazki*, 51–52.
47 Bol'shakova, *Zhizn', obychai*.
48 Pervushin, *Okkul'tny Stalin*.
49 Riumkin, *Seidozero: taina prirody*.
50 Demin, *Zagadki Russkogo Severa*.

### *Zakaznik Seid"iavvr'*

The protection regime of Zakaznik Seid"iavvr' changed in 2003: a stricter limitation on activities was stipulated together with a more specific and wider list of all protected objects. The goals of the *zakaznik* now included the preservation of the traditional Sámi natural environment and lifestyles, and future development of original Sámi culture. The more specific measures that the founding decree provides for achieving such goals are introducing traditional land use by indigenous people, the revival of previously existing types of use of nature in the territory, preservation of artefacts of historical and cultural heritage such as cult-related structures and old village sites, and the revival of folk handicraft and production of art and souvenirs.[51] In accordance with these goals, the following activities are allowed within the borders of the *zakaznik*: reindeer herding and related traditional economic activities that do not violate the protection regime of the *zakaznik*; construction of camps and tourist bases after receiving permission; erecting fences, corrals and other structures for reindeer herding; farming of other animals; traditional subsistence and leisure fishing; gathering of mushrooms and berries; free access to the whole territory and, finally, the organisation of ritual activities at religious and historical places.[52]

This popular symbolic meaning is an important context for understanding the successful re-establishment of Seidozero in 2003. In contrast to its initial establishment under the initiative of a state scientific organisation, the revival of Seidozero's status became a reality after a public lobbying of the local municipal administration of Lovozero and the Murmansk Region authorities. This is in line with what is happening in other regions in Russia, where scholars report an increased role for civil society institutions, such as NGOs, in reinstating protected areas from the Soviet era or creating new ones.[53] Indigenous Sámi political organisations took the lead in this process, supported by national and international environmental and humanitarian NGOs. An important advantage at that time was that non-governmental organisations, including indigenous ones, carried relatively greater weight. Their role, however, has become weaker since the mid-2000s. It proved a beneficial social and political environment for bottom-up agencies to effectively influence local level government. Other positive factors were the already mentioned fame of the lake, which seems to have been a precondition for the development of tourism, a branch of the regional economy that the authorities eagerly point to as an alternative to the previously predominant industry. Finally, the political situation with increased attention being paid to the reformation of the indigenous economy might have encouraged regional authorities to present the *zakaznik* as an example of a successful policy of supporting the restoration of an indigenous traditional economy while at the same time preserving nature and satisfying the desire of the public.

## The *obshchina*

With these provisions, it becomes obvious that Seid"iavvr' is following the example of areas like Laponia, the first site related to reindeer herding to enter the UNESCO list of World Heritage sites. While I have not been able to discover whether the model of Laponia was directly applied, the similarities are obvious. Some of the important differences, however,

51 Decree 2003.

52 Op cit.

53 Wells and Williams, 'Russia's protected areas'.

will be discussed below, which will perhaps help to explain why reindeer herding has not been successful in the Russian case.

In contrast to Laponia, Seid"iavvr' did not come to acknowledge publicly an indigenous economy with a long continuous presence within a natural environment otherwise seen as wilderness by the dominant culture. Some of the territory of the *zakaznik* comprises part of the reindeer pastures of the Cooperative Tundra of Lovozero. As local people and reindeer herders comment, however, these pastures have not been used for a long time. A more important argument from the local perspective, however, is the lack of continuity between the old Sámi reindeer herding culture and the herding methods used in the Cooperative. I do not have the space to engage with the issue of authenticity here, but local people point out the lack of Sámi ethnic continuity within contemporary herding in order to question a Sámi herding tradition.[54] So, as the activists that lobbied for Seid"iavvr assert, and as indicated in the founding decree, one of the goals is to create the necessary conditions for a revival of traditional Sámi culture, including such economic aspects as reindeer herding, within their original environment, after interruption. This lack of direct continuity in the use of the area, economic as well as cultural, I see as an important factor in the failure of the attempt to develop private herding, which I describe below.

One way for indigenous people to rent land and establish traditional economic enterprises is to register a non-profit subsistence organisation called *obshchina*, as mentioned above. In some regions of the north, Chukotka for example, it was embraced quickly and *obshchinas* started being created to replace Soviet state farms for collective reindeer herding as early as the beginning of the 1990s, long before centralised legislation appeared.[55] Among the Kola Sámi, however, the form did not receive any attention until the federal Law 'On the Common Principles of Organization of Obshchinas of the Indigenous Minority Peoples of the Far North, Siberia and Far East of the Russian Federation' came into force in 2000. According to this Law *obshchinas* are forms of self-governing organisations, created with the aim of protecting traditional living territories, and for the protection and development of indigenous traditional ways of life, management and cultures. *Obshchinas* are non-profit organisations that are allowed to develop economic activity for subsistence purposes only. As my fieldwork in various regions of the north reveals, many indigenous people expect *obshchinas* to provide a mechanism whereby they will be allotted land use rights on a long-term basis. The federal legislation, however, stipulates that land can only be given to *obshchinas* within the borders of the so-called 'territories for traditional land use'. So far precise legislation on the formation of such territories has not been worked out, and regional administrations find different solutions to this problem. The Murmansk Region mostly allows *obshchinas* to participate in public competitions for land plots on the same terms as commercial organisations, a practice that has been criticised.[56]

One of the first Sámi *obshchinas*, created with the mediation of the same Sámi organisation that led the lobbying for Seid"iavvr', received serious support from abroad in order to develop private reindeer herding. After a year of struggling with the local authorities, the *obshchina* managed to lease a plot of land close to Seidozero. Unfortunately, the land had been used previously by the Cooperative Tundra, whose administration missed the deadline for registration for the competition. As was to be expected, the Cooperative blamed the

54 Vladimirova, 'We are reindeer people'.
55 Gray, 'The Obshchina in Chukotka'.
56 Kalstad, *The Road to the Last Chance.*

*obshchina* for playing unfairly, even though according to many local people it had not used this particular pasture for decades. This raised the indignation of many local people, who had observed with suspicion the rapid multiplication of different Sámi organisations with foreign help and seen in it the import of foreign ideologies that would not respect the values of the majority of local people. Many simplified the issue as a struggle between collective reindeer herding, represented by the Cooperative, that is supposedly a public good, and private herding, the aim of the *obshchina*, which uses public resources for the good of the few.[57] The conflict of interests also quickly spread within the Sámi community, where other organisations questioned the justice of only a few Sámi getting rights over *Zakaznik* land and benefitting from its fame and symbolic status while launching alternative projects and actively looking for sponsors in order to be able to replace the *obshchina* at Seidozero.[58] The question about the limited scale of conservation of indigenous culture that such initiatives provide has come to the fore worldwide. Institutions such as UNESCO, and conservation initiatives on a local scale, such as Seid"iavvr', share the common problem that they offer 'shelter' to a cultural practice only within the borders of the natural area under protection, which creates further inequality and exclusion among indigenous people, resulting in intra-community conflicts and divisions.

The further development only increased the feeling of injustice expressed in the community. Even though the *obshchina* managed to buy reindeer and build some infrastructure with generous foreign help, its ambition to build self-sufficient reindeer herding was not successful for a number of reasons.[59] Perhaps an indirect result of the location of the *obshchina* grazing land in Zakaznik Seid"iavvr' and the nearby grazing lands of the Cooperative Tundra was the *obshchina* members' expectation that they would be able to benefit through the informal organisation of trips for tourists while their reindeer were allowed to graze mixed with the Cooperative's herds. In order to attract tourists and present Sámi reindeer herding to them, the *obshchina* kept a few reindeer close to its cabin, a strategy that did not seem to bring huge profit, judging by the slow diminishing of its activities and its reindeer after support from abroad ended.[60]

In summary I can say that a number of historical, cultural, and administrative obstacles prevent the successful involvement of Sámi people in traditional livelihoods, as the attempt described above shows. A major hindrance is state ownership and control of land which, while protecting it from illegal privatisation, also makes it into a resource for the private gain of corrupt politicians and administrators, who can choose who will be allowed to rent it. After two and a half decades of attempts, many indigenous people have started to question the ideals of political and economic justice promised by the global indigenous movement, that were eagerly internalised in the 1990s. While Fennoscandic Sámi continue to offer help to Russian Sámi, they cannot understand why in the course of more than 20 years no Kola Sámi has managed or wanted to establish private reindeer herding. Formally, as the Ordinance of Zakaznik Seid"iavvr' also shows, Russian Federation legislation concerning indigenous people promises to guarantee their rights to their culture and traditions, including subsistence. But bureaucratic obstacles, lack of popular support and understanding of the rationale of indigenism among other reasons, create many, in some case insurmountable, hindrances.[61]

57 Vladimirova, *Just Labor*.
58 Interview with NGO INFONOR, April 2006.
59 Vladimirova, *Just Labor*.
60 Vladimirova, 'We are reindeer people'.
61 Donahoe, 'The law as a source'.

## Management

Indigenous Sámi are not represented formally in the government of Seid"iavvr'. On the other hand, the management seem open and supportive of the *obshchina* activity and problems have often been solved through informal negotiations, as the leaders of both the *zakaznik* and the *obshchina* have mentioned to me. The manager of Seid"iavvr' summarised relations in an interview I recorded in 2004 as, 'we do our job, they do theirs, we do not interfere with each other'. The ambition to ease the access of tourists to and within the *zakaznik* while taking maximum care for the preservation of biodiversity and historical heritage has perhaps provided a good common ground for such cooperation. Since the *obshchina*'s dissolution, however, the leader of Seid"iavvr' has shifted his interest mostly to the development of tourism. The ambition to bind together the revival of the indigenous economy within its traditional natural environment and tourism, one of the original objectives of the *zakaznik*, has faded. Traditional economic activity has shrunk to the usual fishing activities, which are not officially banned. The latest attitude of the leader of Seid"iavvr', however, is to use his administrative power to limit it in a way that would not undermine the supply or contribute to the destruction of other natural objects through the use of transportation: 'the Sámi seem to accept the status quo. If anyone wants to fish in Seidozero, they are welcome, but only from the coast; no boats because they leave contamination or damage. The local Sámi don't seem to be interested in anything else.'[62] The future of the *zakaznik*, as he sees it, lies in the improvement of the tourist infrastructure. Special paths and centralised transportation of people from the village to the lake would improve control and limit anthropogenic effects.

It is in the interest of regional authorities to locate territories that are not so attractive to extractive industries or those where conservation, because of its long tradition, has persevered, and mark these for nature protection in order to combine its own goals with indigenous traditional natural resource use. That this is an agenda within the administration of the region becomes obvious when one considers another National Park project, Hibiny Hill. This has not been such an easy success as Seid"iavvr', mostly because its leaders did not agree to limit the protected area to the territories that have no ore supplies that could be extracted.[63]

As Seid"iavvr' shows, such an agenda is difficult to realise, because of a number of historical circumstances and dominant ideas. One of the most obvious obstacles is the widespread idea that the objective of nature protection is to preserve wilderness for scientific study. Thus many generations of indigenous people have been pushed away from their environments and excluded from its use and management, which is hardly unique to Russia, as numerous studies show.[64]

## Concluding remarks

This chapter shows the problems embedded in establishing a novel form of protected area that includes indigenous culture and economy. The attempt of the *obshchina* to develop reindeer herding in the area was raised as an example of the complexities that arise when Sámi people try to take advantage of the special rights to natural resources that Russian

62 Interview recorded in September 2014.
63 Baranovskii, Gar'kusha and Kobiakov, *Proekt Razrabotki Partomchorr*.
64 Dahlberg, Rohde and Sandell, 'National parks and environmental justice'.

legislation promises. Broad legal formulations and the unwillingness of some bureaucrats to cooperate with indigenous people create obstacles to the development of indigenous economic branches.

Zakaznik Seid"iavvr', despite the failure of the *obshchina*, marks a turning point in the relation between conserved territories and indigenous peoples' right to natural resources in Russia. Even though the idea of indigenous reserves, after the model of America, has been long in circulation, the idea of preserving 'wilderness' while allotting it for traditional nature use seems to take a new lease of life. This is hardly surprising in a political environment that benefits continuous growth of the extraction economy, on which the country's wellbeing is desperately dependent. The Soviet nationalisation of the indigenous economy, which led to professionalising its work and dislocating people, put an end to many continuities, in geographical as well as cultural terms. The difficulty of ensuring wide public support, including within the indigenous community, for initiatives such as Seid"iavvr', can be sought in this historical and ideational context. The *obshchina*, which took up the challenge to build a traditional economic enterprise in this difficult context, did not manage to bring it to a successful end because of its lack of experience in both herding and the natural environment of the *zakaznik*, as well as the severe administrative hindrances and lack of popular support. Thus, unfortunately, it did not manage to contribute to a positive change in the conception that traditional culture preservation and revival within its original natural environment is a possible objective for nature conservation in Russia.

The consequences of this failure may be serious for the indigenous community in both symbolic and political terms. The leader of the Sámi Parliament, one of the representative organisations, articulated such risks in an interview I recorded in September 2014: the status quo is not beneficial to the Sámi. After ten years, they cannot see how the administration of the *zakaznik* has helped preserve their culture. Apart from the tourism business plans, and general tolerance towards small informal private tourism businesses at the lake, the leader has contributed little to the improvement of the situation of the *zakaznik*. The leader of the Parliament expressed her worries that faced with so many hindrances, some Sámi have started to give up and accept the idea that perhaps their lives would be easier if they could accept mining and the destruction it brings to their ancestral lands and get their fair share through employment in the sector. The Parliament sees supporting a bigger and federally protected area, the Hibiny Hill National Park, as one way to avoid such a shift. The latter project has been carried out without any clear success for a long time, in contrast to Seid"iavvr', and without indigenous support. One of the bones of contention between its leaders and the Sámi community has been the planned inclusion of Seidozero. The crux of the disagreement is that if the park was created, the land of the *zakaznik* and sacred Sámi territory, would become federal, i.e. be placed under the administration and control of officials in Moscow, who are distant and may not even have heard of Sámi people and their feelings about the lake.

After the failure of the *obshchina* and with the current policy of the *zakaznik* leadership, the Sámi Parliament seems to have become more supportive of the park project. At the level of informal negotiations, the leader of the Parliament has been promised that if the park is created, there will be a regime of co-management, including an indigenous representative on the managing board, and employment opportunities for the Sámi. Becoming a part of a bigger and more widely supported project that can ensure federal status may prove beneficial, if the new park continues the model introduced with Seid"iavvr' to emphasise ethnic culture in unity with its natural environment and ensure its legal protection. However, the only way I see it can be successful is if a shift in the perceptions of wilderness and home occurs, within the indigenous and majority communities. Indigenous and non-indigenous people alike tend to align with Soviet ideology and modernity, and perceive protected areas as 'wild nature' places, wild more in the sense of non-civilised than pristine perhaps, which makes them less attractive for long-term residence. Decades of ideological work have powerfully fostered the value of culture, understood as education and the facilities provided in an urban environment as providing a suitable human home. The kinds of tourism predominant in nature reserves including Seid"iavvr' – wild, adventurous, amateurs of mysticism – only confirm the status of the place as non-home and further alienate indigenous people from it. In order to make initiatives like Seid"iavvr' successful, such divisions need to be re-conceptualised, and the gulf between the ideas of home and 'wild nature' bridged.

## Bibliography


Baranovskii, P., M. Gar'kusha & S. Kobiakov. *Proekt Razrabotki Partomchorr/Partomchorr Mining Project*, 2011. http://hibiny.info/problems/partomchorr.

Beach, Hugh. 'Ecological Man and the Laponia World Heritage Site'. In Kyösti, Julku (ed.), *The Roots of Peoples and Languages of Northern Eurasia*. Oulu: University of Oulu, 2002: 34–45.

Bol'shakova, Nadezhda. *Zhizn', obychai i mify kol'skikh saamov v proshlom i nastoiashchem* [*The Life, Customs, and Myths of Kola Sámi in the past and in the Future*]. Murmansk: Murmasnkoe knizhnoe izdatel'stvo, 2005.

Borissoff, V. A. 'Soviet System of Protected Natural Areas'. *National Parks and Conservation Magazine* 45, no. 6 (1971): 8–14.

Dahlberg, Annika, Rohde, Rick & Klas Sandell. 'National Parks and Environmental Justice: Comparing Access Rights and Ideological Legacies in Three Countries'. *Conservation and Society* 8, no. 3 (2010): 209.

Dahlström, Åsa Nilsson. *Negotiating Wilderness in a Cultural Landscape: Predators and Saami Reindeer Herding in the Laponian World Heritage Area*. Uppsala: Acta Universitatis Upsaliensis, 2003.

Decision. *Decision of the Executive Committee of Murmansk Regional Council of People's Deputees from 24 November 1982 N 538 'About the Organization of Complex State Zakaznik Seidozero'*, 1982.

Decree. *Decree from 31 March 2003 N 96 – PP/5 about Corrections to the Decision of the Executive Committee of Murmansk Regional Council of People's Deputees from 24 November 1982 N 538 'About the Organization of Complex State Zakaznik Seidozero'*, 2003.

Demin, Valerii N. *Zagadki Russkogo Severa* [*Secrets of the Russian North*]. Moscow: Veche, 1999.

Donahoe, Brian. 'The Law as a Source of Environmental Justice in the Russian Federation'. In *Julian Agyeman* and *Yelena Ogneva-Himmelberger* (eds), *Environmental Justice and Sustainability in the Former Soviet Union*, 21–46. Cambridge, MA: MIT Press, 2009.

Federal Law N33-FZ 1995. *Federal Law 'On Protected Natural Areas'*. 33-FZ.

Golovin, A. D. & I. V. Druri. 'Nachalo stacionarnogo izucheniia olenia i olenevodstvo v Murmanskom okruge (olenevodstvo v Lovozerskom raione)' ['The Beginning of Stationary Studies of Reindeer and Husbandry in Murmansk Okrug (Reindeer Herding in Lovozero Municipality']. *Murmanskoe Obshchestvo kraevedeniia. Doklady i soobscheniia* 2 (1928): 53–80.

Gray, Patty A. 'The Obshchina in Chukotka: Land, Property and Local Autonomy'. In *Working Papers/Max Planck Institute for Social Anthropology*, 29. Halle (Saale): Max Planck Institute for Social Anthropology.

Green, Carina. 'Managing Laponia: A World Heritage Site as Arena for Sámi Ethno-politics in Sweden' (Acta Universitatis Upsaliensis). Diss. Uppsala: Uppsala universitet, 2009.

Hønneland, Geir. *Russia and the West: Environmental Co-operation and Conflict*. London: Routledge, 2003.

Kalstad, J. *The Road to the Last Chance. The Politics of the State and the Situation of the Russian Saami (1864–2003).* Tromsø: Tromsø Sámi Museum, 2003.
Kert, G. M. *Saamskie skazki* [*Sámi Stories*]. Murmansk: Murmasnkoe knizhnoe izdatel'stvo, 1980.
Kiselev, A. & T. Kiseleva. *Sovetskie Saamy: Istoriia, ekonomika, kul'tura* [*Soviet Sámi: History, Economy, Culture*]. Murmansk: Murmanskoe knizhnoe izdatel'stvo, 1987.
Kobiakov, K. N. *Sokhranenii cennykh prirodnykh territorii Severo-Zapada Rossii: Analiz reprezentativnosti seti OOPT Arkhangeläskoi, Vologodskoi, Leningradskoi i Murmanskoi oblastei, Respubliki Karelii, Sankt-Peterburga* [*Mapping High Conservation Value Areas in the Russian North-West: Gap-analysis of the Protected Areas Network in Murmansk, Leningrad, Arkhangelsk, Vologda regions, Republic of Karelia, and the city of Saint-Petersburg*]. St. Petersburg: Kola Biodiversity Conservation Center, 2011.
Konstantinov, Yulian. *Reindeer herders: Field-notes from the Kola Peninsula, 1994–95.* Uppsala: Uppsala universitet, 2005.
Konstantinov, Yulian. *Conversations with Power: Soviet and Postsoviet Developments in the Reindeer Husbandry Part of the Kola Peninsula* (Acta Universitatis Upsaliensis). Uppsala: Uppsala University, 2015.
Kriazhkov, Vladimir A. *Korennye malochislennye narody severa v rossiiskom prave* [*Indigenous Numerically Small People of the North in Russian Law*]. Moscow: Norma, 2010.
Löfgren, Orvar. *Längtan till landet Annorlunda: om turism i historia och nutid.* Stockholm: Gidlunds i samarbete med Sveriges turistråd, 1990.
Luk'ianchenko, Tat'iana. *Material'naia kul'tura saamov (loparei) Kol'skogo poluostrova v kontse XIX-XX v* [*Material Culture of the Kola Saami (Lopars) at the end of 19–20 cc.*]. Moscow: Nauka, 1971.
Lutz, Ernst & Julian Oliver Caldecott. *Decentralization and Biodiversity Conservation.* Washington, D. C.: World Bank Publications, 1996.
Marsden, Simon. 'The World Heritage Convention in the Arctic and Indigenous People: Time to Reform?'. *The Yearbook of Polar Law Online* 6, no. 1 (2014): 226–249.
Mels, T. *Wild Landscapes. The Cultural Nature of Swedish National Parks.* Lund: Lund University Press, 1999.
Murashko, Ol'ga. 'Obsuzhdenie Proekta Zakona Rossiiskoi Federacii 'Osnovy pravovogo statusa korennykh narodov severa' ['The Discussion of the Planned Federal Law the Basic Legal Status of the Indigenous People of the North']. *Etnograficheskoe obozrenie* 3 (1995): 110–121.
Novikova, Natal'ia L. *Ohotniki i neftianiki: Issledovanie po iuridicheskoi antropologii* [*Hunters and Oil Workers: Study of Legal Anthropology*]. Moscow: Nauka, 2014.
Ostergren, David M. & Steven J. Hollenhorst. 'Convergence in Protected Area Policy: A Comparison of the Russian Zapovednik and American Wilderness System'. *Society & Natural Resources* 12, no. 4 (1998): 293–313.
Øverland, Indra & Mikkel Berg-Nordlie. *Bridging Divides: Ethno-political Leadership among the Russian Sami.* New York: Berghahn Books, 2012.
Pervushin, Anton. *Okkul'tny Stalin* [*The Occult Stalin*]. Moscow: Iauza, 2006.
Pryde, Philip R. *Conservation in the Soviet Union.* Cambridge: Cambridge University Press, 1972.
Reimers, N. F. & F. R. Shtil'mark. *Osobo okhraniaemye prirodnye territorii* [*Protected Nature Territories*]. Moscow: Mysl, 1978.
Reinius, S. W. *Protected Attractions: Tourism and Wilderness in the Swedish Mountainous Region.* Stockholm: Stockholm University Press, 2009.
Riumkin, Dmitrii. *Seidozero: taina prirody ili drevnykh giperboreicev?* [*Seidozero: The Secret of Nature or of Hyperborea?*]. Zabroska, 2013. *RF.* http://zabroska.su/?p=1063.
Semenov-Tian-Shanskii, Oleg I. *Laplandskii zapovednik.* Moscow: Sovetskaia Rossia, 1984.
Slezkine, Yuri. 'From Savages to Citizens: The Cultural Revolution in the Soviet Far North, 1928–1938'. *Slavic Review* 51, no. 1 (1992): 52–76.

Sobolev, Nikolai A., Shvarts, Evgeny A., Kreindlin, Mikhail L., Mokievsky, Vadim O. & Victor A. Zubakin. 'Russia's Protected Areas: A Survey and Identification of Development Problems'. *Biodiversity & Conservation* 4, no. 9 (1995): 964–983.
Solov'ev, D. K. 'Tipy organizatsii, sposobstvuiushchikh okhrane prirody' ['Types of Organizations that Can Help Protect Nature']. *Sel'skoe khoziaistvo i lesovodstvo*, Petrograd no. 256 (1918): 76–111.
Sörlin, Sverker, ed. *Humanekologi: vägar till överlevnad*. Umeå: Forum för tvärvetenskap, Umeå univ., 1991.
Stammler, Florian & Emma Wilson. 'Dialogue for Development: An Exploration of Relations between Oil and Gas Companies, Communities, and the State'. *Sibirica* 5, no. 2 (2006): 1–42.
Stammler, Florian & Vladislav Peskov. 'Building a "Culture of Dialogue" among Stakeholders in North-West Russian Oil Extraction'. *Europe-Asia Studies* 60, no. 5 (2008): 831–849.
Ushakov, I. *Izbrannye proizvedeniya. /Selected Works/*. 3 vols. Murmansk: Murmanskoe knizhnoe izdatel'stvo, 1997.
Vakhtin, Nikolai. *Native Peoples of the Russian Far North*. London: ERIC, Minority Rights Group International, 1992.
Vladimirova, Vladislava K. 'Just Labor: Labor Ethic in a Post-Soviet Reindeer Herding Community'. Diss. Uppsala: Uppsala Universitet, 2006.
Vladimirova, Vladislava K. '"We Are Reindeer People, We Come from Reindeer": Reindeer Herding in Representations of the Sámi in Russia'. *Acta Borealia* 28, no. 1 (2011): 89–113. DOI:10.1080/08003831.2011.575661.
Weiner, Douglas R. *A Little Corner of Freedom: Russian Nature Protection from Stalin to Gorbachëv*. Berkeley, CA: University of California Press, 1999.
Wells, Michael P. & Margaret D. Williams. 'Russia's Protected Areas in Transition: The Impacts of *Perestroika*, Economic Reform and the Move towards Democracy'. *Ambio* 27, no. 3 (1998): 198–206.

Part 2

# Governance of indigenous space in a global context

# 7 Reimagining governance for 'Yellowstone' modelled national parks in the new era of Indigenous legal recognition

*Jacinta Ruru*

## Introduction

National parks provide an ideal locale for considering Indigenous customary rights and interests in modern landscapes. This is particularly true for national parks modelled on the first national park established in the 'New World', Yellowstone National Park in the US. This is because these parks are places typically owned and managed by the state, protected from private sale, for present and future generations to use and enjoy, and gain from them an appreciation of the country's distinctive scenery, ecological systems, and natural features. The creators of these Yellowstone model national parks (first in the US, and subsequently in Australia, Canada and Aotearoa New Zealand, in that order) devised this new public governance property concept to transform the so-called 'wild' and 'empty' Indigenous 'spaces' of often initially mountainous landscapes into colonial 'places' for recreation, tourism and conservation. But denoting these lands as 'wild' and 'empty' was merely a convenient legal fiction that justified the taking of Indigenous peoples' homelands.

Building on ideas explored in my postgraduate theses, this chapter focuses primarily on the governance of national park landscapes in Aotearoa New Zealand.[1] This work celebrates the fact that the national park label has preserved some last glimpses of what much of our land looked like less than 200 years ago. It is not the end goal of caring for these environments that is questioned here but what is examined is rather how we care for, and what values we prioritise in caring for, these environments. This chapter begins with an introductory context explaining the current national park legislative commitments in Aotearoa New Zealand with reference to its Indigenous peoples. It then provides five reasons why national parks are a useful modern landscape through which to explore Indigenous peoples' customary rights and interests in law. The last two parts of this chapter focus on legislative national park governance ideas generally in Aoteaora New Zealand and then more specifically in a place recently known as a national park: Te Urewera which is in the North Island of Aotearoa New Zealand.

## Context

The 14 national parks in Aotearoa New Zealand exist for the reasons set out in s. 4(1) of the National Parks Act 1980:

> It is hereby declared that the provisions of this Act shall have effect for the purpose of preserving in perpetuity as national parks, for their intrinsic worth and for the benefit,

1 See Ruru, 'Settling indigenous place' and Ruru, 'Treaty of Waitangi and National Parks'.

> use, and enjoyment of the public, areas of New Zealand that contain scenery of such distinctive quality, ecological systems, or natural features so beautiful, unique, or scientifically important that their preservation is in the national interest.

The National Parks Act further stipulates that national parks must be 'preserved as far as possible in their natural state' including all sites and objects of archaeological and historical interest.[2] The soil, water, and forests are to be maintained, and as a general policy 'the native plants and animals of the parks shall as far as possible be preserved and the introduced plants and animals shall as far as possible be exterminated'.[3] Section 4(2)(e) then states:

> Subject to the provisions of this Act and to the imposition of such conditions and restrictions as may be necessary for the preservation of the native plants and animals or for the welfare in general of the parks, the public shall have freedom of entry and access to the parks, so that they may receive in full measure the inspiration, enjoyment, recreation, and other benefits that may be derived from mountains, forests, sounds, seacoasts, lakes, rivers, and other natural features.

The threshold management goal is conservation, defined as: 'the preservation and protection of natural and historic resources for the purpose of maintaining their intrinsic values, providing for their appreciation and recreational enjoyment by the public, and safeguarding the options of future generations'.[4]

Conservation is integral to the national park concept. This work does not aim to undermine that commitment. National parks are an essential management tool that gives priority to conserving biological diversity, but the present law also demands respect for Indigenous peoples. In Aotearoa New Zealand, s. 4 of the Conservation Act 1987 (the umbrella statute to the National Parks Act) states:

> This Act shall so be interpreted and administered as to give effect to the principles of the Treaty of Waitangi.

The Treaty of Waitangi was a document signed in 1840 by the British Crown and over 500 Māori chiefs from throughout the country which provided a blueprint for how the Māori and the British could live together in Aotearoa New Zealand.[5] The Treaty contains three articles written in both Māori and English. However, the translations between the two language versions are not close. In the Māori language version, the Māori retained their sovereignty over their lands but granted the English a right of governance in the country. In the English-language version, the British Crown acquired sovereignty over the country but recognised that the Māori retained ownership of their lands and estates for as long as they wished. Following the signing of the Treaty, the British assumed sovereignty over the country and proceeded to establish a system of governance that mostly alienated the Māori from their lands and culture.

2 National Parks Act 1980, s. 4(2)(a) and (c).

3 Ibid., s. 4(2)(d) and (b).

4 National Parks Act 1980, s. 2 'conservation'. For an interesting discussion of the potential conflict between the twin goals of preservation and use within the US national park legislation, see Mappes, 'National parks', 601–636.

5 For information on the Treaty, see Orange, *The Treaty of Waitangi*; Durie, *Ngā Tai Matatū*; Belgrave, Kawharu and Williams, *Waitangi Revisited*.

Thus the respectful legislative stance articulated in s. 4 of the Conservation Act represents a new direction in Aotearoa New Zealand. The provision is steeped in a legal reconciliation discourse that began to emerge in the 1970s. Courageous Indigenous leaders led this discourse by, for example, taking specific claims to the courts and, in turn, brave judges began for the first time to listen and respond to those Indigenous calls for justice. In the landmark 1987 Court of Appeal decision in the *New Zealand Maori Council* case, the Court stated that the statutory incorporation of the principles of the Treaty of Waitangi in specific instances requires 'the [New Zealand European] and Maori Treaty partners to act towards each other reasonably and with the utmost good faith. That duty is no light one. It is infinitely more than a formality'.[6] This developing jurisprudence in Aotearoa New Zealand, and in many other countries,[7] has been instrumental in creating a platform for the current statutory recognition of the importance of engaging with Indigenous peoples in the governance of national parks.

It is the new direction with regard to the Treaty of Waitangi contained in s. 4 of the Conservation Act 1987 that poses a strong challenge to the twenty-first century concept of the national park landscapes. It is this challenge that frames the primary question explored in my theses and that underpins this chapter. If there is a new commitment to recognising Indigenous peoples in law, what ought this to mean in the context of owning and managing national parks? Or, to situate the question more theoretically, and examine it through the lens of law and geography: if law made colonial space permissible, what are the implications if contemporary law recalibrates its orientation to space and belatedly recognises Indigenous place? Interwoven into exploring these core questions are themes of national identity, peoples' connections to land, the resilience of Indigenous laws, and the power of state law to re-imagine/reconceive its foundations.

## Rationale

National parks provide an ideal basis against which to assess the implications of the new, more inclusively respectful aspirations concerning legal relations. National parks are, after all, 1) the ancestral lands of Indigenous peoples often containing the last remnants of native flora and fauna essential for the survival of Indigenous cultural; 2) the products of colonialism; 3) positioned as symbolic of our national identity and future; 4) subject to a domestic mandatory legal reconciliation discourse; and 5) a topic of interest in international law.

With regard to the first point, the Indigenous worldview is based on an understanding that humans are intimately related to the environment and that the environment records our stories of identity and knowledge. Some specific landmarks are especially important, including, in a Māori context, certain mountains situated in national parks. Some mountain peaks in Aotearoa New Zealand, such as Tongariro, Taranaki/Mount Egmont and Aoraki/Mount Cook, are the ancestors of the tribes that live beneath those summits.

For example, Aoraki was a son of the sky father who paddled in a boat with his brothers searching for the earth mother. Unable to find her, they proceeded to say a prayer to return them to their father but they said the prayer incorrectly forcing their boat to hit a hidden reef. As they scrambled to the high end of the boat, they and their boat turned to stone

6 *New Zealand Maori Council v Attorney-General* [1987] 1 NZLR 641 (CA) at 667. For more information on this case, see Ruru, 'In good faith'.

7 For example, in Canada see s. 35 of the Constitution Act 1982 and in Australia see the Native Title Act 1993.

and in the process of doing so created what today we commonly call the South Island: the boat being the South Island and the four high mountains in the South Island being the four brothers sitting upon the boat (other subsequent legends tell of how a demi-god is in the 'boat of the South Island' and 'fishes up' the North Island that is geographically shaped like a giant fish).[8]

Another story tells of how the great mountains in the North Island came to stand on their present spots. Once upon a time the mountains in the North were grouped in the centre of the island where Tongariro (a male mountain) and Pihama (a female mountain) live. Other male mountains, including Taranaki, fought with Tongariro over the beautiful Pihama. Tongariro won. The other mountains were banished from the area, including Taranaki who fled, carving out a major river in his path. This explains why this peak stands alone on the west coast. These mountains are integral to tribal identity, and each form is regarded with reverence as a sacred ancestor.

Thus, the people of Ngāti Tūwharetoa, who regard Tongariro as a sacred ancestor, acknowledge him in formally introducing themselves: Ko Tongariro te Maunga (Tongariro is the sacred mountain) Ko Taupō te moana (Taupō is the lake) Ko Te Heuheu te (Te Heuheu is the man) Ko Tūwharetoe te iwi (Tūwharetoa is the tribe). All tribes have similar tribal sayings that formally link their people with specific mountains and waters. Significantly, Tongariro, Taranaki and Aoraki are all mountains that are situated within national park boundaries and, as such, are governed by the Department of Conservation.[9]

Moreover, national parks, particularly in the context of Aotearoa New Zealand where they cover a significant part of the country, contain most of the last remaining native flora and fauna. This is important because, as the Waitangi Tribunal has stated, the Government Department of Conservation 'has charge of much of the remaining environment in which mātauranga Māori [Māori knowledge] evolved, and which Māori culture needs for its ongoing survival'.[10] Thus national parks are important to both Indigenous spiritual identity and cultural survival. There is, however, hope for an alignment of aspirations between Indigenous peoples and national park managers because both aspire to meet the similar end goal of retaining these places for the benefit and enjoyment of future generations. Thus, on this first point, national parks provide an ideal focal point for exploring the current commitments to reconciliation.

Moving to the second claim, that parks are the products of colonialism, the national parks of Aotearoa New Zealand were modelled on the US Yellowstone National Park (established in 1872). The British settlers arriving on the shores of the 'new world' wrongly regarded large expanses of land as empty spaces, untouched and wild. In an attempt to fill the void in the landscape and to impose their identities on the land, the national park label proved useful.[11] It enabled the settlers to proclaim to their friends and families back home that they had travelled the seas to live in the most geographically beautiful parts of the world.[12] The colonial ideology empowered the colonisers to be blind to the first peoples' ways of life and lay their own histories and language over the various mountain peaks and river valleys.[13]

8 See Ngai Tahu Claims Settlement Act 1998, Sch. 80.

9 Conservation Act 1987, s. 6(a). For discussion, see Ruru, 'Indigenous peoples' ownership', 111–138.

10 Waitangi Tribunal, *Ko Aotearoa Tenei: A Report*, 297.

11 For example, see Cronon, *Changes in the Land*.

12 See the work of Shultis, 'Natural environments, wilderness'; Shultis, 'The creation of national parks'. See also Kopas, *Taking the Air*; Brown-John, 'Canada's national parks policy' (available to download at www.cpsa-acsp.ca/papers-2006/Brown-John.pdf); and Unger, 'The role of landscape architects'.

13 Bruce Braun has developed these types of arguments in relation to nature and forests, see Bruan, *The Intemperate Rainforest*. See also Deur and Turner, *Keeping It Living*.

Rationalised first as a tourist and recreation tool, it was not until the twentieth century that national parks became firmly embedded in conservation goals. Thus the fact that the first national parks in Aotearoa New Zealand were established in an era that deemed Indigenous peoples 'wild', living on 'wild' lands, provides an ideal opportunity to investigate the ramifications of the current acceptance that national parks overlie Indigenous homelands.

Third, national parks are positioned as symbolic of our national identity and future. Such places thus deserve close attention. If the new Indigenous rights jurisprudence is to be believed (and the Department of Conservation has even compressed, in one instance, the goal of strengthening national identity and upholding Treaty principles)[14] then national parks are places that ought to symbolise transformative relationships, showcasing how respectful relations with Indigenous peoples can be created, and how colonialist ideals of space can be displaced.

Moreover, turning to my fourth point, national parks are subject to a mandatory reconciliation discourse. In Aotearoa New Zealand, the National Parks Act (through s. 4 of the Conservation Act) must be interpreted and administered so as to give effect to the principles of the Treaty of Waitangi. Significantly, in recent years, the Department of Conservation has been making attempts to embrace the new legal discourse of recognising Indigenous peoples and the Crown's rights and responsibilities. Back in 2005 when I began my PhD study, the Director-General of the Department of Conservation stated that the Department is 'committed to supporting new opportunities to work with [Māori] for conservation outcomes, and enhancing [traditional Māori knowledge]'.[15] These aspirations remain true today. For example, in 2014–2015, almost 30 per cent of the Department of Conservation's partnerships involve Māori.[16]

Regarding my fifth point, the international community has been aware and supportive of the need to recognise Indigenous peoples in the management and governance of national parks for some time. Importantly, in 2000, the World Commission on Protected Areas (WCPA), in conjunction with the International Union for Conservation of Nature (IUCN) and the World Wildlife Federation (WWF), published a paper recording a commitment to including Indigenous peoples in the operation of national parks. For instance, it states 'the rights of indigenous . . . peoples inhabiting protected areas must be respected by promoting and allowing full participation in co-management of resources'.[17]

Yet on the international stage, on 23 September 2007 the United Nations General Assembly adopted the Declaration of the Rights of Indigenous Peoples following a 143:4 vote.[18] Aotearoa New Zealand was one of those four countries that voted against the Declaration (Australia, Canada and the United States of America were the other three). However, in 2010, Aotearoa New Zealand changed position and endorsed the Declaration, albeit with attached caveats.[19] The Declaration's preamble comprises 24 paragraphs and 46 articles. At

14 See: New Zealand Department of Conservation, *Statement of Intent 2005–2008*, Department of Conservation, http://www.doc.govt.nz/Documents/about-doc/role/policies-and-plans/statement-of-intent/statement-of-intent-(2005-2008).pdf, 11.

15 New Zealand Department of Conservation, *Department of Conservation Annual Report for year ended 30 June 2005* (Wellington, Department of Conservation, 2005), 88.

16 New Zealand Department of Conservation, *Department of Conservation Annual Report for year ended 30 June 2005* (Wellington, Department of Conservation, 2015), 38.

17 Beltran, *Indigenous and Traditional Peoples*, ix. See also *Convention on Biological Diversity*, www.cbd.int.

18 To view the Declaration see the United Nations website at http://undesadspd.org/IndigenousPeoples/DeclarationontheRightsofIndigenousPeoples.aspx.

19 Aotearoa New Zealand endorsed the Declaration on 19 April 2010; see Sharples, Hon Pita, Minister of Māori Affairs of NZ, 'Announcement of New Zealand's Support', available at http://www.mfat.govt.

the heart of the Declaration is the urgent need for reconciliation in environmental management, including establishing respectful relationships with Indigenous peoples. For instance, one of the paragraphs in the preamble records the commitment to '*Recognizing* that respect for indigenous knowledge, cultures and traditional practices contributes to sustainable and equitable development and proper management of the environment.'

These five rationales together illustrate an important recognition of the role Indigenous peoples ought to play in governing protected areas, including national parks. They provide an essential foundation for the respect of Indigenous peoples' relationships with these lands.

## New legislative conceptions – A general overview

Other chapters in this book already present insights into some of the national parks around the world (such as Haida Gwaii in Canada) and even in Aotearoa New Zealand (namely Tongariro). Thus, this chapter provides only some brief glimpses into the contemporary initiatives for reconciliation in national park governance in Aotearoa New Zealand. It then specifically focuses on a once-known national park – Te Urewera in Aotearoa New Zealand – because it illustrates the possibilities of legislative conceptions.

Governance disputes abound in many countries with national parks. Some stem from who owns the land, others from who should manage the land, and many are a combination of both problems.[20] In Aotearoa New Zealand, the concept of reserving land for national park purposes has an interesting beginning in that an Indigenous tribal group, Ngāti Tūwharetoa, were initially keen to gift summit land (Tongariro) to the Crown to create the country's first national park. Tongariro lies alongside the mountain peaks of Ruapehu and Ngauruhoe in the centre of the North Island and is sacred to Ngāti Tūwharetoa.[21] In 1887, the paramount chief of Ngāti Tūwharetoa, decided that the best way to ensure that the mountain would not be 'cut up'[22] and sold piece by piece to Pākehā, gifted the summit to the Crown for the specific purpose of marking it as our first national park 'for the use of both the Natives and Europeans'.[23] The Crown became the legal owner of Tongariro in 1887, but the Government of the day took some seven years to meet the condition of the gift to give the summit national park status. The Government sought ownership from Ngāti Tūwharetoa of the surrounding Tongariro summit land for inclusion in the national park. Members of New Zealand's legislative assembly, the House of Representatives, believed the land was of no use to Ngāti Tūwharetoa and valuable only for its scenery.[24] The eventual Tongariro National Park Act 1894 allowed the governor to forcibly take the land in return

---

nz/Media-and-publications/Media/MFAT-speeches/2010/0-19-April-2010.php. Canada endorsed the Declaration on 12 November 2010: see Aboriginal Affairs and Northern Development Canada website at http://www.ainc-inac.gc.ca/ap/ia/dcl/stmt-eng.asp. For an excellent discussion of the Declaration see Charters and Stavenhagen, Making the Declaration Work.

20 For example, see this Canadian case *Nunavik Inuit v Canada (Minister of Canadian Heritage)* 1998 Carswell Nat 1504, 164 D.L.R. (4th) 463, [1998] 4 C.N.L.R. 68, 151 F.T.R. 69, (sub nom. *Makivik Corp. v Canada (Minister of Canadian Heritage)*) [1999] 1 F.C. 38, 4 C.N.L.R. 68, 1 F.C. 38, [1998] F.C.J No. 1114 at para [3].

21 For a brief description of the importance of this mountain to Ngati Tūwharetoa see http://www.teara.govt.nz/en/ngati-tuwharetoa/page-5. For more discussion of the creation of national parks in Aotearoa New Zealand, see Ruru, 'Indigenous peoples' ownership', see n. 14.

22 Cowan, *The Tongariro National Park*, 30.

23 Correspondence relative to the gift is contained in *Appendices to the Journals of the House of Representatives* (II) 1887, at G-4.

24 Minister of Lands, Hon, McKenzie (80) *New Zealand Parliamentary Debates* 322 (28 July 1893).

for monetary compensation, albeit a phantom concession considering the government's perceived 'uselessness' of the area to Ngāti Tūwharetoa.[25] The member for Northern Māori, Mr Heke, called it a 'monstrous piece of legislation' that 'was entirely inconsistent with the Treaty of Waitangi'.[26]

Interestingly the seven-year statutory delay is not publicly known, allowing the country to celebrate a century of national parks in 1987. Moreover, it is common to hear the Tongariro National Park heralded as the 'first Western country to reserve a national park in cooperation with its indigenous people'.[27] While the 1887 gift illustrates cooperation, the government's subsequent actions do not. Obviously it has become convenient in portraying the image of good race relations to gloss over the seven-year delay. However, it is likely that this image will soon be confronted head on. In 2013, the Waitangi Tribunal reported that the New Zealand Crown has been, and continues to be, in breach of the principles of the Treaty of Waitangi in creating and managing the Tongariro National Park.[28] The government and relevant Māori tribes are currently negotiating the management of this national park.

Turning to another national park, the country's sixth (created in 1953), now named Aoraki/Mount Cook National Park. Aoraki/Mount Cook is the highest mountain in Aotearoa New Zealand and lies in the South Island within the Aoraki/Mount Cook National Park.[29] It is the tūpuna of Ngāi Tahu, their 'most sacred of ancestors'.[30] The Crown assumed ownership of Aoraki/Mount Cook following Governor Grey's instructions to Henry Kemp to purchase land in the South Island in the late 1840s.[31] Almost immediately after the sale, Ngāi Tahu protested it. In dispute was whether or not the deed of sale included the mountains that run down the centre spine of the South Island. According to Ngāi Tahu, the mountains, including Aoraki/Mount Cook, were never included in the deed of sale. After a century of unsuccessful protest, the late 1980s and 1990s finally saw this issue resolved. The Ngāi Tahu Claims Settlement Act acknowledges the importance of Aoraki to Ngāi Tahu in several instances. For example, the Act states that (who owns Aoraki and manages it as part of its national park estate) the title of the peak will be vested by the Crown in the Ngāi Tahu tribal structure's name for a period of seven days. Ngāi Tahu will then gift the mountain back to the nation, both to ensure that the mountain remains within the National Park, and also that it will serve as an enduring symbol of the tribe's commitment to the co-management, together with the Crown, of areas of great historic, cultural and conservation value. Ngāi Tahu have not yet done this and will not do so until they are satisfied that all the settlement provisions have been implemented as agreed.[32]

25 See Tongariro National Park Act 1894, s 2. For an example of the perceived uselessness of the area see comment by Hon. John McKenzie (86) *New Zealand Parliamentary Debates* 679 (11 October 1894): 'anyone who had seen the portion of the country . . . which he might say was almost useless so far as grazing was concerned, would admit that it should be set apart as a national park for New Zealand'.

26 (86) *New Zealand Parliamentary Debates* 679 (11 October 1894).

27 Shultis, 'Natural environments, wilderness and protected areas', 196.

28 Waitangi Tribunal, *Te Kāhui Maunga*. See also Ruru, 'Rights to water and Te Kāhui Maunga', 15–9 and Ruru, 'Future management of Tongariro National Park', 14–18.

29 The Park name was officially changed to incorporate Aoraki in 1998: see Ngai Tahu Claims Settlement Act 1998, s. 162(1).

30 See Ngai Tahu Claims Settlement Act 1998, Sch. 80.

31 See 'Kemp's purchase' in Waitangi Tribunal *Ngai Tahu Report*, ch. 8.

32 See for example, Otago Daily Times, 'Mt Cook set for double change of ownership' in *Otago Daily Times*, 14 July 2006. http://subs.nzherald.co.nz/topic/story.cfm?c_id=262&objectid=10391211 (accessed 28 November 2015).

The purpose of this general overview has been to illustrate some aspects of the intense importance of the modern landscape of the national park for Indigenous peoples. The last part of this chapter now looks specifically at one landscape in Aotearoa New Zealand.

## New legislative conceptions – Specifically Te Urewera

On the eastern part of the North Island of Aotearoa New Zealand lies Te Urewera. This densely covered native forested land was designated a national park in 1954 and managed as Crown land by the Department of Conservation. The Māori tribe of this area – Ngāi Tūhoe – never consented to their homeland being turned into a national park. After years of negotiation between Ngāi Tūhoe and the Crown, a settlement has now been reached. On 27 July 2014 Te Urewera National Park became simply Te Urewera: 'a legal entity' with 'all the rights, powers, duties, and liabilities of a legal person'.[33] The Te Urewera Act is undoubtedly legally revolutionary, both here in Aotearoa New Zealand and on a world scale.

The Te Urewera Act makes it clear that Te Urewera ceases to be vested in the Crown, ceases to be Crown land, and ceases to be a national park.[34] Te Urewera is now freehold land,[35] managed not by the Department of Conservation but by the new Te Urewera Board. The responsibility of this Board is 'to act on behalf of, and in the name of, Te Urewera'.[36] Te Urewera will still have a management plan like other national parks in New Zealand but the Board, rather than the Department of Conservation, will approve it.[37] For the first three years, the Board has a 50/50 membership of Tūhoe (the Māori tribal group of this place) and Crown appointees (four persons each). Thereafter, the Board will increase by one and the ratio will change to six Tūhoe appointees/three Crown appointees.[38]

The Board, in contrast to almost any other statutory body, including the Department of Conservation, is directed to reflect customary values and law. Section 18(2) states that the Board needs to consider Tūhoe concepts of management and these are described in the legislation in the Māori language.[39] The Act mandates that the Board must strive to make some decisions by unanimous agreement (such as the approval of the Te Urewera management plan) and some decisions by consensus.[40]

The Board must work with the chief executive of the Tūhoe tribal group and the Director-General of Conservation to develop an annual budget. Section 38(2) states that the chief executive and the director-general 'must contribute equally to the costs provided for in the budget, unless both agree to a different contribution'. All revenue received by the Board must be paid into the Board's bank account and used to achieve the intention of this Act.[41] For the purposes of taxation, Te Urewera and the Board are deemed to be the same person.[42] The chief executive of Tūhoe and the Director-General of Conservation are

33 Section 11(1).
34 Section 12.
35 Albeit inalienable except in accordance with Te Urewera Act, see s. 13.
36 Section 17(a).
37 Section 18.
38 Section 21.
39 Aotearoa New Zealand recognised the Māori language as an official language of the country in 1987: see the Māori Language Act 1987.
40 See section 33 and 34.
41 Section 39(1).
42 Section 40(1).

responsible for the operational management of Te Urewera and must prepare an annual operational plan.[43]

The Te Urewera Act stipulates what activities are permitted in Te Urewera and what activities require authorisation and in what form.[44] The National Parks Act does something similar for national parks. Section 58 of the Act lists activities that require an activity permit. These include: taking any plant; disturbing or hunting any animal (other than sports fish); possessing dead protected wildlife for any cultural or other purpose; entering specially protected areas; making a road; establishing accommodation; farming; and recreational hunting. This is a comprehensive list and demonstrates that the tight rules for preserving national park land have been transposed to Te Urewera.

Throughout the Te Urewera Act it is made clear that Te Urewera may still be mined. Section 64(1) is one example of this stating clearly: 'Despite anything in this Act, Te Urewera land is to be treated as if it were Crown land described in Schedule 4 of the Crown Minerals Act 1991.'[45]

Section 3 of the Te Urewera Act is so beautifully expressed that I have copied it here in full:

**Te Urewera**

(1) Te Urewera is ancient and enduring, a fortress of nature, alive with history; its scenery is abundant with mystery, adventure, and remote beauty.
(2) Te Urewera is a place of spiritual value, with its own mana and mauri.
(3) Te Urewera has an identity in and of itself, inspiring people to commit to its care.

**Te Urewera and Tūhoe**

(4) For Tūhoe, Te Urewera is Te Manawa o te Ika a Māui; it is the heart of the great fish of Maui, its name being derived from Murakareke, the son of the ancestor Tūhoe.
(5) For Tūhoe, Te Urewera is their ewe whenua, their place of origin and return, their homeland.
(6) Te Urewera expresses and gives meaning to Tūhoe culture, language, customs, and identity. There Tūhoe hold mana by ahikāroa; they are tangata whenua and kaitiaki of Te Urewera.

**Te Urewera and all New Zealanders**

(7) Te Urewera is prized by other iwi and hapū who have acknowledged special associations with, and customary interests in, parts of Te Urewera.
(8) Te Urewera is also prized by all New Zealanders as a place of outstanding national value and intrinsic worth; it is treasured by all for the distinctive natural values of its vast and rugged primeval forest, and for the integrity of those values; for its indigenous ecological systems and biodiversity, its historical and cultural heritage, its scientific importance, and as a place for outdoor recreation and spiritual reflection.

The Te Urewera Act is significant in a comparable domestic and international context. First, the Act, for the first time in Aotearoa New Zealand's history, marks the permanent removal

43 Sections 50 and 53.
44 See s 55.
45 See also s 56(b) where mining activity authorised by the Crown Minerals Act can be undertaken without authorisation from the Board.

of a national park from the national park legislation. It is significantly different from the Aoraki/Mount Cook seven-day vestment discussed above.

Second, this negotiated settlement is evidence that reconciliation between the Crown and an Indigenous group is possible even when relationships have been extremely tense for a very long time. In the companion Act to the Te Urewera Act, the Tūhoe Claims Settlement Act 2014, some of this history is acknowledged, with attached apologies from the Crown. For example, the Act records that in 1865 'the Crown confiscated much of their most productive land, even though they were not in rebellion'.[46] After the land confiscation, 'the Crown waged war in Te Urewera until 1871'.[47] The Crown was responsible for the execution of unarmed prisoners and the killing of non-combatants. In 1870, Tūhoe were forced out of Te Urewera. As the Act states 'The wars caused Tūhoe to suffer widespread starvation and extensive loss of life.'[48] The atrocities continued with the government using harsh tactics to acquire land. Relevant to this chapter, the Act records:[49]

> In 1954, the Crown established Te Urewera National Park, which included most of Tūhoe's traditional lands. The Crown neither consulted Tūhoe about the establishment of the park nor about its 1957 expansion and did not recognise Tūhoe as having any special interest in the park or its governance. National Park policies led to restrictions on Tūhoe's customary use of Te Urewera and their own adjoining land.

The Act records strongly worded apologies from the Crown. The Crown apologies unreservedly for not honouring Tūhoe, for the wrongful killings, and 'for its unjust and excessive behaviour and the burden carried by generations of Tūhoe who suffer greatly and carry the pain of their ancestors'.[50] More recently, in 2007, about 300 New Zealand armed police raided Ruatoki, a small rural town within the heartland of Tūhoe. The armed raid was made pursuant to the Terrorism Suppression Act 2002 because the police believed that Tūhoe members were running terrorist training camps. While 17 people were arrested on the day, only four people were later brought to trial and then were only found guilty on some firearms charges. In 2014, the police apologised for the raids.[51] Thus, the Te Urewera Act is significant for this country demonstrating that innovative negotiated settlements are possible even where relationships have been strained for a considerable time.

Third, while there are similarities between the Te Urewera Act and the National Parks Act (such as the requirement to have a management plan and to ensure these lands are available for public use and enjoyment) the purpose for the setting aside of the land is subtly, but importantly, different. This is significant. As discussed at the beginning of this chapter, s. 4 of the National Parks Act preserves national parks for their scenery, recreation and science. The National Parks Act does not recognise the importance of lands within national park boundaries as being culturally and spiritually important to the Māori. The National Parks Act is a mono-cultural statute premising only Western values for preserving land. The Te Urewera Act demonstrates a new bi-cultural way of articulating the importance of national

46 Section 8(1) of the Tūhoe Claims Settlement Act 2014.
47 Section 8(3).
48 Section 8(3).
49 Section 8(10).
50 Section 10(3).
51 For example, see http://www.radionz.co.nz/news/national/251999/police-apologise-to-tuhoe-over-raids.

park lands for a multiple of reasons, incorporating both Western and Māori values. Section 4 of the Te Urewera Act reads:

> The purpose of this Act is to establish and preserve in perpetuity a legal identity and protected status for Te Urewera for its intrinsic worth, its distinctive natural and cultural values, the integrity of those values, and for its national importance, and in particular to –
>
> (a) strengthen and maintain the connection between Tūhoe and Te Urewera; and
> (b) preserve as far as possible the natural features and beauty of Te Urewera, the integrity of its indigenous ecological systems and biodiversity, and its historical and cultural heritage; and
> (c) provide for Te Urewera as a place for public use and enjoyment, for recreation, learning, and spiritual reflection, and as an inspiration for all.

Fourth, the Te Urewera Act will be of immense interest internationally for those aspects concerning ownership, management and purpose. Ownership is contested in many countries as several of the chapters in this book demonstrate. These countries may be interested in negotiating a legal personality solution or simply be inspired to devise their own significantly new legal solutions.

The Te Urewera Act is but just one example of how the imagination can be used to create a legislative solution that is acceptable to both the Crown and the Indigenous group. The Hon. Dr Nick Smith, New Zealand's Minister of Conservation (when the Act was passed) stated in 2014:[52] and back in 1998 (when the Ngāi Tahu Claims Settlement Act was enacted, which included the Aoraki/Mount Cook 7-day mechanism):

> It is surprising for me, as a Minister of Conservation in the 1990s who was involved under the leadership of the Rt Hon Jim Bolger – who is in the House – in the huge debate that occurred around the provisions of the Ngāi Tahu settlement in respect of conservation land, how far this country and this Parliament have come when we now get to this Tūhoe settlement in respect of the treasured Te Urewera National Park. If you had told me 15 years ago that Parliament would almost unanimously be able to agree to this bill, I would have said 'You're dreaming mate'. It has been a real journey for New Zealand, iwi [Māori tribes], and Parliament to get used to the idea that Māori are perfectly capable of conserving New Zealand treasures at least as well as Pākehā (European New Zealanders) and departments of State.

Work is now underway to make this new commitment real. The *Te Urewera National Park Management Plan*, approved by the Department of Conservation in 2003, remains in force as the current plan until the new Te Urewera Board creates and approves a new management plan. Progress is happening. In July 2014, the Crown and Ngai Tuhoe announced the appointment of the inaugural Te Urewera Board members. As Nick Smith emphasised with the creation of this new Board: 'This is a very experienced Board capable of moving

52 Hon. Dr Nick Smith, 'Tūhoe Claims Settlement Bill, Te Urewera Bill – Third Readings' (Parliamentary Debate, New Zealand Parliament, 23 July 2014), available online at http://www.parliament.nz/en-nz/pb/debates/debates/50HansD_20140726_00000128/t%C5%ABhoe-claims-settlement-bill-te-urewera-bill-%E2%80%94-third-readings. Note, Hon. Nick Smith was Minister of Conservation for two national governments, first from 16 December 1996 until 10 December 1999 and second from 22 January 2013 until 8 October 2014.

on from this difficult history and enabling Tūhoe and the Crown to work together on its future governance and management.'[53] This Te Urewera solution is a good example of how negotiation can create respectful solutions for caring for landscapes.

## Conclusion

This chapter has presented five reasons why the modern landscapes of national parks require attention. Generally, countries that initially adopted the Yellowstone national park model in the late 1800s are demonstrating some new awareness of the importance of these places for their Indigenous peoples. This is certainly true in Aotearoa New Zealand. Even radical legislative reform is possible as the Te Urewera example has illustrated. The Te Urewera Act of 2014 recognises these lands as the 'homeland'[54] of Tūhoe, but not exclusively. The Act recognises that other Māori tribes value this landscape along with all New Zealanders. It is prized now not just in terms of mono-cultural European New Zealand values, such as those connected with science and recreation, but also for its 'historical and cultural heritage . . . and spiritual reflection'.[55] The respect inherent within this statute has been a long time coming. Coupled with the new provision for its shared management, the Te Urewera negotiated agreement constitutes a modern-day model for a new more respectful approach to valuing and caring for landscapes.

## Bibliography


Belgrave, Michael, Kawharu, Merata & David Williams, eds. *Waitangi Revisited: Perspectives on the Treaty of Waitangi.* South Melbourne, Vic: Oxford University Press, 2005.

Beltran, Javier, ed. *Indigenous and Traditional Peoples and Protected Areas: Principles Guidelines and Case Studies.* ICUN World Commission on Protected Areas, Gland, Switzerland, 2000.

Brown-John, C. Lloyd. 'Canada's National Parks Policy: From Bureaucrats to Collaborative Managers'. Paper presented at the Canadian Political Science Association's Annual Conference, Toronto, June 2006.

Bruan, Bruce. *The Intemperate Rainforest: Nature, Culture and the Power on Canada's West Coast.* Minneapolis: University of Minnesota Press, 2002.

Charters, Claire & Roldofo Stavenhagen, eds. *Making the Declaration Work: The Significance of the Declaration on the Rights of Indigenous Peoples.* Copenhagen: International Work Group for Indigenous Affairs, 2009.

*Conservation Act 1987* (New Zealand).

Convention on Biological Diversity, www.cbd.int.

Cowan, James. *The Tongariro National Park, New Zealand: Its Topography, Geology, Alpine and Volcanic Features, History and Maori Folk-lore.* Wellington: Tongariro National Park Board, 1927.

Cronon, William. *Changes in the Land: Indians, Colonists, and the Ecology of New England.* New York: Hill and Wang, 1983.

*Crown Minerals Act 1991* (New Zealand).

Deur, Douglas & Nancy J. Turner. *Keeping It Living: Traditions of Plant Use and Cultivation on the Northwest Coast of North America.* Washington: University of Washington Press, 2005.

Durie, Mason. *Ngā Tai Matatū: Tides of Māori Endurance.* South Melbourne, Vic: Oxford University Press, 2005.


53 Joint media release from the office of the Minister for Treaty of Waitangi Negotiations and the office of the Minister for Conservation 'The Crown and Ngāi Tūhoe have announced the appointment of the inaugural members of Te Urewera Board', 24 July 2014, available online at http://www.doc.govt.nz/news/media-releases/2014/board-appointed-for-new-era-for-te-urewera/.

54 Section 3(5).

55 Section 3(8).

Kopas, Paul Sheldon. *Taking the Air: Ideas and Change in Canada's National Parks*. Vancouver: UBC Press, 2007.
Mappes, Harmony A. 'National Parks: For Use and "Enjoyment" or for "Preservation"? The Role of the National Park Service Management Policies in that Determination'. *Iowa Law Review* 92, no. 2 (February 2007): 601–636.
*National Parks Act 1980* (New Zealand).
New Zealand Department of Conservation. *Department of Conservation Annual Report for year ended 30 June 2005*. Wellington: Department of Conservation, 2005.
New Zealand Department of Conservation. *General Policy for National Parks*. Wellington, NZ: Department of Conservation for the New Zealand Conservation Authority, 2005.
New Zealand Department of Conservation. *Statement of Intent 2005–2008*. Department of Conservation. http://www.doc.govt.nz/Documents/about-doc/role/policies-and-plans/statement-of-intent/statement-of-intent-(2005–2008).pdf.
New Zealand Department of Conservation. *Department of Conservation Annual Report for year ended 30 June 2015*. Wellington: Department of Conservation, 2015.
*New Zealand Maori Council v Attorney-General* [1987] 1 NZLR 641 (CA).
Ngai Tahu Claims Settlement Act 1998 (New Zealand).
Orange, Claudia. *The Treaty of Waitangi* (2nd edn). Wellington: Bridget Williams Books, 2011.
Otago Daily Times. 'Mt Cook Set for Double Change of Ownership'. *Otago Daily Times* (14 July 2006), http://subs.nzherald.co.nz/topic/story.cfm?c_id=262&objectid=10391211.
Ruru, Jacinta. 'Treaty of Waitangi and National Parks in Aotearoa New Zealand'. Master's thesis, Dunedin: University of Otago, 2002.
Ruru, Jacinta. 'Indigenous Peoples' Ownership and Management of Mountains: The Aotearoa/New Zealand Experience'. *Indigenous L. J.* 3 (2004): 111–138.
Ruru, Jacinta (editor). 'In Good Faith'. Symposium Proceedings Marking the 20th Anniversary of the Lands Case. Wellington, NZ: New Zealand Law Foundation, 2008.
Ruru, Jacinta. 'Settling Indigenous Place: Reconciling Legal Fictions in Governing Canada and Aotearoa New Zealand's National Parks'. PhD diss., Victoria: University of Victoria, 2012.
Ruru, Jacinta. 'Future Management of Tongariro National Park – Te Kāhui Maunga: The National Park District Inquiry Report'. *Māori Law Review* (March 2013): 14–18.
Ruru, Jacinta. 'Rights to Water and Te Kāhui Maunga: The National Park District Inquiry Report'. *Māori Law Review* (April 2014): 15–19.
Sharples, Hon. Pita, Minister of Māori Affairs of NZ. 'Announcement of New Zealand's Support for the Declaration on the Rights of Indigenous Peoples'. Permanent Forum on Indigenous Issues, Ninth Session, 19 April 2010.
Shultis, John. 'Natural Environments, Wilderness and Protected Areas: An Analysis of Historical Attitudes and Utilisation, and their Expression in Contemporary New Zealand'. PhD diss., Dunedin: University of Otago, 1991.
Shultis, John. 'The Creation of National Parks and Equivalent Resources in Ontario and the Antipodes: A Comparative History and Its Contemporary Expression'. In *Changing Parks: The History, Future and Cultural Context of Parks and Heritage Landscapes*, eds. John S. March & Bruce W Hodgins. Toronto: Natural Heritage, 1998: 189–208.
*Te Urewera Act 2014* (New Zealand).
*Tongariro National Park Act 1894* (New Zealand).
Unger, Marina. 'The Role of Landscape Architects in Park Management, Planning and Design with Regard to Indigenous Peoples'. Master of Landscape Architecture thesis, University of Guelph, Guelph, Canada, 1997.
*United Nations Declaration of the Rights of Indigenous Peoples*.
Waitangi Tribunal. *Ngai Tahu Report. Volume Two*. Wai 27. Wellington: Waitangi Tribunal, 1991.
Waitangi Tribunal. *Ko Aotearoa Tenei: A Report into Claims Concerning New Zealand Law and Policy Affecting Māori Culture and Identity*. Wellington, NZ: Legislation Direct, 2011.
Waitangi Tribunal. *Te Kāhui Maunga: The National Park District Inquiry Report Wai 1130*. Wellington, NZ: Legislation Direct, 2013.

# 8 Engaging with uncertainty

## Shared governance in indigenous conservation landscapes

*Michael Adams*

### Introduction

Nature conservation reserves occur across the world, with a spectrum of tenures and management regimes. This chapter examines trajectories of shared governance in conservation between governments and indigenous peoples across two nations, as a contrast to equivalent approaches in contemporary Nordic nations. Australia has the second oldest national park in the world (Royal National Park established in 1879), and two unique World Heritage sites that are jointly managed with local indigenous people (Uluru-Kata Tjuta National Park and Kakadu National Park, both in northern Australia). Aboriginal people have lived in Australia for more than 50,000 years. India has a more recent formal protected area system, but also ancient practices of protecting significant landscapes, and very complex demographic and cultural patterns, including a large number of indigenous groups. Sweden has the oldest protected area system in Europe, as well as the Laponia World Heritage Area, cooperatively managed between the Swedish state and Sámi reindeer herding communities. Across these countries and globally, ideas of the conservation of nature and culture are extensively debated, and a wide range of different forms of conservation are practised.

What has been called the 'classic' model of national parks derived from the later part of the nineteenth century, with examples from the US, Australia and New Zealand. This is the Yellowstone model: government owned and managed, with people present as tourists or managers only. Since the 1970s, this model, while persisting in numerous jurisdictions, has been continuously challenged, with multiple new and different approaches being developed in different nations. A 'new conservation paradigm' has been identified since the late twentieth century. This term has included broad differences, ranging from increased indigenous involvement to increased private sector involvement (including privately owned protected areas) and a focus on significantly larger scales of conservation. The idea of what might constitute a conservation landscape has also broadened to include areas of multiple but compatible land uses. This dynamic policy and management environment interacts with the uncertainty created by changing social and environmental conditions, brought into increasingly sharper focus by discussions of global climate change and its effects.

At the Sixth World Parks Congress held in Sydney, Australia in 2014, there was strong participation by indigenous peoples, and much discussion of shared governance conservation regimes. The Congress resolutions stated:

> The customary territories, lands and marine areas of Indigenous Peoples and local communities embodying traditional lifestyles are among the Earth's most critical, biodiversity-rich land and seas, and constitute Earth's oldest conservation areas and

> living cultures . . . All protected areas established on the territories, lands or seascapes of Indigenous Peoples fully observe their rights and governance systems, and Indigenous Peoples are fully involved in their creation, designation and development.[1]

While this goal is clearly far from being realised in almost all jurisdictions, the 60-year history of the World Parks Congresses provides a snapshot of global conservation policy development, with the recognition of the need to include local peoples evident from the Third Congress in Bali, Indonesia in 1982, and the active participation of indigenous peoples strongly embedded by the Fifth Congress in Durban, South Africa in 2003. In Durban, indigenous activists confronted organisers with the history of indigenous communities being displaced by conservation, leading to progressive resolutions from global conservation organisations to address these issues.[2] While implementation of these resolutions has been unsuccessful or patchy in many nations the resolutions of the Sixth Congress are likely to influence continuing policy development, and provide a benchmark for future conservation actions.[3] In a parallel process, in 2008 the United Nations Declaration on the Rights of Indigenous Peoples was adopted by the UN General Assembly. The declaration is similarly not a legally binding instrument but has also established a new international aspirational standard.

Conversely, 2012 marked the fortieth anniversary of the World Heritage Convention, and there is still no formal process for indigenous communities to be represented in decisions about World Heritage listings. While there are several World Heritage sites that explicitly recognise indigenous cultural values, many World Heritage declarations continue to negatively impact indigenous peoples' rights and livelihoods. There are documented trends in decision-making by the World Heritage Committee which indicate that this situation is escalating. Simultaneously, there are processes attempting to establish much greater recognition and inclusion of indigenous rights in World Heritage planning and management (other chapters in this volume discuss this in detail).[4]

These differing global policy processes highlight the complex situation of conservation in landscapes that are the homelands for indigenous communities. Conservation concepts and politics continue to be contested. While some researchers argue for the demonstrated success of protected areas and the need for their expansion,[5] others assert the failure of protected areas to effectively halt or slow biodiversity loss.[6] Similarly, while there is a global commitment to having protected areas cover 17 per cent of the Earth, others have argued this is clearly insufficient and alternate, community-based, approaches are critical.[7]

Alternate conservation approaches can cover a wide range of models and practices. This chapter focuses on 'shared governance' regimes where national or provincial governments engage with local indigenous peoples in some form of partnership for the ownership and management of protected areas and World Heritage sites. These arrangements are variously described as 'co-management', 'joint-management' and 'shared governance' regimes.

1 IUCN, *A Strategy of Innovative Approaches*.
2 Paulson et al., 'Indigenous peoples' participation'.
3 Colchester et al., 'Conservation and indigenous people'.
4 Gilbert, 'Indigenous peoples' heritage'.
5 Watson et al., 'The performance and potential'.
6 Mora and Sale, 'Ongoing global biodiversity loss'.
7 Butchart et al., 'Shortfalls and solutions'.

They contrast with various types of 'community conserved areas', a concept that usually indicates some form of independent ownership and management regime where indigenous or other local peoples control the processes and the tenure. The two broad categories can also overlap. In this chapter I maintain a distinction between community conserved areas and the various forms of shared governance regimes, but use the terms joint-management, co-management and shared governance interchangeably.

This chapter explores examples of conservation governance in Australia and India, to reveal geographic and cultural influences on conservation, and how these might relate to forms of shared governance and Sámi customary rights in Sweden, explored by other authors in this book. Australia and India both have significant minority indigenous populations with long connections to homelands as well as to particular ecologies and species. They are both 'post-colonial' nations; Australia was a settler state with a British colonial history, with a dominant 'Anglo' settler population; India became an independent nation after British colonial rule with a diverse majority population. As independent states, both countries adopted the broad model of conservation promulgated by the American Yellowstone model. While Australia's first national park was established in 1879, the protected area system began to be formalised in 1967 with the passing of the NSW National Parks and Wildlife Act, explicitly based on the US model.[8] India's first modern national park was Hailey National Park (now Corbett NP), set up in 1938, with the 1972 Wildlife Protection Act beginning the systematic declaration and management of protected areas.[9] While India and Australia are very different in many respects, the policy history of the establishment and development of their protected area networks have common origins in both British colonial administrations and subsequent US models.

I have carried out research fieldwork in Australia, India and Sweden, and the material in this chapter is drawn from analysis of published research, policy documentation, and my own observations and discussions with both researchers and government conservation departments in each nation.

## Australia

Australia has a highly urbanised population of around 24 million, with almost 90 per cent living in mostly coastal urban centres. Currently Aboriginal people comprise only about 3 per cent of the total population and, on all socio-economic measures, have the worst indicators of any social group in the nation. Processes of colonial dispossession since 1770 have resulted in indigenous people continuing to be significantly socially disadvantaged. Aboriginal people and their supporters have worked to redress this disadvantage on multiple fronts, including restitution of homelands through land rights claims and native title processes. By 2015, the outcomes of those efforts have been significant, with 23 per cent of the land area of Australia now under forms of Aboriginal community tenure (see Figure 8.1).

These lands include areas with very significant cultural and natural values, many of which have been incorporated into the Australian national protected area system, as either Indigenous Protected Areas or jointly managed national parks. While Australia is often now seen as a global leader in conservation on indigenous-held land, it is notable that these

8 Worboys, Lockwood and de Lacy, *Protected Area Management*.
9 Saberwal and Rangarajan, *Battles Over Nature*.

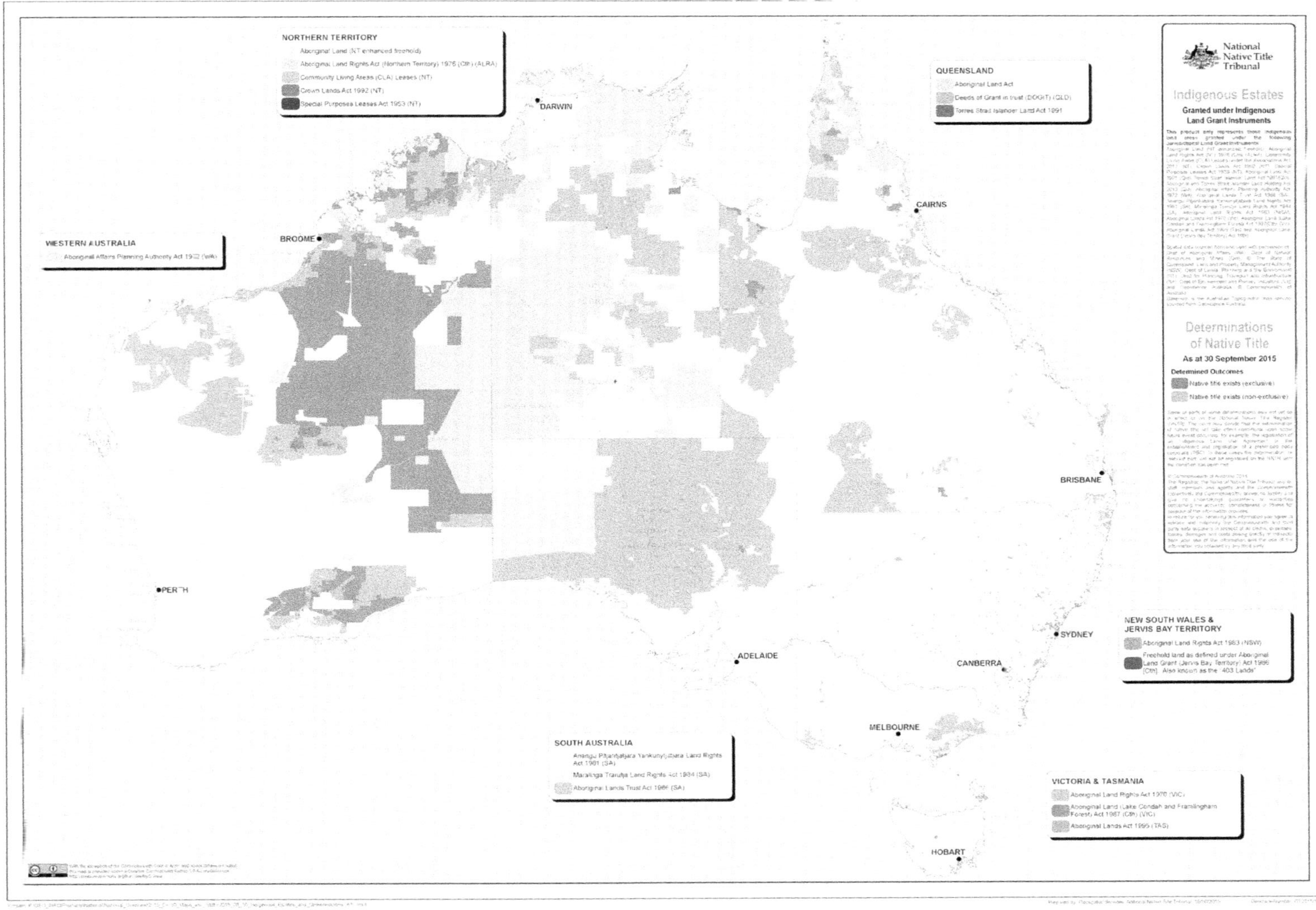


*Figure 8.1* Map of the indigenous estate in Australia in 2010, also showing discrete indigenous communities

Source: Altman, *Alternate Development for Indigenous Territories*

outcomes were very often achieved by Aboriginal protest and litigation, rather than progressive responses by the state.[10]

While 23 per cent is a large percentage of the continent, the distribution of these lands is very uneven, reflecting the residual lands hypothesis often used to describe national park systems – the lands returned to Aboriginal people are typically 'remote' areas few others want.[11] Additionally, a large proportion of the Aboriginal population has not benefitted from these returns, living now in urban or rural areas with little opportunity for successful land claims.

Australia has a robust and extensive conservation reserve system. However, it also has the worst record in the world for modern species extinctions, with 30 endemic land mammal species becoming extinct since British colonisation in 1788 – this is more than one-third of modern global mammal extinctions, and the trajectory is continuing. While the causes of these extinctions remain open to debate, recent analysis suggests 'they largely result from the rapid continental-scale replacement of a purposeful and long-established indigenous land management regime by a substantially more exploitative and transformative set of land management practices and a medley of introduced species' since colonisation.[12]

Changes in protected area management have also included a significant increase in private protected areas.[13] These reserves, often co-funded by government, are included within the National Reserve System, but are independently managed, with no requirement to engage with local Aboriginal people. There is evidence that some private reserve systems have reinforced the displacement of Aboriginal people or blocked access to traditional homelands.[14]

## *Indigenous protected areas*

The Indigenous Protected Areas (IPA) concept was developed in the 1990s in response to the recognition that these extensive indigenous lands held much biodiversity conservation value.[15] The programme allows indigenous landholders to voluntarily agree to manage their lands for conservation, usually in exchange for some level of financial input from the Australian government. Since the first was set up in 1998, IPAs have become a very significant contributor to conservation, comprising 36 per cent of the total national protected area system by 2016, with several additional IPAs in the planning stages (see Figure 8.2). A unique aspect of IPAs is that the type of conservation management carried out is under the control of the indigenous owners, rather than state conservation bureaucracies.

While IPAs have continued to be established across Aboriginal lands, they have also evolved in concept. Several recent additions have used a tenure-blind approach, where a complex array of partner organisations collaborate to manage landscapes. This has been called 'country-based conservation', in recognition of the deep meaning of the Aboriginal English term 'country':

> Country in Aboriginal English is not only a common noun but also a proper noun. People talk about country in the same way that they would talk about a person: they speak to country, sing to country, visit country, worry about country, feel sorry for

10 E.g. Farrier and Adams, 'Indigenous-government co-management'.
11 Joppa and Pfaff, 'High and far'.
12 Woinarski, Burbidge and Harrison, 'Ongoing unravelling'.
13 Fitzsimmons, 'Private protected areas'.
14 Moorcroft and Adams, 'Emerging geographies'.
15 Smyth and Sutherland, *Indigenous Protected Areas*.

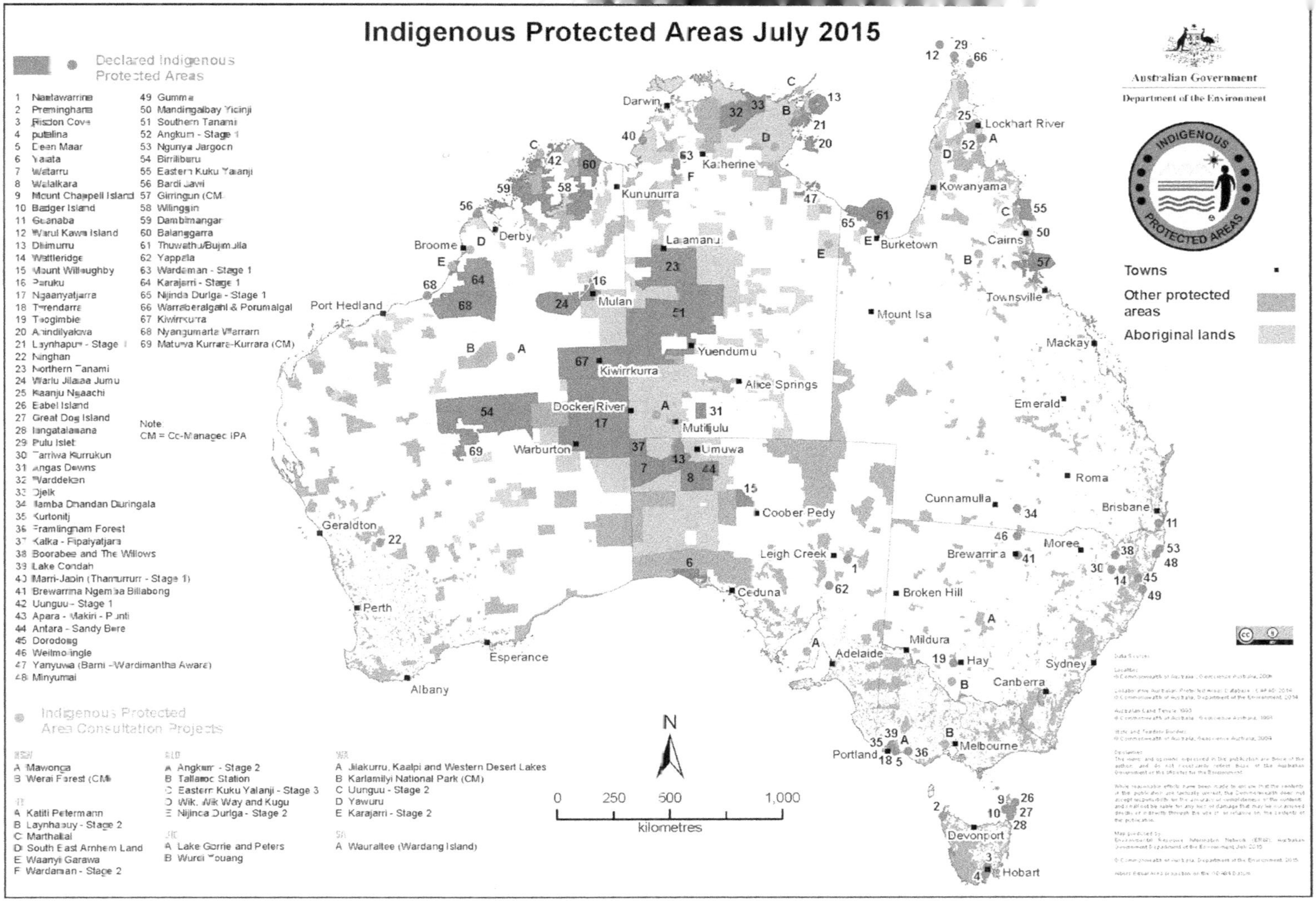


*Figure 8.2* Map of Indigenous Protected Areas

Source: http://www.environment.gov.au/indigenous/ipa/map.html; http://laptop.deh.gov.au/indigenous/ipa/pubs/ipa-map-july2015.pdf

country, and long for country. People say that country knows, hears, smells, takes notice, takes care, is sorry or happy. Country is not a generalised or undifferentiated type of place, such as one might indicate with terms like 'spending a day in the country' or 'going up the country'. Rather, country is a living entity with a yesterday, today and tomorrow, with a consciousness, and a will toward life.[16]

These multi-tenure IPAs are innovative and distinctive, incorporating ideas of landscape-scale connectivity conservation recognising the depth and extent of Aboriginal cultural values in these ecosystems. As the quote above indicates, for Aboriginal people, 'nature' is cultural.

Within a co-management IPA arrangement, local Aboriginal people are responsible for negotiating and coordinating partnerships and securing funding as well as sharing resources and management responsibility. Partnerships are typically 'whole of government' involving local, state and federal agencies and funding sources. Additionally, partners can include non-government organisations and private landholders, determined by the interests and strategic vision of the local Aboriginal people. With the declaration of multi-tenure IPAs the number and diversity of co-management partners involved in protected area management has increased significantly. With increases in the number of actors involved, comes increased potential to produce outcomes that are greater than those that can be delivered by individual efforts alone. In these situations the strengths and weakness of each can be considered complementary. These arrangements have also undoubtedly increased the complexity of protected area governance, and are very challenging to negotiate and implement.[17]

## *Joint management: Uluru-Kata Tjuta*

Uluru-Kata Tjuta National Park has been jointly managed between local Anangu Aboriginal people and Parks Australia, the federal environment bureaucracy, since 1985, and appeared twice on the World Heritage List, first for outstanding 'natural' values in 1987, and then, following criticisms that led to revisions to UNESCO's cultural heritage criteria, for outstanding indigenous cultural landscape values in 1994.[18] Values recognised include:

(that the area is) one of the relatively few places in Australia where landscapes are actively managed by Aboriginal communities on a substantial scale using traditional practices and knowledge that include:

- particular types of social organisation, ceremonies and rituals which form an adaptation to the fragile and unpredictable ecosystems of the arid landscape;
- detailed systems of ecological knowledge that closely parallel, yet differ from, the Western scientific classification;
- management techniques to conserve biodiversity such as the use of fire and the creation and maintenance of water sources such as wells and rockholes.[19]

The recognition of these values acknowledges both ancient Aboriginal occupation and the continuity of their landscape practices into the present. This creates a very strong obligation

16 Rose, *Nourishing Terrains.*
17 Bauman, Haynes and Lauder, *Pathways to the Co-management.*
18 See Adams, *Pukulpa pitjama* for more detail on Uluru-Kata Tjuta.
19 Director of National Parks, *Fifth Uluru-Kata Tjuta*, 150.

on the Australian government to support Anangu customary practice. In addition, the legislative framework for joint management should ensure the primacy of indigenous belief and practice at Uluru-Kata Tjuta. The Anangu Traditional Owners hold inalienable freehold title, but the land is leased back to the Australian government to be managed as a national park. A board of management is responsible for making decisions relating to park management, including preparation of plans of management, and a majority (eight out of 12) of board members must be Anangu.

However, despite the wording of the World Heritage listings, and the legislative obligations of joint-management, there are embedded and ongoing tensions between Western scientific and bureaucratic processes and assumptions, and Anangu society and beliefs. These tensions are expressed in conflicts over the detail of management and policy practices, including fire management, a tourism focus on climbing the monolith of Uluru itself, and Aboriginal employment.

In many Australian Aboriginal landscapes, the use of fire is a central landscape practice. Traditional burning of the Uluru area ceased when the Anangu were forcibly displaced in the 1930s, resulting in large and uncontrolled wildfires in the following decades. The Anangu were able to resume customary burning after regaining title to the land in 1985. Its reintroduction has increased protection from wildfire and there is significant scientific literature demonstrating the positive biodiversity outcomes of northern Australian Aboriginal fire regimes.[20] Anangu fire knowledge is held by particular elders and transmitted orally and experientially to younger people over time. The current management plan states that 'fire management is integral . . . and there are expectations that skills and knowledge will be passed through generations of Anangu and practised in day-to-day management'.[21]

While regular burning has been a feature of park management for some time, the level of Anangu control over and involvement in burning has fluctuated. With expanding bureaucratic regulation of activities in the park, the Anangu face a number of challenges to the level of their involvement. These regulations, for example, exclude the involvement of children. To continue the traditional teaching of grandchildren, the Anangu are having to go off-park, into the surrounding Aboriginal-owned lands, to burn in ways which are culturally appropriate and under their control. There are also quite tight prescriptions, identified from a Western perspective, on when and how burning can be carried out, which are not necessarily reflective of Anangu cultural tradition or knowledge. Anangu decision-making processes do not always mesh well with increasingly regulative planning processes, and limits on the resources available within the organisational structure restrict both the range and number of burns planned. Less flexibility or fewer resources available within the organisational structure to involve and incorporate the Anangu in the adaptive planning and conduct of burning means there is less Anangu involvement in the park's fire management programme. One of the Anangu strengths is the ability to make and adapt fire plans in response to changing environmental circumstances throughout the year.

Many tourists visit Uluru specifically to climb the monolith. The route used by tourists in climbing the rock has great cultural significance to the Anangu, who have long been very opposed to the climb. The inappropriateness of the climb has been formally acknowledged since at least 1991 and discussed in consecutive management plans.[22] The climb has

20 Woinarski, Burbridge and de Lacy, 'Ongoing unravelling'; Gammage, *Biggest Estate*.
21 Director of National Parks, *Fifth Uluru-Kata Tjuta*.
22 Director of National Parks, *Third, Fourth, Fifth Uluru-Kata Tjuta*.

nevertheless continued to be available to tourists through the strong lobbying activities of the tourist industry. Research has started to identify what particular segment of visitors choose to climb, and to investigate how the creation of alternatives may reduce the interest of visitors in the climb. The centrality of Uluru as an Australian icon has also been extensively analysed by researchers, included its contested 'ownership'.[23] The 5th Management Plan (2010–2020) is significant as it identifies for the first time the permanent closure of the climb as an objective and sets out conditions to enable this closure. These include minimising impacts on the tourism industry. While the existence of the climb has clearly been contrary to Anangu wishes for several decades, and the Anangu have expressed disappointment that the climb continues, the explicit objective of permanent closure is a very positive step. However, the wording of the criteria to be met for closure continues to create uncertainty. The move towards closure of the climb will, however, also support the aspirations of some Anangu to develop new, alternate tourism experiences.

Negotiating the relationship between a Western work culture and indigenous cultural frameworks is one of the many challenges at Uluru Kata Tjuta National Park, and there is an ongoing spectrum of approaches to this. There are essentially three sources of employment for Anangu at Uluru Kata Tjuta: the park itself, the tourism industry (including indigenous-owned enterprises), and indigenous organisations and enterprises.

Since the late 1990s, changes in the legislation governing Australian public service activities, including employment and procurement, have increasingly proscribed local, adaptive responses. Employment must be 'merit-based' and there are requirements concerning English language literacy proficiency. As many Anangu are fluent in several indigenous languages before English, and older Anangu are often not literate in English, this creates clear barriers to their employment. The occupational health and safety requirements discussed earlier are standard government regulations, but clearly have the potential to impact on the practice and teaching of culture in a number of ways. A recent IUCN analysis of Booderee National Park, another government administered joint-managed park in south east Australia, also indicates the impact these regulatory and competitive environments have.[24]

Increasing centralisation of administrative control and regulation into state structures reduces flexibility and innovation at Uluru Kata Tjuta itself, a situation recognised by the current management. The park and World Heritage Area are now beginning to transition to a new generation of Anangu Traditional Owners, with only a few of the Anangu involved in the World Heritage nomination remaining alive. This new generation have indicated growing dissatisfaction with government structures and ways of operating, prompting recent and ongoing discussions around 'rethinking management' that might lead to new approaches.[25]

Since 1984 the sole provider of accommodation for visitors to the park has been 'Ayers Rock Resort', located outside and adjacent to the national park. There has been little Aboriginal representation amongst the resort's nearly 600 employees until recently, with only two Aboriginal employees in 2010. However, in 2011 the resort and its company, Voyages, was purchased by the Indigenous Land Corporation,[26] with an ambitious plan to

23 For example Hill, *The Rock*; James, 'Constructing the climb'; Hueneke and Baker, 'Tourist behaviour'; Robinson, Baker and Liddle, 'Journeys through'; Waitt, Figueroa and McGee, 'Fissures in the rock'.

24 Farrier and Adams, 'Indigenous-government co-management'.

25 Director of Parks Australia, 'Kakadu and Uluru-Kata Tjuta'.

26 The Indigenous Land Corporation is a statutory authority established in 1995 with the purpose of assisting indigenous people with land acquisition and land management to achieve economic, environmental, social and cultural benefits. See http://www.ilc.gov.au/.

create an indigenous tourism training academy integrated with the resort.[27] By 2015, more than 200 Aboriginal people, including 60 trainees, had been employed and it is planned to create 350 hospitality jobs for indigenous workers at Uluru and elsewhere in Australia. This is clearly a major development, and while many of the proposed positions will be for Aboriginal people from other parts of Australia, there is likely to be significant benefits for Anangu both in direct employment and training and in increasing the acceptance of indigenous tourism workers in the region.

After 30 years of joint management, it is clear that successes and challenges continue. While there are fluctuating numbers of Anangu staff within the park, there has never been an Anangu park manager and the Anangu continue to be very poorly represented in the local tourism industry. The monolith of Uluru itself is an internationally recognised symbol of Australia and aboriginality but its recognition as a site of sacred significance has been compromised by the continuing presence of the climb. While the Anangu have had a majority of members on the board of management since handback, this clearly does not mean that the Anangu are in control. Powerful external influences such as the tourism industry, and powerful internal influences such as Australian government policies and processes, exert significant pressure. The Anangu have often accommodated these pressures rather than create disharmony and conflict by challenging how they affect their cultural practices.

The values underpinning Western and Anangu societies differ in many fundamental respects that are evident in on-the-ground management activities. Institutional change in Australian society and government, reflected in a greater concern with the regulation of risk management and increasing economic and bureaucratic efficiency, can interact negatively with Anangu cultural tradition. While at least some of these impacts are well outside the control of park management agencies and the Anangu, this incommensurability is reflected in joint management tensions at World Heritage sites and other protected areas across Australia and, while often acknowledged, they remain unresolved.

World Heritage designation at Uluru-Kata Tjuta National Park is a point of pride for the Anangu people: their cultural traditions are acknowledged as being internationally significant, and Anangu customary practice is explicitly recognised as the appropriate way to care for this country. A central challenge for the future is whether Western science and management can facilitate, or even allow, a process that supports the meaningful practice of Anangu traditions of caring for country and the passing on of this knowledge and skill to subsequent generations.

Australia has sometimes been considered a global leader in shared governance arrangements with indigenous peoples in conservation. While this acknowledgement may be deserved in some respects, it is also clear that many of the gains by Aboriginal people have been driven by protest and litigation, rather than by benevolent responses from the state. Shared governance regimes are very diverse, reflecting the diversity of both Aboriginal communities and environmental and tenure contexts, and they are all effectively in a situation of continual negotiation. In some places they are sites for continued political struggle, while in others there are very positive outcomes for local aboriginal people as well as for the conservation of natural and cultural heritage. It will be important to monitor how the recent and rapid increase in private protected areas interacts with indigenous social and environmental justice issues.

27 See http://www.voyages.com.au/corporate/. Voyages was purchased by the Indigenous Land Corporation on behalf of Wana Ungkunytja which represents the business interests of the nearby communities of Mutijulu, Imanpa and Docker River.

## India

India is the world's second most populous country, with 1.25 billion people. It comprises 2.4 per cent of the world's land area, but houses 17 per cent of the world's human population, 8 per cent of the world's mammals and 12 per cent of the world's birds. It is considered one of the global biologically 'megadiverse' countries.[28] In contrast to Australia's highly urban population, India's population is more than 70 per cent rural, with significant numbers living close to and often dependent on forested areas. Indigenous communities, termed Adivasi in India and totalling around 70 million people, comprise around 8% of the population.[29]

Despite a rich and ancient local conservation tradition, since independence in 1947 India has developed a Yellowstone-style national park system, although with significant numbers of people living within many declared protected areas, and ongoing controversy about conservation displacements and human–wildlife conflict. This conservation regime has its roots in the policies of the British colonial administration. Prior to the colonial period, Mughal rulers largely respected local customs and rights, but the British regime was radically different. New forest laws disenfranchised local peoples and reserved forests and their products to the state. These exclusionary laws were based on assumptions that local people's practices included unrestrained, indiscriminate overuse of forests. This logic became the foundation for post-independence conservation: the sense that environments need to be protected from the human communities that live around and within them.[30] As India modernised, these beliefs have continued to justify appropriation of tribal lands and rights to resources in the name of the national interest.[31]

India is also home to many species of large, charismatic mammals: tigers, Asiatic lions, leopards, snow leopards, wolves, several bear species, the Indian rhinoceros and Asian elephants all occupy habitats in India. Again in contrast to Australia, India has had very few extinctions in modern times, the Asian cheetah in 1947 the most notable. This conjunction of one of the world's most populous nations and rich and widespread biodiversity persisting, often in close proximity to human activity, is indicative of particular cultural relationships between humans and animals and plants.

### *Conservation inside protected areas*

Despite the persistence of many species across India's landscapes, most conservation efforts in the last 50 years have focused on national parks and other forms of protected area. The Wildlife Protection Act, passed in 1972, created a process for systematic establishment of national parks, and also banned hunting of almost all species. More than 660 protected areas now cover about 5 per cent of India's land area, with proposals for further expansion.[32] While the expansion of this model of national parks continues, both the effectiveness of these declared protected areas and the usefulness of the concept in India are increasingly questioned. The exclusionary Yellowstone approach had its origin in low-population developed world contexts, and in the different ecological and socio-economic situations of the developing world it may be 'unfit and undesirable'.[33]

28 Chape, Spalding and Jenkins, *World's Protected Areas*.
29 Pathak Broome and Dash, *Recognition and Support*.
30 Saberwal, Rangarajan and Kothari, *People, Parks, Wildlife*.
31 Sharma, *Green and Saffron*.
32 Wildlife Institute of India, *Protected Areas of India*.
33 Rastogi et al., 'Saving the superstar'.

There is a growing literature on 'conservation displacements' of local and indigenous peoples from declared conservation reserves, and India has a particularly negative history regarding conservation refugees, with estimates ranging from 100,000 to 600,000 local people summarily moved to make way for national parks.[34] While there are undoubtedly some successful relocations, there is significant evidence of negative outcomes for both people and biodiversity stemming this approach. In some circumstances, displaced and disenfranchised people have reacted in anger in ways that have impacted on the very values their removal was meant to protect.[35]

Many conservation displacements have been in the name of charismatic species, particularly tigers, the official national animal of India. Tiger researchers have historically argued that tigers and humans cannot coexist, and tigers require large 'inviolate' protected areas for effective conservation. Recent research challenges these assumptions, demonstrating that tigers disperse 'across a highly fragmented and human-dominated landscape',[36] and that 'tigers and people frequently co-occurred at fine scales both inside and outside the park'.[37]

### *Western Ghats World Heritage Area*

The Western Ghats World Heritage (see Figure 8.3) listing provides an illuminating case study of the intersection of global, state and local processes and rights. The Western Ghats is a mountain chain stretching 1,600 km along the western coast of India, with very significant biodiversity values, and is the homeland of numerous Adivasi and other local people. The World Heritage listing includes 39 separate sites in seven clusters, comprising a total of over 800,000 hectares.

In the process leading up to the listing, the international conservation organisation, IUCN, twice (2011 and 2012) assessed the Indian government's proposal. In each of these formal assessments, IUCN recommended that the World Heritage Committee 'defer' listing the sites, for several reasons, including the need for 'increased engagement to ensure the views of all stakeholders, including local indigenous groups are considered, in order to ensure and demonstrate broad-based support for the nomination'.[38] IUCN, as the official assessor, was aware that indigenous and other local groups were protesting against the listing as it was likely to further impact on their already compromised rights in the region. Indigenous groups had taken their concerns to the UN Permanent Forum on Indigenous Issues, stating that the proposal did not recognise their cultural values within the nominated sites, and had not obtained their free, prior and informed consent.

However, at its meeting in St Petersburg in 2012, the World Heritage Committee, after intensive lobbying from the Indian representatives making the proposal, agreed to list the 39 sites as a World Heritage Area, effectively ignoring the advice of their own nominated expert assessor, and demonstrating that they would not engage with the 100,000 Adivasi people whose homelands are part of the listing. The period between the first Indian assessments of the proposed site in 2002 and the listing in 2012 coincided with development, debate and final passing of the Indian Forest Rights Act 2008. This Act, driven by Adivasi protest, recognised that 'forest rights on ancestral lands and their habitat were not

34 Dowie, *Conservation Refugees.*
35 Mohindra and Wangchuk, 'Community-based conservation'
36 Joshi et al., 'Connectivity of tiger populations'.
37 Carter et al., 'Coexistence between wildlife' (discussing Chitwan National Park)
38 IUCN *Evaluations of Nominations.*

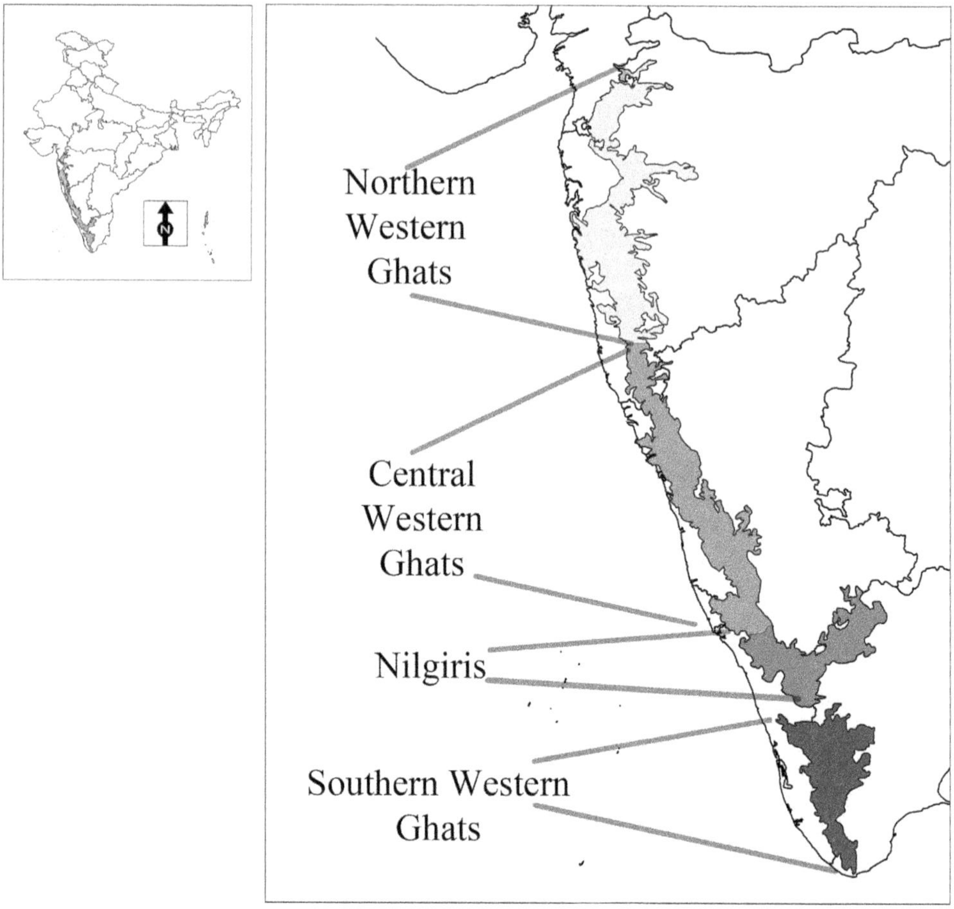


*Figure 8.3* The Western Ghats World Heritage Area

Source: ZA Mirza, RV Sanap, H Bhosale (2014) Preliminary Review of Indian Eumenophorinae (Araneae: Theraphosidae) with Description of a New Genus and Five New Species from the Western Ghats. PLoS ONE 9(2): e87928. doi:10.1371/journal.pone.0087928. UNESCO, http://whc.unesco.org/en/list/1342

adequately recognised in the consolidation of state forests during the colonial period as well as in independent India resulting in historical injustice to the forest dwelling Scheduled Tribes and other traditional forest dwellers who are integral to the very survival and sustainability of the forest ecosystem'.[39] While the Act was a very explicit move to acknowledge prior injustice and establish a new regime of participation and recognition of rights, the World Heritage submissions made no mention at all of the Forest Rights Act.

The decision to list the Western Ghats as a World Heritage Area indicates that the World Heritage Committee 'neither upheld the principles of the UN Declaration on the Rights of Indigenous Peoples nor Indian laws but instead provided prestige and legitimacy to

39 Preamble to Forest Rights Act, quoted in Bijoy, 'Western Ghats'.

something that is patently illegal and unjust with regards to indigenous peoples'.[40] National prestige and global processes combined to dismiss and override local rights.

Sharma provides the background to this outcome: he analyses the relationships between Indian nationalism, politics and environment since independence in 1947. He argues that a 'grand national nature project' was created that overrides local interests: 'in the past, the tribal [sic] was expected to give up his land and forests so that iron mines, steel plants and large dams could be built for the nation . . . this mission was now joined by projects of nature conservation, and in both the interests of the nation were elevated above those of the tribal [sic]'.[41]

### *Conservation outside protected areas*

While formal protected areas are the policy cornerstone of conservation in India, the continuity of cultural traditions is reflected in the large number and extent of 'community conserved areas' in India. Sacred groves and landscapes are found throughout India, serving both to protect specific species and biodiversity assemblages, and providing a source of psychological, religious, cultural and economic benefits to local people. These are widely variable in extent, history, and the management rules and systems that protect them. There is both a continuity of ancient systems, and implementation of entirely new places and processes in response to perceived threats, often still building on community and cultural traditions. These sites have been estimated to number over 100,000, and to cover up to 10 per cent of some regions.[42]

The Wildlife Protection Act (1972) was amended in 2002 to allow for the establishment of 'community reserves' to be managed by local communities, with India's first Marine Conservation Reserve declared in Lakshadweep in 2005, after more than 400 public meetings.[43] The amendment indicates acknowledgement of the importance of these cultural traditions, creating a structure for the formalising of such relationships into law and policy. Shahabuddin however cautions that, if they are not sensitively managed, such processes can work against existing community practices by transferring community control to bureaucratic structures.[44]

In addition to a focus on specific places in the landscape, India has unique cultural traditions of tolerance and reverence for many species, including those that are large and dangerous. India's complex array of religious and cultural beliefs includes the deification and reverence of many wildlife species, with both localised traditions and large religious institutions formalising the protection of particular species. Increasingly, researchers are analysing how these social and cultural traditions influence people's attitudes to the presence and sometimes impact of wild species.[45]

Recent analysis of existing research on Indian big cats (tigers, leopards, snow leopards and Asiatic lions), provocatively entitled 'An ontological crisis?' concluded that the bulk of this research has ignored human wildlife interactions; has taken place almost exclusively within protected areas; and perpetuates the idea that big cats can only thrive in 'pure,

40 Bijoy, 'Western Ghats'.
41 Sharma, *Green and Saffron*, 250.
42 Pathak Broome and Dash, *Recognition and Support*.
43 Shahbuddin, *Conservation at Crossroads*.
44 ibid.
45 E.g. Athreya et al., 'Big cats in our backyard'.

inviolate spaces', despite increasing evidence to the contrary. The authors argue that the biases and gaps in this body of research contribute to 'the erosion of shared histories of relations between humans and large felids', and also by extension, many other species.[46] Athreya et al. demonstrated the ability of several large carnivore species to live in close proximity to dense human settlements and agricultural landscapes with no conflict, even though those carnivores preyed on livestock and domestic dogs. They argue that 'a much greater area of potential "tolerance habitat" is available outside protected areas, and potentially a far greater degree of connectivity between protected areas than generally expected'. Their research integrated ecological and cultural investigations to understand the human–wildlife dynamics of the region.[47]

The trajectory of conservation in India in the last 50 years has consistently ignored cultural traditions and local practices to follow instead a modern science-derived rationalist model that opposes these practices rather than using them to reinforce conservation efforts. The researchers and conservationists described above are arguing that India could be at a point of paradigm shift in conservation philosophy, recognising the strengths of both ancient cultural traditions and the importance of embracing social science research in conservation practice. This contested political and conceptual landscape has now been identified for more than a decade and a vigorous debate continues.[48] Shahabuddin argues for a new paradigm in Indian conservation that is based on equity principles, and suggests that India is on the cusp of change: 'recent effective conservation has been founded on partnerships among different interest groups that find common cause'.[49] However, since the election of the Modi administration in India in 2014 the trumping of environmental interests by national interests has intensified, with recent media headlines declaiming 'Narendra Modi's war on the environment' describing processes to undo policies of fair land acquisition, reverse the fight for tribal rights and undo environmental protection legislation. Modi's party, the Bharatiya Janata Party (BJP), has been described as having a 'radical anti-environment agenda'.[50]

## Strategies and outcomes

The Australian and Indian case studies indicate a suite of strategies and outcomes that have varying levels of success. The increasing recognition of indigenous and local rights in conservation landscapes in global policy forums is not always reflected in national policies and management outcomes. Even as Australia hosted the 2014 World Parks Congress, foregrounding indigenous involvement in conservation, tensions continued to unfold across the shared governance regimes in national parks and World Heritage sites.

Drawn-out but eventually successful legal cases have returned lands and rights to some Australian indigenous communities, creating shifts in power that allow those communities to negotiate shared governance conservation regimes. In many cases, however, the ongoing realities of management in those sites are contested and difficult, with unequal resources disadvantaging indigenous communities. One element that is clear is that shared governance regimes are emergent, unpredictable and fluid, with a clear need for commitment in the long term to enable equity for the indigenous partners.

46 Ghosal et al., 'An ontological crisis'.
47 Athreya et al., 'Big cats in our backyard'.
48 E.g. Rangarajan, 'Politics of ecology' in Saberwal and Rangarajan, *Battles Over Nature*.
49 Shahabuddin, *Conservation at Crossroads*, 205.
50 Mohan, 'Narendra Modi'; Dorschner, 'India needs environmental opposition'.

For India, while Rai and Bawa argue that it is 'time to rethink, revise and reject the modern idea that people and wildlife have to be isolated and managed separately, scientifically, and by expert knowledge alone', the on-the-ground management realities mostly ignore this.[51] What is promising is a continuing groundswell not just from tribal communities asserting their rights, but from conservation researchers and activists promoting community-based conservation and the critical significance of indigenous knowledge traditions in ensuring successful conservation outcomes.

Each nation has a different pattern of outcomes. In both, indigenous protest and litigation is significant. In Australia, legal recognition of indigenous rights to land has had important tenure outcomes, and Australia as a nation has been keen to claim credit for innovative approaches to shared conservation governance. The actual daily outcomes for the indigenous communities in those relationships however can vary considerably, with communities constrained to continue resistance and protest to maintain rights guaranteed in law. In India, there is a long history of management outcomes failing to meet legislative requirements, so rights for Adivasi peoples have consistently been ignored. International policy processes, whether via the World Parks Congress or World Heritage organisations, are not consistently successful in influencing outcomes. Both Australia and India have resisted international pressure over indigenous rights and also conservation outcomes for World Heritage sites. In India the listing of the Western Ghats despite expert recommendation not to do so, and in Australia the threat to list both Kakadu and the Great Barrier Reef World Heritage sites as 'world heritage in danger' indicate the intransigence of national governments in the face of international pressure.

## Conservation, geography and culture

Despite their shared British colonial histories, a key difference between India and Australia is that, as a settler regime, Australia initially largely displaced indigenous peoples from their country in order to take control of tenure and production. In India the British regime focused on maximising exploitation of the colonised landscape's resources – India became a supplier of cheap raw materials. These histories result in varying patterns of cultural relationships to land and biodiversity, and different policy frameworks responding to these.

Australia now has 23 per cent of its land area under some form of indigenous control – on those lands, depending on significant resource constraints, indigenous communities have high levels of control over conservation management, and in many cases have voluntarily entered into partnerships with governments and others to implement it. On other tenures, indigenous people usually have very little control, either of ecosystem or species management.

India has a unique tradition of diverse religious respect, translated in this case into on going relationships with ecosystems and particular species. Little land is under indigenous control, and negotiations continue over implementing access rights under both the Wildlife Protection Act and the Forest Rights Act. Cultural relationships with animals have, however, facilitated conservation through 'tolerance habitat' on non-conservation tenures – a very significant outcome in conservation terms but little acknowledged in formal policy.

On the largest scale, Australia, Sweden and India demonstrate global inequities: the extravagance and high living standards of the developed world is built on the depletion

51 Rai and Bawa, 'Inserting politics', 427.

and disadvantage of other peoples and places. On the national scale, each country also demonstrates social and spatial inequities, where certain cultural groups in particular places are marginalised and disempowered. In Australia, the maps (Figures 8.1 and 8.2) indicate that shared conservation governance regimes are disproportionately found in 'remote' locations: this is a result of a combination of factors. These are the primary regions for return of indigenous lands (in these remote areas no-one else competes for these tenures); and indigenous populations predominate in these regions, although there are also significant urban and rural indigenous populations. India's intense cultural and environmental diversity mean that the patterns are spatially less obvious: Indigenous populations are disadvantaged almost everywhere, although there continue to be correlations between high biodiversity and high cultural diversity. As in Australia, recognition and rights for Sámi in Sweden are concentrated in the north, remote from major population centres, and coinciding with a concentration of national parks.

Politically, India is an emerging power, the third largest economy in the world, although with wide socio-economic disparities and continuing extreme poverty. Australia and Sweden, while small economically and in population terms, are established developed nations with high living standards, although indigenous people in Australia continue to have low socio-economic status. Both Australia and India are subject to political and policy shifts depending on the nature of individual governments. The dominance of the Congress Party in India since independence gave conservation and the environment some prominence, building in part on the ideas of Mahatma Gandhi but transitioning into modernist rational conservation approaches. The rise of the BJP in the current government seems likely to change this significantly, and prioritise development and modernisation at the expense of both tribal communities and conservation. Successive recent conservative governments in Australia have reversed conservation measures, so Australia 'is no longer an enlightened model for protected areas. . .the Great Barrier Reef, a World Heritage site, is suffering from overfishing and the construction of three new harbours for exporting coal, a major contributor to climate change'.[52]

The histories of conservation and indigenous peoples' rights in Australia and India, while from two very different nations, nevertheless reflect continuities of colonial attitudes in both places. Australia has had better outcomes in recognising rights to indigenous lands, but only in remote, residual landscapes not wanted by others. As the situation at Uluru Kata Tjuta National Park indicates, even where there are strong institutional structures for recognising and respecting rights, outcomes for Aboriginal people can be unsuccessful. Since independence India has had a history of successively legislating to protect the rights of Adivasi people in forests, but a parallel history of failing to implement that legislation, resulting in ongoing dispossession and injustice. In both countries, the cultural traditions of those indigenous peoples have the potential to creatively and positively inform current conservation practice. While this is increasingly recognised in emerging research, both bureaucratic structures and the philosophies of modern environmental movements combine to discount the relevance of these knowledge traditions.

## Conclusions

There are of course very significant differences between Australia, India and Sweden, in history, geography, culture and economics. But as both conservation and minority social

52 McNeely, 'A political future'.

justices issues have become global phenomena, analysing comparative international experience can provide valuable lessons and resources. All three countries have colonial histories of injustice towards indigenous peoples, where this injustice has been used to benefit the majority state. India is a relatively young modern nation with huge complexities in culture, geography and economic development, but also with very significant ancient and continuing cultural resources well suited to engaging with contemporary conservation challenges. Between Sweden and Australia the levels of current disadvantage for indigenous peoples are very different, but in both nations the ongoing presence of colonial attitudes continues to affect those communities. In Australia there have been some clear outcomes for Aboriginal people over the last three decades, and these have increasingly interacted with conservation outcomes. In Sweden, the Sámi do not suffer significant socio-economic disadvantage, but are increasingly dispossessed of traditional homelands. The Laponia experience may be the beginning of a positive new approach to collaborative and shared approaches to governance and knowledge-sharing in conservation landscapes.

Emerging trends in global conservation, including the 'new conservation paradigm' with all its diversity, offer opportunities to consider the advantages of complementary approaches to knowledge. The rationalist approaches favoured by state conservation regimes provide a particular suite of useful knowledge resources, often on large national scales. The cultural relationships between indigenous peoples and their homelands could provide a complementary set of resources, deeply embedded in long time frames and on local to regional scales. Each of these traditions has strengths and limitations that could be usefully analysed to expand the toolkit available for creative responses to impending and potentially very challenging environmental changes. Engaging these different cultures demands respect and acknowledgement of both difference and historic disadvantage.

## Bibliography


Adams, M. '*Pukulpa pitjama* Anangu*ku ngurakutu* – Welcome to Anangu Land: World Heritage at Uluru-Kata Tjuta National Park'. In *World Heritage Sites and Indigenous Peoples' Rights*, eds. S. Disko & H. Tugendhat. Copenhagen: IWGIA, 2014: 289–312.

Altman, J. C. *Alternate Development for Indigenous Territories of Difference*. Canberra: Centre for Aboriginal Economic Policy Research Topical Issue, No. 5/2011; 2011.

Athreya, V., Odden, M., Linnel, J., Krishnaswamy, J. & U. Karanth. 'Big Cats in Our Backyard: Persistence of Large Carnivores in a Human Dominated Landscape in India'. *PLoS ONE* 8, no. 3 (2013): 1–8.

Bauman, T., Haynes, C. & G. Lauder. *Pathways to the Co-management of Protected Areas and Native Title in Australia*. Canberra: AIATSIS Research Discussion Paper 32, 2013.

Bijoy, C. R. 'Western Ghats of India: A Natural Heritage Enclosure?'. In *World Heritage Sites and Indigenous Peoples' Rights*, eds. S. Disko & H. Tugendhat. Copenhagen: IWGIA, 2014: 223–244.

Butchart, S. H. M., M. Clarke, R. J. Smith, R. E. Sykes, J. P. W. Scharlemann, M. Harfoot, G. M. Buchanan, A. Angulo, A. Balmford, B. Bertzky, T. M. Brooks, K. E. Carpenter, M. T. Comeros-Raynal, J. Cornell, G. F. Ficetola, L. D. C. Fishpool, R. A. Fuller, J. Geldmann, H. Harwell, C. Hilton-Taylor, M. Hoffmann, A. Joolia, L. Joppa, N. Kingston, I. May, A. Milam, B. Polidoro, G. Ralph, N. Richman, C. Rondinini, D. B. Segan, B. Skolnik, M. D. Spalding, S. N. Stuart, A. Symes, J. Taylor, P. Visconti, J. E. M. Watson, L. Wood & N. D. Burgess. 'Shortfalls and Solutions for Meeting National and Global Conservation Area Targets'. *Conservation Letters* (2015). doi:10.1111/conl.12158.

Carter, N. B., Shrestha, J., Karki, N. & J. Liu Pradhan. 'Coexistence between Wildlife and Humans at Fine Spatial Scales'. *Proceedings of the National Academy of Sciences* 109, no. 38 (2012): 15360–15365.

Chape, S., Spalding, M. & M. Jenkins. *The World's Protected Areas*. Berkeley: UC Press, 2008.
Colchester, M., Ferrari, M. Farhan, Nelson, J., Kidd, C., Zaninka, P., Venant, M., Regpala, L., Balawag, G., Motin, B. & B. Lasimbang. *Conservation and Indigenous Peoples: Assessing the Progress since Durban*. FPP Series on Forest Peoples and Protected Areas, 2008.
Director of National Parks. *Third Uluru (Ayers Rock-Mount Olga) National Park Management Plan*. Canberra: Australian National Parks and Wildlife Service, 1991.
Director of National Parks. *Fourth Uluru-Kata Tjuta National Park Management Plan 2010–2020*. Canberra: Parks Australia, 2000.
Director of National Parks. *Fifth Uluru-Kata Tjuta National Park Management Plan 2010–2020*. Canberra: Parks Australia, 2010a.
Director of National Parks. *Uluru-Kata Tjuta National Park Tourism Directions: Stage 1*. Canberra: Department of Sustainability, Environment, Water, Population and Communities, 2010b.
Director of Parks Australia. 'Kakadu and Uluru-Kata Tjuta World Heritage Areas'. Paper presented to the Symposium Keeping the Outstanding Exceptional: The Future of Australia's World Heritage, Cairns, 9–10 August 2012.
Dorschner, J. 'India Needs an Environmental Opposition Party'. *American Diplomacy*. http://www.test.unc.edu/depts/diplomat/item/2015/0106/ca/dorschner_green.html, 2015.
Dowie, M. *Conservation Refugees*. Cambridge, MA: MIT Press, 2011.
Farrier, D. & M. Adams. 'Indigenous-Government Co-Management of Protected Areas: Booderee National Park and the National Framework in Australia'. In *Guidelines for Protected Area Legislation*, ed. B. Lausche, 1–40. 'Special Protected Area Types' Gland, Switzerland: IUCN, 2011.
Fitzsimons, J. A. 'Private Protected Areas in Australia: Current Status and Future Directions'. *Nature Conservation* 10 (2015): 1–23. DOI:10.3897/natureconservation.10.8739.
Gammage, B. *The Biggest Estate on Earth: How Aborigines Made Australia*. Sydney: Allen & Unwin, 2011.
Ghosal, S., Athreya, V., Linnel, J. & P. Vedeld. 'An Ontological Crisis? A Review of Large Felid Conservation in India'. *Biodiversity and Conservation* 22, no. 11 (2013): 2665–2681.
Gilbert, J. 'Indigenous Peoples' Heritage and Human Rights'. In *World Heritage Sites and Indigenous Peoples' Rights*, eds. S. Disko & H. Tugendhat. Copenhagen: IWGIA, 2014: 55–64.
Green, C. 'The Laponian World Heritage Area: Conflict and Collaboration in Swedish *Sápmi*'. In *World Heritage Sites and Indigenous Peoples' Rights*, eds. S. Disko & H. Tugendhat. Copenhagen: IWGIA, 2014: 85–102.
Head, L., Adams, M., McGregor, H. & S. Toole. 'Australia and Climate Change'. *WIRES Climate Change* 5 (2014): 175–197.
Hill, B. *The Rock: Travelling to Uluru*. St. Leonards: Allen & Unwin, 1994.
Hueneke, H. & R. Baker. 'Tourist Behavior, Local Values, and Interpretation at Uluru: "The Sacred Deed at Australia's Mighty Heart"'. *GeoJournal* 74 (2009): 477–490.
IUCN. *IUCN Evaluations of Nominations of Natural and Mixed Properties to the World Heritage List*. http://whc.unesco.org/archive/2011/whc11-35com-inf.8B2e.pdf, 2011.
IUCN. *IUCN Evaluations of Nominations of Natural and Mixed Properties to the World Heritage List*. http://whc.unesco.org/archive/2012/whc12-36com-8B2inf-en.pdf, 2012.
IUCN. *A Strategy of Innovative Approaches and Recommendations for Respecting Indigenous and Traditional Knowledge and Culture in the Next Decade*. http://worldparkscongress.org/downloads/approaches/Stream7.pdf, 2014.
James, S. 'Constructing the Climb: Visitor Decision-making at Uluru'. *Geographical Research* 45, no. 4 (2007): 398–407.
Joppa, L. N. & A. Pfaff. 'High and Far: Biases in the Location of Protected Areas'. *PLoS ONE* 4, no. 12 (2009): e8273. DOI:10.1371/journal.pone.0008273.
Joshi, A., Vaidanathan, S., Mondol, S., Edgaonkar, A. & U. Ramakrishnan. 'Connectivity of Tiger (*Panthera Tigris*) Populations in the Human-influenced Forest Mosaic of Central India'. *PLoS ONE* 8, no. 11 (2013): 1–11.

McNeely, J. 'A Political Future for Protected Areas'. *Oryx* 49, no. 2 (2015): 189–190.

Mohan, R. 'Narendra Modi's War on the Environment'. http://america.aljazeera.com/multimedia/2015/4/narendra-modis-war-on-the-indian-environment.html, 2015.

Mohindra, V. & Wangchuk, R. 'Community-based Conservation and Livelihood Strategies for the Protection of the Snow Leopard and Its Habitat in Ladakh, India'. In *Conservation in a Crowded World*, eds. J. Merson, R. Cooney & P. Brown. Sydney: UNSW Press, 2012: 34–54.

Moorcroft, H. & M. Adams. 'Emerging Geographies of Conservation and Indigenous Land in Australia'. *Australian Geographer* 45, no. 4 (2014): 485–504.

Mora, C. & P. F. Sale. 'Ongoing Global Biodiversity Loss and the Need to Move beyond Protected Areas: A Review of the Technical and Practical Shortcomings of Protected Areas on Land and Sea'. *Marine Ecology Progress Series* 434, no. 9 (2011): 251–266.

Pathak Broome, N. & T. Dash. 'Recognition and Support of ICCAs in India'. In *Recognising and Supporting Territories and Areas Conserved By Indigenous Peoples and Local Communities: Global Overview and National Case Studies*. eds. A. Kothari with C. Corrigan, H. Jonas, A. Neumann & H. Shrumm. Secretariat of the Convention on Biological Diversity, ICCA Consortium, Kalpavriksh, and Natural Justice, Montreal, Canada. Technical Series no. 64, 2012.

Paulson, N., Laudati, A. Doolittle, A., Welch-Devine, M. & P. Pena. 'Indigenous Peoples' Participation in Global Conservation: Looking beyond Headdresses and Face Paint'. *Environmental Values* 21, no. 3 (2012): 255–276.

Rai, N. & K. Bawa. 'Inserting Politics and History in Conservation'. *Conservation Biology* 27, no. 2 (2013): 425–428.

Rastogi, A., Hickey, G., Badola, R. & S. Hussein. 'Saving the Superstar: A Review of the Factors Affecting Tiger Conservation in India'. *Journal of Environmental Management* 113 (2012): 328–340.

Robinson, C., Baker, R. & L. Liddle. 'Journeys through an Australian Sacred Landscape'. *Museum International* 55 (2003): 74–77.

Rose, D. B. *Nourishing Terrains*. Canberra: Australian Heritage Commission, 1996.

Saberwal, V. & M. Rangarajan. *Battles over Nature*. Delhi: Permanent Black, 2003.

Saberwal, V., Rangarajan, M. & A. Kothari. *People, Parks and Wildlife: Towards Coexistence*. Hyderabad, India: Orient Longman, 2004.

Shahabuddin, G. *Conservation at the Crossroads*. Delhi: Permanent Black, 2010.

Shahabuddin, G. & M. Rao. 'Do Community-conserved Areas Effectively Conserve Biological Diversity? Global Insights and the Indian Context'. *Biological Conservation* 143, no. 12 (2010): 2926–2936.

Sharma, M. *Green and Saffron: Hindu Nationalism and Indian Environmental Politics*. Delhi: Permanent Black, 2012.

Smyth, D., & J. Sutherland. *Indigenous Protected Areas: Conservation Partnerships with Indigenous Landholders: A Report*. Canberra: Environment Australia, 1996.

UNESCO. *Western Ghats World Heritage*. http://whc.unesco.org/en/list/1342, nd.

Waitt, G., Figueroa, R., & L. McGee. 'Fissures in the Rock: Rethinking Pride and Shame in the Moral Terrains of Uluru'. *Transactions of the Institute of British Geographers* 32, no. 2 (2007): 248–263.

Watson, J. E., Dudley, N., Segan, D. B. & M. Hockings. 'The Performance and Potential of Protected Areas'. *Nature* 515, no. 7525 (2014): 67–73.

Wildlife Institute of India. *Protected Areas of India*. http://www.wiienvis.nic.in/Database/Protected_Area_854.aspx, nd.

Woinarski, J., A.W. Burbidge & P. L. Harrison. 'Ongoing Unraveling of a Continental Fauna: Decline and Extinction of Australian Mammals since European Settlement', *Proceedings of the National Academy of Sciences* (2015). doi:10.1073/pnas.1417301112.

Worboys, G., Lockwood, M. & T. de Lacy. *Protected Area Management*. South Melbourne: Oxford University Press, 2001.

# 9 A space for Sámi values? Sámi reindeer herding and Norwegian national parks

*Jan Åge Riseth*

## Introduction

Reindeer (*Rangifer tarandus tarandus*) has been a keystone species in Scandinavia since the Ice Age. The Sámi are the indigenous people of central and northern Scandinavia, and have a long history of living off reindeer. In ancient times this was by way of hunting, but since the seventeenth century it has been by nomadic herding, where the families followed the animals on their annual migrations through the landscape. Nowadays, reindeer herders live a more semi-nomadic life based in a small number of dwellings, but still keep a check on the animals throughout the year.

Legal nature protection is a relatively recent phenomenon in Norway, dating back just over 50 years. Norway was the first country to ratify (in 1990) ILO Convention 169 concerning indigenous and tribal peoples, and thus has a good reputation internationally for the treatment of its indigenous people. However, from time to time, conflicts surface about national parks in Sámi areas, especially connected with reindeer herding. The aim of this contribution is to understand why such conflicts occur, and what can be done about them.

As of 31 December 2014, 17 per cent of the land area of mainland Norway was protected under the provisions of the Nature Diversity Act. The current 37 national parks constitute almost 10 per cent of the land area.[1] Norway's first national park was established in 1962, and the first nationwide plan for national parks and large protection areas was adopted in 1964. Even in the 1960s, reindeer herding was largely based on human and animal muscle power all year round. It is unlikely that anyone envisioned that the mechanisation of reindeer herding (the use of snowmobiles, ATVs and, to some extent, helicopters) would become a difficulty in relation to nature protection.

From the late nineteenth century the position of reindeer herding in mainstream society was characterised by a disparaging attitude towards both reindeer herding and Sámi. The Reindeer Herding Act of 1933 was based on the idea that reindeer herding lacked stamina and was on the verge of extinction; it was only tolerated useage (*precario*). However, this view was certainly about to change by the 1960s. In 1968 came the first two judgments from the Norwegian Supreme Court establishing that reindeer herding rights and property ownership rights had equally strong protection. A considerable amount has happened since then. A branch agreement for reindeer herding, based on the pattern of the agricultural agreement, was adopted (1976) and new Reindeer Herding Acts were introduced (1978 and 2007). A specific section on Sámi rights was included in the Norwegian Constitution in 1988 and a representative body, the Sámi Parliament was established in 1989. The year after Norway ratified ILO Convention 169. The

1 Norwegian Environment Agency, Miljøstatus.

section on Sámi rights is also reflected in the preamble of several important acts, including the Nature Diversity Act (2009). Regional boards with Sámi representation have been established for protected areas. This progress has created clear expectations concerning greater influence for reindeer herding in land use and nature management. Although the majority of Sámi reindeer herders perceive that the advantages of national parks outweigh the disadvantages,[2] it seems that the expectations are not even close to being met.

Some of the potential for conflict emerged in a speech at a function to celebrate the 50th anniversary of the Børgefjell National Park in the summer of 2013. Nils P. Joma, who manages reindeer in Tjåehkere Sijte, discussed the history of the Sámi. He asked 'What if the Sámi had not existed?' He noted that: 'From ancient times, the Sámi regarded these areas as theirs, and that is still the case even today.'[3] His speech conveyed mixed feelings; pride in their own history and recognition that their areas have become a national park, but also hurt at having to explain that they have always been there. We may also wonder why the speaker referred to the situation as being both in the past and the present. It appears that he had a need to emphasise that they are *still* their areas. Do the Southern Sámi perhaps feel that they have lost control of the areas that have been protected?

In Reisa National Park there is more direct conflict. Two reindeer herding representatives claim that the existing draft management plan 'is slowly but surely pushing reindeer herding out of the national park, with provisions. . . . that prohibit the practising of the ordinary reindeer herding which is currently carried out in our reindeer grazing districts'.[4]

Both these examples deviate from what one would immediately expect in a country perceived as a leader when it comes to indigenous policy. This chapter attempts to uncover the conflicts that gave rise to these statements. I have formulated the following research questions:

(1) Have established institutions contributed to creating conflicts between the protection of natural habitats and Sámi reindeer herding?
(2) How can these conflicts be resolved?

I will start by accounting for my theoretical approach, methodology and source data for this chapter. I will then go through the various factors that I perceive to be the most important for the analysis before I present some important findings from two different regions. The discussion that follows leads towards answers to the research questions.

## Theory, methodology and source data

This chapter rests on a broad methodological and empirical basis. The methods employed are data analysis and interviews. The written material covers media reports, local contemporary descriptions, government reports, legislation, case documents from environmental management authorities and national as well as international presentations of environmental and indigenous processes. With respect to my own material, I have used seven interviews from two different research projects carried out in the period 2003–2013, four of which are quoted directly.

2 Riseth and Holte, 'Rennäring och nationalparker', 269–290.
3 Joma, Speech at the 50 years anniversary.
4 Solaas, 'Søker ikke dispesasjon', 10.

My theoretical approach is institutional analysis. From a fundamental perspective, this academic tradition defines the frameworks and social conditions for actions. People are always influenced by standards or rules about what constitutes acceptable or sensible action in various situations. Institutions may also be described as constant social structures that give meaning and stability to social life. Various social arenas are controlled by different institutions.[5] Institutions may be *regulatory*, such as laws and regulations, *normative*, such as values and norms, and *cultural cognitive*, including signs and symbols that tell us what is meaningful.[6]

In order to analyse institutions and interaction about the use of natural resources and nature management, I have adopted a theoretical analytical tool, the so-called Institutional Analysis and Development (IAD) Framework.[7] This framework was developed in the 1980s and has since been used in a large number of analyses of common pool resource situations. The core of the framework is an *action arena* made up of *actors* and *action situations. Action situations* refer to natural and social space where actors meet and are defined by the purpose of the analysis. The relevant action arenas comprise a number of biophysical and institutional factors. In this contribution, I will present a simplified analysis taking my point of departure in three combined factors that contribute to the constitution of the action arenas. The action arenas I have studied are two regions with both Sámi reindeer herding and established national parks.

## Constituting factors

### *Reindeer herding and nature protection in Norway*

The reindeer has a major impact on the development of vegetation in the mountains and forests of Scandinavia. The positive effect of reindeer herding on the landscape, biodiversity and climate are generally little known. All grazing animals help to limit shrub growth and forest expansion. The significance of the reindeer is greatest in the summer grazing areas where, in addition to keeping the landscape open, it also contributes to a meadow flora on rich bedrock that has a wealth of species. Some rare alpine plant species are dependent on reindeer grazing for their survival.[8] In addition, reindeer grazing contributes to limiting the effects of climate change as lower vegetation cover reduces global warming so that a higher proportion of the radiation exposure is reflected back into the atmosphere.[9] The use of ATVs contributes to vegetation changes in areas with sparse vegetation cover as well as in wet habitats. In my view, the extent of this damage is mostly a matter of aesthetic ideals. In some places, heavily used hiking trails and T-marking by the Norwegian Trekking Association (DNT) contributes to obvious changes in the landscape.

Sámi reindeer herding is practised over approximately 40 per cent of Norway's land area – almost all of northern Norway with the exception of Lofoten and some other islands, most of Trøndelag south to Trondheim, Trollheimen and the inland areas of Sør-Trøndelag and Hedmark roughly as far as Femunden. This area is called the Sámi reindeer herding area

5 Vatn, *Institutions and the Environment.*

6 Scott, *Institutions and Organizations.*

7 Ostrom, *Understanding Institutional Diversity.*

8 Olofson and Oksanen, *Effects on Reindeer Density*; Riseth and Oksanen, *Ressursøkonomiske og økologiske perspektiver.*

9 Olofson et al., 'Herbivores inhibit climate driven'.

and constitutes the land area on which the Sámi have recognised rights to practise reindeer herding. Jotunheimen has reindeer herding run by Norwegian mountain farmers, while other mountain areas in southern Norway have populations of wild reindeer. As of 1 April 2015, Sámi reindeer herding in Norway comprised 211,606 reindeer managed by 534 Siida-shares (family units) with a total of 3150 associated persons.[10]

Figure 9.1 depicts the development of national park area in Norway and compares the Sámi reindeer herding area with the remainder of south Norway. Twenty-three of the 37 national parks in mainland Norway are within the Sámi reindeer herding area, which itself covers 40 per cent of the land area and in 2013 accounted for 58 per cent of the accumulated national park area.

A scientific evaluation of protected areas in Norway focused on the extent to which the protected areas are representative of the nature of the country. Framstad and colleagues[11] found wide variation in the representation of different habitat types and stated that mountain areas had relatively little need of protection and also were less exposed to threats than most habitat types. Statistics for relative representation of habitat types shows that roughly twice as much mountain land is protected than the percentage of land would indicate.[12] This pattern illustrates what Arnesen and Riseth[13] referred to as *the inverse protection paradox*: The actual protection appears to be approximately inversely proportionate to the need for protection.

Nature protection of land through formal, legally based decisions dates back to the establishment of Yellowstone National Park in Wyoming, US, in 1872. 'The conservation

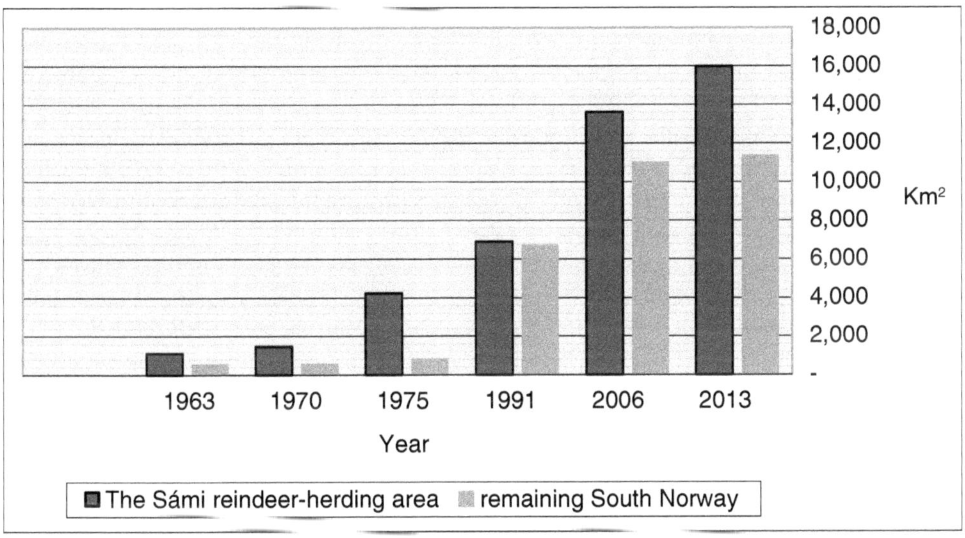


*Figure 9.1* Accumulated national park area. The Sámi reindeer herding area and remaining south Norway (separate comparison based on the Norwegian Environment Agency, 2015)

10 Norwegian Agricultural Agency, 2015.
11 Framstad et al., *Naturfaglig evaluering*.
12 Riseth, 'Premisser for bruk og vern'.
13 Arnesen and Riseth, 'Protection and equity?'.

practice in Yellowstone became the model for subsequent establishment of protected areas worldwide.'[14] The core of the practice known as *the Yellowstone model* is *the protection of valuable and beautiful nature for the enjoyment of visiting guests.*[15] This model has inspired nature protection enthusiasts for one and a half centuries and has dominated the establishment and management of protected areas in many countries worldwide.

The model is based in part on the illusion that it is protecting 'wilderness' or 'untouched' nature and what is worse is that in many countries it is based on oppression and marginalisation of indigenous and local people in the areas that are protected. Yellowstone National Park was established towards the end of the white people's conquest of the West, while the US army still led brutal wars against the tribes of native Americans opposed to being placed in the reservations. The original residents became outlaws in their own areas and their use of natural resources was ignored.[16] For indigenous peoples in many countries, the establishment of national parks and protected areas has resulted in their being marginalised, dispossessed and stripped of their role as resource managers in their own areas. A number of studies confirm this is the case for almost everywhere in the world.[17] Adams[18] sums up the situation, writing that until the 1990s the conventional meaning of establishing national parks was oppression of the local people's use of natural resources and the enforced loss of established rights and patterns of resource use.

In Norway nature protection arose as a separate expert-based sector in the space of two to three decades after the end of the Second World War with the adoption of two conservation Acts (1954 and 1970), an expert body (the Norwegian Nature Conservation Council, 1955) and a separate Ministry for the Environment (1972). In the 1960s an organisation society emerged in which popular movements to a greater extent developed professional bodies with the competence and capacity to enter into dialogue with the authorities.[19] The 1970s saw extensive popular movements, where the battles involving the EEC and watercourse developments were important. Seippel[20] concludes that the conservation and environmental movement in the 1970s and 1980s paved the way for conservation and other environmental issues. A lasting effect was the institutionalisation of nature and environmental protection during the 1970s and 1980s.[21] Further development of land protection was institutionalised through the establishment of the County Governor's Environmental Protection Department (1982) and the second National Protection Plan.[22] This plan was based on the Nature Conservation Act of 1970 and its main objective was to preserve larger continuous untouched, or essentially untouched, natural habitats because the area classified as 'without major infrastructure development' had been significantly reduced during the twentieth century.

Since the adoption of the second National Protection Plan, the national parks in the reindeer herding areas have had three purposes: firstly nature conservation, secondly outdoor

14 Benjaminsen and Svarstad, *Politisk økologi*, 93.
15 Ward, *The West*, 326.
16 Jacoby, *Crimes against Nature*.
17 Chatty, 'Enclosures and exclusions', 2–7; Neuman, *Imposing Wilderness*; Hitchcock, 'We are the first people', 797–824; Poirier and Ostergren, 'Evicting people', 331–352; Fearnside, Conservation policy; Nicholas, Protect the forest better; Smardon and Faust, 'Introduction: International policy', 160–192.
18 Adams, 'Nature and the colonial mind'.
19 Selle, 'Organisasjonssamfunnet'.
20 Seippel, 'Trees, ecology and biological diversity'.
21 Slagstad, *De nasjonale strateger*; Berntsen, *Grønne linjer*.
22 NOU 2001:28, *Naturmangfoldloven*; St.meld. 62, Ny landsplan.

recreation and finally 'Protecting the natural resource base within the national park is important for Sámi culture and industry utilisation. The area shall be able to be used for reindeer herding.'[23] Even though reindeer herding is one of the purposes of protection, it is in principle placed after outdoor recreation.

After consultations with the Sámi Parliament (of Norway), the purpose (s. 1) of the Nature Diversity Act states that, in addition to protecting nature, the act shall also provide 'a basis for human activity, culture, health and well-being . . . including a basis for Sámi culture'. In addition, s. 14 of the Act was reformulated and given a different emphasis. When decisions are made that directly affect Sámi interests, due importance shall be attached . . . to the natural resource base for Sámi culture'.[24] Thus the Act makes it clear that safeguarding the material basis for Sámi culture is one of its purposes and that this is to be emphasised.

Despite this provision, the national parks still have purpose clauses that prioritise outdoor recreation ahead of reindeer herding. During the consultations, the Sámi Parliament stated that it may be appropriate to establish IUCN's protection category VI – *resource management area* – as a new category because this 'will safeguard sustainable use and harvesting' in a better manner,[25] but this was not supported by the Ministry which stated that resource use was not an objective with area protection (op. cit.).

The nature management sector has a strong scientific tradition and has not been particularly open to other types of knowledge, such as traditional popular knowledge.[26] The knowledge monopoly and limited openness can jointly lay the foundation for a model of power and co-option rather than genuine participation.[27] The monopoly of natural science of what is considered legitimate knowledge is broken by s. 8 of the Nature Diversity Act, which obliges the authorities to consider not only scientific knowledge, but also 'knowledge that is based on many generations of experience acquired through the use of and interaction with the natural environment, including traditional Sámi use'.[28]

During the implementation of the second National Protection Plan, the Government, in 2003, adopted the so-called Mountain Text (Fjellteksten) as an initiative to promote commercial tourism in protected areas, thereby contributing to local value creation.[29] This has in part created very strong negative reactions within the Sámi reindeer herding industry due to expectations of increased traffic disrupting reindeer herding in protected areas, and because as a result of this the Sámi reindeer herders feel ignored and excluded in their own areas.[30]

In connection with the second National Protection Plan, on the initiative of the Storting, four local management trials were initiated,[31] which resulted in new regional boards for protected areas. During the consultations on the Nature Diversity Act, local participation was an important point for the Sámi Parliament, which in its plenary resolution said, amongst other things, the following about Sámi influence in the management of protected areas:

> The Sámi Parliament refers to the fact that the act allows for a specially appointed body to be the management authority for protected areas. The Sámi Parliament will actively

23 Forskrift, *Verneplan Verdal-Snåsa-Lierne.*
24 Ot. Prp., *Naturmangfoldloven.*
25 Ot. Prp., *Naturmangfoldloven*, 36.
26 Aasetre, *Moderne naturforvaltning.*
27 Arnesen and Riseth, 'Konfliktfyllda naturskyddsprocesser'.
28 Ot. Prp., *Naturmangfoldloven*, 34–35.
29 Fedreheim, 'Value creation'.
30 Solaas, 'Sámisk utelatt i merkevarestrategi'.
31 Falleth and Hovik, *Lokal forvaltning.*

> follow up the work involving evaluation of local management of protected areas, so that protected areas that directly affect Sámi interests may be added to a special management body with Sámi participation, which is appointed by the Sámi Parliament, cf. Articles 6, 7 and 15 of the ILO Convention 169 concerning indigenous and tribal peoples in independent states.[32]

Regional boards were appointed for protected areas, including national parks, in 2010. In Sámi areas, these boards included representatives[33] appointed by the Sámi Parliament.

In the so-called commons law project, Sámi customs were surveyed as part of the basis for the work of the Sámi Rights Committee. One of the reports contained the following important ascertainment:

> In reality, there are probably two legal systems at work in large parts of Northern Norway; the commons law legal system and the Norwegian state legislation. Depending on individuals' respective ethnic identities, their familiarity with local customs and their levels of knowledge etc., they adapt to one or the other of the two legal systems, which leads to unwanted conflicts.[34]

Moreover, Helander (ibid.) explained that it is often difficult for Sámi to understand the sense and logic of government legislation, and that they would prefer to continue with their proven practices. She also points out that the government's application of law is an expression of the execution of power and, when this execution of power is not perceived as legitimate, those who execute it also lose credibility.

### *Norway and the Sámi*

During the nineteenth century the Norwegian nation state was founded and established. The nation-building process contributed to the idyllisation of rural life. Farmers and nature received a prominent place in the national romantic art.[35] The emergence of farmers as an important political force coincided with nature becoming a national symbol, as was expressed in landscape paintings, folk tales, folk music and poetry.[36] Norwegian nationalism is regarded as a moderate form,[37] but the nation did not give space to everyone.

The Sámi were among those excluded from the national community. Under Danish rule until 1814, 'the Sámi had in principle been one of many equal peoples or nations'.[38] However, from the mid-nineteenth century, the new Norway developed a completely opposite policy. The Norwegian authorities wanted to 'create a separate Norwegian-national platform in relation to other states and peoples, not least their Nordic neighbours'.[39]

As a result of this, the Sámi became a marginalised minority (op. cit.). Leading historians defined the Sámi from both the history and the people. Within the space of a few decades, it

32 Sametinget [Sámi Parliament], Naturmangfoldlov.
33 One or more, but never in majority.
34 Helander, *Sámiska rättsuppfatningar.*
35 Witoszek, *Norske naturmytologier.*
36 Ween and Abram, *Norwegian Trekking Association.*
37 Store norske leksikon, 'Nasjonalisme'.
38 Pedersen, 'Samenes historie', 174.
39 op. cit., 177.

became the recognised teaching that the Sámi were inferior people, a view which formed an ideological basis for the policy of Norwegianisation and the undermining of Sámi rights.[40] Urban elites played important roles in the development of a Norwegian national identity. Mountain hiking was organised and promoted by the Norwegian Trekking Association (DNT), which was established in 1868. The DNT was also among the first initiators of active nature conservation in Norway.

The disparagement of the Sámi has had extensive political ramifications from the mid-nineteenth century almost up to today. The assimilation policy had a major effect on Sámi language and Sámi cultural expressions. In the long run, the majority of Sámi people probably lost their original language (op. cit.). Reindeer herding was stigmatised as a primitive industry in danger of extinction and was forced to give way to 'better justified interests'. It was subject to a highly restrictive and controlling regime. This led to dramatic changes in land use,[41] socio-economic costs of unknown scope[42] and left a direct mark on the Sámi reindeer herders' legal status right up until the turn of the millennium.[43] The first step towards reversing this highly repressive policy came in 1959 when the Sámi Committee submitted its recommendation, which was an indirect result of the UN Universal Declaration on Human Rights of 1948.[44] Formal equality between the Sámi and Norwegian cultures did not come until 1988 when a specific section on Sámi rights was included in the Norwegian Constitution.

## *International challenges*

The modern Sámi political movement also experienced strong growth in the 1970s. Interestingly enough, it was the nationwide protest movement against a hydropower development (Alta-Kautokeino) that grew from being a nature protection issue into an indigenous people's issue, which started a Sámi political revolution in Norway.[45] Nine years after the government's decision concerning the clarification of Sámi rights, the Sámi Parliament was established. This evolved into the core institution in the new Sámi public life.[46]

Strikingly enough, the establishment of the Sámi Parliament did not lead to increased Sámi influence within nature management. However, the process leading to the adoption of the Finnmark Act (2005),[47] acting as a new arena, opened the way for consultations and interaction between Sámi interests and the government. No less than 18 years after its establishment, through an agreement with the Ministry for Environment,[48] the Sámi Parliament achieved recognition of the fact that Sámi interests should have a special role in matters relating to nature conservation in their own areas.

In the last decades before the turn of the millennium, key international processes were implemented that were to influence Norway in terms of both environmental protection and policies related to indigenous peoples. The processes that followed the United Nations

40 Pedersen, 'Samenes historie', 173–192.
41 Riseth, *Reindrift og ressursforvaltning*.
42 Fjellheim, *Gåebrien Sijte*.
43 Ravna, *Finnmarksloven*.
44 Aarseth, *Norsk Samepolitikk*.
45 Hjorthol, *Alta. Kraftkampen*.
46 Bjerkli and Selle, *Samer, makt og demokrati*.
47 Hernes and Oskal, *Finnmarksloven*; Bjerkli and Selle, *Samepolitikkens utvikling*.
48 https://www.regjeringen.no/no/dokumenter/avtale-mellom-sametinget-og-miljoverndep/id481195/ (accessed 27 August 2015).

Conference on Environment and Development in 1992 (the Rio Summit), in particular the Convention on Biological Diversity (CBD), but also Agenda 21, have given the traditional knowledge and practices of indigenous peoples a central place in global discussions concerning sustainable resource use and sustainable development. Article 8(j) of the CBD requires the parties that have ratified the Convention, through national legislation, to respect, preserve and maintain the knowledge and practices of indigenous and local communities relevant for the conservation and sustainable use of biological diversity, while Article 10(c) requires the parties to protect and encourage customary use of biological resources in accordance with traditional cultural practices that are compatible with conservation or sustainable use requirements. However, a discourse analytical study of the CBD and connected texts[49] reveals that the CBD provides indigenous people with only a narrow space for political agency regarding influence over and participation in the management of biological resources.

> The inclusion of indigenous subjects seems to be based mainly on the possible contributions they can make to the objectives of the conventions and the work of the state parties to the convention, not on their possible rights as peoples to self-determination and collective rights to land, water and resources, or as possible parties in their own rights.[50]

Reimerson sees this as a colonial legacy (op. cit.) that may affect and limit the space of agency for indigenous peoples.

The fifth meeting of the Conference of the Parties (COP5) to the Convention adopted a work programme for the implementation of Article 8(j), which includes strengthening the capacity of indigenous peoples to participate in decision-making processes and policy formulation.[51] A project at the Nordic Sámi Institute (NSI) considered how the CBD and Agenda processes should be applied to Sámi conditions. The conclusion was:

> Transferring of authority to the superior Sámi organ is a necessary but insufficient measure. Democratization of decision-making processes in environmental management will also require that local Sámi communities and local organisations are strengthened so that their knowledge and points of view can be expressed, and that methods are developed that attribute them equality and importance.[52]

While the CBD is a legally binding agreement, Agenda 21 is a political indication of intent. It contains a chapter concerning the recognition and strengthening of the role of indigenous peoples and their communities and a chapter that focuses on the initiatives of local authorities.[53] Mona Schanche[54] analysed public documents in order to see whether both these international environmental agreements influenced policy development for resource management in Sámi areas. She found, for instance, that only one of the three relevant ministries made the necessary arrangements to involve the Sámi Parliament.

49 Reimerson, 'Between nature and culture', 992–1009.
50 Op. cit., 1004.
51 Schanche, 'Innledning'.
52 Op. cit., 6.
53 Posey and Dutfield, *Beyond Intellectual Property*.
54 Schanche, *Urfolk, rettigheter og ressurser*.

The exclusion of indigenous and local communities and a lack of participation in the establishment and management of protected areas was a key topic at the fourth World Parks Congress in Caracas in 1992 and, to an even greater extent, at the fifth World Parks Congress in Durban in 2003. This Congress may be seen as a breakthrough for the understanding that effective conservation requires viewing protection not only as an environmental issue, but also as a *social* issue. The Congress attached importance to poverty eradication, social justice and societal involvement in conservation issues, including new forms of protection.[55]

The International Union for Conservation of Nature (IUCN) revised its protection categories in 1994 and recognised that indigenous peoples may own and manage protected areas. The new categories aim to promote sustainable use while also maintaining biodiversity,[56] including *Managed Resource Protected Area.*[57] There is an increasing international trend to involve indigenous and local communities in the establishment and management of protected areas.[58]

## Coordination in local and regional action arenas

The Sámi believe nature is based on animism, i.e. that everything in nature, including plants and hills, has a soul. Many indigenous cultures are animistic in the sense that for them nature is alive and there is a social space in which humans and non-humans can interact. Sámi reindeer herders have strong ties to their ancestral areas, which they perceive as living beings with their own relationships to animals and humans. Human actions are sanctioned but people must have respect for the environment otherwise the balance in life will be disturbed.[59]

This understanding of nature is well evidenced by the establishment of protected areas.[60] The question asked by the Lule Sámi during a protective process 'What have we done wrong that it needs to be protected?'[61] is probably fairly typical of the Sámi perception that the protection being established is aimed at them as Sámi and at the local community. They perceive the protection as a statement of distrust from mainstream society. It is possible to understand Joma's anniversary speech, referred to above, in the same context. The Sámi University College's reports in connection with protection planning also document that local Sámi use of natural resources is both extensive and balanced, and that responsible harvesting of natural resources forms an important part of people's everyday lives.[62]

### *Indre Namdal and Snåsa*

In terms of reindeer herding, protection and protection processes, the reindeer grazing districts of Tjåehkere (Østre Namdal), Låarte (Luru) and Skæhkere (Skjækerfjell) and the

55 Andrade, 'Science and society', 4–5.
56 Stolton and Oviedo, 'Using the categories'.
57 Category VI- *Managed Resource Protected Area*: Protected area managed mainly for the sustainable use of natural ecosystems. Area containing predominantly unmodified natural systems, managed to ensure long-term protection and maintenance of biological diversity, while at the same time providing a sustainable flow of natural products and services to meet community needs.
58 NOU, *Naturmangfoldloven.*
59 Helander, *Sámiska rättsuppfattningar*; Westerfjeld, *Sørsamisk naturforståelse*, 217–219.
60 Bye and Jåma, *Mijjieh låartesne.*
61 Andreassen, 'Ka galt har vi gjort', 115.
62 Riseth and Solbakken, 'Naturbruk i Kautokeino'.

municipalities of Røyrvik, Luru and Snåsa constitute a reasonably delimited region. The rural areas of Indre Namdal were colonised relatively late by the Norwegian agricultural community. The clearing of farms in Lierne did not gather pace until the latter half of the eighteenth century.[63] In agricultural history, 'the big transformation in the farming community' refers to the concept of transition from subsistence to a monetary economy in Norwegian rural communities. As regards Snåsa, this transition has been dated to 1880, but for Lierne the breakthrough came after the Second World War and for some clusters of farms as late as the 1960s. This is something that must have coloured the identity and values of the people from Lierne.[64] The municipality is characterised by strong traces of the predator policies and a dramatic decline in grazing animals. A reindeer herder in Lierne says:

> The predator policies[65] – have been the death of this rural community. Sheep and reindeer and everything. . . . Perhaps 1000 sheep left in all of Lierne. They were reorganized from sheep to milk quotas, good for some . . . The primary industry is almost gone. A lot of the new stuff is in the form of projects, so as soon as it is finished there is not a chance in the world. The municipality and nurses etc. remain. Some construction workers. The slate [quarry] and the bakery are very good. . . . Not so much farming left to combine such jobs with. Then there is a little more pace so that shops and the like function. If these disappear, it will be very bad. I can't understand how the bakery can survive. The only thing they have locally is good water.
>
> (Interview with reindeer herder in Lierne, 21 January 2013)

Not only are the Sámi reindeer herders strongly attached to their areas, they have long felt that they were the only ones who took care of them. 'The problem with establishing the parks is that there are now so many others who will have rights at our expense' (interview with reindeer herder in Snåsa 18 March 2013). 'If it had not been for reindeer herding, there would not have been any basis for having a national park here. Then there would have been ski slopes and the like everywhere here. It is those who have stopped many developments' (interview with reindeer herder in Lierne 21 January 2013). In addition to Norway's second national park, Børgefjell, the region got the country's fourth national park, Gressåmoen, in 1970. A reindeer herder comments as follows:

> But if we are to gain knowledge from this old park, when Gressåmoen was established they introduced many restrictions there too. Among other things, we were supposed to apply annually to use snowmobiles there, but we didn't do that and no one has talked about that again either. But we don't really know about such matters. Even if we avoid [restrictions in reality] and don't do it for many years, after all it's still written in the papers.
>
> (Interview with reindeer herder in Snåsa 18 March 2013)

The second National Protection Plan covered both a major expansion of Gressåmoen, which became Blåfjella-Skjækerfjella, and the new Lierne National Park. The conflicts surrounding the establishment process have been discussed both by Riseth[66] and Ween.[67] When it came

63 Hermanstrand and Kosmo, *Røyrvik: samene i Østre Namdal.*
64 Estil, *Kulturmøte – kulturkonflikt.*
65 Increasing predator populations due to protection of lynx, brown bear, wolverine and eagles since 1980s
66 Riseth, *Indigenous perspective.*
67 Ween, *produksjon av natur/sted.*

to limiting the park area, the group that achieved the most was probably the local population of Lierne. The local residents' commitment may be viewed in the light of their connection with the uncultivated lands as well as the results of the predator policies.[68]

The Sámi reindeer herders felt that they had been pushed to the sidelines in the process leading to the protection decisions, and that they had gained too little influence in the management.[69] In response they resigned from the interim administrative council of the new Blåfjella-Skjækerfjella/Låarte-Skæhkere National Park, and they also boycotted the official opening at Lifjellet in Lierne municipality on 26 June 2006 involving HRH Crown Princess Mette Marit. Official Sápmi was represented by the vice-president of the Sámi Parliament, Johan Mikkel Sara (Kautokeino): 'This was a formidable challenge internally in the Southern Sámi community and, as such, the Blåfjella-Skjækerfjella National Park has regrettably received negative symbolic value in sections of the Southern Sámi society.'[70] Sara's speech shows how ambivalent is the Sámi people's relation to land protection. The vice-president pointed out that Sámi interest in Norway, and particularly in reindeer herding, had supported the creation of national parks to protect their own areas from external pressure, but he then said:

> However, we must note that this unconditional support is no longer present. . . . The delimitation . . . has been adapted to the requirements of competing interests and, not least, that it has been opened for the commercialisation of the protected area that will increase the pressure on already vulnerable areas.[71]

Although Lierne National Park did not create such local conflicts, it is not without problems. Some find it difficult to stay current with what is happening in the national park as: 'Reindeer herding has not been so limited by the national park. Included in a working committee, but have not been allowed to continue . . . Don't get to know anything. Was fine while I was on the working committee' (interview with reindeer herder in Lierne 21 January 2013). The national park can also bring a lot of unwanted activity:

> SNO [the State Nature Inspectorate] suddenly dives into the park. Various projects. I get. . . . [very] . . . annoyed by it. They come with different research, Arctic foxes, feeding stations. . . . Must be able to give an opinion, they are on our grazing areas. They drive here and there and everything is permitted. They take all sorts of liberties. Ordinary local residents are not even allowed to drive to go fishing.
>
> (Interview with reindeer herder in Lierne 21 January 2013)

The new regional boards in the protected areas have provided significant representation for Sámi interests, and the reindeer herders from these districts serve on such boards. Moreover, it is an interesting development that, despite the above-mentioned conflicts concerning the protected areas, the reindeer herders from all three districts are participating with their own natural and cultural tourism projects in the programme 'Natural heritage as a creator of value' (Naturarven som verdiskaper). However, it is clearly evident that such participation

68 Aune, Johansen and Trana, *Blåfjella Skjækerfjella og og Lierne.*
69 Riseth, op. cit.
70 Aune, Johansen and Trana, op. cit., 220.
71 Sara, Tale [Speech]. Åpningen av, 1.

is on their own terms.[72] This may suggest a promising future with fewer conflicts between reindeer herding and protected areas.

## *Nord-Troms*

Reisa National Park was established in 1986. Reindeer herding is not mentioned as a purpose in the regulations for protection in this national park, as it is in the first National Protection Plan. It is mentioned only in connection with motorised traffic.[73] There have been conflicts between reindeer herding and environment protection authorities ever since the national park was established and, as referred to above, there is also an open conflict concerning the present proposal for the management plan. The internal dialogue with environmental protection authorities started with a meeting in January 1984 at which the reindeer herders asked what limitations would be imposed on reindeer herding. The conclusion from the authorities' representative was that no such limitations would be imposed. When the park was established, this proved to be incorrect (interview with reindeer herder 18 June 2013): 'the reindeer herders who use these areas found that there were negative consequences for reindeer herding even though we were promised that there would not be any'.[74] The regulations for protection specified that those practising reindeer herding had to apply for exemptions to use ATVs on bare ground:[75]

> Since the establishment of Reisa National Park, negotiations have taken place between those practicing reindeer herding and the public administration . . . [about] . . . motorised traffic in the national park. Even during the consultation process . . . [before] the establishment of the national park, there were discussions about motorised traffic and the reindeer grazing district proposed that those practicing reindeer herding should not have to apply for permission to use motor vehicles.[76]

Reindeer herders have been reported for illegal driving and their own proposal for solving the problem was ignored by the bureaucracy.[77] There are two different opinions on either the parties agreed on a plan for ATV use in the district,[78] or the county governor granted exemptions based on fixed routes without those practising reindeer herding applying (interview with reindeer herder 18 June 2013).

The work on the management plan in Reisa has been a long and resource-demanding process. In 1996, the county governor drew up a draft management plan, but it was never adopted, one of the reasons being that reindeer herders opposed it.[79] Reisa National Park still (August 2016) does not have a valid management plan. One of the contentious points in the ongoing work involving the management plan applies to the knowledge base and cultural landscapes. It is claimed that, among other things, the draft plan does not accord with s. 8 of the Nature Diversity Act, which stipulates that the authorities shall attach importance

72 Ween and Riseth, 'Indigenous hospitality'.
73 Forskrift om vern for Reisa nasjonalpark.
74 Eira, *Medforvaltning som ideal*, 66.
75 Forskrift om vern for Reisa nasjonalpark, op.cit.op. cit.
76 Eira, op. cit., 67.
77 Op. cit., 67–68.
78 Op. cit., 68.
79 Op. cit., 71.

to knowledge that is based on many generations of experience (based on Article 8(j) of the Convention on Biological Diversity) in that the County Governor refused to include elements of cultural history (interview with reindeer herder 18 June 2013).

Two reindeer herding representatives who have been involved in the work on the management plan for this national park have sharply criticised the park protection regulations. The reindeer herders are not willing to accept that they should have to apply for exemption to use modern technical aids. Representative Peer Gaup points out that in addition to being an industry reindeer herding is also a way of life, and that a management plan must be based on all parties agreeing on the basics, a position which has been used as a starting point in, for instance, the Swedish national parks in Laponia.[80] There have also been other conflicts, including the reindeer herders being instructed to remove mobile shepherd huts under threat of fines.[81] The national park administrator confirms that dialogue has been lacking, but that it is improvements under way opening for joint and acceptable solutions for both reindeer herders and administration.[82]

## Discussion

In the Introduction I asked (1) how established institutions have contributed to creating conflicts between the protection of natural habitats and Sámi reindeer herding in Norway and (2) how these conflicts can be resolved.

I have gone back to the nineteenth century in order to gain an historical understanding of the events leading up to our time. On the one hand nationalism in the new Norway gave nature and mountains a strong symbolic value, while on the other hand it contributed to the neglect of the Sámi as indigenous people in large sections of the country. The symbolic value of the mountains probably partly explains why they account for a disproportionate amount of the protected area. The history of Norwegianisation and the inferior position of the Sámi reindeer herders, even in the 1960s, can basically explain why reindeer herding was ignored in the work involving the first National Protection Plan. Although nature management has never had the strict regimes found in many other countries, the Norwegian national park model undoubtedly has its roots in the Yellowstone model's rhetoric about wilderness/untouched nature.

This rhetoric is still alive in both the administration and among organised conservationists.[83] Legislation and environmental management have been set up in a way that obscures the Sámi reindeer herders and deprives them of the role of resource managers in their own areas. The only mention of reindeer herding in the regulations for national parks from the first National Protection Plan concerns the limitations being imposed. The preparatory work for the second National Protection Plan discussed relations with reindeer herding and noted that: 'In line with this, reindeer herding connected to the Sámi areas is in a unique position in relation to other business interests in the national parks.'[84] The report to the Storting states that one:

> does not consider the wish to ensure the resource base for reindeer herding as an independent basis for national park protection . . . [but that] . . . a supplementary basis for areas that would otherwise qualify as national parks . . . recommended to attach

80 Solaas, 'Søker ikke dispensasjon'.
81 http://www.nordlys.no/nyheter/article7302644.ece (accessed 18 April 2014).
82 Rune Benonisen (pers. communication).
83 Benjaminsen and Svarstad, *Politisk økologi*.
84 NOU, *Naturmangfoldloven*, 83.

> importance to the interests of reindeer herding by the establishment and management of national parks . . . the restructuring that has taken place since the last National Protection Plan was dealt with must be taken into consideration to a reasonable extent.[85]

As mentioned, the practical result of this was that reindeer herding became the 'third purpose'.

The obvious question then is whether this will have any practical significance. The attitude of the reindeer herders towards protection changed during the protection plan process for Blåfjella/Skjækerfjella when the park was reduced in size and the efforts involving commercialisation, in line with the provisions of the Mountain Text (Fjellteksten), created expectations of increased pressure and greater disturbance.[86] In her review of the protection plan process for Blåfjella/Skjækerfjella National Park, Ween[87] demonstrates that the grounds for protection changed over the space of the 20 years the protection process lasted, i.e. that different discourses dominate in different periods. She points out that it may be seen as an *ontological* struggle, i.e. a struggle over the reality in which the national park should be understood. The authorities say that they take reindeer herding into consideration and attach importance to it, while the Sámi reindeer herders still feel that their arguments are not taken into consideration.[88]

In answer to the first research question, we can say that established thinking and practice in the protection of natural habitats has contributed to creating conflicts between protection and Sámi reindeer herding through the marginalisation of the Sámi reindeer herders as resource managers in their own areas. The authorities have ignored the fact that national parks where Sámi reindeer herding takes place are not primarily 'untouched nature', but rather Sámi cultural landscapes where the Sámi reindeer herders have clear rights, and that the Sámi people still see themselves as responsible resource managers in their own areas. A more profound aspect of this is the Sámi reindeer herders' understanding of nature and their inherited ties to ancestral landscapes. This also involves expectations that s. 8 (knowledge base) of the Nature Diversity Act should allow for the recognition of local cultural history as important in the current management of protected areas. The present draft management plan for Reisa National Park states that the management authority and the local national park centre will conduct 'surveying and obtaining of traditional knowledge about reindeer herding as a way of life and use'.[89] It is not stipulated that those who practise reindeer herding should be involved in this work.

With regard to how these conflicts can be resolved, the starting point must be that effective nature protection is reliant on support from those who live in and by the nature to be protected. This understanding is established in the international discourse dating from the 1990s. It points towards co-management, which is a form of administration based on mutual trust.[90] Sandström and colleagues[91] note that Norway, Sweden and Finland have not fulfilled their international obligations in this area concerning nature management.

The Sámi Parliament's consultation with the authorities has led to the opening up of the knowledge base and the management model. Regarding the knowledge base, whether or

85 St.meld., *Naturmangfoldloven*, 40.
86 Riseth, 'An indigenous perspective', 177–185.
87 Ween, 'Blåfjella-Skjækerfjella nasjonalpark'.
88 Op. cit.
89 Fylkesmannen i Troms, *Reindrift*, 8, 56.
90 Carlsson and Berkes, 'Co-management'; Borrini-Feyerabend et al., *Sharing Power*.
91 Sandström, Hovik and Falleth, *Omstridd natur*.

not this will have any practical significance remains an open question. I recently (September 2015) visited several national parks in Australia. While there, I found that guides and park managers consistently and in detail provided an account of the knowledge and natural resource use practices of the indigenous people in relation to the various elements of nature that we saw. They also explained that they all had to be certified to perform this work and that this was linked to the management models for each of the protected areas. It seems that the establishment in 2010 of regional boards in protected areas with Sámi representatives is the Sámi Parliament's main achievement in connection with the Nature Diversity Act and the protection of natural habitats. In both the cases discussed, it is worth noting that the Sámi reindeer herders in northern and southern Norway feel they have been deceived by the environmental authorities. Inevitably, this must have led to a mistrust that still exists. Lájlá Eira[92] has studied the practice of co-management in two national parks with reindeer herding, both of which are from the first National Protection Plan. Although she finds clear differences between the two cases, she does not find trust:

> A common feature of the two fields is that previous experience involving management, dating right back to the establishment of the national parks, influences the current management practices. Those practicing reindeer herding are sceptical since they believe they did not have the possibility to influence during the establishment of the national parks that they perceived they needed, and have since had a retreat that means that they do not perceive that their interests and rights were adequately attended to in the earlier phases of the establishment. For this reason, those practicing reindeer herding are still sceptical towards the administration.[93]

Concerning the ideal of co-management, Eira (op. cit.) concludes:

> As mentioned, the division of powers in co-management shall be shared between the users and the state. In the new management model, the power is moved, in terms of the administrative authority, to the local national park boards. The interviews with the reindeer herders in both fields indicate that that their perception is that the power is not shared . . . At the same time, one may question whether the power is divided in the new management model, since it is the Ministry for Environment that has the supreme authority for the national parks.[94]

Today it seems as if the Sámi representatives on the regional boards stand relatively alone without any apparatus to monitor and support them. In this context, there may be grounds for recalling the NSI project concerning requirements for following up international processes, which in a quote[95] in the section on internationalisation, pointed to the requirement to strengthen Sámi communities and local organisations so that their knowledge and points of view can be expressed. This is primarily a challenge for the Sámi Parliament. It is also worth noting that at an early stage the Sámi Parliament wanted 50 per cent Sámi representation on the new management boards.[96] It may prove that the current representation is

92 Eira, *Medforvaltning*.
93 Op. cit., 81.
94 Op. cit, 81.
95 Schanche, 'Innledning'.
96 Riseth, 'An indigenous perspective'.

insufficient. This may stimulate a new discussion about the need for a Sámi majority (similar to that practised in Australia) or a *consensus* model (decisions based on agreement), as in Laponia (Sweden) and in the Northwest Territories in Canada.[97]

Regarding specific management challenges, there are grounds for highlighting two main problems for Sámi reindeer herders who now have national parks in their areas: a problem concerning *administration* and a problem concerning *pressure on grazing area*.[98] The former centres on the protection authorities' attempt to regulate reindeer herding in accordance with the regulations for protection, in particular the requirement to apply for an exemption for the use of ATVs on bare ground. This has been a bone of contention since the 1980s.[99] Based on Helander's[100] perspective of two different legal understandings and Ween's[101] notion of an ontological struggle, it appears that the county governor in Troms and the Sámi reindeer herders in the Reisa National Park have lived in parallel universes for the past three decades. If the county governor has granted exemptions that reindeer herders have not applied for, neither party has anything to worry about even though there is no actual dialogue. However, there are also examples of regulations for new protection areas that makes it possible that the herders ATV use in reality is a subject for the Reindeer Herding Act.[102]

The problem concerning pressure on grazing area is not new either, but it has received special attention in the wake of the Mountain Text, which created expectations of an increased influx of tourists under the auspices of commercial operators. It is difficult to assess the extent of this pressure, but the point is more that if the intentions of the Mountain Text prove to be correct, it will undoubtedly constitute an extra burden for reindeer herders. This problem is greatest in national parks, which include summer grazing areas for reindeer.[103]

Pressure on grazing was also discussed at this year's national park conference. A representative of Innovation Norway promoted the idea of branding national parks as a tourist product without mentioning the existence of reindeer herding. Several reindeer herders and reindeer politicians have reacted sharply to the fact that this discussion occurred without any presentation of the Sámi reindeer herding perspective.[104] One of those who reacted is Arild Inga, who in addition to being a reindeer herder runs a tourism business and is a member of a national park board. In an opinion piece in a newspaper, he reacted sharply to both the pressure on grazing areas resulting from focusing on national parks as a tourist product and on the restrictions that are still imposed on reindeer herding in national parks.[105]

## Conclusion

Although there has been some progress in recent years as a result of the agreement between the Ministry for Environment (now the Ministry for Climate and Environment) and the Sámi Parliament and later with the Nature Diversity Act, insufficient consideration is still given to the fact that Sámi reindeer herders have clear rights and should not be ignored. I believe I have demonstrated that this is the root of the conflicts between Sámi reindeer herders and protected areas.

97 Svensson, *Forvaltningssystem og forvaltningspraksis.*
98 Riseth, op. cit.; Riseth and Holte, 'Rennäring och nationalparker'; Eira, op. cit.
99 Eira, op. cit.
100 Helander, *Sámiska rättsuppfattningar.*
101 Ween, 'Blåfjella-Skjækerfjella nasjonalpark', 95–109.
102 Forskrift om vern av Kvænangsbotn landskapsvernområde.
103 Riseth and Holte, 'Rennäring och nationalparker'.
104 Solaas, 'Sámisk utelatt i merkevarestrategi'.
105 Inga, 'Nasjonalparker som reiselivsprodukt', 21.

If the authorities wish to reduce the conflicts with those who practise reindeer herding, shifting the focus is essential. The thinking in the Yellowstone model that the national parks are primarily for the visitors must be abandoned, at least in Sámi areas. Reindeer herding must be prioritised more highly among the purposes, and those visiting the national park must do so on the reindeer herders' terms, as is the case with those invited to the projects run by reindeer herders in Nord-Trøndelag. In order to accomplish this, at the very least, the regulations for protection need to be changed so that reindeer herding has a stronger position in relation to recreational use. This is necessary because these prioritised purposes form the basis for the day-to-day work of the national park boards and national park administration. This must also involve ensuring that the management plans for national parks safeguard the Sámi reindeer herders' understanding of nature and relation to the cultural landscape in accordance with the tradition of reindeer herding. The overarching authorities and the Sámi Parliament must contribute to the Sámi reindeer herders being able to pursue their industry and their way of life without the risk of being treated as environmental criminals. It would be preferable if the legislation is amended so that *resource management area* becomes a protection category and that after closer consideration some national parks are adapted to it. Moreover, the regulations and practice must be amended to prevent stricter demands being placed on reindeer herding than would otherwise apply under the Reindeer Herding Act, including the use of ATVs on bare ground, also for protection areas established before the new acts of nature diversity (2009) and reindeer herding (2007).

Comprehensive efforts are also required to reduce the old mistrust. One specific measure would be to develop an apparatus centred on the Sámi representatives on the regional boards and strengthening the connection between them, the reindeer grazing districts and local communities and the Sámi Parliament. Time will tell whether there is also a need for major reforms of the administrative model.

## Bibliography


Aarseth, B. *Norsk Samepolitikk 1945–1990. Målsetting, virkemidler og resultater.* Oslo: Vett & Viten/Norsk Folkemuseum, 2006.

Aasetre, J. *Moderne naturforvaltning: Mellom rasjonalitet og dyrking av urørt natur.* Arbeider fra Geografisk institutt, serie A, 25. Trondheim: NTNU, 1999.

Adams, W. M. 'Nature and the Colonial Mind'. In *Decolonizing Nature: Strategies for Conservation in a Post-colonial Era*, ed. W. M. Adams & M. Mulligan, 16–50. London and Sterling, VA: Earthscan, 2003.

Andrade, G. 'Science and Society at the World Park Congress'. *Conservation Biology* 19, no. 1 (2005): 4–5.

Andreassen, L. 'Ka galt har vi gjort når det må vernes?: Dilemmaer ved etablering av nasjonalpark i lulesamisk område'. In *Samiske landskap og Agenda 21: kultur, næring, miljøvern og demokrati (seminar 2001: Karasjok). Samiske landskap og Agenda 21*, ed. S. Andersen. Guovdageaidnu: Sámi instituhtta, Diedut 2002 (1): 115–127.

Arnesen, T. & J. Å. Riseth. 'Konfliktfyllda naturskyddsprocesser i Norge'. In *Omstridd natur. Trender och utmaningar i nordisk naturförvaltning*, eds. C. Sandström, S. Hovik & E. I. Falleth, 83–104. Umeå: Borea, 2008.

Arnesen, T. & J. Å. Riseth. 'Protection and Equity? Local and Indigenous Encounters with the Grand Scheme of Area Protection in Norway'. In *Nordic Tourism: Issues and Cases*, eds. M. Hall, D. Muller & J. Sarinen, 77–80. Bristol: Channelview, 2009

Aune, T., Johansen, S. & K. Trana. *Blåfjella-Skjækerfjella og Lierne nasjonalparker: Blå fjell og gylne drømmer.* Nordli: Lierne Nasjonalparksenter, 2009.

Bay-Larsen, I. A. 'Bureaucrats and Boundaries. The Changing Intersection between Experts, Local Communities and Environmental Administration in Nature Protection'. PhD thesis. Tromsø: University of Tromsø, 2012.

Benjaminsen, T. A. & H. Svarstad. *Politisk økologi. Miljø, mennesker og makt.* Oslo: Universitetsforlaget, 2010.

Berntsen, B. *Grønne linjer. Natur- og miljøvernets historie i Norge.* Oslo: Unipub, 2011.

Bjerkli, B. & P. Selle, eds. *Samer, makt og demokrati. Sametinget og den nye samiske offentligheten.* Oslo: Gyldendal Akademisk, 2003.

Bjerkli, B. & P. Selle, eds. *Samepolitikkens utvikling.* Oslo: Gyldendal, 2015.

Borrini-Feyerabend, G., Pimbert, M., Farvar, M. Taghi, Kothari, A. & Y. Renard. *Sharing Power. A Global Guide to Collaborative Management of Natural Resources.* London: Earthscan, 2007.

Bye, A. & B. Å. Jåma. *Mijjieh låartesne: rein, folk og natur i Luru reinbeitedistrikt, Nord-Trøndelag.* Levanger: Own publishing, 2011.

Carlsson, L. & F. Berkes. 'Co-management: Concepts and Methodological Implications'. *Journal of Environmental Management* 75 (2005): 67–76.

Chatty, D. 'Enclosures and Exclusions: Conserving Wildlife in Pastoral Areas of the Middle East'. *Anthropology Today* 14 (1998): 2–7.

Convention on Biological Diversity. COP 7 Decision VII/28. Kuala Lumpur, 9–20 February 2004. http://www.cbd.int/decisions/?m=COP-07&id=7765&lg=0 (accessed 6 December 2008).

Eira, L. H. *Medforvaltning som ideal og praksis. Studie av forvaltningspraksisen i to nasjonalparker med reindrift.* Masteroppgave i Samfunnsplanlegging og kulturforståelse: University of Tromsø, 2013.

Estil, B. *Kulturmøte – kulturkonflikt: en studie av rovdyrsproblematikken i Lierne i et historisk perspektiv.* Hovedoppgave i historie: NTNU, 1998.

Falleth, E. I. & S. Hovik. *Lokal forvaltning av store verneområder: Erfaringer fra fire forsøk.* NIBR-rapport 2008 No. 11. Oslo: Norsk institutt for by- og regionforskning, 2008.

Falleth, E. I. & S. Hovik. 'Local Government and Nature Conservation in Norway: Decentralisation as a Strategy in Environmental Policy'. *Local Environment* 14, no. 3 (2009): 221–231.

Fearnside, P. M. 'Conservation Policy in Brazilian Amazonia: Understanding the Dilemmas'. *World Development* 31 (2003): 757–779.

Fedreheim, G. E. 'Value Creation on Norway's Green Gold: An Analysis of Policy Formulation and Implementation in the Field of Nature Conservation'. PhD in Sociology; No. 12, Bodø: University of Nordland, 2013.

Fjellheim, S. *Gåebrien Sijte- en sameby i Rørostraktene.* Røros: Own publishing, 2012. Forskrift om vern av Kvænangsbotn landskapsvernområde/Bađaávžži ja Gearbbet suodjemeahcci/ Niemenaikun ja Kärpikän suojeluala, Kvænangen kommune, Troms.

Forskrift om vern for Reisa nasjonalpark/Ráisa álbotlas meahcci, Nordreisa kommune, Troms. Lovdata. FOR-1986–11–28 nr 2112.

Forskrift om verneplan for Verdal-Snåsa-Lierne. Vern av Blåfjella-Skjækerfjella/Låarte-Skæhkere nasjonalpark, Verdal, Steinkjer, Grong, Snåsa og Lierne kommuner, Nord-Trøndelag. Lovdata. FOR-2004–12–17–1691.

Framstad, E., T. Blindheim, L. Erikstad, P. G. Thingstad & S.-E. Sloreid. *Naturfaglig evaluering av norske verneområder.* Rapport 535. Oslo/Trondheim: NINA, 2010.

Fylkesmannen i Troms. Forvaltningsplan for Reisa nasjonalpark/Ráisa álbmotlas meahcci og Raisduottarhaldi landskapsvernomrade/Ráisduottarháldi suodjemeahcci (2014). Utkast fra Fylkesmannen i Troms og arbeidsutvalget 'Reisagruppa' overlevert Reisa nasjonalparkstyre i 2014. *Reindrift*, 8, 56.

Hajer, M. J. *The Politics of Environmental Discourse: Ecological Modernization and the Policy Process.* Oxford, UK: Oxford University Press, 1995.

Helander, E. *Samiska rättsuppfattningar.* Juridica Lapponica 30. University of Lapland. Rovaniemi, 2004 [first printed in NOU 2001: 34, 2001].

Helander-Renvall, E. 'Animism, Personhood and the Nature of Reality: Sámi Perspectives'. *Polar Record* 46 (2010): 44–56.

Hermanstrand, H. & A. Kosmo. *Røyrvik: samene i Østre Namdal.* Røyrvik: Røyrvik Kommune, 2009.

Hernes H-K. & N. Oskal, eds. *Finnmarksloven.* Oslo: Cappelen Akademisk, 2008.

Hitchcock, R. K. ' "We Are the First People": Land, Natural Resources and Identity in the Central Kalahari'. *Journal of Southern African Studies* 28 (2002): 797–824.

Hjorthol, L. M. *Alta. Kraftkampen som utfordret statens makt.* Oslo: Gyldendal Akademisk, 2006.

Inga, A. P. 'Nasjonalparker som reiselivsprodukt i et reindriftssamisk perspektiv'. *Ságat* 71 (17 April 2015): 21.

Jacoby, K. *Crimes against Nature: Squatters, Poachers, Thieves, and the Hidden History of American Conservation.* Berkeley: University of California Press, 2001.

Joma, N. P. *Speech at the 50 Years Anniversary of Børgefjell nasjonalpark,* 2013.

Neuman, R. P. *Imposing Wilderness: Struggles over Livelihood and Nature Preservation in Africa.* Berkeley: University of California Press, 1998.

Nicholas, C. 'Who Can Protect the Forest Better? Pitching Orang Asli against Professionals in Protected Area Management in Peninsular Malaysia'. International Symposium on Eco-Human Interactions in Tropical Forests. Kyoto: Kyoto University, Society of Tropical Ecology, 2005.

Norwegian Agricultural Agency [Landbruksdirektoratet]. *Ressursregnskap for reindriftsnæringen.* Alta: Rapport No 36, 2015.

Norwegian Environment Agency [Miljødirektoratet]. *Miljøstatus i Norge. Vernet areal, Norge.* http://www.miljostatus.no/Tema/Naturmangfold/Vernet-natur/Vernet-areal-Norge/ (accessed 22 April 2015).

NOU 1986:13. *Ny landsplan for nasjonalparker.* Oslo, Bergen, Stavanger, Tromsø: Universitetsforlaget, 1986.

NOU 2004:28. *Naturmangfoldloven.* Oslo, Bergen, Stavanger, Tromsø: Universitetsforlaget, 2004.

Olofsson, J. & L. Oksanen. 'Effects of Reindeer Density on Vascular Plant Diversity on North Scandinavian Mountains'. *Rangifer* 25, no. 1 (2005): 5–18.

Olofsson, J., Oksanen, L., Callaghan, T., Hulme, P. E., Oksanen, T. & O. Suominen. 'Herbivores Inhibit Climate Driven Shrub Expansion on the Tundra'. *Global Change Biology* 15 (2009): 2681–2693.

Ostrom, E. *Understanding Institutional Diversity.* Princeton and Oxford: Princeton University Press, 2005.

Ot. Prp. 52 (2008–2009). *Om lov om forvaltning av naturens mangfold (naturmangfoldloven).* Tilråding fra Miljøverndepartementet, 3 April 2009.

Pedersen, S. 'Samenes historie; fra undertrykking til kulturelt likeverd'. In *Likeverd. Grunnlaget for demokrati,* ed. A. Holt-Jensen & S. Dyrvik, 173–192. Oslo: Res Publica, 2015.

Poirier, R. & D. Ostergren. 'Evicting People from Nature: Indigenous Land Rights and National Parks in Australia, Russia and the United States'. *Natural Resources Journal* 42 (2002): 331–352.

Posey, D. & G. Dutfield. *Beyond Intellectual Property: Towards Traditional Resource Rights for Indigenous People and Local Communities.* Ottawa: International Development Research Centre, 1996.

Ravna, Ø. *Finnmarksloven- og retten til jorden i Finnmark.* Oslo: Gyldendal Juridisk, 2013.

Reimerson, E. 'Between Nature and Culture: Exploring Space for Indigenous Agency in the Convention on Biological Diversity'. *Environmental Politics* 22, no. 6 (2013): 992–1009.

Riseth, J. Å. 'An Indigenous Perspective on National Parks and Sámi Reindeer Herding in Norway'. *Geographical Research* 45, no. 2 (June 2007): 177–185.

Riseth, J. Å. . Premisser for bruk og vern: Forskningsresultater og innspill'. In *Seminar om forskning innenfor vern og bruk av verneområder og randsoner : oppsummering av foredrag og innspill på seminar 13.–14. januar 2009.* Retrieved 9. July 2016 http://www.forskningsradet.no/prognett-miljo2015/Arrangement/Seminar_om_forskning pa_bruk_og_vern__Kunnskapsformidling_og_kunnskapsbehov/1224698155445&lang=no.

Riseth, J. Å. *Reindrift og ressursforvaltning.* Drammen: Vett & Viten, 2015.

Riseth, J. Å. & A. Holte. 'Rennäring och nationalparker i Norge'. In *Omstridd natur: Trender och utmaningar i nordisk naturförvaltning*, eds. C. Sandström, S. Hovik & E. I. Falleth, 269–290. Umeå: Borea, 2008.

Riseth, J. Å. & L. Oksanen. 'Ressursøkonomiske og økologiske perspektiver på grenseoverskridende reindrift'. In *Grenseoverskridende reindrift før og etter 1905*, eds. E. G. Broderstad, E. Niemi & I. Sommerseth, 93–113. Skriftserie, nr. 14. Senter for samiske studier. Tromsø: Universitetet i Tromsø, 2007.

Riseth, J. Å. & J. I. Solbakken. 'Naturbruk i Kautokeino i et kulturhistorisk lys'. *Utmark* 1/2010. http://www.utmark.org/utgivelser/pub/2010-1/Riseth_Solbakken_Utmark_1_2010.html (accessed 16 November 2015).

Sametinget. *Naturmangfoldlov*. Sametingets plenum. Sak 44/08, 2008.

Sandström, C., Hovik, S. & E. I. Falleth, eds. *Omstridd natur: Trender och utmaningar i nordisk naturförvaltning*. Umeå: Borea, 2008.

Sara, J. M. Tale [Speech]. *Åpningen av Blåfjella-Skjækerfjella og Lierne nasjonalparker*, 2006.

Schanche, A. 'Innledning'. In *Naturressurser og miljøverdier i samiske områder: forvaltnings- og forskningsutfordringer*, ed. A. Schanche, 3–19. Rapport 1 i prosjektet 'Miljø, kultur og kunnskap. Bruk og forvaltning av naturressurser i Sámiske områder'. Kautokeino; Dieđut 2/2001.

Schanche, M. *Urfolk, rettigheter og ressurser: Politiske prosesser omkring miljø- og ressursforvaltning i samiske områder i Norge*. Oppgave i statsvitenskap. Trondheim: NTNU, Unpublished, 2001.

Scott, W. R. *Institutions and Organizations*. Thousand Oaks, London and New Delhi: SAGE, 2001.

Seippel, Ø. 'Trees, Ecology and Biological Diversity'. In *Protecting Nature: Organizations and Networks in Europe and the USA*, ed. C. S. A. van Koppen & W. T. Markham, 165–186. Cheltenham, UK and Northampton, USA: Edward Elgar, 2007.

Selle, P. 'Organisasjonssamfunnet- ein statsreiskap?'. In *Ein stat? Fristillingas fire ansikt*, ed. T. Grønlie & P. Selle, 145 pp. Oslo:Samlaget, 1998 (referred in Slagstad, 2001).

Slagstad, R. *De nasjonale strateger*. Oslo: Pax, 2001.

Smardon, R. C. & B. B. Faust. 'Introduction: International Policy in the Biosphere Reserves of Mexico's Yucatan Peninsula'. *Landscape and Urban Planning* 74 (2006): 160–192.

Solaas, S. 'Samisk utelatt i merkevarestrategi for nasjonalparker'. *Ságat* (21 April 2015).

Solaas, S. 'Søker ikke om dispensasjon'. *Ságat* (21 April 2015).

Spence, M. D. *Dispossessing the Wilderness: Indian Removal and the Making of National Parks*. New York: Oxford, 1999.

St.meld. 62 (1991–92). *Ny landsplan for nasjonalparker og andre større verneområder i Norge*. Oslo: Miljøverndepartementet, 1992.

Stolton, S. & G. Oviedo. 'Using the Categories to Support the Needs and Rights of Traditional and Indigenous Peoples in Protected Areas'. Chapter 2.12. In *Speaking a Common Language: The Uses and Performance of the IUCN System of Management Categories for Protected Areas*, ed. K. Bishop, N. Dudley, A. Phillips & S. Stolton. Cardiff: Cardiff University, IUCN-The World Conservation Union and UNEP-World Conservation Monitoring Centre, 2004.

Store norske leksikon, 'Nasjonalisme'. https://snl.no/nasjonalisme (accessed 25 August 2015).

Svensson, G. *Forvaltningssystem og forvaltningspraksis i nordlige-arktiske verneområder*. Nordreisa: Halti nasjonalparksenter. Unpublished Report, 2013.

Vatn, A. *Institutions and the Environment*. Cheltenham: Edward Elgar, 2005.

Ward, G. C. *The West: An Illustrated History*. Boston: Little Brown & Co, 1996.

Ween, G. B. 'Blåfjella-Skjækerfjella nasjonalpark: Naturforvaltning som produksjon av natur/sted'. *Norsk Antropologisk Tidsskrift* 8 (2009): (1–2), 95–109.

Ween, G. & S. Abram. 'The Norwegian Trekking Association: Trekking as Constituting the Nation'. *Landscape Research* 37, no. 2 (2012): 155–171.

Ween, G. & J. Å. Riseth. 'Indigenous Hospitality and Tourism, past Trajectories and New Beginnings'. In *Arctic Indigenous Tourism*, eds. A. Viken & D. Müller. Bristol: Channelview, 2016 (in press).

Witozek, N. *Norske naturmytologier*. Oslo: Pax, 1998.

Wulff, G. Editorial. 'Presses ut av nasjonalparken'. *Ságat* (24 April 2015).

# 10 International arenas, local space for agency and national discourse as mediator

## Protected areas in Swedish and Norwegian Sápmi

*Elsa Reimerson*

### Introduction

In an increasingly globalised world, discourses articulated in and through international arenas[1] shape and influence national and local protected area discourses, and the outcomes of international negotiations have substantial effects on the space for agency of individuals and groups on national and local levels. The number and scope of international institutions, organisations and knowledge systems aimed at solving environmental problems are growing, as is the influence of international conservation authorities. International law governs much national protected area legislation, and discourses of protected areas are intertwined within and across political and administrative levels.[2] International arenas for nature conservation and protected areas have also proved important for Indigenous advocacy, as part of Indigenous peoples' strategies to legitimise and support their claims to land rights, participation and political influence.[3]

Discourses of area protection have traditionally been concentrated on preserving and maintaining (the idea of) 'untouched' or 'wilderness' areas, and have largely ignored or suppressed Indigenous land and resource use.[4] In recent decades, the arguments and ideologies underpinning area protection have changed, introducing concepts such as biological diversity protection and sustainable development along with rights-based approaches, increased recognition of local and traditional knowledge and a growing focus on local participation.[5] International arenas for nature conservation and area protection increasingly focus on Indigenous peoples' role in and contribution to conservation policies and have become important instruments through which they can gain protection for their natural resources, knowledge, traditions and lifestyles.[6] Indigenous peoples are visible

1 I use the word 'arenas' to refer to the both material and non-material spaces for discourse formation and negotiation constructed through conventions, authorities, organisations, and meetings on the international level. Cf. Fraser, 'Rethinking the Public Sphere'.

2 Sonnenfeld and Mol, 'Globalization and the transformation of environmental governance'; Zimmerer, 'Geographical perspectives'; Büscher and Whande, 'Whims of the winds of time?'.

3 Fourmile, 'Indigenous peoples'; Barsh, 'Indigenous peoples'.

4 Stevens, 'Legacy of Yellowstone'; Adams, 'Nature and the colonial mind', Colchester, 'Conservation policy and Indigenous peoples'; Chatty and Colchester, *Conservation and Mobile Indigenous Peoples*; Colchester, *Salvaging Nature*; Anaya, *Indigenous Peoples in International Law*.

5 Zachrisson, *Commons Protected for or from the People*; Hovik, Sandström and Zachrisson, 'Management of protected areas'; Agrawal and Ribot, 'Accountability in decentralization'; Lane, 'Affirming new directions'; Stevens, 'A new protected area paradigm'.

6 Barsh, 'Indigenous peoples'; Fourmile, 'Indigenous peoples', Morgan, 'Advancing Indigenous rights at the United Nations'; Berkes, Colding and Folke, 'Rediscovery of traditional ecological knowledge'; Heinämäki, 'Protecting the rights of Indigenous peoples'.

and active on the international level, making use of international arenas as platforms for advocacy and attempts to influence policy.[7] International law can be an important tool for advancement of the political goals of Indigenous peoples, and international activism can be a way for them to bypass national levels where they are not sufficiently or accurately represented.[8]

However, both scholars and Indigenous representatives have also problematised the major international conventions for nature conservation and area protection. Critics argue that these texts are largely constructed and upheld by non-Indigenous people, that their organisations and decision-making bodies include representatives of nation-states where Indigenous peoples are still struggling for recognition of their rights and that they do not always provide adequate mechanisms for Indigenous influence and participation. They have also been criticised for upholding and reproducing colonial discourses and structures, and for failing to safeguard, or even violating, Indigenous rights.

Progress made in the international arena can strengthen the position of Indigenous peoples on the national and local levels, but these processes are seldom simple or straightforward. The relationship between political and administrative divisions on different scales and levels is complex, reciprocal and mutually influencing. The formation of discourses on the international level affects national and local discourses, but does not determine them.[9] National and local discourses affect global discourse formation, and may reinforce, resist or rearticulate international discourses as these are introduced into the national or local context. A country's implementation of international conventions means adopting internationally established discourses, but it also means incorporating them in, or adjusting them to, potentially different or even contradictory national discourses.

In this chapter, I examine how discourses articulated in and through international arenas for protected area and nature conservation affect Indigenous peoples' space for political agency on national and local levels, and discuss the potential of international arenas as political tools for the promotion of Indigenous rights in national contexts. I investigate two cases of protected areas governance and management in Norwegian and Swedish Sápmi, analyse how discursive constructions of Sámi influence and participation relate to the Convention on Biological Diversity and the World Heritage Convention and discuss the effects of these constructions on Sámi space for agency in relation to protected areas.

## Background

In 2012, the Swedish government transferred parts of the management of the Laponia World Heritage site in northern Sweden to a newly established not-for-profit organisation comprising municipal, state and Sámi actors. Representatives of local Sámi reindeer herding communities (RHCs) hold the majority on the board of directors of the management organisation. Sámi cultural heritage is an important part of the justification for the listing of Laponia as a World Heritage site, and the World Heritage Convention (WHC) was fundamental for the Sámi RHCs' influence over the management of the site.[10]

7 Keck and Sikkink, *Activists beyond Borders*; Niezen, *Origins of Indigenism*; Dahl, *Indigenous Space*.

8 Koivurova and Heinämäki, 'Participation of indigenous peoples'; Schroeder, 'Agency in international climate negotiations'; Dahl, *Indigenous Space*; Niezen, *Origins of Indigenism*.

9 Büscher and Whande, 'Whims of the winds of time?'.

10 UNESCO World Heritage Centre, 'Laponian area'; Reimerson, 'Sami space for agency'.

Two years previously, in 2010, the Norwegian government had introduced a reform that allows for the transfer of the management of national parks and other large protected areas to local management boards, with Sámi representation in areas of importance for Sámi culture. The reform was justified partly by commitments under the Convention on Biological Diversity (CBD).[11] These recent examples of efforts to increase Sámi influence over protected areas, and the international arenas for protected areas to which they are linked, will serve here as the empirical basis for the discussion of the relationship between global discourses and national or local space for agency.

In both Norway and Sweden, a large proportion of the areas set aside for protection or conservation includes or covers traditional Sámi territories, and large parts of Sápmi are set aside as protected areas. Protected area establishment and management has been, and continues to be, the subject of negotiations and conflicts over resource utilisation and nature conservation in relation to Sámi Indigenous rights. Both Norway and Sweden have made commitments through international protected area and nature conservation conventions, and their political and administrative systems are similar. However, there are significant differences in how the two states have responded to and dealt with international commitments, as well as in their approaches to Sámi rights.

Sweden's first national parks, established in 1909, were the first in Europe. Norway adopted its first nature protection laws in 1910, but did not establish national parks until the early 1960s. Both countries have historically centralised the management of protected areas to national and regional state authorities. Today, Norway has moved further towards a delegation of authority over protected areas and places greater emphasis on sustainable use, whereas Sweden prioritises strict regulation and has a less comprehensive strategy for decentralisation.[12]

Both Norway and Sweden have recognised the Sámi as an Indigenous people, and both have signed the UN Declaration on the Rights of Indigenous Peoples (UNDRIP). Norway is commonly considered comparatively more active in its engagement with Indigenous issues, and the Sámi people in Norway have a stronger political and legal standing than in Sweden.[13] Norway has ratified ILO Convention No. 169 on Indigenous and Tribal Peoples (ILO 169) and has subsequently established agreements with the Norwegian Sámi Parliament concerning consultation procedures, including specific guidelines for proceedings on protected areas in Sápmi.[14] Sweden has not ratified ILO 169, nor established consultation agreements.

The Laponia World Heritage site was included on the World Heritage List in 1996 based on both natural and cultural values, with the living cultural heritage of the Sámi as a central part of the justification for inscription.[15] Since 2012, Laponia has been managed by a

11 Prop 1 S (2009–2010), 222; Fauchald , Guldbrandsen and Zachrisson, 'Internationalization of protected areas'; Reimerson, 'Discourses of decentralization'.

12 Fauchald, Guldbrandsen and Zachrisson, 'Internationalization of protected areas'; Zachrisson, *Commons Protected for or from the People*; Zachrisson, 'The designation of Fulufjället National Park'; Hovik, Sandström and Zachrisson, 'Management of protected areas'.

13 Minde, 'Sámi land rights in Norway'; Allard, 'The Nordic countries' law on Sámi territorial rights'; Josefsen, Mörkenstam and Saglie, 'Different institutions within similar states'.

14 ILO, 'Convention No. 169'; Procedures for Consultations between State Authorities and the Sámi Parliament; Ministry of the Environment and Sámediggi – Sametinget, 'Avtale mellom Sametinget og Miljøverndepartementet'.

15 UNESCO World Heritage Centre, 'Laponian area'.

not-for-profit organisation, Laponiatjuottjudus,[16] comprised of representatives from Sámi reindeer herding communities (RHCs), the Norrbotten County Administrative Board (CAB), the Swedish Environmental Protection Agency (SEPA) and the two municipalities within whose territories Laponia is situated. RHC representatives hold the majority on the organisation's board of directors.[17] The management arrangement for Laponia is unique in Sweden, both in terms of local influence and control over protected area management and in terms of Sámi influence and rights.[18]

The Norwegian reform of protected area management, implemented in 2010, provides for local governance of a broad range of large protected areas.[19] Under the reform, the Ministry of Climate and Environment delegates the management of protected areas to inter-municipal National Park Boards (NPBs) consisting of elected political representatives nominated by local and regional councils and, in Sámi areas, the Sámi Parliament.[20] The level of Sámi representation is determined by the importance of each area for Sámi culture and industry.[21] Forty-one NPBs have been established, of which 20 include Sámi Parliament representatives.[22] When the reform is fully implemented, local boards will manage a majority of Norway's large protected areas.[23]

## Analytical framework

This chapter employs a discourse theoretical approach. 'Discourse' refers here to historically specific systems of rules and practices that form the meaning or identities of objects and subjects, legitimise certain knowledge and define who can make authoritative claims to hold such knowledge.[24] Social phenomena are given meaning through the connection of concrete subjects or objects to specific linguistic signs, defined by their relation and difference to other signs.[25] While both possible and necessary, such fixations of meaning are always partial, never complete or inevitable.[26] They need to be reproduced in order to maintain their stability, and are thereby processes of power.[27] By mapping the formation of meaning and critically scrutinising the relationships of power that are both productive of and produced by it, discourse analysis offers ways in which to challenge dominant notions, thereby opening the way for change.[28]

I am interested in the ways dominant discourses construct the conditions for Indigenous subjects to act, speak, participate or exert influence in relation to protected area governance

16 *Tjuottjudus* is a term for management or administration in the Lule Sámi language.
17 Laponiaprocessen, 'Statutes for Laponiatjuottjudus'; Laponia, 'Management plan'.
18 Zachrisson, 'Conflict resolution mechanisms'; Hovik, Sandström and Zachrisson, 'Management of protected areas'; Beach, 'World Heritage and Indigenous peoples'.
19 Prop 1 S (2009–2010), 218–226.
20 Norges nasjonalparks- og verneområdestyrer, 'Om styrene'; Norwegian Environment Agency, 'Hvem forvalter verneområdene?'.
21 Prop 1 S (2009–2010), 224.
22 Sámediggi – Sametinget, *Nye styremedlemmer for nasjonalpark- og verneområdestyrene*; Norges nasjonalparks- og verneområdestyrer, 'Nasjonalpark- og verneområdestyrer'.
23 Fauchald and Gulbrandsen, 'The Norwegian reform'.
24 Howarth, *Discourse*, 9; Foucault, *Archaeology of knowledge*, 54, 55–61.
25 Howarth, *Discourse*, 18–23.
26 Laclau and Mouffe, *Hegemony & Socialist Strategy*, 110–111.
27 Howarth, *Discourse*, 104; Foucault, *Power/Knowledge*, 98,119, 198; Jørgensen and Phillips, *Discourse Analysis*, 13.
28 Howarth, *Discourse*, 129; Jørgensen and Phillips, *Discourse Analysis*, 25–26.

and management. I understand agency – the ability or capacity of an individual or group to act – as constructed through the discursive positioning of different individuals or groups, shaped by structures and relationships of power and dependent on context.[29] I use *space for agency* as a concept to describe and analyse the effects of these positionings, relationships and contexts.[30]

Discourses position subjects within discursive structures, produce them as social actors and define the ways in which they can gain recognition as political agents.[31] Certain subject positions may restrict the space for agency of an individual or group, if they limit their ability to be recognised as knowledgeable subjects or to speak with authority within a certain topic area.[32] Conversely, other positions may enable space for political agency, if they work to strengthen and add legitimacy to certain claims made from those positions.[33]

Discourses of nature conservation and heritage protection are evolving and changing, but colonial constructs continue to influence discourses on both protected areas and Indigenous rights.[34] They include the separation of nature from culture, the 'othering' and subjugation of Indigenous subjects, the failure to recognise Indigenous land use and land rights, and the view of Indigenous territories as 'wilderness'.[35] Indigenous and other non-Western peoples, along with scholars and heritage practitioners, have criticised policies and practices of nature conservation and heritage protection for carrying colonial notions of Indigenous peoples and of human–nature relations, upholding Eurocentric, universalising discourses, limiting Indigenous representation and reproducing colonial power relations.[36] This has consequences for the space for agency produced in and through the international arenas in focus in this study, as experiences of colonisation and unequal power relationships continue to shape contemporary relationships between Indigenous peoples and majority populations.[37]

## *Analytical tools and material*

In tracing the formation of meaning and the shaping of spaces for agency in protected area discourses, I make use of two sets of analytical tools. The first borrows from Carol Bacchi's application of the concept of *problematisations*. Bacchi suggests that all policy proposals rely on specific representations of problems, or problematisations, which fix elements within discourse in accordance with particular interpretations of the world; attribute identities to

29 Davies, 'Concept of agency'; Mouffe, 'Democratic citizenship'; Smith, *Laclau and Mouffe*.

30 Laclau and Mouffe, *Hegemony & Socialist Strategy*; Smith, *Laclau and Mouffe*; Jørgensen and Phillips, *Discourse Analysis*; Reimerson, 'Between nature and culture'; Reimerson, 'Sami space for agency'.

31 Howarth, *Discourse*, 108–109; Laclau and Mouffe, *Hegemony & Socialist Strategy*, 115; Foucault, *Archaeology of Knowledge*, 55–61.

32 cf. Mörkenstam, *Om 'Lapparnes privilegier'*; Reimerson, 'Between nature and culture'; Reimerson, 'Sami space for agency'.

33 cf. Tennberg, 'Indigenous peoples as international political actors'.

34 Adams, 'Nature and the colonial mind'; Stevens, 'Legacy of Yellowstone'; Büscher and Whande, 'Whims of the winds of time?'.

35 Poirier and Ostergren, 'Evicting people from nature'; Stevens, 'Legacy of Yellowstone'; Adams, 'Nature and the colonial mind'; Pickerill, 'From wilderness to WildCountry'; Uggla, 'What is this thing called "natural"?'; Plumwood, 'Decolonizing relationships with nature'.

36 See e.g. IIFB Opening statements to COP9, COP10, COP11 and Working Group 8(j)-7; Byrne, 'Western hegemony'; Suchet, '"Totally wild"?', Colchester, 'Conservation policy and indigenous peoples'; Colchester et al., *Conservation and Indigenous Peoples*; Labadi, 'Representations of the nation'; Smith, *Uses of Heritage*; Baird, *Politics of Place*.

37 Smith, *Decolonizing Methodologies*; Anaya, *Indigenous Peoples in International Law*.

individuals and groups; and shape subjects' space for political agency.[38] By examining the representations of problems in protected area policy texts, their underlying assumptions can be revealed and their consequences for subjects' space for agency explored. This approach exposes the relationships between the construction of nature conservation as an area of politics, its delimitations and priorities, and the articulation of subjects in relation to that political domain.

The second set of analytical tools draws on discourse theory concepts developed by Ernesto Laclau and Chantal Mouffe. Here, the focus is on the production of meaning through the establishment of relations between elements in discourse. These processes, or *articulations*, invest linguistic signs, subjects, subject positions and other social phenomena with meaning and order them in relation to each other, thus achieving a temporary fixation of the discourse.[39] Signs or concepts are sorted and linked in *chains of equivalence* that define how and what an object or a subject is, and is not, in relation to other chains.[40] These constructions make some of the possible identifications relevant, or privileged, while others are ignored. This approach allows me to map the process through which Indigenous peoples are discursively positioned as subjects and agents in nature conservation and protected area discourse.

The combination of these approaches enables investigation of the foundational assumptions of protected area discourses as well as the fixation of meaning of particular concepts. It allows for a discussion of discursive tensions, hegemonic formations, power relations and the effects of these processes on the space for Indigenous agency in discourses of protected areas.[41]

The empirical material analysed in this study includes policy proposals, legislative texts and other official texts, and interviews. I have not differentiated between kinds of texts – they are each part of the discursive processes studied, and each contributes to the understanding of how meaning is constructed through discourse.[42] I have coded the texts through the identification of themes drawn both from theoretical assumptions and emerging from the empirical material, and searched the material for problem representations and articulations of central concepts.

## Results

### *The WHC and Laponia*

The World Heritage Convention (WHC) provides the legal framework and the administrative and financial support for the World Heritage List, which is an inventory of cultural and natural sites deemed to be of 'outstanding universal value'.[43] Since the establishment of the World Heritage Convention in 1972, the sites included on the World Heritage List have primarily represented cultural heritage sites related to European national identity. The WHC has done well in protecting European churches and castles, but has more seldom

38 Bacchi, *Analysing Policy*, 16–32.
39 Laclau and Mouffe, *Hegemony & Socialist Strategy*, 105.
40 Laclau and Mouffe, *Hegemony & Socialist Strategy*, 127–130; Howarth, *Discourse*, 106–107.
41 Bacchi, *Analysing Policy*, 2–21; Laclau and Mouffe, *Hegemony & Socialist Strategy*, 127–130; Jørgensen and Phillips, *Discourse Analysis*, 43–45.
42 Howarth, *Discourse*, 10.
43 UNESCO World Heritage Centre, *World Heritage Information Kit.*

recognised heritage forms and values that diverge from Western models.[44] Many of the World Heritage sites listed for natural values are located in the territories of Indigenous peoples, but the existence and role of those peoples or the cultural heritage values associated with Indigenous landscapes have often not been reflected in World Heritage nomination and management.[45]

The World Heritage Convention and the work of the World Heritage Committee have been criticised for upholding a Eurocentric, universalising discourse, for reproducing colonial structures and for constraining the agency of Indigenous peoples.[46] Indigenous peoples and human rights organisations have raised concerns about violations of Indigenous rights in the implementation of the Convention.[47] Only state parties to the WHC have voting rights in the World Heritage Committee, the main body in charge of the implementation of the WHC. There is little official input from Indigenous representatives to the Committee, and efforts to establish an advisory body of Indigenous experts on World Heritage have thus far failed.[48] The 'Operational Guidelines for the Implementation of the World Heritage Convention' encourage state parties to ensure participation of a wide variety of stakeholders in the identification, nomination and protection of World Heritage sites, but does not mention Indigenous peoples.[49] The focus instead is on local communities and non-governmental organisations.

Nevertheless, the WHC is the only convention that has tried to engage with cultural landscapes and as such, it potentially provides a way for Indigenous peoples to protect their lands, culture and heritage.[50] In recent decades, the World Heritage Committee claims to have made efforts to diversify the World Heritage List and support underrepresented countries.[51] Following criticism and recommendations from the UN Permanent Forum on Indigenous Issues (UNPFII) and others, the World Heritage Committee is also working to improve mechanisms whereby Indigenous peoples can become involved in World Heritage practices and ensure the safeguarding of their rights and interests in the work under the WHC.[52]

As of October 2015, there are 15 Swedish sites inscribed on the World Heritage List, the majority being cultural sites, situated in the southern part of the country.[53] Laponia was listed as a World Heritage site in 1996. An earlier World Heritage nomination draft for Laponia had only considered the natural values of the site, but after criticism from both Sámi and Swedish actors, it was nominated and accepted as a mixed site – the only one in

44 Meskell, 'UNESCO and the fate of WHIPCOE'.

45 IWGIA, 'World Heritage Sites and Indigenous Peoples'; Baird, *Politics of Place.*

46 Smith, *Uses of Heritage*; Waterton, Smith and Campbell, 'The utility of discourse analysis'; Labadi, 'Representations of the nation'; Byrne, 'Western hegemony'; Baird, '"The breath of the mountain is my heart"'; Baird, *Politics of Place.*

47 Disko and Tugendhat, *International Expert Workshop.*

48 Meskell, 'UNESCO and the fate of WHIPCOE'; Gillespie, *Protected Areas and International Environmental Law.*

49 UNESCO World Heritage Centre, 'Operational Guidelines'.

50 Rössler, 'World Heritage cultural landscapes'; Disko and Tugendhat, *International Expert Workshop.*

51 Rössler, 'World Heritage cultural landscapes'; UNESCO World Heritage Centre, 'Global strategy'.

52 NGO/IPO Joint Submission to the UNPFII, *Continuous Violations of FPIC in WHC*; NGO/IPO Joint Submission to the UNPFII, *The Lack of Implementation of UNDRIP in WHC*; Disko and Tugendhat, *International Expert Workshop*; UNESCO World Heritage Centre, *World Heritage and Indigenous Peoples.*

53 UNESCO World Heritage Centre, 'Sweden'.

Sweden, and one of only a handful in the world to include the living culture of an Indigenous people.[54] It includes four national parks and two nature reserves and covers 9,400 square kilometres in the northernmost county of Sweden, Norrbotten. Reindeer husbandry still takes place throughout the whole Laponian Area, and Laponia includes the lands of nine active reindeer herding communities (RHCs).[55]

After inscription, the RHCs in the Laponian area made it clear that they would not accept a management organisation without strong Sámi influence and control, but state and municipal authorities were not initially prepared to meet the RHCs' demands. It took almost 15 years to reach an agreement on the management of Laponia.[56] In 2009, a government-commissioned committee, assembled by the Norrbotten County Administrative Board (CAB) and with a mandate to develop a new management arrangement with strong Sámi influence, presented a joint proposal for a new organisational structure for Laponia.[57] The not-for-profit organisation Laponiatjuottjudus was established in 2011. In 2012, the CAB formally decided to transfer management of the Laponian area to Laponiatjuottjudus, and the decision was implemented on 1 January 2013.

The World Heritage listing of Laponia brought to the fore issues of Sámi participation and influence in Swedish protected area management, and the WHC is fundamental to the organisation of the management of Laponia. The living Sámi cultural heritage in the area was a major factor in the inclusion of the site on the World Heritage List, and the RHCs used this as a strategic tool to further their claims in both the process leading up to the nomination and in the negotiations after inclusion.[58] After the inscription, the RHCs produced a visionary document including a proposed management programme for Laponia, *Mijá ednam*, in which they argued that a strong Sámi influence in the management of Laponia is a necessity for the safeguarding of the World Heritage values of the site.[59] *Mijá ednam* establishes a longstanding and coherent Sámi presence in the Laponian area; stresses the importance of Sámi reindeer herding for the cultural and natural values of Laponia; and proposes that the World Heritage listing be used to protect and promote Sámi culture and industry.[60]

The management plan for Laponia echoes the views of *Mijá ednam* and largely uses the same, or similar, language when describing the importance of Sámi reindeer herding for Laponia's World Heritage values. The plan describes Laponia as a Sámi cultural landscape, and Sámi culture – in particular Sámi reindeer herding – as a condition for the World Heritage values of Laponia.[61] Interviews with those directly involved in the management organisation further confirmed the links between Sámi influence and the notion of Sámi culture as a condition for the World Heritage values of Laponia. Interviewees also described the WHC

54 Nilsson Dahlström, *Negotiating Wilderness*, 226–267.

55 A reindeer herding community (Swe. *Sameby*, lit. 'Sámi village') is an economic association for reindeer herders. It also refers to the geographical area in which the RHC is entitled to pursue reindeer husbandry.

56 Nilsson Dahlström, *Negotiating Wilderness*, 323–346; Green, *Managing Laponia*, 101–123; Zachrisson, 'Conflict resolution mechanisms', 10–15.

57 CAB Norrbotten 'Hemställan Laponiadelegation'; Swedish Government 'Regleringsbrev 2007 Naturvårdsverket'.

58 Green, *Managing Laponia*, 152–184.

59 Mijá ednam, *Samebyarnas Laponiaprogram*, 69.

60 Mijá ednam, *Samebyarnas Laponiaprogram*, 13–19, 37–61.

61 Laponia, 'Management plan', 16–17, 33–43, 102–103.

and UNESCO as important factors in the design and continued work of the management organisation.[62]

The problem representations in these articulations focus on the protection and preservation of the natural and cultural heritage values of Laponia. The safeguarding of Sámi culture and the influence of the RHCs over the management of Laponia follow from the importance of Sámi culture and reindeer herding for the World Heritage status of the site. Arguments for Sámi influence over the management of Laponia rely on a chain of equivalence that articulates *Laponia* as a *Sámi cultural landscape* and *Sámi culture, knowledge and practices* as a *condition for World Heritage values*.[63] Through this articulation, Sámi reindeer herders are positioned as bearers and guardians of Laponia's World Heritage values and their participation in and influence over the management of Laponia as necessary to safeguard those values.

*Mijá ednam* also positions the Sámi as an Indigenous people and articulates a problem representation related to the obligations of the Swedish state to the Sámi people according to both international and national commitments.[64] The Laponia management plan reproduces these articulations, which can be understood through a chain equating *Sámi* with *Indigenous*, linking *Sámi rights* to *Indigenous rights* according to international law and including *rights to land, water and natural resources*.[65] However, the consequences of this positioning for the management of Laponia are less clear in the documents. The arguments for Sámi influence rely mainly on the positioning of the Sámi reindeer herders as bearers and guardians of Laponia's World Heritage values.

These two chains are articulated in parallel. They are not necessarily contradictory or mutually exclusive, but they rely on different logics and have potentially different consequences. The positioning of Sámi reindeer herders as bearers and guardians of World Heritage values invests Sámi influence and participation with a largely functional or instrumental value. While it enables space for Sámi agency as knowledge-holders and stewards of natural and cultural values, it qualifies Sámi influence in a more far-reaching way than does the positioning of the Sámi as an Indigenous people with rights according to international law.[66] Nonetheless, RHC representatives and Sámi activists have been able to make use of the intimate connection between Laponia's status as a World Heritage site and the conditions for Sámi culture and reindeer herding in the area to further their claims in the negotiations over the management of the site as well as to protest exploitation of grazing areas outside of Laponia.[67]

The parallel articulations of the Sámi in relation to the Laponia World Heritage site indicate a tension in the discourse. Which representation becomes more influential affects the relationship between Sámi rights within and outside of Laponia. It will probably have consequences for the prospects of using the progress made in Laponia to argue for strengthened Sámi rights and influence elsewhere in Swedish Sápmi, and it directly affects the possibilities of upholding the cultural heritage values of the site. All the affected RHCs have grazing

62 Reimerson, 'Sami space for agency', 819. Interviews were conducted by me in 2013 and include six persons who at that time were either serving as members of the board of directors for one of the parties (the RHCs, the municipalities, the CAB and the SEPA) or employed at the Laponiatjuottjudus office. See Reimerson, 'Sámi space for agency', 813–814.

63 Reimerson, 'Sami space for agency', 819.

64 Mijá ednam, *Samebyarnas Laponiaprogram*, 23–31, 67–72.

65 Laponia, 'Management plan', 10–13, 14–15, 136–147; Reimerson, 'Sami space for agency', 818–819.

66 Reimerson, 'Sami space for agency', 820–822.

67 Interview with RHC representative, September 2013; Green, *Managing Laponia*, 145–147; Lundberg et al., 'Threat against Laponian area'.

lands both inside and outside Laponia, and the areas outside the protected area are often more critical than the areas situated within Laponia. The Sámi cultural heritage of Laponia, as protected through the World Heritage listing, is thereby vulnerable to developments in areas over which the management organisation has little or no influence.[68]

## *The CBD and the Norwegian reform*

The Convention on Biological Diversity (CBD) is a legally binding treaty with three main objectives: 1) the conservation of biological diversity; 2) the sustainable use of the components of biological diversity; and 3) the fair and equitable sharing of the benefits arising out of the utilisation of genetic resources. Although not primarily a regime under which protected areas can be inscribed, the CBD provides a definition of protected areas that can be viewed as a lowest common denominator, and it is one of the main international arenas for nature conservation legislation and policy.[69] Furthermore, the CBD is one of the most important international instruments through which Indigenous peoples can seek protection for their natural resources, knowledge, traditions and lifestyles. The CBD is the only convention that explicitly protects Indigenous peoples' intellectual property rights, and it has become a major focus for advancing their environmental claims.[70]

The CBD's main provisions for issues regarding Indigenous peoples are Article 8(j) and its related provisions (Articles 10(c), 17.2, and 18.4). These provisions focus on the preservation, maintenance and application of the traditional knowledge, innovations and practices of indigenous and local communities.[71] The CBD Programme of Work for Protected Areas (PoWPA, adopted in 2004) includes several goals and suggested activities of relevance to Indigenous peoples under the convention. The PoWPA urges parties to the convention to ensure the full and active participation of Indigenous and local communities in the implementation of the convention, encourages the establishment of protected areas that benefit Indigenous and local communities and sets targets to enhance and secure the involvement of Indigenous and local communities in the establishment and management of protected areas.[72] The Aichi Biodiversity Targets, adopted in 2010, also stress the respect for and integration of traditional knowledge and the participation of Indigenous and local communities at all relevant levels.[73]

Indigenous peoples participate actively in CBD arenas.[74] The International Indigenous Forum on Biodiversity (IIFB), created at the third Conference of the Parties (COP) in 1996, forms a caucus for Indigenous representatives attending CBD meetings and works to coordinate strategies, provide advice and influence decisions. Since the fifth COP in 2000, it has

68 Interview with municipality representative, March 2013; Interview with CAB representative, August 2013; Nilsson Dahlström, *Negotiating Wilderness*, 269–270.

69 Chandra and Idrisova, 'Convention on biological diversity'; Gillespie, *Protected Areas and International Environmental Law*, 9, 27; Harrop and Pritchard, 'A hard instrument goes soft'; Morgera and Tsioumani, 'Yesterday, today and tomorrow'.

70 Barsh, 'Indigenous peoples', 848; Posey, 'Protecting Indigenous peoples' rights to biodiversity'; Fourmile, 'Indigenous peoples'; Richardson, 'Indigenous peoples, international law and sustainability'.

71 The CBD consistently refers to 'indigenous and local communities', not 'Indigenous peoples'. As a result of persistent advocacy on the part of Indigenous peoples' organisations, the 12th Conference of the Parties to the CBD agreed to use the term 'indigenous peoples and local communities' in future decisions and secondary documents under the convention. See COP-CBD, 'COP12 Decision XII/12'.

72 SCBD, 'Programme of work on protected areas'.

73 COP-CBD, 'COP10 Decision X/2. Annex'.

74 Oldham, 'Negotiating diversity'.

been acknowledged as an advisory body to the COP on the implementation of Article 8(j) and related provisions.[75]

The CBD's approach to Indigenous peoples has been criticised on several counts. Some of the major objections include the reluctance to recognise Indigenous peoples as *peoples*, the failure to distinguish between Indigenous and non-indigenous local communities, and the affirmation of state sovereignty over natural resources.[76] The ways in which the CBD addresses Indigenous peoples includes colonial notions and power relations, and the Convention offers a narrow and qualified recognition of Indigenous peoples as relevant subjects.[77] The inclusion of Indigenous subjects in the CBD is based mainly on the possible contributions they can make to the objectives of the Convention, rather than on any intrinsic Indigenous rights to self-determination or collective rights to natural resources.[78] Furthermore, the Convention qualifies continued Indigenous access to land on the nature of Indigenous land use as being (understood as) customary, traditional, and sustainable.[79] The lack of recognition of Indigenous rights as such also means that Indigenous people have no legal standing in pursuing remedies under the CBD for any alleged breach of the Convention.[80]

In 2001, the Norwegian government commissioned an inquiry committee to review Norway's legislation on the conservation and sustainable use of biological diversity. An important part of the committee's mandate was to ensure the fulfilment of international commitments, particularly the CBD.[81] Based on the inquiry committee's final report from 2004, the government introduced a new bill – the Nature Diversity Act (NDA) – in Parliament in 2009.[82] The passing of the NDA was followed by the introduction of a new management model for protected areas, which authorises the Ministry of Climate and Environment[83] to delegate the management of national parks and other large protected areas to inter municipal National Park Boards (NPBs). The reform guarantees Sámi representation on NPBs in areas of Sámi interest, with the degree of Sámi representation determined by each area's importance for Sámi culture and industry.[84]

NPBs are established if a majority of the affected municipalities in each area agree to the delegated management authority. They are appointed by the Ministry of Climate and Environment after nominations from municipal councils, county councils, and the Sámi Parliament. Their mandate includes development and revision of protected area management plans, enforcement of and exemptions from protected area regulations, and management activities to safeguard the conservation values of protected areas.[85] The ministry retains the authority to approve management plans, and may revoke the NPBs' delegated authority if it finds its decisions or activities to be inconsistent with legislation or regulations.[86]

75 IIFB, 'About'; COP-CBD, 'COP5 Decision V/6'.
76 IIFB, Opening statements at COP9, COP10, COP11 and Working Group 8(j)-7; Fourmile, 'Indigenous peoples', 227; Woodliffe, 'Biodiversity and Indigenous Peoples', 265–266.
77 Reimerson, 'Between nature and culture'.
78 Reimerson, 'Between nature and culture'; Bluemel, 'Separating instrumental from intrinsic rights'; Barsh, 'Indigenous peoples'.
79 Barsh, 'Indigenous peoples', 848.
80 Fourmile, 'Indigenous peoples', 228–229.
81 NOU 2004:28, 57–58.
82 Ot.prp. nr 52 (2008–2009).
83 1972–2013 Ministry of the Environment, 2014 – Ministry of Climate and Environment.
84 Prop 1 S (2009–2010), 224.
85 Cf. Ministry of the Environment, 'Vedtekter Midtre Nordland Nasjonalparkstyre 110610'
86 Prop 1 S (2009–2010), 225.

Articulations of Sámi participation in the budget bill introducing the reform and the legislative history of the NDA largely hinge on a problem representation focusing on Norway's commitments under international law and international agreements on nature conservation and protected areas. The problem is presented in terms of threatened conservation values resulting, at least in part, from weak or insufficient management. The solution is strengthened management based on local influence, participation and knowledge, consistency, consideration and use of appropriate and relevant knowledge and well-established measures to ensure compliance.[87] The government budget bill introducing the reform presents it as a solution to an established need to strengthen protected area management, described as a requirement under the CBD.[88]

The NDA inquiry committee's report and the NDA bill describe the ecosystem approach, as defined and developed under the CBD, as a guiding framework for nature conservation and protected area management.[89] The committee report, the NDA bill and the budget bill introducing the reform all establish the Sámi as holders of traditional knowledge and emphasise Norway's obligations under Article 8(j) to protect, preserve and promote that knowledge.[90] The budget bill introducing the reform also refers to the CBD PoWPA's requirement for full and effective participation of Indigenous peoples in protected area management, and concludes that a new management arrangement must secure Sámi participation in all protected areas that concern Sámi interests.[91] In relation to this problem representation, *Sámi participation* is linked to *traditional knowledge* and *sustainable use*.[92]

The texts analysed also present an articulation of the Sámi as an Indigenous people with rights to self-determination and influence according to international and national law. Referring to ILO 169, the consultation agreement between the Norwegian government and the Sámi Parliament and the guidelines for proceedings on protected areas in Sápmi, they establish that Norway is obligated to guarantee Sámi participation in processes regarding the use, management and conservation of natural resources in Sámi areas.[93] Here, the problem is represented as the full and effective implementation of Norway's obligations under ILO 169, and *Sámi participation* is articulated as a *right* held by the Sámi as an *Indigenous people*.[94]

The problem representation linked to Norway's obligations under the CBD and the chain equating *Sámi participation – traditional knowledge – sustainable use* allows space for Sámi agency as holders of traditional knowledge and stewards of environmental values. This positioning of the Sámi in relation to protected area management reflects the CBD's functional approach to indigenous participation, and may qualify or restrict space for agency by ascribing it instrumental rather than intrinsic value or by drawing on stereotypical notions of traditionality.

The chain equating *Sámi participation – right – Indigenous peoples* positions the Sámi as rights-holders and Norway as having obligations to protect those rights. It connects to international Indigenous rights law, particularly ILO 169, and allows space for Sámi agency

87 Prop 1 S (2009–2010), 222–223.
88 Prop 1 S (2009–2010), 219–20, 222–223.
89 NOU 2004:28, 148–51, 186–89; Ot.prp. nr 52 (2008–2009), 51–52, 84, 94–95, 97, 206.
90 NOU 2004:28, 464–66; Ot.prp. nr 52 (2008–2009), 89–93; Prop 1 S (2009–2010), 222.
91 Prop 1 S (2009–2010), 55, 222.
92 Reimerson, 'Discourses of decentralization'.
93 NOU 2004:28, 469, 486–87; Ot.prp. nr 52 (2008–2009), 47; Prop 1 S (2009–2010), 222.
94 Reimerson, 'Discourses of decentralization'.

through consultations and consideration regardless of traditional knowledge or environmental stewardship. As such, it invests the concept of Sámi participation with an intrinsic rather than instrumental value, and may be less restrictive than the articulation linked to the CBD.

## Concluding discussion

International protected area arenas can be used to further or strengthen Indigenous peoples' claims to rights in relation to or influence over the management of protected areas on their traditional lands. Indigenous peoples have lobbied for and used the acknowledgement of the close relationship between cultural and biological diversity, and the recognition of their knowledge and practices as beneficial for the conservation and sustainable use of biodiversity, to gain influence over the work under the CBD. In the Norwegian protected area management reform, the CBD and its PoWPA contribute to the legitimisation and justification of Sámi participation and influence. In the case of Laponia, UNESCO and the WHC have been useful in the RHCs' strategies to gain influence over the management of the World Heritage site and shape their space for agency in relation to the natural and cultural resources of Laponia.

International discourses may also set limits to the articulation of claims and the political strategies possible or acceptable on the national or local level. The specific context of Laponia, along with the focus of the WHC, seems to have enabled certain political claims and strategies, while making others less useful or possible. There is a discourse centred on the Sámi as an Indigenous people with rights according to international law, but all concrete suggestions, demands and arguments are based on the links between the Sámi reindeer herders and the properties of the area under protection in this particular area, under these particular circumstances. The emphasis on Sámi influence as a condition for the preservation of the World Heritage values of Laponia, rather than as a consequence of Sámi rights as an Indigenous people, could affect the space for agency of the RHCs, and might limit the possibilities of using Laponia as an argument for increased Sámi influence over protected area management elsewhere.

Furthermore, national contexts and discourses mediate the impact of discourses articulated in and through international arenas. The CBD stresses Indigenous participation as a functional right, qualified by its potential contribution to conservation objectives rather than justified based on the intrinsic rights of Indigenous peoples as *peoples*. The Norwegian reform reflects this approach, but it also articulates a discourse that constructs Sámi rights as Indigenous rights, linked to Norwegian obligations under international Indigenous rights legislation such as ILO 169. The commitments to ensure participation in the implementation of the CBD serve to further support Norway's obligations to its Indigenous people, but do not add anything qualitatively different to the discourse. By contrast, Laponia stands out as an exception in Swedish Sápmi, and the WHC added a crucial dimension to Sámi claims for influence. The more established Norwegian discourse of Sámi rights as Indigenous rights, along with the greater Norwegian emphasis on local participation in nature conservation in general, thus constructs a space for Sámi political agency that differs significantly from the Swedish part of Sápmi.

The results of this study highlight the importance of international political and legal discourses in the construction of national and local spaces for agency, but also point to the significance of the specific subject positions they articulate and the ways in which national discourses mediate their impact. The formation of discourses on the global level does not simply determine discourse and practice on the local level. It goes both ways – or, rather, it goes in several directions: discourses on different levels mutually constitute, influence and reinforce each other, and discourses articulated on one level may be contested and reconfigured on others. The discourses and structures of international arenas for protected areas and nature conservation shape the possibilities of using them as political tools to promote Indigenous rights – limiting them in some ways, but also providing opportunities for influence and participation. Unequal power structures continue to characterise discourse formation and policy implementation from the global to the local level, and critical scrutiny of the conditions for indigenous political agency is necessary in order to achieve change. By deconstructing these processes, we open the way for change.

## Bibliography


Adams, W. M. 'Nature and the Colonial Mind'. In *Decolonizing Nature: Strategies for Conservation in a Post-colonial Era*, eds. W. M. Adams & M. Mulligan, 16–50. London: Earthscan Publications, 2003.

Agrawal, A. & J. Ribot. 'Accountability in Decentralization: A Framework with South Asian and West African Cases'. *The Journal of Developing Areas* 33, no. 4 (1999): 473–502.

Allard, C. 'The Nordic Countries' Law on Sámi Territorial Rights'. *Arctic Review on Law and Politics* 2, no. 2 (2011): 159–183.

Anaya, J. *Indigenous Peoples in International Law* (2nd edn). Oxford: Oxford University Press, 2004.

Bacchi, C. *Analysing Policy: What's the Problem Represented to Be?* Frenchs Forest: Pearson, 2009.

Baird, M. F. 'The Politics of Place: Heritage, Identity, and the Epistemologies of Cultural Landscapes'. PhD diss., University of Oregon, 2009.

Baird, M. F. '"The Breath of the Mountain Is My Heart": Indigenous Cultural Landscapes and the Politics of Heritage'. *International Journal of Heritage Studies* 19, no. 4 (2013): 327–340.

Barsh, R. L. 'Indigenous Peoples'. In *The Oxford Handbook of International Environmental Law*, eds. D. Bodansky, J. Brunnée & E. Hey. Oxford: Oxford University Press, 2007: 829–852.

Beach, H. 'World Heritage and Indigenous Peoples: The Example of Laponia'. In *Upholders of Culture: Past and Present*, ed. B. Sundin, 90–98. Stockholm: Royal Swedish Academy of Engineering Sciences (IVA), 2001.

Berkes, F., Colding, J. & C. Folke. 'Rediscovery of Traditional Ecological Knowledge as Adaptive Management'. *Ecological Applications* 10, no. 5 (2000): 1251–1262.

Bluemel, E. B. 'Separating Instrumental from Intrinsic Rights: Toward an Understanding of Indigenous Participation in International Rule-Making'. *American Indian Law Review* 30, no. 1 (2005): 55–132.

Büscher, B. & W. Whande. 'Whims of the Winds of Time? Emerging Trends in Biodiversity Conservation and Protected Area Management'. *Conservation and Society* 5, no. 1 (2007): 22–43.

Byrne, D. 'Western Hegemony in Archaeological Heritage Management'. *History and Anthropology* 5, no. 2 (1991): 269–276.

CAB Norrbotten 2006. Hemställan om inrättande av Laponiadelegation mm (dnr. M2006/2962/Na).

Chandra, A. & A. Idrisova. 'Convention on Biological Diversity: A Review of National Challenges and Opportunities for Implementation'. *Biodiversity and Conservation* 20, no. 14 (2011): 3295–3316.

Chatty, D. & M. Colchester. *Conservation and Mobile Indigenous Peoples: Displacement, Forced Settlement and Sustainable Conservation*. Oxford: Berghahn, 2002.

Colchester, M. *Salvaging Nature: Indigenous Peoples, Protected Areas and Biodiversity Conservation*. Montevideo: World Rainforest Movement, 2003.

Colchester, M. 'Conservation Policy and Indigenous Peoples'. *Environmental Science & Policy* 7, no. 3 (2004): 145–153.

Colchester, M., Ferrari, M. F., Nelson, J., Kidd, C., Zaninka, P., Venant, M., Regpala, L., Balawag, Grace T., Motin, B. & B. Lasimbang. *Conservation and Indigenous Peoples: Assessing the Progress since Durban*, FPP Series on Forest Peoples and Protected Areas. Morcton-in Marsh: Forest Peoples Programme, 2008.

COP-CBD. 'COP5 Decision V/6'. Montreal: Secretariat of the Convention on Biological Diversity, 2000. http://www.cbd.int/decision/cop/?id=7148 (accessed 3 January 2012).

COP-CBD. 'COP12 Decision XII/12. Article 8(j) and Related Provisions'. Montreal: Secretariat of the Convention on Biological Diversity, 2014. https://www.cbd.int/doc/decisions/cop-12/cop-12-dec-12-en.pdf (accessed 6 May 2014).

COP-CBD. 'COP10 Decision X/2. Annex: Strategic Plan for Biodiversity 2011–2010 and the Aichi Biodiversity Targets'. Montreal: Secretariat of the Convention on Biological Diversity, 2010. https://www.cbd.int/decision/cop/?id=12268 (accessed 25 March 2015).

Dahl, J. *The Indigenous Space and Marginalized Peoples in the United Nations.* New York: Palgrave Macmillan, 2012.

Davies, B. 'The Concept of Agency: A Feminist Poststructuralist Analysis'. *Social Analysis: The International Journal of Social and Cultural Practice* 30 (1991): 42–53.

Disko, S. & H. Tugendhat. *International Expert Workshop on the World Heritage Convention and Indigenous Peoples.* Copenhagen, Denmark, 20–21 September 2012. Copenhagen: International Work Group for Indigenous Affairs, 2013.

Fauchald, O. K. & L. H. Gulbrandsen. 'The Norwegian Reform of Protected Area Management: A Grand Experiment with Delegation of Authority?'. *Local Environment* 17, no. 2 (2012): 203–222.

Fauchald, O. K., Gulbrandsen, L. H. & A. Zachrisson. 'Internationalization of Protected Areas in Norway and Sweden: Examining Pathways of Influence in Similar Countries'. *International Journal of Biodiversity Science, Ecosystem Services & Management* 10, no. 3 (2014): 240–252.

Foucault, M. *Power/Knowledge: Selected Interviews and Other Writings 1972–1977.* Translated by L. M. Colin Gordon, John Mepham & Kate Soper. Edited by C. Gordon. New York: Random House/Vintage Books, 1980.

Foucault, M. *The Archaeology of Knowledge*, Routledge Classics. London: Routledge, 2002.

Fourmile, H. 'Indigenous Peoples, the Conservation of Traditional Ecological Knowledge, and Global Governance'. In *Global Ethics and Environment*, ed. N. Low. London: Routledge, 1999: 215–246.

Fraser, N. 'Rethinking the Public Sphere: A Contribution to the Critique of Actually Existing Democracy'. *Social Text* 25–26 (1990): 56–80.

Gillespie, A. *Protected Areas and International Environmental Law.* Leiden: Martinus Nijhoff, 2007.

Green, C. 'Managing Laponia: A World Heritage Site as Arena for Sámi Ethno-politics in Sweden'. PhD diss., Uppsala University, 2009.

Harrop, S. R. & D. J. Pritchard. 'A Hard Instrument Goes Soft: The Implications of the Convention on Biological Diversity's Current Trajectory'. *Global Environmental Change* 21, no. 2 (2011): 474–480.

Heinämäki, L. 'Protecting the Rights of Indigenous Peoples – Promoting the Sustainability of the Global Environment?'. *International Community Law Review* 11, no. 1 (2009): 3–68.

Hovik, S., Sandström, C. & A. Zachrisson. 'Management of Protected Areas in Norway and Sweden: Challenges in Combining Central Governance and Local Participation'. *Journal of Environmental Policy & Planning* 12, no. 2 (2010): 159–177.

Howarth, D. *Discourse*, Concepts in the social sciences, 99–0594137–1. Buckingham: Open University Press, 2000.

IIFB. 'About'. International Indigenous Forum on Biodiversity, 2015. http://iifb.indigenousportal.com/about/ (accessed 24 February 2015).

ILO (International Labour Organization) 'Convention No. 169 Concerning Indigenous and Tribal Peoples in Independent Countries', 1989. http://www.ilo.org/dyn/normlex/en/f?p=NORMLEXPUB:12100:0::NO::P12100_ILO_CODE:C169 (accessed 3 May 2015).

IWGIA. 'World Heritage Sites and Indigenous Peoples'. Copenhagen, Denmark: International Work Group for Indigenous Affairs, n.d. http://www.iwgia.org/culture-and-identity/world-heritage-sites-and-indigenous-peoples (accessed 24 February 2015).

Jørgensen, M. & L. Phillips. *Discourse Analysis as Theory and Method [Electronic Book]*. London: Sage, 2002.

Josefsen, E., Mörkenstam, U. & J. Saglie. 'Different Institutions within Similar States: The Norwegian and Swedish Sámediggis'. *Ethnopolitics* 14, no. 1 (2014): 32–51.

Keck, M. E. & K. Sikkink. *Activists beyond Borders: Advocacy Networks in International Politics*. Ithaca, NY: Cornell University Press, 1998.

Koivurova, T. & L. Heinämäki. 'The Participation of Indigenous Peoples in International Norm-Making in the Arctic'. *Polar Record* 42, no. 221 (2006): 101–109.

Labadi, S. 'Representations of the Nation and Cultural Diversity in Discourses on World Heritage'. *Journal of Social Archaeology* 7, no. 2 (2007): 147–170.

Laclau, E. & C. Mouffe. *Hegemony & Socialist Strategy*. London: Verso, 1985.

Lane, M. B. 'Affirming New Directions in Planning Theory: Comanagement of Protected Areas'. *Society & Natural Resources* 14, no. 8 (2001): 657–671.

Laponia. 'Tjuottjudusplána/Förvaltningsplan/Management Plan', 2012. http://laponia.nu/wp-content/uploads/2014/08/Laponia-forvaltningsplan-eng-web-150327_2.pdf (accessed 21 March 2016).

Laponiaprocessen. 'Stadga för föreningen Laponiatjuottjudus [Statutes for Laponiatjuottjudus]'. 2011. http://laponia.nu/wp-content/uploads/2014/08/Stadgar-Laponiatjuottjudus.pdf (accessed 21 March 2016).

Lundberg, T., K. Kuoljok, J.-E. Länta & H. Blind. 'The Threat against Laponian Area, Sweden', 2013. http://www.whatlocalpeople.se/wp-content/uploads/2013/02/130204-The-threat-against-Laponia-Area.pdf (accessed 7 October 2015).

Meskell, L. 'UNESCO and the Fate of the World Heritage Indigenous Peoples Council of Experts (WHIPCOE)'. *International Journal of Cultural Property* 20, no. 2 (2013): 155–174.

Mijá ednam. *Samebyarnas Laponiaprogram*. Jokkmokk: Mijá ednam, 1999.

Minde, H. 'Sami Land Rights in Norway: A Test Case for Indigenous Peoples'. *International Journal on Minority and Group Rights* 8, no. 2–3 (2001): 107–125.

Ministry of the Environment. 'Vedtekter Midtre Nordland Nasjonalparkstyre 110610'. 2011. http://nasjonalparkstyre.no/Documents/Midtre_Nordland_dok/Vedtekter%20MNNPS/Vedtekter%20Midtre%20Nordland%20nasjonalparkstyre.pdf?epslanguage=no (accessed 2 September 2014).

Ministry of the Environment and Sámediggi – Sametinget. *Avtale mellom Sametinget og Miljøverndepartementet om retningslinjer for verneplanarbeid etter naturvernloven i samiske områder*. Oslo: Ministry of the Environment, 2007. https://www.regjeringen.no/nb/dokumenter/avtale-mellom-sametinget-og-miljoverndep/id481195/ (accessed 25 August 2015).

Morgan, R. 'Advancing Indigenous Rights at the United Nations: Strategic Framing and Its Impact on the Normative Development of International Law'. *Social & Legal Studies* 13, no. 4 (2004): 481–500.

Morgera, E. & E. Tsioumani. 'Yesterday, Today and Tomorrow: Looking Afresh at the Convention on Biological Diversity'. *Edinburgh School of Law Working Paper* 21 (2011). http://dx.doi.org/10.2139/ssrn.1914378 (accessed 24 February 2015).

Mörkenstam, U. 'Om "Lapparnes privilegier". Föreställningar om samiskhet i svensk samepolitik 1883–1997'. PhD diss., Stockholm: Stockholm University, 1999.

Mouffe, C. 'Democratic Citizenship and the Political Community'. In *Dimensions of Radical Democracy: Pluralism, Citizenship, Community*, ed. C. Mouffe, 225–239. London: Verso, 1992.

NGO/IPO Joint Submission to the UNPFII. 'Continuous Violations of the Principle of Free, Prior and Informed Consent in the Context of UNESCO's World Heritage Convention'. UN Permanent Forum on Indigenous Issues, Tenth Session, New York, 16–27 May 2011, 2011.

NGO/IPO Joint Submission to the UNPFII. 'Lack of Implementation of the UN Declaration on the Rights of Indigenous Peoples (UNDRIP) in the Context of UNESCO's World Heritage Convention'. UN Permanent Forum on Indigenous Issues, Eleventh Session, New York, 7–18 May 2012, 2012.

Niezen, R. *The Origins of Indigenism: Human Rights and Politics of Identity*. Berkeley: University of California Press, 2003.

Nilsson Dahlström, Å. 'Negotiating Wilderness in a Cultural Landscape: Predators and Saami Reindeer Herding in the Laponian World Heritage Area'. PhD diss., Uppsala University, 2003.

Norges nasjonalparks- og verneområdestyrer 'Nasjonalpark- og verneområdestyrer'. n.d. http://nasjonalparkstyre.no (accessed 6 October 2015).

Norges nasjonalparks- og verneområdestyrer 'Om styrene', 2014. http://nasjonalparkstyre.no/Om-styrene/ (accessed 6 October 2015).

Norwegian Environment Agency 'Hvem forvalter verneområdene?'. Trondheim: Norwegian Environment Agency. n.d. http://www.miljødirektoratet.no/no/Tema/Verneomrader/Forvaltning-av-verneomradene/ (accessed 18 August 2015).

NOU 2004:28. Lov om bevaring av natur, landskap og biologisk mangfold.

Oldham, P. 'Negotiating Diversity: A Field Guide to the Convention on Biological Diversity'. Lancaster: Lancaster University/Cesagen, 2001–2002. http://www.cesagen.lancs.ac.uk/virtual/biodiversity/ (accessed 24 February 2015).

Ot.prp. nr. 52 (2008–2009). Om lov om forvaltning av naturens mangfold (naturmangfoldloven).

Pickerill, J. 'From Wilderness to Wild Country: The Power of Language in Environmental Campaigns in Australia'. *Environmental Politics* 17, no. 1 (2008): 95–104.

Plumwood, V. 'Decolonizing Relationships with Nature'. In *Decolonizing Nature: Strategies for Conservation in a Post-colonial Era*, eds. W. M. Adams & M. Mulligan, 51–78. London: Earthscan Publications, 2003.

Poirier, R. & D. Ostergren. 'Evicting People from Nature: Indigenous Land Rights and National Parks in Australia, Russia, and the United States'. *Natural Resources Journal* 42, no. 2 (2002): 331–351.

Posey, D. A. 'Protecting Indigenous Peoples' Rights to Biodiversity'. *Environment: Science and Policy for Sustainable Development* 38, no. 8 (1996): 6–45.

Procedures for Consultations between State Authorities and the Sámi Parliament, 2005. https://www.regjeringen.no/en/topics/indigenous-peoples-and-minorities/Sámi-people/midtspalte/PROCEDURES-FOR-CONSULTATIONS-BETWEEN-STA/id450743/ (accessed 25 August 2015).

Prop. 1 S (2009–2010). Proposisjon til Stortinget (forslag til stortingsvedtak) for budsjettåret 2010. Miljøverndepartementet.

Reimerson, E. 'Between nature and Culture: Exploring Space for Indigenous Agency in the Convention on Biological Diversity'. *Environmental Politics* 22, no. 6 (2013): 992–1009.

Reimerson, E. 'Sami Space for Agency in the Management of the Laponia World Heritage Site'. *Local Environment* 21, no 7 (2016): 808–826.

Reimerson, E. 'Discourses of Decentralization: Local Participation and Sámi Space for Agency in Norwegian Protected Area Management'. Unpublished Manuscript.

Richardson, B. J. 'Indigenous Peoples, International Law and Sustainability'. *Review of European Community & International Environmental Law* 10, no. 1 (2001): 1–12.

Rössler, M. 'World Heritage Cultural Landscapes: A UNESCO Flagship Programme 1992 – 2006'. *Landscape Research* 31, no. 4 (2006): 333–353.

Sámediggi – Sametinget. Nye styremedlemmer for nasjonalpark- og verneområdestyrene. Press release 16 June 2014. http://www.sametinget.no/Miljoe-areal-og-kulturvern/Naturmangfold/Nye-styremelemmer-for-nasjonalpark-og-verneomraadestyrene (accessed 14 October 2014).

SCBD (Secretariat of the Convention on Biological Diversity). 'Programme of Work on Protected Areas'. Montreal: SCBD, 2004. https://www.cbd.int/doc/publications/pa-text-en.pdf (accessed 8 April 2015).

Schroeder, H. 'Agency in International Climate Negotiations: The Case of Indigenous Peoples and Avoided Deforestation'. *International Environmental Agreements: Politics, Law and Economics* 10, no. 4 (2010): 317–332.
Smith, A. M. *Laclau and Mouffe: The Radical Democratic Imaginary*. London: Routledge, 1998.
Smith, L. T. *Decolonizing Methodologies: Research and Indigenous Peoples*. London: Zed, 1999.
Smith, L. *Uses of Heritage*. New York: Routledge, 2006.
Sonnenfeld, D. A. & A. P. J. Mol. 'Globalization and the Transformation of Environmental Governance: An Introduction'. *American Behavioral Scientist* 45, no. 9 (2002): 1318–1339.
Stevens, S. 'The Legacy of Yellowstone'. In *Conservation through Cultural Survival: Indigenous Peoples and Protected Areas*, ed. S. Stevens, 13–32. Washington, DC: Island Press, 1997.
Stevens, S. 'A New Protected Area Paradigm'. In *Indigenous Peoples, National Parks, and Protected Areas: A New Paradigm Linking Conservation, Culture, and Rights*, ed. S. Stevens, 47–83. Tucson: University of Arizona Press, 2014.
Suchet, S. '"Totally Wild?" Colonising Discourses, Indigenous Knowledges and Managing Wildlife'. *Australian Geographer* 33, no. 2 (2002): 141–157.
Swedish Government 2006. Regleringsbrev för budgetåret 2007 avseende Naturvårdsverket.
Tennberg, M. 'Indigenous Peoples as International Political Actors: A Summary'. *Polar Record* 46, no. 3 (2010): 264–270.
Uggla, Y. 'What Is This Thing Called "Natural?" The Nature–culture Divide in Climate Change and Biodiversity Policy'. *Journal of Political Ecology* 17, (2010): 79–91.
UNESCO World Heritage Centre. 'Global Strategy', 1992–2015. http://whc.unesco.org/en/globalstrategy/ (accessed 24 February 2015).
UNESCO World Heritage Centre. 'Laponian Area', 1992–2015. http://whc.unesco.org/en/list/774 (accessed 5 October 2015).
UNESCO World Heritage Centre. 'Sweden', 1992–2015. http://whc.unesco.org/en/statesparties/se (accessed 7 October 2015).
UNESCO World Heritage Centre. *World Heritage Information Kit*. Paris: UNESCO World Heritage Centre, 2008.
UNESCO World Heritage Centre. *World Heritage and Indigenous Peoples (World Heritage no. 62)*. Paris and London: UNESCO and Publishing for Development Ltd, 2012.
UNESCO World Heritage Centre. 'Operational Guidelines for the Implementation of the World Heritage Convention', 2013. http://whc.unesco.org/en/guidelines (accessed 24 February 2015).
Waterton, E., Smith, L. & G. Campbell. 'The Utility of Discourse Analysis to Heritage Studies: The Burra Charter and Social Inclusion'. *International Journal of Heritage Studies* 11, no. 4 (2006): 309–325.
Woodliffe, J. 'Biodiversity and Indigenous Peoples'. In *International Law and the Conservation of Biological Diversity*, ed. C. Redgwell & M. Bowman. London: Kluwer Law International, 1996: 255–270.
Zachrisson, A. 'Commons Protected for or from the People. Co-management in the Swedish Mountain Region'? PhD diss. Umeå: Umeå University, 2009.
Zachrisson, A. 'Conflict Resolution Mechanisms in Co-management: The Laponia World Heritage (Paper IV)'. In *Commons Protected For or From the People: Co-management in the Swedish Mountain Region?* PhD diss. Umeå: Umeå University, 2009.
Zachrisson, A. 'The Designation of Fulufjället National Park: Efficient Co-management through Downward Accountability?'. *Local Environment* 14, no. 3 (2009): 259–271.
Zimmerer, K. S. 'Geographical Perspectives on Globalization and Environmental Issues: The Inner-connections of Conservation, Agriculture, and Livelihoods'. In *Globalization and New Geographies of Conservation*, ed. K. S. Zimmerer, 1–44. Chicago: University of Chicago Press, 2006.

# 11 World Heritage bureaucracy – How it works and how it affects indigenous peoples

*Carina Green and Jan Turtinen*

## Introduction

The World Heritage Convention[1] is one of the best-known and most widely accepted of UNESCO's treaties: it has been ratified by more than 190 states.[2] Its aim is to safeguard the cultural and natural heritage associated with irreplaceable and exceptional manifestations of a specific entity, phenomena or practice and to protect these from the presumed detrimental effects of globalisation, decay, damage and destruction. At present, over 1,000 sites are inscribed on the World Heritage List as belonging to the common heritage of humankind.[3] An increasing number of these sites involve the interest of indigenous peoples, as many of the protected areas are situated on traditional indigenous lands. Furthermore, for some of the sites, the cultural expressions of the local indigenous people are considered to have outstanding universal values and are therefore being protected by the Convention.

Indigenous peoples worldwide are demanding more control over and influence on World Heritage procedures. Many nation states welcome the interest from indigenous communities, as it is considered to improve indigenous and non-indigenous relationships and to advance recognition of indigenous peoples' heritage. They often recognise the contribution that indigenous peoples' knowledge can make to strong and effective management of these sites.[4]

In this chapter we examine how the framework of the World Heritage Convention shapes the conditions for indigenous peoples to influence the nomination process for new World Heritage areas and to participate in the management of already established sites. We argue that bureaucratic structures and practices, and the normative heritage discourse they rest on and recreate, are in large part the reason for the slow rate at which indigenous peoples gain influence and control over World Heritage processes. By 'World Heritage bureaucracy' we mean the employment of bureaucratic forms of organisation for the identification and management of heritage sites: in other words, the institutional system of roles and responsibilities, procedures, practices and perspectives with which the Convention is implemented. This framework establishes the conditions under which indigenous peoples can achieve

1 UNESCO, *Convention Concerning the Protection of the World Cultural and Natural Heritage*, 16 November 1972.

2 UNESCO, World Heritage Centre, *States Parties, Ratification Status*, http://whc.unesco.org/en/statesparties/ (accessed 15 August 2015).

3 UNESCO, World Heritage Centre. *World Heritage List*, http://whc.unesco.org/en/list/ (accessed 15 August 2015).

4 See for example Reimerson, *Nature, Culture, Rights*, 2–3.

representation, cooperation, involvement and control.[5] International institutions, just like nation states, use bureaucracy as a means to organise and control. Such a hierarchical and standardised form of organisation is ill-suited to dealing with local complexity.[6] Therefore, even though the same framework is being implemented on a global scale, the specific context of each locality means that the interpretation, impact and outcome of the Convention will differ.[7] We employ ethnographic data from three different sites to investigate how normative conservation regime (some would argue *colonial* conservation regimes) may be recreated through the World Heritage Convention, but also how a World Heritage process in itself may create space for increased authority and control for indigenous peoples.

The methodology applied in this study includes, along with ethnographic data collection, the study and analysis of literature, public documents, webpages, and other sources. We believe that an ethnographic methodology produces data, knowledge, and understanding that reveal the nuances and complexity that is always inherent in any indigenous-state relations in World Heritage processes.

Short-term fieldwork in the form of participant observation and semi-structured interviews were conducted in Laponia in Sweden; Tongariro National Park, New Zealand; and Cape York, Australia. The first two areas are established World Heritage sites, while the third is in the process of preparing a nomination to the World Heritage List which could be submitted within a few years. The interviews were characterised by a mutual sharing of information in informal dialogue; they were not recorded directly, but notes were made immediately afterwards. This technique was employed to foster a warm and trusting environment for our interviews. We continue to have discussions and communication with many of the people we met in the course of our fieldwork. For our interviews we mostly sought out state officials, consultants, official representatives of indigenous groups and the like. Their accounts of their personal experiences and their different perspectives provided us with insights into World Heritage processes as well as factual material that complement data from other sources. The knowledge and understanding of those processes that we gained in the course of our fieldwork form the basis for some of the statements we make and the information we provide in the case studies below.

It is worth mentioning that this chapter presents the outcome of a rather minor project. From an anthropological perspective, the amount of time spent in the field, around nine weeks in total, was minimal. (However, we have researched and worked with similar issues for a long time, so we have been able to draw on previous experience and knowledge.)

## *The World Heritage Convention and indigenous peoples*

UNESCO's interest in indigenous peoples and their involvement in the organisation's operations have grown over time. Just as their traditional lands are often targeted for natural protection, the cultural traits of indigenous peoples are often referred to as being important and worth protecting. It has been argued that the common – often exaggerated – perception of indigenous peoples as 'non-modern', local rather than global, and living in close contact

5 Nadasdy, 'The anti-politics of TEK: The institutionalization of co-management discourse and practice', *Anthropologica*, 47, no. 2 (2005).

6 Barnett and Finnemore, *Rules for the World*, 18; Scott, *Seeing Like a State*, 44.

7 Compare Reimerson, *Nature, Culture, Rights*, 59; Green and Turtinen, 'Indigenous peoples and World Heritage sites – Normative heritage discourses and possibilities for change', in *International Indigenous Development Research Conference 2014 Proceedings*.

with nature, makes them important targets for the preservation goals of the World Heritage Convention.[8] In the eyes of UNESCO, they are seen to be especially exposed to the negative global impacts of climate change, land degradation and the like.[9]

The experience of being indigenous undeniably differs. What is shared among indigenous peoples is the colonial experience, although the nature of this also varies greatly due to historical and other factors. It is not our intention in this article to treat indigenous peoples as a homogeneous whole. But holding a specific legal position within international law compared to other minority groups that are not labelled 'indigenous', their position vis-à-vis their own national authorities and the international community (as represented by UNESCO) often becomes strong and well-defined. It is also worth noting that from an international perspective the concept 'indigenous people' is often used without problematisation or contextualisation. From the UNESCO perspective, 'indigenous peoples', as a category, is treated as a simplified classification that fits well into the bureaucratic rhetoric and into the whole World Heritage concept.

The links with indigenous peoples and their international political movement have grown stronger over the years. In 2000–2001 a group of international indigenous representatives attempted to create an indigenous advisory body (WHIPCOE) that would work directly under the World Heritage Committee.[10] They did not succeed, but there is now a renewed effort to strengthen collaboration with indigenous peoples.[11]

The United Nations Declaration on the Rights of Indigenous Peoples[12] has also played a large role in bringing indigenous peoples' rights to the fore within UNESCO. A policy is under development to harmonise UNESCO's work, including the World Heritage Convention, with the goals expressed in the Declaration. A further step was taken by the World Heritage Committee at its 39th session in Bonn, Germany, in 2015 in the form of amendments to paras 40 and 123 of the Convention's Operational Guidelines.[13] These paragraphs highlight the right of indigenous peoples to be participants in the nomination processes and to exercise shared responsibility with the state concerned. The principle of applying free, prior and informed consent in relation to indigenous peoples was introduced.

In spite of such lofty phrases, however, actual support for indigenous peoples' involvement in the shaping and management of World Heritage sites might look very different in a local context than it does from a UNESCO perspective. As our case studies show, the Convention, national and regional politics and the normative bureaucratic perspectives and practices set a very strict agenda for what can be done and how it can be done.

## *World Heritage bureaucracy and normative heritage discourse*

International organisations such as UNESCO operate through normative power and bureaucratic means. They use bureaucratic organisation and expertise to make their operation

8 Wall, 'Partnerships involving indigenous peoples in the management of heritage sites', in *Tourism and Cultural Conflicts*; Green, *Managing Laponia*, 97.

9 UNESCO, *UNESCO and Indigenous Peoples: Partnership for Cultural Diversity*, http://portal.unesco.org/culture/en/ev.php-URL_ID=35393&URL_DO=DO_TOPIC&URL_SECTION=201.html (accessed 31 August 2015).

10 Green, *Managing Laponia*, 97–100.

11 Disko and Tugendhat, *International Expert Workshop on the World Heritage Convention and Indigenous Peoples*, 62.

12 United Nations. The General Assembly. *United Nations Declaration on the Rights of Indigenous Peoples*, Resolution 61/295, 2007.

13 UNESCO. World Heritage Committee, 39th session, decision 39 COM 11, 2015.

project appear legitimate, objective and universal. The work that they carry out entails global rationalisation and standardisation.[14] International organisations know and deal with the world through bureaucracy in order to make it amenable to interventions and control.[15] Standardised procedures, professional assessments and formal decisions make sense of diverse local realities and make it possible to act upon them. The World Heritage Convention, in various ways, is no exception to these predispositions.

All natural and cultural phenomena that are to be listed must meet the criteria for World Heritage status, and be described according to the Convention's categories and vocabulary. There are, in other words, certain boxes that all sites must be fitted into. Nominations to the list must be evaluated by experts before an international committee – the World Heritage Committee – takes a decision. The Committee consists of representatives of 21 states; it usually meets once a year. The International Council on Monuments and Sites (ICOMOS) and the World Conservation Union (IUCN) are the appointed expert advisory bodies to the Committee. They are large professional organisations with huge influence over the international environmental and cultural heritage agenda. A nomination or a management arrangement must meet these bureaucratic conditions and comply with the experts' professional judgements. Hence, the Convention privileges certain forms of knowledge over other ways of understanding the world.[16]

Dan Brockington et al. have shown how major international (non-governmental) organisations play an important role in the bureaucratic practices that recreate environmental policies and conservation practices, making them internationally uniform and dominated by a limited set of values and goals.[17] As our case studies indicate, these processes involve a specific kind of techno-scientific knowledge that is 'often mobilised to implement elite understanding of ecological-conservation practices, at the cost of silencing alternative types of knowledge that may be more closely associated with the interest of local communities'.[18] According to Paul Nadasdy such consequences result from the employment of bureaucratic forms of management and control.[19]

The World Heritage Convention has been developed and moulded in a specific cultural context that is neither historically nor fully shared by many indigenous peoples: it exemplifies a very specific understanding of culture and of heritage. It can thus be said to be part of what Laurajane Smith refers to as the 'authorised heritage discourse'.[20] This discourse stems from the narratives of the elite class in European history, and UNESCO is one of its authorisers. Their experience and ideas of cultural values based on time depth, aesthetics and the importance of monumentality and tangible heritages are the foundation of the cultural heritage discourse at work today, within and outside of UNESCO.[21] Smith's concept refers

14 Barnett and Finnemore, *Rules for the World*, 18.

15 Compare Barnett and Finnemore, *Rules for the World*, 16–44.

16 Smith, *Uses of Heritage*, 12.

17 Brockington, Duffy and Igoe, *Nature Unbound*, 2008.

18 Igoe, Neves and Brockington, 'A spectacular eco-tour around the historic bloc: Theorising the convergence of biodiversity conservation and capitalist expansion', *Antipode* 42, no. (2008): 491–492; Compare Reimerson, *Nature, Culture, Rights*, 49–50.

19 Nadasdy, 'The anti-politics of TEK: The institutionalization of co-management discourse and practice', *Anthropologica*, 47, no. 2 (2005).

20 Smith, *Uses of Heritage*, 11.

21 Green and Turtinen, 'Indigenous peoples and World Heritage sites – Normative heritage discourses and possibilities for change', in *International Indigenous Development Research Conference 2014 Proceedings*, 61.

to cultural heritage, but applies also to hegemonic natural heritage management, although the historical roots here are different.

The discourse is institutionalised through the Convention's rhetoric, rules, practices and organisation and is further normalised by the officials and experts who implement it internationally and nationally. Through the lens of the current authorised heritage discourse they determine what counts as worthy of protection and in what way it should be protected. The discourse values certain ways of knowing, categorising and practising heritage conservation over others, and is further reinforced by national laws and regulations through which the Convention is implemented. For many actors involved in the implementation it becomes difficult (impossible, some would say) to do things differently and to think about natural and cultural heritage in different ways.

## *Cape York*

In Queensland, Australia, the government has long aspired to nominate a large part of the Cape York Peninsula to the World Heritage List.[22] This vast area in northeast Australia comprises the traditional lands of several aboriginal communities (Traditional Owners). Its rainforests and savannahs are considered to have high natural values from the point of view of science and natural resource management.

The idea of making Cape York a potential World Heritage site dates to 1982 when, on the tenth anniversary of the World Heritage Convention, IUCN published an indicative inventory of the world's most outstanding natural areas.[23] Over time several investigations have been carried out to clarify how the area could qualify as part of World Heritage.[24] The results of these investigations reveal that natural values are perceived as less problematic whereas cultural values need further investigation. One of the reports states that:

> while the potential of Cape York to reach the threshold of outstanding universal value that is required for inscription on the World Heritage List on natural criteria is relatively well recognised and researched, the same cannot be said for cultural values. . . . A significant amount of research and documentary, archival and recorded material exists (Smyth and Valentine 2008) but the evidence to underpin a claim for outstanding universal value is yet to be clarified as is the interest of Traditional Owners, other residents of the region and other stakeholders in having their places and/or cultural values included in a World Heritage nomination.[25]

Worth noting here is *who* it is who needs the knowledge and the nomination and from what point of view and for what purpose. To the aboriginal communities, the lands and cultural and social traditions are, needless to say, well known. However, many conversations during

22 Valentine, *Compiling a Case for World Heritage on Cape York Peninsula*, 2–7.

23 IUCN, *The World's Greatest Natural Areas*, 53–3; Valentine, *Compiling a Case for World Heritage on Cape York Peninsula*, 2.

24 For example Valentine, *Compiling a Case for World Heritage on Cape York Peninsula*; Smyth and Valentine, *Pathways to Securing Cultural and Natural Heritage of International Conservation Significance on Cape York Peninsula*; Smith, *Review of Properties Nominated for Inscription on the World Heritage List under the Cultural Landscape Category*.

25 Smith, *Review of Properties Nominated for Inscription on the World Heritage List under the Cultural Landscape Category*, 6.

our fieldwork confirmed that aboriginal communities seldom attach 'value' to cultural and natural phenomena as expressed by the Convention. But to the state – and in the end also to UNESCO's World Heritage Committee and its advisory bodies – this information needs to be recorded, put into the nomination and categorised and *valued* according to the Convention's criteria for World Heritage status.

If and when the authorities do start to prepare a nomination dossier, the input of the Traditional Owners will be limited by and translated into this normative and bureaucratic framework. A nomination is an application, and the authorities need to present a candidate with a good chance of making it onto the List. A successful nomination requires that the information and the arguments provided meet the views of the experts that assess it and also of the World Heritage Committee that takes the decision on inscriptions. The authorities are well aware of this, and have carried out analyses of the categories and the criteria, as well as of previous successful and unsuccessful nominations, to find applicable categories and criteria. Possible pathways to local support for the nomination have also been investigated.[26]

Thus, to a large extent the framework for characterising the area is already set before the Traditional Owners are involved in the gathering of information. The natural values in the area have in fact already been identified and defined by natural heritage professionals and scholars on the basis of the criteria for natural heritage. As for the cultural values, the investigations will inevitably limit the influence of the Traditional Owners by framing the consultations in terms of how the relevant authorities consider the applicability of the information to the nomination.[27]

The Convention is so strongly rooted in Western science and expert evaluation and advice that the knowledge systems of the Traditional Owners stand little chance of being recognised on their own terms. They will be considered only partially, and can only be so if the nomination is to be successful. The Convention, like any other bureaucracy, only considers information that is relevant to its own needs.[28] Indigenous peoples' knowledge tends to be considered only partially, and is valued from a primarily Western scientific point of view and translated into the normative framework of natural and cultural resource management.[29] What Cape York illustrates is that in the case of World Heritage these tendencies are amplified by the nomination procedure.

The report cited above also points to the authorities' need for local support, a prerequisite for all nominations today. This requirement was introduced into the Convention's Operational Guidelines by the World Heritage Committee to strengthen the safeguarding of the sites.[30] To this end, the authorities have undertaken a long process of consultation with stakeholders in the area. Gaining support has been a challenge: there are contending interests and differing opinions on what the consequences of the World Heritage status

26 Smyth and Valentine, *Pathways to Securing Cultural and Natural Heritage of International Significance on Cape York.*

27 Compare Nadasdy, 'The anti-politics of TEK: The institutionalization of co-management discourse and practice', *Anthropologica*, 47, no. 2 (2005): 224.

28 Compare Scott, *Seeing Like a State*, 77.

29 See for example Igoe, Neves and Brockington, 'A spectacular eco-tour around the historic bloc: Theorising the convergence of biodiversity conservation and capitalist expansion', *Antipode* 42, no. (2008); Nadasdy, 'The anti-politics of TEK: The institutionalization of co-management discourse and practice', *Anthropologica*, 47, no. 2 (2005); Smith, *Uses of Heritage*; Waterton, Smith and Campbell, 'The utility of discourse analysis to heritage studies: The Burra Charter and social inclusion', *International Journal of Heritage Studies* 12, no. 4 (2006).

30 Cameron and Rössler, *Many Voices, One Vision*, 122.

would be. The potential nomination is part of the struggle over the area's future, involving aboriginal communities, the government, pastoralists, miners, NGOs and others.[31] The aboriginal NGOs and communities are divided; not all of them have been interested in participating, or agreeing to, the nomination. There are land tenure issues that aboriginal communities want to see resolved before a nomination takes place.[32] The government has passed legislation limiting traditional uses of the land.[33] There is also a legacy from other World Heritage sites to tackle, notably the neighbouring Wet Tropics where there was a lack of consultation in the nomination process and where the Traditional Owners are not happy with established management structures.

The government has taken account of these previous experiences and has instituted a 'free, prior and informed consent' strategy, which means that the nomination will only proceed for areas where Traditional Owners have given their articulated consent.[34] The strategy demonstrates a willingness to come to terms with a problematic past. However, implementing 'free, prior and informed consent' has at times been a challenge. The Western knowledge system expressed through the authorised heritage discourse and bureaucratic practices is very different from the modes of understanding of the Traditional Owners in Cape York. Concepts such as 'heritage' and 'value' are not clear to many of them and have to be explained by the officials working with the consultations, along with the idea of the nomination itself and why it might be a good idea. Indigenous knowledge and practices will eventually be included in the nomination and management of this site, but the current work seems to lack real insight and engagement of the Traditional Owners in general.

How much influence the communities will eventually have is uncertain for the moment since the work has been halted. New state and commonwealth governments with other plans for the Cape York Peninsula have been elected.[35] Nick Skilton et al. argue that the prospects for meaningful and respectful consultations seem limited due to the way the authorities have been seeking support by pushing the nomination through by means of political interests rather than by engaging local aspirations and involvement.[36] We would add that regardless of the approach, the Convention's bureaucratic procedures and organisational setup limit local influence and control.

## *Laponia*

The Laponian World Heritage site was inscribed to the list in 1996.[37] Situated in the north of Sweden in the traditional Sámi area (Sápmi), it stretches over 9,000 square kilometres

31 Skilton, Adams and Gibbs, 'Conflict in common: Heritage-making in Cape York', *Australian Geographer* 45, no. 2 (2014); Holmes, 'Contesting the future of Cape York Peninsula', *Australian Geographer* 42, no. 1 (2011); Holmes, 'Cape York Peninsula, Australia: A frontier region undergoing a multifunctional transition with indigenous engagement', *Journal of Rural Studies* 28, no. 3 (2012).

32 Valentine, *Compiling a Case for World Heritage on Cape York Peninsula*, 53.

33 Skilton, Adams and Gibbs, 'Conflict in common: Heritage-making in Cape York', *Australian Geographer* 45, no. 2 (2014): 158.

34 Skilton, Adams and Gibbs, 'Conflict in common: Heritage-making in Cape York', *Australian Geographer* 45, no. 2 (2014): 157.

35 Skilton, Adams and Gibbs, 'Conflict in common: Heritage-making in Cape York', *Australian Geographer* 45, no. 2 (2014): 149.

36 Skilton, Adams and Gibbs, 'Conflict in common: Heritage-making in Cape York', *Australian Geographer* 45, no. 2 (2014): 162.

37 UNESCO. World Heritage Centre. *Laponian Area*, http://whc.unesco.org/en/list/774/ (accessed 15 August 2015).

and consists of established and well-known national parks and nature reserves. Laponia is a 'mixed site', which means that both natural and cultural criteria are included in the nomination. The cultural values include both remnants of the reindeer herding Sámi culture in the area and the present Sámi reindeer herding traditions.

The local Sámi were not involved in the nomination process from the beginning.[38] At first, the authorities sought to nominate the area only as a natural heritage site. But they were advised by the evaluating experts and other authorities to increase the size of the site and to include the Sámi culture in the area. The local Sámi community was duly consulted to some extent and the Sámi political and cultural establishment assisted the application by writing the section dealing with cultural heritage, which was then more or less simply added to the natural criteria in the nomination.

After inclusion on the list in 1996 the local Sámi began to demand more influence and a better position in negotiations with the authorities.[39] They were afraid that they would not have a sufficient influence on the management of the new site, even though Sámi cultural heritage was among the actual values to be protected and the site was situated on the lands where they practised reindeer herding. They also quickly realised that the World Heritage status as such could provide an arena for advanced self-governance in general.

Under the current operational rules, a World Heritage site must have adequate protection and management arrangements to guarantee the safeguarding of its values.[40] A management plan should be in place, or at least well on its way, before the site is listed, but back in 1996 this was not a prerequisite. This meant that the process of producing a management plan and a management organisation for Laponia started after it was actually set up. Before that the Swedish Environmental Protection Agency and the regional county administration had been responsible, but now the local Sámi began to organise with the intention of having their voices heard. This led to a long and intense debate between the local Sámi and various authorities.[41]

Early on, the local Sámi formed a working group focused on Laponia-related issues.[42] At this early stage in the process, the Sámi pointed out that, as an indigenous people, they had the right to an influential position in any future management structure. They demanded that they should form a majority on a future management board, a demand that was strongly rejected by the authorities. At this stage, the thought of Sámi-controlled management of these iconic national parks was inconceivable. Moreover, the idea of a Sámi-designed management and conservation system seemed to the authorities implausible, unnecessary and undoable. The county administration had the government's mandate to manage the area by enforcing national legislation, goals and guidelines, and to alter this mandate would require major changes in directives. The Sámi, however, felt that they had the support of the international community, including UNESCO, even if this support was based on rather simplistic, universal rhetoric rather than concrete commitments. The Sámi often referred to this international support to strengthen their demands in discussions with the authorities.[43]

38 Green, 'The Laponian world heritage area. Conflict and collaboration in Swedish Sápmi', in *World Heritage Sites and Indigenous Peoples' Rights*, 90.

39 Green, *Managing Laponia*, 107.

40 UNESCO. The World Heritage Committee. *Operational Guidelines for the Implementation of the World Heritage Convention*, 8 July 2015, chapter II.F.

41 For an in-depth account of the disagreement on how to organise the management of Laponia, see Green, *Managing Laponia*.

42 *Mijá Ednam*, http://docplayer.se/4526192-Mija-ednam-samebyarnas-laponiaprogram.html (accessed 15 August 2015).

43 Green, *Managing Laponia*, 101–123.

The negotiations between the local Sámi and the authorities broke down.[44] The Sámi strategy was to refrain from entering into real negotiations until they were promised a majority of the seats on the management board along with a new management plan that adhered to Sámi perceptions and put reindeer herding first. The stand-off lasted for about ten years. Many different factors led the authorities to resume negotiations on Sámi terms. The government agreed to institute the management structure that the Sámi representatives had envisioned, with increased Sámi and local non-Sámi influence, more democratic decision structures, and the incorporation of Sámi stories, practices and knowledge of the landscape.[45] Today Laponia has a progressive management organisation, called Laponiatjuottjudus, which to a significant extent is Sámi-driven.

The rather unconventional structure of Laponiatjuottjudus challenges the normative way of thinking about nature and culture conservation. Sámi influence is strong, and the Sámi hold the majority on the board, and a Sámi representative is currently the chair. However, decisions are taken by consensus. The board includes representatives of the regional and local authorities and the Swedish Environmental Protection Agency as well as the local Sámi community.[46]

The Sámi-inspired management structure also influences the way that the practical conservation and management work is carried out. The personnel employed at the Laponiatjuottjudus office are well acquainted with Sámi culture and with the reindeer herding business; most of them have Sámi backgrounds. Official documents, such as the management plan, are written both in Swedish and in Sámi and have a form and rhetorical style that differ to some extent from what is normally found in documents of this sort.[47] According to informants, articulating what is 'Sámi' management in relation to 'Swedish' management is an on-going project throughout the organisation. The management plan spells out the importance of respect among the actors. Transparency and the incorporation of the aspirations of both Sámi and non-Sámi locals are said to be of paramount importance. Local participation is implemented through a public deliberation – ***rádedibme*** – that is held once or twice a year. Here interested local individuals, entrepreneurs and others can meet and discuss important issues and proposed changes in the management structure. A holistic and sustainable perspective on the Laponian area is said to be vital if the integrity of the site is to be maintained. At the same time protection without development is not considered appropriate.[48] Instead, effective and modern management should incorporate both 'traditional knowledge' and new technologies. In the management plan, Laponia is viewed as an arena for learning, a concept called *Searvelatna*. *Searvelatna* expresses the point that management is a process in need of constant change and evaluation.[49]

Having said that, Laponiatjuottjudus in many respects resembles any other administrative unit in the 'Western' world. The people working within the organisation are still 'bureaucrats' in that they must follow rules and regulations and goals and aims that have been set up nationally to govern the conservation of the area; but they do it in a slightly different way, with the Sámi story of the landscape and the reality of modern reindeer herding at the

44 Green, *Managing Laponia*, 101–123.
45 Swedish Code of Statues (SFS), *Laponiaförordning* (Laponia regulation), 2011:840.
46 Laponiatjuottjudus, http://laponia.nu/about-us/laponiatjuottjudus/ (accessed 15 August 2015).
47 Laponiatjuottjudus, *Laponia, Tjuottjudusplána – Management plan*.
48 Green, 'The Laponian World Heritage area. Conflict and collaboration in Swedish Sápmi', in *World Heritage Sites and Indigenous Peoples' Rights*, 97.
49 Green, *Managing Laponia*.

forefront. The organisation has also become an important platform for integrating Sámi perspectives and practices into nature and culture conservation.[50]

It is also important to point out that the indigenous community was already acquainted with the structure, bureaucracy and vocabulary of the World Heritage Convention. To a great extent, Sámi worldviews and knowledge overlap that of other people in the Nordic countries. The framework and bureaucratic practices involved in the whole World Heritage process were thus no more foreign to the average Sámi than to the average Swede. The Sámi were able to use World Heritage status to increase their influence and implement Sámi-based management of the site.

The experience described to us in the course of our fieldwork leads us to conclude that difficult issues remain to be addressed. The parties involved in the site continue to have different perspectives. The Sámi in the organisation sometimes feel that the authorities with whom they collaborate continue to measure and value 'new' Sámi-inspired initiatives (such as producing informational material, organising meetings, etc.) from an 'old' normative perspective. In other words, there is a feeling that there is still some de-colonising work to be done before a just and equal partnership can be reached in the management of Laponia.

### *Tongariro National Park*

Tongariro National Park, situated on New Zealand's North Island, was added to the World Heritage List in 1990 on the basis of natural criteria only.[51] In recognition of its cultural values it was re-inscribed as a Cultural Landscape in 1993, the first site to be so designated after the introduction of the category into the Convention's Operational Guidelines in 1992. The new category opened the way for the Convention to recognise intangible cultural values and the importance of human interaction with the environment.[52]

According to Herdis Hølleland, Tongariro contributed to this advance in several ways.[53] When Tongariro was originally nominated in 1987 it was presented as a mixed site as regards its natural values and, as a sacred site for the Māori community, for its intangible cultural values. The cultural values did not fit into the existing categories and criteria included in the rules, and the nomination was referred back to the national authorities who revised it to focus on natural values only.

However, this nomination and others with similar cultural aspects pointed to the need for change. A number of thematic studies of various landscapes and expert meetings were conducted before the rules were changed. The persons active in the management of Tongariro, both from the Department of Conservation, which is the government's state agency for heritage and resource management, and from the largest Māori tribe (*iwi*) in the area (Tuwharetoa), were instrumental in developing the Cultural Landscape category.[54] They cooperated with the UNESCO World Heritage Centre and heritage experts to broaden the understanding and application of the new category in order to address the cultural,

50 Reimerson, 'Sámi space for agency'. *Local Environment* (2016).

51 UNESCO. World Heritage Centre, *Tongariro National Park*, http://whc.unesco.org/en/list/421 (accessed 15 August 2015).

52 UNESCO. World Heritage Centre, *Tongariro National Park*, http://whc.unesco.org/en/list/421 (accessed 15 August 2015).

53 Hølleland, *Practicing World Heritage*, 107–121.

54 See also Hølleland, *Practicing World Heritage*, 119–121.

spiritual and immaterial aspects of heritage connected to the landscape, aspects that had been omitted from the revised application, and were missing in relation to many other existing and potential sites. The Cultural Landscape category has the potential to alter normative approaches to landscapes and nature conservation. To some extent the new category paved the way to raise the significance of Māori connections to the area and to more formally include Māori-based knowledge and practices in the area. For instance, the protection of spiritual values, not only natural values, has been vital in preventing the development of construction near the peaks of the mountains. Trails have been drawn so that they do not intrude on areas of high cultural or spiritual significance.

Initially the local Māori community used the cultural landscape inscription to claim more formal influence and control over the management of the park. In this respect the Convention had a certain ethno-political role to play. However, according to several informants, since the inscription the Convention has gradually decreased in importance. The Treaty of Waitangi is far more significant to Māori communities as an instrument of ethno-political power than the Convention and other international agreements on natural and cultural heritage protection and indigenous people's rights.

The Treaty of Waitangi, regarded as one of the founding documents of the New Zealand state, regulates Māori–state relations and responsibilities.[55] The meaning of the treaty is much debated and is interpreted differently. Nevertheless, it has been instrumental in establishing a legal basis for Māori efforts to recover traditional land and to claim compensation for losses. The Department of Conservation must put the Treaty of Waitangi into effect under s. 4 of the Conservation Act.[56] Section 4, in theory, gives Māori communities, in matters that relate to the management of their traditional areas, the right to insight, codetermination, cooperation and consultation. Section 4 alludes to extensive rights concerning the protection of cultural values that are connected to the managed natural areas.[57] There is some room for interpretation, however, and s. 4 has been implemented differently in different areas. Nevertheless, from an international perspective, the Māori in New Zealand have a powerful political, economic and social position compared to many other indigenous peoples. They are strongly organised and are able to act as a counterpart to the authorities in many segments of society. As far as the work of the Department of Conservation is concerned, informants point to the fact that extensive consultation with Māori communities is carried out on many different scales and on many different issues.

The management of Tongariro is no exception to the general conservation policy that applies to all national parks in New Zealand. Although there can be close and frequent contacts between the Department of Conservation and the Māori communities, the relationship is occasionally tainted with mistrust, and with lack of dialogue and respect. During our fieldwork we heard about the recent reorganisation of the Department of Conservation and its effect on communication between local Māori communities and that authority. Both Māori representatives and state officials complained that established lines of communications had been disrupted and that officials were more remote.

55 Orange, *An Illustrated History of the Treaty of Waitangi*.

56 Department of Conservation, *Treaty of Waitangi Responsibilities*, http://www.doc.govt.nz/about-us/our-policies-and-plans/conservation-general-policy/2-treaty-of-waitangi-responsibilities/ (accessed August 2015).

57 Compare Dahlström and Green. 'Indigenous traditional knowledge and sustainable development in the World Heritage sites of Laponia in Sweden and Tongariro in New Zealand', in *Science for Sustainable Development: The Social Challenge with Emphasis on the Conditions for Change: Proceedings of the 2nd VHU Conference on Science for Sustainable Development, Linköping, Sweden, 6–7 September 2007*.

People pointed to the relocation of applications and decisions regarding concessions for certain uses or activities in the area from the local office in Turangi in the traditional lands of Tuwharetoa close to the national park, to the city of Hastings some 200 km away. At the local office four people had worked with applications and decisions and, we were told, had become fairly competent. The relocation of the task to the office in Hastings meant that the relationship with Tuwharetoa and the routines, skills and trust that had been built up over time were lost. All of this had now to be re-established with new people far away who did not have the same level of knowledge of the *iwi* and the local circumstances. The Māori rely on personal relationships, mutual respect and trust, so to them the change was disrespectful. The new organisation hampered the cooperation between the officials in Turangi and the local *iwi,* which had up until then been a vital key in the management of the site. Among the local Māori representatives in Tongariro there was a feeling that the possibilities for carrying on a mutually respectful dialogue to strengthen co-management were now declining. Some even suggested that the situation was so precarious as to call for an address to the World Heritage Committee, or even to propose the withdrawal of Tongariro from the World Heritage List.

## *Concluding discussion*

Perspectives that alter from the normative are generally difficult to acknowledge when World Heritage sites are to be implemented, in spite of the clearly stated policy of the World Heritage Committee to make room for a valid and effective inclusion of indigenous peoples and their perceptions. The nomination and management of the World Heritage sites that we have included in our study have been shaped in an arena where many different trajectories meet to affect the outcome. These trajectories include national and international conservation goals and agendas, democratic developments and participatory actions, ethno-political endeavours, changing power patterns, and so forth. In spite of its strict bureaucratic structure and global uniformity, however, the World Heritage Convention has the potential to have a profound effect on local situations and relations among stakeholders. In our study, Laponia is the clearest example of this.

However, World Heritage processes also have the potential to reinforce a strictly normative practice of nature and culture conservation, enforcing Laurajane Smith's 'authorised heritage discourse'.[58] The Convention deals with territories and subjects from a Western scientific and professional point of view, and can therefore be interpreted as perpetuating postcolonial state intervention and control. The process is initiated and controlled by state authorities and their personnel and consultants, even if the aim of the entire project is to nominate the site as one where the indigenous communities are presented as consenting partners in the process. To some degree, this can be labelled a form of 'structural violence' where bureaucratic structures and practices and normative understandings of heritage direct the outcome that is wanted and needed by disregarding alternative narratives or approaches.[59]

In the case of Cape York, the Traditional Owners are formally involved, but, as we have seen, the process is managed through state control and according to specific forms. Here, the World Heritage bureaucracy adds yet another layer of structure that must be

58 Smith, *Uses of Heritage*, 11.

59 Compare MacNeil, 'Shafted', *Ethnologica Scandinavica* 45 (2015). See also Skilton, Adams and Gibbs, 'Conflict in common: Heritage-making in Cape York', *Australian Geographer* 45, no. 2 (2014): 163.

accommodated. While the whole idea of conserving culture and nature seems foreign to most Traditional Owners, for them to participate in a World Heritage nomination, they must accept or at least adapt to the World Heritage conservation regime.[60] In the case of Laponia, we can look back on a process where the local indigenous Sámi were not initially included and had to fight for their position as recognisable actors and partners in the eyes of the authorities. However, since they, like other actors, mastered the bureaucratic framework, they were able to incorporate and use its rhetoric and support for indigenous issues. The management plan adopted following the World Heritage appointment created an opportunity for the Sámi communities to change the power relations with the state.

The long process leading to the implementation of the management plan has become a platform for Sámi revitalisation and an opportunity for the stakeholders to think outside the strict framework of the normative conservation discourse.[61] The changes have not been rapid nor without friction; they can be said to have occurred within a bureaucratic framework. Nevertheless, alternative notions, wordings and practices are being put in place that are initiated by Sámi and inspired by the Sámi reality. This has the potential to slowly change the normative conservation discourse, but it is not a sudden paradigmatic transformation.

Tongariro illustrates that categories and criteria are decisive for the recognition of indigenous peoples under the Convention. There the Cultural Landscape category brought to prominence Māori interpretations, stories and knowledge. However, when it comes to indigenous influence on a more practical level, World Heritage status as such does not play a decisive role. Voices are now being raised to alert the World Heritage Committee to the gravity of their situation or even to propose a withdrawal of the site from the World Heritage List. Deletion is a long process that is most unlikely to occur; but for the issue even to be raised with the state and the World Heritage Committee would entail reactivation of the Convention as an ethno-political instrument. The Convention would play a role in the relation of the Māori to the state that has been minimal since the site's inclusion on the List. This suggests that the Convention's role may vary over time.

The relation between the local Māori representatives and the Department of Conservation has been characterised by rather regular and respectful meetings and consultations. So far, personal contacts have been an important part of successful communication among actors in the area. The view was often expressed in the course of our fieldwork that reorganisations have weakened this relatively open dialogue. A bureaucracy should ideally serve only the interest that it was designed to serve: officials should be neutral and impartial and not rely on personal relations. Tongariro shows that, in reality, personal relations can be an important key to strong and effective communication among stakeholders. It illustrates James C. Scott's argument that there must be room for practical knowledge, informal processes and improvisations in a bureaucracy, because a bureaucratic organisation cannot easily deal with complexity.[62] Informality might actually enable it to function and to facilitate indigenous influence.

These three cases illustrate that the World Heritage Committee, the expert organisations and the national arena authorities find it difficult to examine their preconceived notions and practices and to change, or adapt, the way conservation management is structured and implemented. The will to improve the situation may be there, from UNESCO to national,

60 Compare Nadasdy, 'The anti-politics of TEK: The institutionalization of co-management discourse and practice', *Anthropologica*, 47, no. 2 (2005): 227.

61 Reimerson, 'Sámi space for agency in the management of the Laponia World Heritage site', *Local Environment*, (2015): 15.

62 Scott, *Seeing Like a State*, 6.

regional and local authorities. Indigenous peoples also see the Convention as a means to gain further self-governance and increased their influence and control over the management of their traditional areas. But the power inherent in the bureaucratic organisation and practice and its role in recreating and reinforcing normative beliefs and conducts is often underestimated.[63] The World Heritage Convention is, ultimately, a conservative instrument that has proven relatively unreceptive to non-Western worldviews and conservation perspectives. Change is coming about, but slowly and often within the limits of established normative understandings and bureaucratic structures.

## References

Barnett, Michel & Martha Finnemore. *Rules for the World. International Organizations in Global Politics.* New York: Cornell University Press, 2004.

Brockington, Dan, Duffy, Rosaleen & Jim Igoe. *Nature Unbound: Conservation, Capitalism, and the Future of Protected Areas.* London: Earthscan Publishers, 2008.

Cameron, Christina & Mechtild Rössler. *Many Voices, One Vision: The Early Years of the World Heritage Convention.* Farnham: Ashgate, 2013.

Dahlström, Åsa & Carina Green. 'Indigenous Traditional Knowledge and Sustainable Development in the World Heritage sites of Laponia in Sweden and Tongariro in New Zealand'. In *Science for Sustainable Development: The Social Challenge with Emphasis on the Conditions for Change: Proceedings of the 2nd VHU Conference on Science for Sustainable Development, Linköping, Sweden, 6–7 September 2007*, ed. Björn Frostell. Uppsala: Föreningen Vetenskap för Hållbar Utveckling, 2008.

Department of Conservation. *Treaty of Waitangi Responsibilities.* http://www.doc.govt.nz/about-us/our-policies-and-plans/conservation-general-policy/2-treaty-of-waitangi-responsibilities/.

Disko, Stefan & Helen Tugendhat. *International Expert Workshop on the World Heritage Convention and Indigenous Peoples.* Copenhagen: International Work Group for Indigenous Affairs, 2013.

Green, Carina. *Managing Laponia: A World Heritage as Arena for Sámi Ethno-Politics in Sweden.* Uppsala: Uppsala University Press, 2009.

Green, Carina. 'The Laponian World Heritage Area: Conflict and Collaboration in Swedish Sápmi'. In *World Heritage and Indigenous Peoples' Rights*, eds. Stefan Disko & Helen Tugendhat, 85–102. Copenhagen: IWGIA, 2014.

Green, Carina & Jan Turtinen. 'Indigenous Peoples and World Heritage Sites – Normative Heritage Discourses and Possibilities for Change'. In *International Indigenous Development Research Conference 2014 Proceedings*, 65–65. Auckland: Nga Pae o te Maramatanga, Maori Centre of Research Excellence, University of Auckland, 2015.

Hølleland, Herdis. *Practicing World Heritage: Approaching the Changing Faces of the World Heritage Convention.* Oslo: University of Oslo, 2012.

Holmes, John. 'Contesting the Future of Cape York Peninsula'. *Australian Geographer* 42, no. 1 (2011): 53–68.

Holmes, John. 'Cape York Peninsula, Australia: A Frontier Region Undergoing a Multifunctional Transition with Indigenous Engagement'. *Journal of Rural Studies* 28, no. 3 (2012): 252–265.

Igoe, Jim, Neves, Katja & Dan Brockington. 'A Spectacular Eco-Tour around the Historic Bloc: Theorising the Convergence of Biodiversity Conservation and Capitalist Expansion'. *Antipode* 42 (2008): 486–512.

63 Compare Nadasdy, 'The anti-politics of TEK: The institutionalization of co-management discourse and practice', *Anthropologica*, 47, no. 2 (2005): 228; Waterton, Smith and Campbell, 'The utility of discourse analysis to heritage studies: The Burra Charter and social inclusion', *International Journal of Heritage Studies* 12, no. 4 (2006).

IUCN. *The World's Greatest Natural Areas: An Indicative Inventory of Natural Sites of World Heritage Quality*. Gland: IUCN, 1982.

Laponiatjuottjudus. *Laponia, Tjuottjudusplána – Management plan*.

Laponiatjuottjudus. *Laponiatjuottjudus*. http://laponia.nu/about-us/laponiatjuottjudus/.

MacNeil, Kristina S. 'Shafted'. *Ethnologica Scandinavica* 45 (2015): 73–88.

*Mijá Ednam – Samebyarnas Laponiaprogram*. http://docplayer.se/4526192-Mija-ednam-samebyarnas-laponiaprogram.html.

Nadasdy, Paul. 'The Anti-Politics of TEK: The Institutionalization of Co-Management Discourse and Practise'. *Anthropologica* 47, no. 2 (2005): 215–232.

Orange, Claudia. *An Illustrated History of the Treaty of Waitangi*. Wellington: Bridget Williams Books Ltd, 2004.

Reimerson, Elsa. *Nature, Culture, Rights: Exploring Space for Indigenous Agency in Protected Areas*. Umeå: Umeå University, Department for Political Science, 2015.

Reimerson, Elsa. 'Sami Space for Agency in the Management of the Laponian World Heritage Site'. *Local Environment*, 21, no. 7 (2016): 808–826.

Scott, James C. *Seeing like a State. How Certain Schemes to Improve the Human Condition Have Failed*. New Haven: Yale University Press, 1998.

Skilton, Nick, Adams, Michael & Leah Gibbs. 'Conflict in Common: Heritage-Making in Cape York'. *Australian Geographer* 45, no. 2 (2014): 147–166.

Smith, Anita. *Review of Properties Nominated for Inscription on the World Heritage List under the Cultural Landscape Category*. Melbourne: La Trobe University, 2011.

Smith, Laurajane. *Uses of Heritage*. London: Routledge, 2006.

Smyth, Dermot & Peter Valentine. 'Pathways to Securing Cultural and Natural Heritage of International Conservation Significance on Cape York Peninsula'. Discussion Paper Prepared for the Queensland Environment Protection Agency, 2008. http://www.ehp.qld.gov.au/cape-york/pdf/smyth-valentine-2008.pdf.

Swedish Code of Statutes (SFS). *Laponiaförordning* (Laponia Regulation), 2011: 840.

UNESCO, The General Conference. *Convention Concerning the Protection of the World Cultural and Natural Heritage*. 16 November 1972.

UNESCO, The World Heritage Committee, 39th Session, decision 39 COM 11, 2015.

UNESCO, World Heritage Committee. *Operational Guidelines for the Implementation of the World Heritage Convention*. Chapter II.F. 8 July 2015.

UNESCO. *UNESCO and Indigenous Peoples: Partnership for Cultural Diversity*.http://portal.unesco.org/culture/en/ev.php-URL_ID=35393&URL_DO=DO_TOPIC&URL_SECTION=201.html.

UNESCO, World Heritage Centre. *Laponian Area*. http://whc.unesco.org/en/list/774/.

UNESCO, World Heritage Centre. *States Parties, Ratification Status*. http://whc.unesco.org/en/statesparties/.

UNESCO, World Heritage Centre. *Tongariro National Park*. http://whc.unesco.org/en/list/421.

UNESCO, World Heritage Centre. *World Heritage List*.

United Nations, The General Assembly. *United Nations Declaration on the Rights of Indigenous Peoples*, Resolution 61/295, 2007.

Valentine, Peter. *Compiling a Case for World Heritage on Cape York Peninsula. Final Report for QPWS*. Townsville: James Cook University, 2006.

Wall, Geoffrey. 'Partnerships Involving Indigenous Peoples in the Management of Heritage Sites'. In *Tourism and Cultural Conflicts*, eds. Michael D. Robinson & Priscilla Boniface, 269–286, New York: CABI Publishing, 1999.

Waterton, Emma, Smith, Laurajane & Gary Campbel. 'The Utility of Discourse Analysis to Heritage Studies: The Burra Charter and Social Inclusion'. *International Journal of Heritage Studies* 12, no. 4 (2006): 339–355.

# 12 Sámi participatory rights in area protection and management

## The influence of the related CBD's programme in Finland and Norway

*Antje Neumann*

### Introduction

The Convention on Biological Diversity (CBD) of 1992, although not constituting indigenous peoples' rights and clearly implying numerous limitations in this respect, recognises, however, some of them, particularly in its preamble and in Article 8(j). At the same time, the CBD recognises protected areas as cornerstones of biodiversity conservation, expressed especially in Article 8(a) to (e), according to which each party to the Convention is obliged to establish national protected area systems. Under these provisions, a specific Programme of Work on Protected Areas (PoWPA) was established to support the implementation of the Convention's objectives. One of its targets, reflecting in particular the relations between indigenous peoples and area protection, is Programme Element 2 which contains the specific goal of enhancing and safeguarding the involvement of indigenous and local communities in the management of existing, and the establishment and management of new, protected areas.

Finland and Norway, both inhabited by the Sámi, an indigenous people,[1] are contracting parties to the CBD. As such, they have committed themselves to achieve the Convention's objectives and to implement its provisions into their national systems. According to their respective national strategies on biological diversity, they have also expressed their commitment to meet the targets of the PoWPA, in particular those of Programme Element 2.2. Thus, the enhancement and securing of the Sámi involvement in the establishment and management of protected areas are definite targets within their national protected areas agendas. Against this background, the article examines the extent to which both states meet the PoWPA's targets, and contrasts the respective results of domestic implementation. With this objective, the article aims to contribute to this volume by analysing the legal situation of the Sámi in Finland and Norway, particularly in terms of participatory rights in the context of area protection.

The overall analytical approach used in this chapter combines the area protection context, provided here by the CBD in particular and its provisions in Article 8(a)–(e), with the indigenous peoples' rights context. The latter is represented by the International Covenant on Civil and Political Rights (ICCPR) of 1966 and the ILO Convention No. 169 Concerning

1 The Sámi people are the indigenous people of the northern part of the Scandinavian Peninsula and large parts of the Kola Peninsula. They call their traditional living territory *Sápmi*. The majority of the Sámi population – around 50–65,000 people – live in Norway; in Finland they number approximately only 8,000. See: International Work Group for Indigenous Affairs (IWGIA), *Sápmi*, http://www.iwgia.org/regions/arctic/sapmi (accessed 10 November 2015).

Indigenous and Tribal Peoples in Independent Countries (ILO Convention 169) of 1989. While both states are parties to the ICCPR, to date only Norway has ratified ILO Convention 169.[2] Methodologically, the article looks at the measures taken by both states to meet their legal obligations arising from international biological conservation and human rights agreements. Measures within the framework of this article cover both legal (e.g. domestic laws, regulations, guidelines and management plans)[3] and policy instruments (e.g. national strategies and programmes). In addition, the thematic and periodic national reports, which provide specific information on implementing measures of CBD provisions, serve as sources for the analysis. Relevant literature and journal articles dealing with Sámi participation in protection and management and based on related case-studies have also been taken into account.

Structurally, the chapter starts with an overview of the CBD's commitments to area protection and indigenous peoples, focusing on the Convention's PoWPA and the development of the Programme Element 2.2. Measures that both states have taken to achieve the targets of Programme Element 2.2 are examined. A division is made between measures dealing with area protection, those related to Sámi participatory rights, and measures as outlined in the respective national reports to the CBD. An analysis is then made of the progress of both states in meeting their commitments under the PoWPA, as well as the restraints and challenges that remain to be tackled on the path to ensure full and effective participation of Sámi people in the establishment and management of protected areas. The chapter concludes by highlighting some of the results achieved and critical gaps that need further consideration in the move towards recognising Sámi participatory rights in the context of area protection and management.

## The CBD's commitments to area protection and indigenous peoples

The system of protected areas constitutes one of the cornerstones of biodiversity conservation since they maintain key habitats, provide refuges, allow for species migration and movement, and ensure the maintenance of natural processes across the landscape.[4] As of 2014, there were 209,000 protected areas, situated in 193 countries, covering more than 32 million km$^2$ worldwide.[5] The importance of protected areas for biological diversity is expressed in Article 8(a)–(e) of the CBD, which explicitly includes the objectives of establishing systems of protected areas and the development of guidelines for the selection, establishment and management of protected areas.[6] Beyond their contribution to biodiversity conservation, protected areas also provide livelihoods for nearly 1.1 billion people; they are the primary source of drinking water for over a third of the world's largest cities and a major factor in ensuring global food security.[7] More than 370 million indigenous peoples, who

2 In Finland, a lengthy prepared government bill to ratify ILO Convention 169 was withdrawn by the Finnish Parliament in March 2015.

3 In many jurisdictions, management plans have the status of legal documents. See Thomas et al., *Guidelines for Management Planning*, 2003, 9. In the given context, also the management plans of protected areas in Finland and Norway are regarded as legal documents since they contain specific provisions mandatory for their addressees and are prepared and approved according to defined procedural regulations.

4 Convention on Biological Diversity (CBD), *Protected Areas – An Overview*, CBD's webpage, http://www.cbd.int/protected/overview/default.shtml (accessed 12 November 2015).

5 Deguignet et al., *2014 United Nations List of Protected Areas*, 1.

6 Article 8(a) and (b) CBD.

7 Convention on Biological Diversity (CBD), *Protected Areas*, above note 4.

live in some 90 countries worldwide, participate significantly in these livelihoods.[8] Indigenous peoples and biological diversity have several aspects in common: many or most of the world's major centres of biodiversity coincide with areas occupied or controlled by indigenous peoples. The traditional territories of indigenous peoples encompass up to 22 per cent of the world's land surface, and simultaneously coincide with areas that hold 80 per cent of the planet's biodiversity.[9] In literature, it is also recognised that indigenous peoples contribute decisively to the maintenance of biological diversity and ecosystems within their territories.[10]

The CBD, although not establishing indigenous peoples' rights[11] and clearly implying numerous deficiencies in this respect,[12] does recognise some of them. The dependency of indigenous and local communities on biological diversity and their unique role in conserving life on earth is, for example, enshrined in the preamble of the Convention. The most important operating provision for the recognition of indigenous peoples rights is Article 8(j) of the CBD, together with related provisions in Articles 10(c), 17(2) and 18(4). These provisions promote particularly the preservation and maintenance of indigenous peoples' knowledge, innovations and practices, and their traditional lifestyles, and encourage the equitable sharing of the benefits arising from the utilisation of such knowledge, innovations and practices. However, they also relate to indigenous peoples' participatory rights, especially regarding access to genetic resources and the sharing of the benefits arising from the utilisation of such resources. Nowadays this subject is regulated by the Nagoya Protocol on Access to Genetic Resources and the Fair and Equitable Sharing of Benefits Arising from their Utilization to the Convention on Biological Diversity (Nagoya Protocol), adopted in 2010.

Under Article 8(a)–(e) and (j) of the CBD special working groups were established, followed by the adoption of respective programmes of work, which are not only internal documents of the working groups but contain specific targets for the parties to the Convention. From a legal point of view, they are mostly considered as 'soft law' and as such are not legally binding.[13] The same applies to the guidelines established under certain provisions of the CBD. However, by establishing basic principles and setting up key issues for consideration the programmes of work and the guidelines are of major importance for implementing the Convention's objectives. In the context of area protection and management, the PoWPA and its relation to indigenous peoples' participatory rights is of particular relevance and will be presented in more detail below. References will also be made to the Akwé:Kon Guidelines under Article 8(j) of the CBD,[14] since they play a major role in the Finnish implementation process.

8 United Nations Permanent Forum on Indigenous Issues (UNPFII), *State of the World's Indigenous Peoples*, UNPFII-webpage, http://undesadspd.org/IndigenousPeoples/LibraryDocuments/StateoftheWorldsIndigenousPeoples.aspx (accessed 10 November 2015).

9 Sobrevila, *The Role of Indigenous Peoples*, 5.

10 Stevens, *Conservation through Cultural Survival*, 2.

11 Carino, *Indigenous People's Rights and the International Regime on Access and Benefit-sharing*, 2007, www.twn.my/title2/resurgence/206/cover9.doc.

12 Reimerson, 'Between nature and culture', 992–1009.

13 See for the legal classification of the CBD and its COP 'actions': Makagon, *Analyzing the Binding Nature.*

14 The Akwé:Kon Guidelines were adopted by CBD COP VII (2004), Decision VII/16. They are voluntary and legally non-binding. The guidelines aim to provide general advice on the incorporation of cultural, environmental, including biodiversity-related, and social considerations of indigenous and local communities into new or existing impact-assessment procedures.

### *The Programme of Work on Protected Areas (PoWPA)*

The Programme of Work on Protected Areas (PoWPA) affects and relates to many of the other key matters under the CBD, and is also linked to all the thematic programmes. Thus, it is one of the most important cross-sectional issues under the Convention. The PoWPA was adopted at the seventh COP in 2004[15] and has the overall objective to establish and maintain ecologically representative national and regional systems of protected areas in the terrestrial context by 2010, and in the marine context by 2012.[16] With regard to indigenous peoples, the programme recalls the obligations of parties towards indigenous and local communities stated in Article 8(j) of the CBD and related provisions, and notes that the establishment, management and monitoring of protected areas should take place with the *full and effective participation* of, and full respect for the rights of, indigenous and local communities, consistent with national law and applicable international obligations.[17] The PoWPA comprises four interlinked elements intended to be mutually reinforcing and cross-sectional in their implementation.

Programme Element 2 is particularly relevant regarding indigenous peoples' participation in area protection and management as it includes the goal to *enhance and secure involvement of indigenous and local communities* and relevant stakeholders. Under this goal, it explicitly establishes the target of '*full and effective participation* by 2008, of indigenous and local communities, in full respect of their rights and recognition of their responsibilities, consistent with national law and applicable international obligations, and the participation of relevant stakeholders, in the management of existing, and the establishment and management of new, protected areas'.[18] In order to achieve that goal, parties to the convention are encouraged to implement specific plans and initiatives to involve indigenous and local communities effectively, support participatory assessment exercises, and promote an enabling environment for the involvement of indigenous and local communities in decision making, e.g. through legislation, policies, capacities, and resources.[19]

In the subsequent COPs, the implementation of the PoWPA was a continuing subject of discussions and decisions among the parties to the Convention. In 2006, for example, Decision VIII/24 (relating to protected areas and the respective programme of work) recognised as a priority 'the need for adequate technical, institutional and financial capacities for the implementation of the programme'.[20] While dealing further with the implementation of the programme, COP IX in 2008 in Decision IX/18[21] focused particularly on options for mobilising adequate and timely financial resources for the implementation of the programme.

In 2010, when comprehensive, effectively managed, and ecologically representative national and regional systems of protected (terrestrial) areas should have been established, a review of the progress of the implementation of the PoWPA and on opportunities for its further development after 2010 was prepared for the IUCN's World Commission on Protected Areas (WCPA).[22] According to this review, the PoWPA, although seen as the most

15 Decision VII/28 (2004).
16 Ibid., para. 18.
17 Ibid., para. 22.
18 Ibid., see target under goal 2.2 (emphasis added)
19 Ibid., Programme Element 2, goal. 2.2, paras. 2.2.1–2.2.5.
20 Decision VIII/24 (2006).
21 Decision IX/18 (2008).
22 IUCN WCPA, *Next Steps: Convention on Biological Diversity Programme of Work on Protected Areas, 2010.*

successful CBD initiative with measurable targets, was assessed as lacking implementation in terms of completeness and variability.[23] The review further stated that the PoWPA had generally been more effective concerning 'technical' issues (e.g. gap analysis) than with social targets (e.g. governance and participation).[24] The analysis was critical regarding Programme Element 2.2 – *enhance and secure involvement of indigenous and local communities and relevant stakeholders* – as, although some progress had been made in some areas, it was way behind meeting the targets at global level.[25] As a result of this review, COP X, held in October 2010, adopted a decision to strengthen decisively the implementation of the PoWPA.[26] This decision led to an invitation to the parties at the national level to develop long-term action plans for the implementation of the PoWPA, and to integrate them into revised national biodiversity strategies and action plans and relevant sector plans and budgets.[27]

In considering the development of long-term action plans for the implementation of the PoWPA, the following COP, held in 2012, welcomed the progress made by the parties.[28] As regards the remaining tasks, it specifically called on parties to strengthen recognition of and support for community-based approaches to conservation and sustainable use of biodiversity in situ, including *indigenous and local community conserved areas*, other areas within IUCN governance types and initiatives led by indigenous and local communities that meet the objectives of Aichi Biodiversity Target 11 and support the voluntary use of the Indigenous and Community Conserved Areas Registry managed by the United Nations Environment Programme World Conservation Monitoring Centre.[29]

A review of the overall global progress in implementing the PoWPA, based primarily on information provided by the fourth national reports and a series of CBD regional workshops, showed that c. 7 per cent of the parties had succeeded in enhancing and securing the involvement of indigenous and local communities in the establishing and management of protected areas; that 'significant progress up to a status of nearly complete' was achieved by c. 20 per cent of the parties to the convention; and that progress was 'fully underway' in a further 10 per cent.[30] Compared to the other programme elements, the implementation process of Programme Element 2.2 was one of the items where most 'significant progress' had been made.[31]

## Measures to implement PoWPA Element 2.2 in Finland and Norway

Given the complex nature of the PoWPA Element 2.2 targets – establishing and managing protected areas to conserve biological diversity and ensuring indigenous peoples' rights to participate in these activities – the following text considers three different categories of measures: those regarding the implementation of protected areas according to Article 8(a)–(e) of the CBD, those aiming at the implementation of the Sámi right to full and effective

23 Ibid., 8.
24 Ibid.
25 Ibid., 9.
26 Decision X/31 (2010).
27 Ibid. para. 1(b) and (c).
28 Decision XI/24 (2012).
29 Ibid., para. 1(e).
30 Convention on Biological Diversity (CBD), *Global Summary of PoWPA Implementation*, CBD's webpage, http://www.cbd.int/protected/implementation/default.shtml (accessed 12 November 2015).
31 Ibid.

participation, and those highlighted in the national reports Finland and Norway have submitted to the COPs of the CBD. While the first two categories are legal in character and concern primarily regulatory measures, the third category comes from a policy context and predominately comprises measures of non-legal nature (although measures of a legal nature might also be referred to in the third category).

### *Measures in the area protection context*

Protected areas in Finland and Norway constitute a substantial part of the total territorial areas of both countries. Both countries have made significant efforts to increase the extent of protected areas and thereby to protect biological diversity during the last decade. In Finland, the completion of the European Union Natura 2000 network contributed to achieve the targeted goals. As of 2014, the established network of protected areas covered about 12.5 per cent of the total surface area.[32] If other areas, like that of the Natura 2000 network sites, are included the total area of protection increases to 15 per cent.[33] Of Finland's terrestrial areas, about 12 per cent are included in the Natura 2000 network together with 19 per cent of the inland waters.[34] Protected areas can be either on state-owned or privately owned lands. They can be established by law, statute or a decision by Finland's environmental administration. Most protected areas are situated on state land and are managed by Metsähallitus' Natural Heritage Services (a state-owned enterprise which administers state-owned forests and water areas).[35]

The main legal instruments Finland adopted to establish and manage protected areas are the Nature Conservation Act of 1996,[36] the Decree on Nature Conservation of 1997, the Forest Act of 1996 and the Act on Wilderness Reserves of 1991. This legislation categorises protected areas as: national parks, strict nature reserves, mire reserves, protected herb-rich forests, protected old-growth forest areas, grey seal protection areas, other protected areas on state-owned land, protected areas on private land and wilderness areas. The Nature Conservation Act was amended in 2004 and 2005 in order to comply with EU legislation and the CBD.[37]

The proportion of terrestrial protected areas in Norway, comprising 17 per cent of the total surface area, slightly exceeds that in Finland.[38] Protected areas in Norway are established under Chapter V of the Nature Diversity Act, which came into force on 1 July 2009.[39] While the whole Act has to be seen as a measure implementing the CBD's objectives, the provisions for protected areas contribute particularly to the attainment of the PoWPA goals.[40] Specifically as regards protected areas, the new legislation was introduced to enhance protection efforts and ensure greater consistency and clarity for landowners and local communities involved by establishing, among other things, clear goals for protected areas, obligatory management plans for large protected areas and increased funding for management.[41]

32 Ahokumpu et al., *Fifth National Report*, 11.
33 Finland, *Implementation of the Convention.*
34 Ibid.
35 Metsähallitus, *A Network of Protected Areas.*
36 *Finland's Nature Conservation Act of 20 December 1996.*
37 Finland's Ministry of the Environment, *Nature Conservation Legislation.*
38 Norwegian Directorate for Nature Management, *State of the Environment Norway*, 2013.
39 Norwegian Nature Diversity Act of 19 June 2009.
40 Norway, *Norway's Fourth National Report*, 69.
41 Norwegian Environment Ministry, *New Nature Diversity Act.*

According to the Nature Diversity Act, the protected areas system in Norway covers the following categories: national parks, protected landscapes, nature reserves, habitat management areas and marine protected areas. Additional legislation relevant to area protection and management include the Forestry Act of 2005, the Planning and Building Act of 2008, and the Water Resource Act of 2000.

As regards the area protection context it should be noted that both states favour conservation models that also allow for traditional uses such as hunting, fishing, mushroom and berry picking. This is laid down in s. 33(1)(f) of the Norwegian Nature Diversity Act, which promotes the conservation of 'natural environments that reflect human use through the ages (cultural landscapes)', and in s. 14(1)–(4) of the Finnish Nature Conservation Act which explicitly allows the picking of berries and mushrooms for human consumption and other practical purposes.

### *Measures regarding Sámi participatory rights*

As an indigenous people, the Sámi have the right to full and effective participation as an expression of their right to self-determination.[42] The most important legal frameworks for this, at least from a hard-law perspective, are provided by the ICCPR and ILO Convention 169, both of which are legally binding. In respect of the ICCPR, the Human Rights Committee (HRC) has clarified in its General Comment 23 in relation to Article 27 that the protection of indigenous rights to land, territories and resources is strongly linked to the right to effective participation.[43] In ILO Convention 169, it is Article 6(1) that imposes the general legal obligation to consult with indigenous peoples regarding legislative or administrative measures that directly affect them.[44] Although, in the latter context, the original obligation to be 'consulted' does not imply the right to consent; meanwhile the right of effective participation for indigenous peoples has been endorsed by several human rights bodies.[45] In terms of state legal obligations, it should be noted that Finland, although it has not yet ratified ILO Convention 169, already uses it as a starting point for its international commitments regarding indigenous peoples.[46]

Sámi participatory rights have been developed in both countries, as shown for example, by the change of conditions governing political participation and influence.[47] In Norway,

42 Like the term 'indigenous people', their 'right to full and effective participation' is barely defined. Despite specific expressions within the Universal Declaration of Human Rights (UDHR) of 1948 (in particular Article 21 UDHR), the right of indigenous peoples to full and effective participation can be seen as embedded in the overarching right to self-determination; or as expressed by the UN Development Group Guidelines on Indigenous Peoples Issues, the right to self-determination may be expressed 'through full and effective participation of indigenous peoples at every stage of any action that may affect them direct or indirectly'. United Nations Development Group, *Guidelines on Indigenous Peoples' Issues.* February 2008.

43 In so far as it has stated that 'The enjoyment of those rights [those under Article 27] may require positive legal measures of protection and measures to ensure the effective participation of members of minority communities in decisions which affect them.' See: Human Rights Committee (HRC), *General Comment no. 23: The rights of minorities (Art. 27)*, 1994, para. 7.

44 See, among others, Trask, *Indigenous Peoples Participation in Decision Making – A Paper Prepared for the UN Expert Mechanism on the Rights of Indigenous Peoples*, 2010, http://www2.ohchr.org/english/issues/indigenous/ExpertMechanism/3rd/docs/contributions/MililaniTrask.doc.

45 Ibid.

46 Heinämäki et al., 'The protection of the culturally', 206.

47 Josefsen, 'The Sámi and the national', 7.

the Sámi Parliament was already established in 1989[48] – the first in the Nordic States – in Finland a respective parliament only came into operation six years later, in 1996.[49] However, constitutionally, the Sámi have a stronger position in Finland than in Norway: according to the reworked Finnish Constitution of 1999, the Sámi are recognised as an indigenous people with the right to maintain and develop their own language and culture;[50] whereas in Norway, state authorities are merely required to create conditions enabling the Sámi people to preserve and develop their language, culture and way of life.[51] Although the Sámi thus have stronger constitutional rights in Finland than in Norway, it is argued that these have not been converted into practical political action to any particular extent.[52]

The degree of specification in respect to Sámi participatory rights also differs. In Norway, a special agreement, setting out 'Procedures for Consultation between Central Government Authorities and the Sámi Parliament' (Procedures for Consultation), was concluded between the Minister for Local Government and Regional Development and the President of the Sámi Parliament on 11 May 2005.[53] These procedures aim, among others, to facilitate agreement between government authorities and the Norwegian Sámi Parliament whenever issues arise concerning the implementation of legislation or measures that may directly affect Sámi interests.[54] In addition, specific 'Guidelines for Consultations in Relation to Area Protection' (Guidelines for Consultation) were agreed between the Norwegian Ministry for the Environment and the Sámi Parliament on 31 January 2007.[55] These guidelines are to ensure that consultations connected with any proposal for nature protection in Sámi areas will be conducted in good faith and with the goal of achieving agreement between the state authorities and the Sámi Parliament.[56] Furthermore, these guidelines contain specific procedures for the consultation process, such as specific timeframes and regulations governing the composition of planning and management boards.[57] Such explicit regulations do not exist in Finland. Apart from the constitutional guarantee of their cultural autonomy[58] and the obligation for all governmental authorities to negotiate with the Sámi Parliament in all far-reaching and important measures,[59] so far, respective fora or bodies that could structure the obligation to negotiate and a specific procedure to operationalise it, are still lacking.[60]

### *Measures outlined in the national reports*

While the national reports, referred to below, may include references to the measures already mentioned above (in particular relevant legislation), they add important information regarding policy measures taken in the present context. At the same time, they reveal a prioritisation among the various measures chosen and also hint at certain

48 Norway's Sámi Parliament Act 1987.
49 Finland's Sámi Parliament Act 1995.
50 Article 17 (3) Finnish Constitution 1999.
51 Article 108 Norwegian Constitution 1814 (2014).
52 Josefsen, above note 47, 11.
53 Norway's Procedures for Consultations 2005.
54 Human Rights Committee (HRC). *Replies by the Government of Norway.*
55 Norway's Guidelines for Consultation 2007.
56 Ibid., s. 1.
57 Ibid., ss. 5 and 6.
58 Article 17 (3) Finnish Constitution 1999.
59 Article 9 (1) (2) Finland's Sámi Parliament Act 1995.
60 Josefsen, above note 47, 11.

deficiencies. The most relevant reports evaluated here are, for Finland, its fourth and fifth National Report to the CBD 2009 and 2014, its National Biodiversity Strategy and Action Plan 2012, and its Progress Reports on the Implementation of the PoWPA 2012 and 2014. For Norway, the relevant reports are the fourth and fifth National Report to the CBD 2009 and 2014, and its Progress Report on the Implementation of the PoWPA 2012.

It is remarkable that Finland, within its national strategies, closely followed the CBD developments and priorities as set out especially by the Convention's Strategic Plan for Biodiversity 2010–2020 and the Aichi Biodiversity Targets 2010.[61] In its fourth National Report 2009, Finland explicitly referred to its implementation progress of the PoWPA and listed seven specific measures it had taken regarding Programme Element 2.2. These included the legal obligation to negotiate with the Sámi Parliament and reindeer herding cooperatives in all matters affecting the status of the Sámi as an indigenous people, and the establishment of protected area cooperation groups and of co-managed protected areas.[62] However, the report, self-critically, also pointed out that 'the co-management approach including decision-making mechanisms and management planning and practices needs close re-evaluation in terms of involving local and indigenous communities and other stakeholders in practice', and that 'there could be more focus on how to find a way to develop measures for co-management of PAs [protected areas] as it is seen from wider perspective'.[63] In this context, the report stressed the challenge 'that the social, cultural, economic and ethnical circumstances vary so much from south to north of the country, [that] the creation of common guidelines or policy may not feasible'.[64] This is also reflected in the literature, which points out that the engagement of Sámi people in forestry and reindeer herding, and the engagement of Finns and Sámi in reindeer herding, differ widely and create a broad diversity.[65]

In compliance with the CBD Strategic Plan for Biodiversity 2010–2020 and the Aichi Biodiversity Targets of 2010, Finland, at the end of 2012, approved a new 'Strategy for the Conservation and Sustainable Use of Biodiversity' for 2012–2020.[66] Although the PoWPA is not especially addressed in this new strategy, it is nevertheless covered by it. Thus, in connection with Aichi Biodiversity Target 11, the strategy sets the target that by 2020 'Finland's network of protected areas and the measures applied to conserve biodiversity in the use of other areas together cover at least 17 per cent of the terrestrial environments and inland waters of the country, and 10 per cent of coastal and marine areas.'[67] Aichi Biodiversity Target 18 is especially important for PoWPA Programme Element 2.2, since it lays down that, by 2020, 'Finland's implementation of the CBD allows for the full and effective participation of the Sámi community at all relevant levels in line with decisions set out in

61 Strategic Plan for Biodiversity 2011–2020 and the Aichi Biodiversity Targets were adopted in Decision X/2 (2010). Its purpose is to promote effective implementation of the CBD through a strategic approach, comprising a shared vision, a mission, and strategic goals and targets (called 'the Aichi Biodiversity Targets').

62 Finland, *Fourth National Report*, 142.

63 Ibid., 143.

64 Ibid.

65 See, e.g., Mazzullo, *Environmental Conservation*, 397.

66 Finland *Government Resolution on the Strategy.*

67 Ibid. Target 11.

the CBD and by COPs.'[68] According to this goal, Finland, in its Action Plan related to the PoWPA of 2012[69] (as requested by CBD COP Decision X/31) established as key actions:

- the application of the Akwé:Kon Guidelines in the Sámi homeland area to mitigate conflicts between reindeer husbandry and other land use and negative impacts on nature in the region, safeguarding Sámi culture and traditional knowledge, and
- the reconciliation of hunting and nature conservation in protected areas through participatory management planning.[70]

Although the application of the Akwé:Kon Guidelines does not count directly in implementing the targets of the PoWPA, and here in particular those of Programme Element 2.2, both instruments have a lot in common as regards indigenous peoples' general involvement in biodiversity conservation. During the last few years, Finland started to be very committed to implementing the Programme of Work related to Article 8(j) under the CBD. One outcome of this commitment was the decision to test the application of the Akwé:Kon Guidelines on the preparation of the management plan for the Hammastunturi wilderness area in Upper Lapland, where a joint working group was established, including Sámi representatives who were all holders of traditional knowledge. The final report for this test case was submitted to the CBD in 2013. It concluded, as the most important result, that both the Sámi and Metsähallitus (the competent authority) viewed the procedure as outlined in the Akwé:Kon Guidelines as useful for both sides, and highlighted the whole process as a workable framework for cooperation.[71]

With reference to these efforts, Finland, in its Progress Report on the Implementation of the PoWPA in 2014, noted the substantial progress it has made not only as regards the practical implementation of the Akwé:Kon Guidelines in the management planning in the Sámi homeland, but also in respect of the enhancement and involvement of the Sámi people in the management of protected areas, as required by Programme Element 2.2 of the PoWPA.[72] In the same context, Finland referred to its second key action – the reconciliation of hunting and nature conservation in protected areas through participatory management planning – as fully completed by the established routine in all management planning for protected areas.[73]

Unlike Finland, Norway's fourth National Report, also dated from 2009, does not deal explicitly with the specific programmes of work established under the CBD[74] and therefore made no particular reference to the PoWPA. However, regarding progress achieved towards the CBD 2010 target and the strategic plan, the Norwegian report stated that recent developments in Norwegian Sámi policy were highly relevant for the implementation of the CBD (e.g., references were made to the Finnmark Act of 2005 and the Procedures for Consultation between the State Authorities and the Sámi Parliament of 2005 (as mentioned above)).[75]

68 Ibid. Target 18.
69 Finnish Government, above note 66.
70 Ibid. 'Priority and timeline for key actions of the PoWPA' Action 1 under Programme Element 2.
71 Juntunen and Stolt, *Application of Akwé:Kon Guidelines*, 59.
72 Heinonen et al., *Implementation of the Convention.*
73 Ibid.
74 Norway. *Norway's Fourth National Report.*
75 Ibid.

Norway's latest reports, both the Progress Report on the Implementation of the PoWPA of 2012[76] and the fifth National Report of 2014,[77] mentioned previous legislative efforts – the Procedures for Consultation 2005 and the new Nature Diversity Act 2009 with its specific recognition of the Sámi culture. The reports also stressed the new reform of governance of protected areas adopted in 2009. This reform can be seen largely as a response to reports that Norwegian protected areas have had previously poor performance and deficiencies in involving local interests.[78] Along with this reform, management responsibilities for national parks and other large protected areas have been transferred to the local level, to local management boards, which give the municipalities involved a greater sense of control and responsibility.[79] As of 2014, 43 local management bodies have been established,[80] and more than three-quarters of the total protected area on the Norwegian mainland will be subject to local management regimes as soon as the reform is fully implemented.[81] From a participatory point of view, the local management boards include representatives from municipalities and county councils, and also from the Norwegian Sámi Parliament in areas involving Sámi interests.[82] Through this transfer of management responsibilities to the local level new opportunities to take into account local knowledge, including traditional knowledge of Sámi people, might be facilitated for the management of protected areas.[83]

## Progress and deficiencies

The outline of legislative and policy measures in Finland and Norway to ensure full and effective participation of the Sámi people in the context of area protection and management, and especially to meet their commitments under Programme Element 2.2. of the PoWPA, shows that notable results have been achieved by both. However, the states have set different emphases and followed different approaches: Finland, on the one hand, followed closely the international policy setting of the CBD, particularly the Convention's Strategic Plan for Biodiversity 2010–2020 and the Aichi Biodiversity Targets of 2010, and even confirmed this commitment in its stated aim that it 'will take the lead in international cooperation on the implementation of Article 8(j) of the Convention'.[84] While doing so, it very much favoured a certain policy setting by launching related governmental resolutions and establishing expert groups. It also used regulatory approaches through the application of the Akwé:Kon Guidelines in the development of a management plan for a wilderness area, an approach that has been used for other conservation areas meanwhile,[85] and that will be implemented in the management of natural resources and land areas in future.[86] Although the application of the Akwé:Kon Guidelines, as noted previously, does not directly aim to

76 Norway. *Norway's CBD Notification.*
77 Norway. *Norway's Fifth National Report.*
78 Fauchald and Gulbrandsen, *The Norwegian Reform of Protected Area Management: A Grand Experiment with Delegation of Authority?* 2012, 218.
79 Norway, above note 76, 68.
80 Norway, above note 77, 68.
81 Fauchald and Gulbrandsen: above note 78, 209.
82 Norway, above note 77, 68.
83 Ibid.
84 Finnish Government, above note 66.
85 The Akwé:Kon Guidelines have also been applied to the preparation of the management plans of Urho Kekkonen national park and Käsivarsi wilderness area. Metsähallitus, email to the author, 1 December 2015.
86 Juntunen and Stolt, above note 71, 9.

enhance indigenous peoples in area protection and management (as targeted under the PoWPA), its successful implementation can, however, provide a tangible tool to support the effective participation of indigenous peoples in land-use planning, and facilitate more engagement of the local Sámi people in this process.[87]

Norway, on the other hand, put more emphasis on reconciling domestic concerns by reaching specific agreements with the Sámi Parliament (e.g. the Procedures for Consultation 2005 or the Guidelines for Consultations 2007) or by developing an administrative reform related to protected areas in order to better meet local interests. Especially due to this reform of 2009 increased participation of Sámi representatives in the newly established local management boards could be achieved. According to an early evaluation of the reform, presented at the end of 2011, 22 representatives of the Norwegian Sámi Parliament participated at that time in the 29 local management boards then established.[88] They represented 12 per cent of the overall membership of these boards.[89] Thus Sámi participation in the management of protected areas could actually be increased through the reform.

Despite these achievements in involving the Sámi in area protection and management, considerable deficiencies remain in both states as regards the Sámi right to full and effective participation. Finland, as indicated in its fourth National Report to the CBD, still faces difficulties in balancing the interests of Sámi with those of other people who live in the same area and practise the same way of life[90] – difficulties that become especially relevant in the context of area protection and management. In addition to this, concerns remain that the Sámi people, notwithstanding the progressive implementation of the Akwé:Kon Guidelines in wilderness areas of the Sámi homeland, lack participation and decision-making powers over matters of fundamental importance to their culture and way of life, including rights to land and resources.[91] This becomes especially apparent with regard to Finland's existing legislation. While, at a first glance, s. 9(1)–(2) of the Finnish Sámi Parliament Act seems to provide a strong obligation for negotiating with the Sámi Parliament on matters of area protection and management this obligation is weakened by being reduced to '*hearing*' and '*discussing*', rather than voting or exercising other decisive rights. Moreover, s. 9(2), second sentence, then adds a further weakness to participation, by stating that 'Failure to use this opportunity in no way prevents the authority from proceeding in the matter.' Despite this, specifying regulations concerning state obligations to consult the Sámi in matters of area protection and management either do not exist in Finland or do not focus on the Sámi people in particular.[92] Therefore, the Human Rights Committee in its latest Concluding Observation 2013, requested Finland, among others, to 'increase its efforts to revise its legislation to fully guarantee the rights of the Sámi people in their traditional land, ensuring

87 Heinämäki et al., above note 46, 224.

88 Fauchald and Gulbrandsen, above note 78, 213.

89 Ibid. As regards these numbers, it has to be noted that the Norwegian reform of protected areas 2009 applies to the total extent of protected areas in Norway, and not only to those in the Sámi homeland. Thus, an evaluation of Sámi representatives in the local management boards concerning the Finnmark area would show a higher percentage of Sámi representatives.

90 Anaya, *The Situation of the Sámi People*, section III (D), para. 29.

91 Human Rights Committee (HRC). *Concluding Observations*, para. 16.

92 The latter, e.g., applies to Finland's Nature Conservation Act 1996, which refers, in the context of participation in drafting nature conservation programmes, only to parties whose interests or rights are affected by such programmes, but not to the Sámi people in particular. See: s. 8 Finland's Nature Conservation Act 1996.

respect for the right of Sámi communities to engage in free, prior and informed participation in policy and development processes that affect them.'[93]

As regards Norway, it has to be noted that the 2009 reform of protected areas, although de facto leading to increased participation of the Sámi people in area protection and management through their representation in the newly established local management boards, did not have the explicit aim of enhancing Sámi participatory rights but rather focussed on local stakeholders generally. In 2006, severe confrontations between Sámi reindeer herders and relevant Norwegian state authorities had been reported in respect of the establishment of two national parks, the Blåfjella-Skjækerfjella and Lierne National Park, both situated in the heartland of the indigenous reindeer managing areas of the Sámi.[94] Later studies on the governance of protected areas in Norway confirmed these unresolved conflicts and identified the lack of enabling rules (clear-cut procedures), failures to involve Sámi reindeer herders in informed discussion about rules and ability to modify these rules (collective choice), and in the conflict resolution mechanism used in these cases.[95] More recent investigations, taking into account the 2009 reform, stressed the fact that the establishment of the local management boards provides a novel example of adaptive governance that can foster resilient livelihoods for various groups of actors that depend on protected areas.[96] However, these investigations also pointed to continuing shortcomings in appropriate Sámi participation in the decision-making process.[97] Moreover, the authors of these later studies also stressed the time component that is critical for the Sámi involved to achieve the outcome of coproduction of knowledge and learning.[98] Alongside this specific comment, although in the more general context of the Procedures for Consultation of 2005, Sámi representatives criticised a lack of disclosure and late involvement in certain cases and called for clearer internal routines on the part of the Norwegian government in this area.[99] In consequence, the ILO body examining the application of ILO Convention 169 requested Norway in its latest observation to 'continue to pursue its efforts to address the challenges identified and to provide information enabling it to examine the manner in which the procedures established ensure the effective consultation and participation of the indigenous peoples concerned in decisions which may affect them directly, giving full effect to the requirements of the Convention'.[100]

Summarising the progress made during recent years and the remaining deficiencies it can be noted that Finland, although not yet having ratified ILO Convention 169 and thus lacking legislation to implement it, has compensated for this weakness by launching respective policy measures to enhance Sámi participation in landscape planning and management (especially through the application of the Akwé:Kon Guidelines). In doing so, it used regulatory approaches through the development of adequate management plans for wilderness and other protected areas, and indicated that it would continue this approach in the management of natural resources and land areas in future. Norway, in contrast, has not foregrounded its regulatory setting towards Sámi participatory rights in the context of

93 Human Rights Committee, above note 91.
94 Riseth, 'An indigenous perspective'.
95 Hovik, Sandström and Zachrisson, 'Management of protected areas'.
96 Risvoll et al., 'Does pastoralists' participation'.
97 Ibid., 6/11.
98 Ibid.
99 Committee of Experts on the Application.
100 Ibid.

protection and management (in particular, the Procedures of Consultation of 2005 and the Guidelines for Consultation of 2007). Instead, it has focussed on administrative measures (the 2009 governance reform of protected areas) that in fact also led to increased participation of Sámi in the management of protected areas.

## Conclusion

During the last decade, Finland and Norway, both parties to the CBD and, as such, committed to the Convention's objectives, made significant progress towards realising the PoWPA adopted within the CBD framework, and here in particular as regards Programme Element 2.2 – the enhancement and securing of the Sámi involvement in the establishment and management of protected areas.

Finland, for its part, has put a lot of emphasis on the international policy setting exemplified by the CBD's Strategic Plan for Biodiversity 2010–2020 and the Aichi Biodiversity Targets 2010. Here, it also stated its ambition to take the lead in international cooperation on the implementation of Article 8(j) of the CBD. In fulfilling this commitment, it implemented, the first country to do so, the Akwé:Kon Guidelines at the national level by applying them in the preparation of the management plan for a wilderness reserve situated in the Sámi homeland, followed by further applications. The successful application of these guidelines, intended to be continued in managing natural resources and land areas in future, has shown positive results in supporting effective participation of indigenous peoples in land-use planning and in enhancing the engagement of the local Sámi people in this process.

Norway, in contrast, has largely focussed on domestic issues and rather addressed implicitly the PoWPA's targets, including that of Programme Element 2.2. In doing so, it referred to its governance reform of protected areas 2009, which aimed at improving the consideration of local interests in the context of area protection. Through these efforts, Sámi representatives (along with other local stakeholders) became increasingly involved in the newly established local management boards. The reform thus provides a successful example of adaptive governance in the establishment and management of protected areas.

Despite the progress in both countries, deficiencies remain regarding the full and effective participation of Sámi people in area protection and management. In Finland, although the country is performing strongly in matters of international conservation policy, lasting weaknesses can be seen with respect to indigenous peoples' rights issues. This becomes especially apparent in weak and non-explicit procedural rights for the Sámi in the decision-making process. Thus, the ratification of ILO Convention 169 remains a key step to be taken, in order also to fully comply with the targets set under the CBD. Norway, having progressively ratified ILO Convention 169, however, faces challenges in respect of applying existing legal instruments concerning Sámi rights. This refers particularly to its Procedures for Consultation with the Sámi Parliament and its Guidelines for Consultations in relation to area protection. These regulatory instruments should be more explicitly and effectively applied in order to directly strengthen Sámi participation in the context of area protection and management.

## Bibliography

Ahokumpu, Anna-Liisa, Ari-Pekka Auvinen, Marja Pylvänäinen & Marina von Weissenberg. *Fifth National Report to the Convention on Biological Diversity*. Finland's Ministry for the Environment, 5 May 2014.

Anaya, James. *The Situation of the Sámi People in the Sápmi Region of Norway, Sweden and Finland*. Report of the Special Rapporteur on the situation of human rights and fundamental freedoms of indigenous people, Human Rights Council (HRC), A/HRC/18/XX/Add.Y, 12 January 2011.
Committee of Experts on the Application of Conventions and Recommendations (CEACR). *Observation*. CEACR document, adopted 2014, published 104th ILC session 2015.
Deguignet, Marine, Juffe-Bignoli, Diego, Harrison, Jerry, MacSharry, Brian, Burgess, Neil & Naomi Kingston. *2014 United Nations List of Protected Areas*. Cambridge: UNEP-WCMC, 2014.
Fauchald, Ole Kristian & Lars H. Gulbrandsen. 'The Norwegian Reform of Protected Area Management: A Grand Experiment with Delegation of Authority?'. *Local Environment* 17, no. 2 (2012): 203–222.
Finland. *Fourth National Report on Convention on Biological Diversity in Finland*. Ministry for the Environment, 24 June 2009.
Finland. *Implementation of the Convention on Biological Diversity's Programme of Work on Protected Areas*. 30 March 2012.
*Finland's Sámi Parliament Act of 14 July 1995 (974/1995)*.
*Finland's Nature Conservation Act of 20 December 1996 (1096/1996)*.
*Finnish Constitution of 11 June 1999 (731/1999)*.
Finnish Government. *Government Resolution on the Strategy for the Conservation and Sustainable Use of Biodiversity in Finland for the Years 2012–2020 (2012), Saving Nature for People*. 20 December 2012.
Heinämäki, Leena, Herrmann, Thora Martina & Antje Neumann. 'The Protection of the Culturally and Spiritually Important Landscapes of Arctic Indigenous Peoples under the Convention on Biological Diversity and First Experiences from the Application of the Akwé: Kon Guidelines in Finland'. In *The Yearbook of Polar Law*, eds. Gudmundur Alfredsson & Timo Koivurova (Editors-in-Chief), Hjalti Ómar Ágústsson (Special Editor), 189–225. Leiden/Boston: Brill/Martinus Nijhoff Publishers, 2014.
Heinonen, Mervi, Juvonen, Sanna-Kaisa & Kari Finland Lahti. *Implementation of the Convention on Biological Diversity's Programme of Work on Protected Areas: CBD Programme of Work on Protected Areas in Finland – Analysis of Implementation of Key Actions 2012–13*. 9 June 2014.
Hovik, Sissel, Sandström, Camilla & Anna Zachrisson. 'Management of Protected Areas in Norway and Sweden: Challenges in Combining Central Governance and Local Participation'. *Journal of Environmental Policy & Planning* 12, no. 2 (2010): 159–177.
Human Rights Committee (HRC). *General Comment No. 23: The Rights of Minorities (Art. 27)*, UN document CCPR/C/21/Rev./Add.5, 8 April 1994.
Human Rights Committee (HRC). *Replies by the Government of Norway to the List of Issues (CCPR/C/NOR/Q/5) to be Considered in Connection with Examination of the Fifth Periodic Report of Norway (CCPR/C/NOR/2004/5)*. UN document CCPR/C/NOR/Q/5/Add.1, 8 March 2006.
Human Rights Committee (HRC). *Concluding Observations on the Sixth Period Report of Finland*. UN document CCPR/C/FIN/CO/6, 22 August 2013.
IUCN WCPA. *Next Steps: Convention on Biological Diversity Programme of Work on Protected Areas*. Gland: IUCN, 2010.
Josefsen, Eva. 'The Sámi and the National Parliaments – Channels for Political Influence'. *Galdu Cala, Journal of Indigenous Peoples' Rights* 2 (2007): 7–28.
Juntunen, Suvi & Elina Stolt. *Application of Akwé: Kon Guidelines in the Management and Land Use Plan for the Hammastunturi Wilderness Area*. Finland: Metsähallitus, 2013.
Makagon, J. Eli. 'Analyzing the Binding Nature of COP Decisions through the Convention on Biological Diversity'. Natural Justice, New York (2012).
Mazzullo, Nuccio. 'Environmental Conservation and Local Interests in Finnish Lapland'. *Conservation and Society* 3, no. 2 (2005): 388–406.

Metsähallitus. *A Network of Protected Areas Conserves Finland's Nature*, in Metsähallitus' webpage, June 2, 2015. http://www.metsa.fi/web/en/network-of-protected-areas (accessed 10 November 2015).
Norway. *Norway's Fourth National Report to the Convention on Biological Diversity.* 24 April 2009.
Norway. *Norway's CBD Notification: 18 Contributions from Norway, National Initiatives, Activities and Action Plans Contributing to the Implementation of the Strategic Plan for Biodiversity 2011–2020.* 17 April 2012.
Norway. *Norway's Fifth National Report to the Convention on Biological Diversity.* 4 July 2014.
*Norway's Sámi Parliament Act (The Sámi Act concerning the Sameting and other Sámi legal matters) of 12 June 1987.*
*Norway's Procedures for Consultations of 11 May 2005.*
*Norway's Guidelines for Consultation of 31 January 2007.*
*Norway's Nature Diversity Act of 19 June 2009.*
*Norwegian Constitution of 17 May 1814 with later amendments.*
Norwegian Directorate for Nature Management, *State of the Environment Norway*, 2013.
Norwegian Environment Ministry. *New Nature Diversity Act Will Secure Norway's Natural Environment*, Press release, 3 April 2009. https://www.regjeringen.no/en/aktuelt/new-nature-diversity-act/id553630 (accessed 11 November 2015).
Reimerson, Elsa. 'Between Nature and Culture: Exploring Space for Indigenous Agency in the Convention on Biological Diversity'. *Environmental Politics* 22, no. 6 (2013): 992–1009.
Riseth, Jan Åge. 'An Indigenous Perspective on National Parks and Sámi Reindeer Management in Norway'. *Geographical Research* 45, no. 2 (2007): 177–185.
Risvoll, Camilla, Fedreheim, Gunn Elin, Sandberg, Audun & Shauna Burn Silver. 'Does Pastoralists' Participation in the Management of National Parks in Northern Norway Contribute to Adaptive Governance?'. *Ecology and Society* 19, no. 2 (2014): 71, 11 pages.
Sobrevila, Claudia. *The Role of Indigenous Peoples in Biodiversity Conservation – The Natural but often Forgotten Partners.* Washington: The International Bank for Reconstruction and Development/The World Bank, 2008.
Stevens, Stan. *Conservation through Cultural Survival: Indigenous Peoples and Protected Areas.* Washington, DC: Island Press, 1997.
Thomas, Lee, Middleton, Julie & Adrian Phillips. *Guidelines for Management Planning of Protected Areas.* Gland and Cambridge: IUCN, 2003: ix + 79 pp.
United Nations Development Group (UNDG). *Guidelines on Indigenous Peoples' Issues.* The Guidelines were drafted by a group of UN organizations and specialised agencies under the aegis of the Inter-Agency Support Group on Indigenous Peoples'Issues, and approved by the UNDG on 1 February 2008.

# 13 Contrasting nature, contrasting rights – Concluding remarks

*Christina Allard, Elsa Reimerson and Camilla Sandström*

What is the main point in comparing conservation aims, protected areas and Indigenous peoples across different states? Despite international cooperation efforts, binding treaties and voluntary instruments, legislation and policies may differ considerably among neighbouring countries. Comparisons provide new perspectives on the protected area regimes of other countries, as well as valuable insights relevant to one's own jurisdiction. The most important result of comparisons is often the reflection concerning the assumptions, historical trajectories and hidden agendas of national regimes, which one does not easily detect without the contrasts with other conservation systems.

International norms are always interpreted and moulded to fit the national legal system, the history and current understanding of the relationship between the state and its Indigenous peoples and ethnic groups. As indicated by several authors in this volume, issues of environmental protection and conservation law are bound up with another internationally 'hot topic', namely the Indigenous rights discourse with its strong focus on Indigenous rights and self-determination. How closely these two strands of discourse are connected is unique to each country, as is shown by the case studies, comparisons and country reports presented in this collection.

The purpose of this book is to provide a multidisciplinary and comparative analysis of how the customary livelihoods of Indigenous peoples have adapted to modern industrialised landscapes and how emergent approaches have contributed to global changes regarding Indigenous rights and models for nature conservation. It is noticeable that 'the Yellowstone model' lingers on, but also that new ways of genuinely addressing the role of Indigenous and local peoples in nature conservation have emerged. We stand at a crossroads. The Indigenous rights discourse calls on us to find the means to reinterpret the relationships between majority societies and Indigenous communities. The conservation discourse addresses the need to involve not only Indigenous communities, but also other local stakeholders, ethnic groups and the general public, in decision-making concerning environmental matters.[1]

As the title suggests, this book is an account of Indigenous customary rights in modern landscapes. Scholars from different disciplines were invited to investigate protected areas on Sámi lands in Nordic and Russian, historical and contemporary contexts. These contributions illuminate the considerable divergences between the different nation states. Others have provided examples for comparison from around the world, notably Australia, Aotearoa New Zealand, Canada and India. The literature on protected areas and

1 See here in particular the Århus Convention, 1998 (Convention on Access to Information, Public Participation in Decision-Making and Access to Justice in Environmental Matters).

Indigenous rights largely lacks in-depth scholarly articles in English covering Sápmi and the Sámi people. The book addresses this gap. It provides insights into developments that are of great interest for an international audience and offers a point of departure for international comparison.

The last chapter provides a few comments and remarks, drawing both on the collective, interdisciplinary knowledge of the authors here, notably with reference to Indigenous rights, nature resource policy and conservation, and on insights from the contributions offered by all the authors. In this we compare and contrast the various protected area regimes and our specific cases.

## The influence of borders

Borders of various kinds have significant meaning for Indigenous peoples, perhaps especially so in Sápmi where the establishment of national borders split the Sámi people among nation states. The Nordic countries share a longstanding history of wars and unions, and the northernmost regions, the Laplands in Sweden and Finland and the Finnmark in present-day Norway – their names denoting core Sámi areas[2] – were historically common lands without fixed borders. Previously this was an area of international political importance and a playground for sovereignty claims and power struggles. Since the Middle Ages, the Sámi have been under the dominion of stronger powers. They commonly paid tax to more than one kingdom; the Danish/Norwegian and the Swedish/Finnish kings, and/or the Russian tsar.[3]

Finland was part of the kingdom of Sweden for over 600 years until it came under the control of the Russian Empire in 1809. The national border between Sweden and Finland was drawn in 1810.[4] The national border between Russia and Norway was settled in 1826, and the Finnish–Russian border was confirmed in 1833. Norway belonged to the kingdom of Denmark from the 1400s until 1814, but in the same year was subsumed into a new union under the Swedish king. This union lasted until 1905, when Norway gained full sovereignty. The national border between Norway and Sweden in the very north was established in 1751. An addendum to the border treaty, the so-called Lap Codicil, emphasised that Sámi customary rights and movement should continue regardless of the border.[5]

The years 1852 and 1889 marked significant changes that had domino effects throughout Sápmi. At that time the borders between Finland/Norway and Finland/Sweden, respectively, were closed for seasonal reindeer herding migrations[6] resulting in over-grazing in certain regions, to which the states responded partly with forced relocation of Sámi families to the southern parts of the reindeer herding area. This caused conflicts with the local Sámi in these areas, which in some regions remain highly visible even today. The borders are still closed. Today, only the Norwegian/Swedish border is open for cross-border reindeer

2 Sámi were historically called Laps in Sweden/Finland and were commonly called Finns in Norway, thus the name of these areas the Lap's lands, Lapland, and the Finn's lands (*mark* in Scandinavian), Finnmark.

3 See e.g. Hansen and Olsen, *Samenes historie*, 151–152, 155–157, 169–172; Lundmark, *Så länge vi har marker*, 25–29. For a comparison of the taxation system see also Elenius et al., *The Barents Region*, Ch. 1–3.

4 For a short historical account, see the expert report *Nordisk samekonvensjon*, 106–109. See generally e.g. Gustafsson, *Nordens historia*; Elenius, *Nordiska gränser i historien*.

5 See further Pedersen, *Lappekodisillen i nord 1751–1859*.

6 See *Nordisk samekonvensjon*, 109.

herding, regulated by a bilateral treaty, but the redrafting of the treaty is currently quite a contentious area.[7]

The establishing of national borders meant tangible changes for the Sámi. The historical context is crucial for an understanding of the contemporary situation and the differences in legislation and recognition of Sámi rights among the nations.

Another set of borders that has influenced the Sámi are contemporary administrative boundaries of various kinds. In this context, both fixed pasture borders for reindeer herding communities and the boundaries of protected areas are significant as they influence the daily lives of the Sámi. Generally, it is forbidden to keep reindeer or hunt outside the boundaries of a reindeer herding community and, in the same vein, the specific provisions applicable for each national park, nature reserve and the like have to be complied with.

Since reindeer herding is carried out over vast areas, commonly spread over several municipalities and even counties, reindeer herders have to deal with several state bodies – often with different sets of policies and understandings concerning competing land uses, for building permits, planning and environmental permits, etc.

Certain administrative areas provide stronger protection for Sámi culture and livelihoods. One such is the Wilderness Areas in northern Finland, established though a parliamentary Act. Another is the administratively demarked northern areas of the Sámi Homeland in Finland and Finnmark County in Norway. In both, there are certain provisions that offer stronger protection for Sámi culture and customary activities, such as reindeer herding. The Norwegian Finnmark Act from 2005 interestingly also mentions that the provisions of the Act are to be applied in accordance with ILO Convention no. 169 and other international treaties concerning Indigenous peoples and minorities. What this means in practice remains to be fleshed out.

Even if some administrative borders, such as a few protected areas or the Sámi Homeland in Finland, call for greater protection of Sámi customary activities, such borders, depending on policies, are nevertheless a complicating factor for the Sámi. Generally, they must be said to impede any aspiration and capability regarding self-government as long as the Sámi are not part of the decision-making related to the area. Moreover, there can be a mismatch between administrative and ecological borders, for instance where good pasture areas are closed or made inaccessible to reindeer herding communities, for conservation or other purposes.

There are also imaginary borders. The notion of 'nature' and 'culture' as binary opposites creates an artificial distinction that affects Indigenous peoples, and the Sámi are no exception. The problematic and conceptual understanding of nature and the Sámi presence has historical roots, as Hjulman's chapter highlights with respect to Sweden's first national parks. Among the Nordic countries today, Norwegian preparatory works for conservation legislation have displayed this tension between Sámi understanding and contemporary Western conservation perspectives, as shown briefly by Allard in her chapter. This creates tensions in conservation discourses where modern, Western science and beliefs commonly outweigh the custom-based traditional (ecological) knowledge and belief system of the Sámi and other Indigenous peoples.

Ruru, in her chapter, points out the centrality of the concept 'wild' in relation to colonisation. The concept of 'wilderness' has been used both to indicate that proposed

7 On the politics see Broderstad, 'Cross-border reindeer husbandry'.

national parks were 'empty' land, devoid of human presence, and to justify settlers' claims to land and nature in Aotearoa New Zealand and elsewhere. The belief that nature can be separated from culture is evident in many conservation regimes, for instance as demonstrated by Elenius in his chapter regarding the concept of wilderness in Finland. It was used both for the creation of a myth and a historical narrative for the newborn Finnish nation after its separation from Sweden in 1809, and when the Wilderness Areas were established in 1991.

The chapter by Herrmann, Heinämäki and Morin stresses that the World Heritage regime continues to uphold the distinction between cultural and natural properties, which becomes more problematic in sites located in Indigenous territories. Indigenous peoples commonly perceive the landscape holistically, asserting that natural and cultural values are inseparable and connected to social, cultural, economic and legal structures, including customs. However, Vladimirova, in her chapter on the Russian Sámi, points to the problem that not only the majority communities but also the Sámi tend to perceive protected areas as 'wild nature' places, aligned with Soviet ideology and modernity – not primarily as longstanding traditional homelands with culture embedded in them.

## Longstanding struggles and Sámi–state relations

Conflicts and struggles surrounding the establishment, governance and management of protected areas on the lands of Indigenous peoples arise in several contexts – between Indigenous communities and the state, between Indigenous and non-Indigenous local communities and within Indigenous communities themselves. State confiscation of Indigenous peoples' lands for the purposes of nature conservation has led to longstanding tensions. Conflicting views of conservation and use and the possibility of combining them continue to create friction. Restrictions imposed as a consequence of area protection change the conditions for Indigenous peoples' livelihoods as well as those for co-existence and cooperation between Indigenous and non-Indigenous communities on the local level, and the design and implementation of management systems can be contentious issues. The contributions to this volume provide both historical and contemporary examples of how these tensions and conflicts can play out, and how they are intimately connected to issues of the territorial and environmental rights of Indigenous peoples.

Ultimately, many of the conflicts that are present at the local level, or even within Indigenous communities, have their roots in the practices or (historical) decisions of the states. To give just one example, since the first regulation of Sámi rights in Sweden in the late nineteenth century the legislator has recognised only Sámi reindeer herders as right-holders, leaving the majority of Sámi people without special rights (for instance regarding hunting and fishing rights) thereby splintering the Sámi community.[8] Taking such complexities into consideration is crucial to understanding the bigger picture where conservation and Indigenous rights tensions come together. With such inbuilt conflicts, the potential for collaboration and coexistence between different indigenous groups might be disrupted and any coexistence impeded. As explicitly or implicitly evident from several chapters in this volume, diverse forms of relationships and tensions on different levels influence the decisions about the designation and management of protected areas.

8 See further Mörkenstam, 'The power to define'.

### *State, competent authorities and Indigenous peoples*

Success stories of co-management, collaboration or cooperation over protected areas are often the result of conflicts, tensions and long struggles by Indigenous communities to gain recognition regarding their territorial rights. Green and Turtinen, Reimerson and Adams put forward the Laponia World Heritage site as a largely successful example of shared management of natural and cultural values on Indigenous lands, but the process leading up to the new management organisation was mired in conflict. State and municipal authorities initially refused to meet the Sámi reindeer herding communities' demands for influence and control over the management of the site, and negotiations were at a standstill for almost ten years before the parties could come to an agreement.[9] The conflict between the Swedish state, Jokkmokk and Gällivare municipalities and Sámi reindeer herding communities over the management of the Laponia World Heritage site was eventually resolved, and the reindeer herding communities secured substantial influence and control.[10]

Green and Turtinen also discuss the importance of the geographical and administrative proximity of conservation management organisations or authorities. Protected areas, as well as Indigenous communities, are often located far from cities and administrative centres. Closeness facilitates meetings, physically as well as conceptually, and contributes to the management organisation's legitimacy, functioning and ability to reduce conflict. In Tongariro National Park, the relocation of staff and responsibilities from a local office to a city some 200 kilometres away has disrupted established lines of communication between local Māori and the Department of Conservation and led to informants questioning the possibilities of continuing a mutually respectful and strong co-management arrangement. In Laponia, mechanisms for local participation and knowledge-sharing and high levels of cultural and linguistic competence among management staff constitute crucial components of the adaptation of management structures to Sámi organisational practices. Successful co-management requires several interrelated matters to be kept in mind.

Another obstacle revealed in the various cases in this volume is the states' lack of respect and recognition of Indigenous organisations and practices, including traditional (ecological) knowledge. Hjulman describes how Swedish conservation ideologies in the early twentieth century lacked knowledge and understanding of the interconnectedness between Sámi land use and the natural values of conservation landscapes. In Russian Sápmi, as discussed by Vladimorova, scientists have been the primary actors in nature conservation, and little attention has been paid to Sámi knowledge and histories. Similarly, Riseth argues that the Norwegian conservation regime rests heavily on a scientific tradition, tends to ignore cultural aspects of conservation landscapes and lacks understanding and integration of Sámi knowledge and practices. Adams' account of the management of Uluru-Kata Tjuta highlights conflicts over the details of management and policy practices resulting from insufficient consideration of Indigenous beliefs and practices, and concludes that the Indian state has consistently ignored Indigenous peoples' cultural traditions and practices. Tensions have also been very much apparent with respect to Aotearoa New Zealand's national parks, emphasised by Ruru and Green and Turtinen, but there are also promising new developments, such as Te Urewera on the North Island.

9 See e.g. Nilsson Dahlström, *Negotiating wilderness*; Green, *Managing Laponia*.
10 Reimerson, 'Sami space for agency'.

### *Local and intra-community tensions*

Even if not always explicit or immediately recognisable, tensions or conflicts on local levels often originate in issues of Indigenous rights. The notion of formal equality between persons and groups complicates the special rights discourse for Indigenous communities. However, their territorial rights, ownership or usufruct rights, are founded on protracted use recognised through doctrines in domestic property law. The fact that such rights have been neglected by the state – for instance, where they are not formally codified in written law, or where the state has refrained from making proper legal investigations – does not mean that they do not exist. In this sense, such territorial rights are not special rights but recognised customary rights with connotations to the human right to property and non-discrimination vis-à-vis the majority population. If such rights indeed exist, there will naturally be a differentiation of rights between Indigenous and non-indigenous local communities.

Neumann and Itkonen discuss how the differentiation between Sámi and non-Sámi local communities has been a cause of tension in Finland, and how competition over access and rights to nature has caused conflicts between reindeer herding and other land uses. Hjulman finds corresponding disputes in his historical study of Abisko and Muddus National Parks in Swedish Sápmi. Itkonen further highlights how changes in intra-Sámi community relationships have led to friction on the local level in the Skolt Sámi area in Finland, and Vladimorova notes similar problems in the Russian Kola peninsula. In addition, Elenius demonstrates how the influence from global Indigenous legislation and policy, as well as from environmentalist movements, radicalised the Sámi political movement in Finland and has led to different local strategies among Finnish Sámi.

### *Diverging perspectives*

The chapters by Elenius, Hjulman, Herrmann, Heinämäki and Morin, Riseth, and Green and Turtinen all address problems arising from differing perspectives on conservation – what should be protected, how and by whom. Riseth, relating to the situation in Norway, discusses examples of conflict between Sámi reindeer herders and the state's conservation interests over national parks. He argues that established conservation ideas and practices are one root to conflict because they marginalise Sámi reindeer herders as resource managers and ignore Sámi cultural landscapes and the longstanding Sámi knowledge and practices related to these landscapes. Hjulman, in turn, shows how early twentieth century authorities and conservationists struggled to fit Sámi land use into their understanding of protected areas, and how Sámi actors had to navigate in a world of insufficient recognition of their traditions and practices in order to continue their traditional livelihoods in Abisko and Muddus National Parks. Elenius traces the ethnic relations between Sámi and other ethnic groups in Sweden and Finland, and shows how historically fostered inter-ethnic relations have led to different conservation systems in the two countries, despite a shared history within the Swedish kingdom. For instance, in contrast to Sweden, the establishment of the specific Wilderness Areas in the far north of Finland has meant protection for reindeer herding against effective industrialised forestry. On the other hand, it has positioned the Sámi as a 'nature people', largely deprived of any development.

The case of the SGang Gwaay World Heritage site, analysed by Herrmann, Heinämäki and Morin, illustrates the complexity of cultural heritage protection, as do the problems arising from attempts to categorise and value the cultural heritage of the traditional owners of the proposed Cape York World Heritage site according to World Heritage Conservation standards, discussed by Green and Turtinen. In the Canadian SGang Gwaay World Heritage site, tension arose over whether totem poles should be left to naturally decompose – as prescribed by Haida tradition – or be subjected to restoration efforts to preserve them for future generations. In Cape York, the World Heritage nomination process placed expectations on the traditional owners that they would frame their knowledge and their cultural and social traditions according to notions of 'value', as defined by the World Heritage framework, which did not correlate well with their own understandings of their relationship to the area.

These examples highlight longstanding tensions and struggles with respect to area protection at different levels and by many stakeholders, including Indigenous communities, the state, and local and conservationist groups. The Sámi and other Indigenous peoples have fought, and continue to fight, for their rights, their worldviews and their space for agency in a constantly changing society. However, conflict is not necessarily a bad thing. The process of resolving conflicts has the potential to renew and rearticulate relationships. As such, tensions and frictions can be part of a formative process that may encourage new thinking and lead to models of protected area management that are more adequately suited to solving the challenges of today.

## Contrasting our cases – Shared governance models

In parallel with the longstanding struggles and tensions described above, the traditional top-down ways of promoting conservation – 'the Yellowstone model' – have largely been dismissed as being too protectionist and exclusionary, and therefore inappropriate and even counterproductive regarding conservation. The growing belief that top-down governance of national parks risks jeopardising local support (with the consequent undermining of conservation goals) has led to what is often defined as the 'new conservation paradigm' based in the development of alternative and more inclusive approaches under the assumption that they will enhance legitimacy.[11]

The new conservation paradigm is influenced by the overarching societal trend often framed as a transition from government to governance, stressing the fact that steering is no longer the privilege of governments alone, but now includes power sharing between various actors.[12] Kooiman orders this shared responsibility into hierarchical governance, self-organising governance and co-governance modes.[13] Hierarchical governance refers to governmental steering where the participation of non-governmental actors is minimal. Self-governance refers to a situation where non-governmental actors organise themselves and co-management includes governmental and non-governmental actors working together to achieve common goals.[14] In a similar vein, the International Union for Conservation of Nature (IUCN) has developed a tool for comparing various modes of governance in relation to protected areas where the self-organising mode of governance (types C and D) is split into two categories: private governance and governance by Indigenous peoples and local communities.[15]

11 Berkes, 'Rethinking community-based conservation'; Lockwood, 'Good governance'; Kothari, Camill and Brown, 'Conservation as if people mattered'.
12 Visseren-Hamakers et al., 'Conservation partnerships'.
13 Kooiman, *Governing as Governance.*
14 Löf, *Challenging Adaptability.*
15 Borrini-Feyerabend et al., *Governance of Protected Areas.*

*Table 13.1* IUCN governance types for protected areas[16]

| | |
|---|---|
| Type A. Governance by government | Federal or national ministry/agency in charge; sub-national ministry/agency in charge; government-delegated management (e.g. to NGO) |
| Type B. Shared governance | Collaborative management (various degrees of influence); joint management (pluralist management board); transboundary management (various levels across international borders) |
| Type C. Private governance | By individual owner; by non-profit organisations (NGOs, universities, cooperatives); by for-profit organisations (individuals or corporate) |
| Type D. Governance by Indigenous peoples and local communities | Indigenous peoples' conserved areas and territories; community conserved areas – declared and run by local communities |

We will use the IUCN typology (Table 13.1) to compare how the new conservation paradigm, in one way or another, has been implemented in the national conservation policy in the cases presented in this book. While Australia was quite early in establishing shared governance arrangements in conservation with Indigenous peoples, the Scandinavian countries in contrast have only recently opened the way for Indigenous influence: Norway through a national conservation policy, and Sweden on an ad hoc basis.[17]

Three of the cases analysed in this book can be defined as various forms of shared governance (type B), while protected area governance in Finland and Russia falls under type A, namely hierarchical governance. In Australia, since 1985, the Uluru-Kata Tjuta National Park has been managed jointly by the local Anangu aboriginal people and Parks Australia, the federal environment bureaucracy. The co-management arrangement is recognised within a legislative framework for shared governance with the purpose of ensuring the primacy of Indigenous belief and practice. At Uluru-Kata Tjuta, this means that a board of management, where a majority (eight out of 12) must be Anangu, is responsible for making all decisions relating to planning and management of the park.

Another example of a shared governance arrangement is the SGang Gwaay UNESCO World Heritage site in Canada, which is preserved as a sacred place by the Haida Nation. According to the chapter by Herrmann, Heinämäki and Morin, SGang Gwaay has more integrated involvement in decision-making than other Canadian examples of co-management and has been identified as an example of best practices for aboriginal co-management of World Heritage sites. Formally, it means that the Haida are involved as full members in all the decision-making processes concerning the management of the Gwaii Haanas National Park Reserve, the National Marine Conservation Area Reserve, and the Haida Heritage Site. The majority conditions are, however, less important as mutual agreements are to be reached through consensus.

In Sweden, the recently established World Heritage site, Laponia, can also be defined as a form of shared governance partnership (type B). Powers are devolved to a management organisation – Laponiatjuottjudus – where decisions are to be reached based on consensus in accordance with the commonly developed values of the organisation.

16 Ibid., 29.
17 Holmgren, Sandstrom and Zachrisson, 'Protected area governance in Sweden'.

If Uluru-Kata Tjuta National Park, S*G*ang Gwaay and Laponia are all examples of various forms of shared governance (type B above), the Norwegian situation can still, despite the attempts to include the Sámi people in the management of NPs, be defined as governance by government (type A), albeit with some elements of shared governance. More specifically it can be termed government-delegated management since the primary task of the management boards, where the Sámi parliament is represented, is to implement the national policy although with local adaptations.

If the inclusion of Indigenous people in the cases described above can be viewed as various forms of compromise between the state and Indigenous peoples, we can see a completely different development in Aotearoa New Zealand. The development of the governance of Te Urewera NP, which in 2014 became Te Urewera: 'a legal entity' with 'all the rights, powers, duties, and liabilities of a legal person', can be defined as an example of type D – governance by Indigenous peoples. Ruru defines the development as an example of 'new legislative imagining' – with a new, more respectful approach to valuing and caring for landscapes, incorporation of customary law and practices and reconciliation. The recent institutional change has opened up the possibility of including the Māori in conservation outcomes, and enhancing traditional Māori knowledge and has been followed by the instigation of more partnerships. In 2014–2015, almost 30 per cent of the Department of Conservation's partnerships involved Māori.

With the Te Urewera Act, the Te Urewera ceased to be Crown land, ceased to be a national park and was subsequently turned into freehold land. As such, it is no longer managed by the Department of Conservation but by the new Te Urewera Board. This Board has the responsibility 'to act on behalf of, and in the name of, Te Urewera'. The phasing out of the government, however, will be gradual. For the first three years, the Board will have a 50/50 membership of Tūhoe (the local Māori tribal group) and Crown appointees (four people each). Thereafter, the Board will increase by one and the ratio will change to six Tūhoe and three Crown appointees.

Australia and Aotearoa New Zealand can be seen as two of the most progressive countries of those included in this book in relation to the promotion of new modes of governance that include Indigenous peoples in conservation. While this may be deserved in some respects, it is also clear from the preceding chapters and the comparison presented in this chapter that many of the advances by Indigenous people have been driven by protest and legal action, rather than by benign responses from the governments.

As we have seen above, shared governance arrangements are very diverse, reflecting the diversity of both Indigenous communities and environmental and tenure contexts. They are furthermore in a situation of recurrent negotiations and, as we will see, often dependent on national and international, legal and policy developments.

## Does international law provide aid?

Several contributions to this volume highlight the importance of the international context for both nature conservation and Indigenous rights and the interconnectedness between the two fields of international law and policy. The territories of Indigenous peoples are also areas that are home to a vast majority of the world's biological diversity and other natural values, and most conservation bodies and scholars now readily acknowledge the contribution of Indigenous peoples to the maintenance of biological diversity and the functioning of ecosystems. Ruru points out that the international community is becoming increasingly aware and supportive of the need to recognise and support Indigenous peoples in the management and governance of protected areas. Adams notes that the 'new conservation paradigm' of recent decades has emphasised increased Indigenous involvement in conservation as well as a broadening of the concept of conservation landscapes to encompass areas with multiple land uses, and Indigenous cultural landscapes. Many of the most important international instruments for conservation and area protection, including the UN Convention on Biological Diversity and the UNESCO World Heritage Convention, reflect these developments.

As discussed in the chapters by Neumann and Reimerson, the Convention on Biological Diversity (CBD) commits signatory states both to the protection of biological diversity and the protection of Indigenous peoples' traditional knowledge, practices and innovations. CBD guidelines, protocols and work programmes encourage states to secure indigenous peoples' rights to participate in the governance and management of protected areas on their lands, and Indigenous peoples' organisations and representatives have established ways in which to influence CBD processes and decisions. Through its attempts to engage with cultural landscapes, the World Heritage Convention (WHC) has the potential to act as an instrument to protect Indigenous peoples' lands and cultural heritage. Green and Turtinen remark that recent amendments to the WHC highlight Indigenous peoples' right to participate and share responsibility in the nomination and management of World Heritage sites. Herrmann, Heinämäki and Morin stress that UNESCO has clear obligations to protect human rights and argue that conservation under the World Heritage Convention can contribute greatly to the cultural survival of Indigenous peoples, as well as to the protection of their lands, waters and traditional knowledge.

International law and policy can strengthen the negotiating position of Indigenous peoples on national and local levels and support their claims to influence and participate in protected area governance and management. Neumann's study of the implementation of the CBD and its Programme of Work on Protected Areas (PoWPA) in Finland and Norway shows that the states' measures to meet their commitments under the CBD have resulted in noticeable changes in terms of Sámi participation in protected area management. In her analysis of the recently established local management boards for protected areas in Norway, Reimerson concludes that the Norwegian discourse, in arguing for Sámi participation in protected area management, emphasises Norway's commitments under international law.

In the process leading up to the new management arrangement for the Laponia World Heritage site in Swedish Sápmi, discussed specifically by Green and Turtinen and Reimerson, UNESCO and the WHC served to support the claims of the Sámi reindeer herding communities and allowed the development of a management organisation with strong Sámi influence. However, as Adams points out in his chapter regarding India, international law may also hamper local and customary uses and belief systems, as has been the case with the Western Ghats World Heritage site, where national prestige and global processes combined to dismiss and override local rights.

While international law and policy on conservation arguably hold promise for Indigenous peoples' control and influence over protected areas on their lands, they are subject to ongoing and extensive criticism from Indigenous rights perspectives. Critics point to the lack of representation, insight, influence and participation of Indigenous peoples, as well as outright violations of Indigenous rights. Empirical examples from the studies in this volume illustrate these problems. Green and Turtinen argue that the bureaucratic structures and practices of UNESCO and the WHC and its universalising, standardising ambitions regarding heritage categorisation and protection make it ill-suited to dealing with local complexity and unreceptive to Indigenous and other non-Western worldviews and perspectives. In the case of a proposed World Heritage site on Indigenous lands in Cape York, Green and Turtinen find that the structure of the nomination procedure has amplified tendencies to consider Indigenous peoples' knowledge only partially, value it from a primarily Western scientific point of view and misrepresent it through translation into a hegemonic framework of conservation.

The combined results of this volume nevertheless indicate that despite persisting problems, international law and policy may serve to support and reinforce Indigenous peoples' claims to land, influence or participation in protected area governance and management – through binding commitments by states under international law or through the establishment of principles, norms and best practices. However, outcomes and consequences on the national and local levels vary considerably depending on national implementation strategies and existing legal and political frameworks.

Neumann's comparison of Finland and Norway shows that domestic legislation and Sámi rights systems limit and shape the implementation of commitments under the CBD. Elenius' comparison of Sweden and Finland demonstrates that national myths and memories are strong forces behind both nature conservation strategies and the way reindeer herding has been implemented in nature conservation legislation. He points out that inter-ethnic relations, nation building and nature conservation are intimately linked.

Reimerson's contrasting of the Laponia management organisation with the Norwegian protected area management boards suggests that the comparatively stronger protection of Sámi rights in Norway, compared to Sweden, reduces the importance of international conservation law as a supporting structure, whereas the international context became a more important factor for the Sámi in the Swedish case. Green and Turtinen come to a similar conclusion regarding the case of Tongariro National Park in Aotearoa New Zealand, where the WHC had some ethno-political significance for the local Māori community when the site was listed as a World Heritage site but where the Treaty of Waitangi has proved far more important as a legal basis for Māori land and compensation claims.

As illustrated by the contributions to this volume, the globalised and interconnected framework of conservation legislation and policy provides a crucial context for the understanding of Indigenous rights in relation to protected landscapes. Global attention to their rights and to patterns of colonialism by majority societies has strengthened Indigenous peoples internationally and nationally, but recognition of Indigenous rights and strategies to implement international law vary considerably among countries – even between neighbouring and otherwise similar states, as shown by Allard in her comparison of protected area regimes in the Nordic states. Indigenous peoples find ways of using international arenas to their advantage and international bodies may put pressure on individual states to secure the full and effective inclusion of Indigenous peoples in protected area governance and management.

In her account of the case of Te Urewera, where both Western and Māori values are incorporated into the legislation, Ruru gives a valuable example of radical legislative reform and the possibility of integrating bi-cultural values in legislation. A similar attempt, although not as courageous, is discernible in the aim of the Norwegian Nature Diversity Act of 2009, which emphasises the protection of the environment as a 'basis for Sámi culture'. This is a way of re-imagining conservation legislation in general that potentially makes space for Indigenous rights and worldviews.

## Conclusions and looking ahead

Although new and emergent approaches have contributed to global changes in Indigenous rights and nature conservation models, this book reveals a number of challenges related to the implementation of these rights, both in terms of their codification and through various reforms in the governance of protected areas. Regardless of country, at least three overarching and, to some extent, related patterns obstructing the implementation of Indigenous rights in conservation regimes can be discerned. First, the legacy of colonialism has had an impact, and still does, on the political and social organisation among Indigenous peoples. Secondly, the institutional path dependency of national as well as international law, which tends to close down around specific institutional solutions and bureaucratic practices, largely neglects the needs and conditions of Indigenous peoples. Thirdly, there are obvious difficulties in combining Indigenous values and views with Western understandings of conservation.

### *Colonial legacy*

As we have seen in several chapters, a variety of forms of shared governance within nature conservation are increasingly being encouraged and implemented. This can, with the support of international conventions, be viewed as a way of leaving behind the state-controlled, top-down colonial management system that dominated the twentieth century. In this regard, the development of shared governance regimes has been recognised as part of a decolonisation process because of its capacity, compared to state-controlled systems, to accommodate multiple goals and stakeholders. However, as has been highlighted, by Adams for instance, despite different histories, the policies concerning Indigenous peoples and nature conservation still tend to reflect colonial attitudes. Although Australia has done better in recognising Indigenous peoples' land rights than many other countries, these rights are disproportionately found in remote, residual landscapes not wanted by others and thus with no competition for tenures.

In Sweden, where the Laponia World Heritage site has been defined as a success story regarding the inclusion of the Sámi in the management of the area, it can also be seen as the exception rather than the rule. In its present form, the Swedish government has shown no interest in transferring the Laponia model to other protected areas in Sápmi. In India where the Adivasi forest rights have been successively strengthened over the years, there is persistent failure to implement them.

The limited success in introducing shared governance arrangements, and thus a very slow decolonisation process, can partly be understood as being due to the relatively weak, and often fragmented, social and political organisational structures among Indigenous people. The weak organisation is a direct result of the legacy of colonialism, but also of contemporary government policy and legal change, demographic processes, such as urbanisation, and forced displacements, and commercialisation and commodification of ecosystems services. There is often reluctance among state authorities to hand over power to Indigenous peoples just because traditional local authorities are weak. Indigenous peoples seem to be punished twice over.

### *Institutional path dependency and structural violence*

Another reason Indigenous peoples tend to achieve influence over traditional land at such a slow pace is what Green and Turtinen frame as the 'bureaucratic structures and practices' and the discourses these bureaucracies rest on and recreate. Their study of the bureaucracy and the institutional system of roles and responsibilities in implementing World Heritage sites shows that hierarchical and standardised forms of organisation are often ill-suited to handling local complexity. Although Indigenous peoples are formally involved in the process of establishing and managing the World Heritage sites, they are often run and controlled by the state in accordance with procedures generated by the state. The World Heritage bureaucracy thus adds yet another layer of structures that must be accommodated and accepted by the Indigenous peoples, often causing conflicts and tensions regarding roles and responsibilities.

The discrepancy between traditional local forms of organisation and the bureaucracy that surrounds the World Heritage Convention was one of the reasons why it took so many years to reach an agreement regarding the Laponia World Heritage site. Similar patterns can be discerned in other chapters where the negotiations between Indigenous peoples regarding, for example, shared governance arrangements frequently take place within the state-controlled system. Since institutions are often enmeshed in systems and can only be changed incrementally by organisations, the scope for alternative pathways is limited. This type of process where rigid bureaucratic structures and practices direct the outcome of the process can be defined as a form of 'structural violence', that is social arrangements, embedded in the political and economic organisation of Western societies, which constrain Indigenous people's agency.

### *Indigenous values and views versus Western views on conservation*

Another important pattern that we can find throughout the contributions in this book is how different values or even clashes between values or belief systems may influence the outcome of negotiations over shared governance practices. This is particularly visible in how the biophysical environment is interpreted, that is whether it constitutes an integral part of the cultural identity and social integrity of the users or if it is regarded as something to be protected from traditional use and users.

As we have seen in, for example, the case of the S*G*ang Gwaay World Heritage site, the traditional ecological knowledge (TEK) of the Haida First Nation, which can be viewed as a body of knowledge, practices and representations that describes the relationships of the people, including their ancestors and their physical environment, has been the subject of negotiations and compromises with the responsible Canadian conservation agency.

The importance of TEK has been highlighted in various conventions, such as the Convention on Biodiversity and most recently by the Intergovernmental Science-Policy Platform on Biodiversity and Ecosystem Services (IPBES),[18] an intergovernmental body that assesses the state of biodiversity and of the ecosystem services it provides to society. However, TEK is primarily recognised as valuable for the protection of biodiversity and ecosystem services and not as a value in itself. The reduction of Indigenous values and views as a means to achieve an end, for instance biodiversity, rather than as an end in themselves impedes the possibilities of reaching agreements on the governance and management of protected areas.

Furthermore, the attempts to integrate TEK and science, which often constitute a purpose – though not explicit – of shared governance arrangements, assumes that TEK can easily be fitted into Western conceptions of knowledge. As such it is defined like any other form of scientific data to be integrated into existing management bureaucracies. As we have seen in several chapters, predominant views on TEK tend to compel the Indigenous peoples to adapt their way of expressing their values and views to the practices of, for example, the World Heritage bureaucracy. At best the integrated knowledge can be used as

18 IPBES, http://www.ipbes.net/.

a common basis for shared governance. However, experience shows that the new and integrated knowledge often serves to concentrate power to the state-controlled administration rather than the Indigenous peoples.[19]

### *What are the alternatives?*

By comparing conservation aims, protected areas and Indigenous peoples across different countries this final chapter highlights the inherent linkages between the environmental and socio-political dimensions of nature conservation. In doing so, it also explores the problems and prospects that many Indigenous peoples face when claiming greater control over traditional lands. On the basis of what we know today, what kind of policy approaches can be expected in the future?

There are at least three alternatives. We have, firstly, the current approach, which can be defined as a case-by-case approach. Despite the rather progressive moves regarding the legal development of Indigenous rights on the international level and the fact that many countries have integrated Indigenous rights into national legislation, there is no clear-cut legal framework for Indigenous rights and nature conservation in any of the countries represented in this book. As we have seen, each case, despite involving similar international conventions such as the World Heritage Convention, is treated independently. Learning across cases seems limited and the institutional path dependency on the national level obstructs initiatives to open up alternative pathways. The advantages of this approach lie, of course, in the potential to adapt to local conditions and possibly also to gain political acceptance as no fundamental changes in either politics or practices are required. It also takes into account the historical dimension of each country and the coexistence of ethnic groups, which cannot be underestimated when trying to obtain legitimacy for new decisions. The disadvantages are the ad hoc processes, the piecemeal solutions to problems and the absence of general guidelines for the legal interpretation of Indigenous rights in protected areas. The current case-by-case option is therefore at best a temporary approach and not satisfactory in the long term.

A second option would be to further promote various forms of shared governance as stipulated by the IUCN and in practice recognise the rights of Indigenous peoples in the governance of protected area management on traditional lands. The involvement of Indigenous peoples would thus no longer be the exception to the rule, but rather the general basis for the governance and management of protected areas when situated within Indigenous homeland regions. The advantages of this option, which could also include local communities in general, lie in the potential to reconcile the interests of Indigenous communities and conservation aims and thus take into account local conditions. The disadvantage, as we see in several of the contributions to this volume, is the co-option of Indigenous knowledge and the risk of increasing conflict rather than reconciliation around conservation efforts.

A third opportunity could be to take an even further step and, as in the case of Aotearoa New Zealand, essentially reduce the powers of central governments while placing responsibility for conservation on the holders of traditional rights. The advantages here, which would require institutional innovation, are that the scope and power of Indigenous communities are specified through a clarification of territorial rights and provision of a degree of autonomy. Such a change would also entail a move away from a single focus on conservation

19 Nadasdy, 'Adaptive co-management'.

to a holistic approach taking into consideration not only ecological processes but also cultural and social aspects. However, reducing the powers of central governments in this way would probably be seen as a disadvantage by those with vested interests in conservation and other local and national aspects.

Regardless of the alternatives sketched above, there is current, steady, but somewhat slow, progress towards seeking reconciliation between the state and Indigenous peoples, in particular with respect to diverging views on territorial rights and conservation aims. This trend is happening on the international as well as national and local levels, and often involves legal and policy development and innovation. The near future will provide us with answers that will emerge from conservation tensions and power struggles, possibly offering other new forms of shared governance models.

## Bibliography

Berkes, Fikret. 'Rethinking Community-based Conservation'. *Conservation Biology* 18, no. 3 (2004): 621–630.

Borrini-Feyerabend, Grazia, Dudley, Nigel, Jaeger, Tilman, Lassen, Barbara, Broome, Neema Pathak, Phillips, Adrian & Trevor Sandwith. *Governance of Protected Areas: From Understanding to Action.* Best Practice Protected Area Guidelines Series No. 20, Gland: IUCN, 2013.

Broderstad, Else Grete. 'Cross-border Reindeer Husbandry: Between Ancient Usage Rights and State Sovereignty'. In *The Proposed Nordic Saami Convention: National and International Dimensions of Indigenous Property Rights*, eds. Nigel Bankes & Timo Koivurova, 149–174. Oxford: Hart, 2013.

Elenius, Lars, ed. *Nordiska gränser i historien. Linjer och rum, konstruktion och dekonstruktion.* Joensuu: University Press of Eastern Finland, 2015.

Elenius, Lars, Tjelmeland, Hallvard, Lähteenmäki, Maria & Alexey Golubev, eds. *The Barents Region: A Transnational History of Subarctic Northern Europe.* Oslo: Pax Forlag, 2015.

Green, Carina. 'Managing Laponia: A World Heritage Site as Arena for Sámi Ethno-politics in Sweden'. PhD diss., Uppsala: Uppsala University, 2009.

Gustafsson, Harald. *Nordens historia. En europeisk region under 1200 år.* Lund: Studentlitteratur, 2007.

Hansen, Lars Ivar & Bjørnar Olsen. *Samenes historie fram til 1750.* Oslo: Cappelen Akademisk Forlag, 2004.

Holmgren, Lina, Sandström, Camilla & Anna Zachrisson. 'Protected Area Governance in Sweden: New Modes of Governance or Business as Usual?'. *Local Environment* (2016) (forthcoming). Published on-line: http://www.tandfonline.com/doi/full/10.1080/13549839.2016.1154518.

Kooiman, Jan. *Governing as Governance.* London: Sage Publications Ltd, 2013.

Kothari, Ashish, Camill, Philip & Jessica Brown. 'Conservation as If People also Mattered: Policy and Practice of Community-based Conservation'. *Conservation and Society* 11, no. 1 (2013): 1–15.

Lockwood, Michael. 'Good Governance for Terrestrial Protected Areas: A Framework, Principles and Performance Outcomes'. *Journal of Environmental Management* 91, no. 3 (2010): 754–766.

Löf, Anette. 'Challenging Adaptability: Analysing the Governance of Reindeer Husbandry in Sweden'. PhD diss., Umeå: Umeå University, 2014.

Lundmark, Lennart. *Så länge vi har marker: Samerna och staten under sexhundra år.* Stockholm: Prisma, 1999.

Mörkenstam, Ulf. 'The Power to Define: The Saami in Swedish Legislation'. In *Conflict and Cooperation in the North*, eds. Kristiina Karppi & Johan Eriksson, 113–145. Umeå: Norrlands universitetsförlag i Umeå, 2002.

Nadasdy, Paul. 'Adaptive Co-Management and the Gospel of Resilience'. In *Adaptive Co-Management: Collaboration, Learning, and Multilevel Governance*, eds. Derek Armitage, Fikret Berkes & Nancy Doubleday, 208–227. Vancouver: University of British Columbia Press, 2007.

Nilsson Dahlström, Åsa. 'Negotiating Wilderness in a Cultural Landscape: Predators and Saami Reindeer Herding in the Laponian World Heritage Area'. PhD diss., Uppsala University, 2003.

*Nordisk samekonvensjon: utkast fra finsk-norsk-svensk-samisk ekspertgruppe*, 2005.

Pedersen, Steinar. *Lappekodisillen i nord 1751–1859: Fra grenseavtale og sikring av samenes rettigheter til grensesperring og samisk ulykke*. Kautokeino: Sámi University College, 2008.

Reimerson, Elsa. 'Sami Space for Agency in the Management of the Laponian World Heritage Site'. *Local Environment*, 21, no. 7 (2016): 808–826.

Visseren-Hamakers, Jacoba, Ingrid, Leroy, Pieter & Pieter Glasbergen. 'Conservation Partnerships and Biodiversity Governance: Fulfilling Governance Functions through Interaction'. *Sustainable Development* 20 (2012): 264–275.

# Index

For Product Safety Concerns and Information please contact our EU representative GPSR@taylorandfrancis.com
Taylor & Francis Verlag GmbH, Kaufingerstraße 24, 80331 München, Germany

www.ingramcontent.com/pod-product-compliance
Ingram Content Group UK Ltd.
Pitfield, Milton Keynes, MK11 3LW, UK
UKHW050050200926
475702UK00019B/2767

* 9 7 8 0 3 6 7 5 9 5 6 9 2 *